P9-CEA-099

Commentary
on the
OLD TESTAMENT

Commentary
on the
OLD TESTAMENT
IN TEN VOLUMES

by

C. F. KEIL and F. DELITZSCH

VOLUME IV

Job

by F. DELITZSCH

Two Volumes in One

WILLIAM B. EERDMANS PUBLISHING COMPANY
Grand Rapids, Michigan

COMMENTARY ON THE OLD TESTAMENT
by C. F. Keil and F. Delitzsch
Translated from the German

Volumes translated by James Martin
THE PENTATEUCH
JOSHUA, JUDGES, RUTH
THE BOOKS OF SAMUEL
THE BOOKS OF THE KINGS
THE PROPHECIES OF ISAIAH
THE PROPHECIES OF EZEKIEL
THE TWELVE MINOR PROPHETS

Volumes translated by Andrew Harper
THE BOOKS OF THE CHRONICLES

Volumes translated by Sophia Taylor
THE BOOKS OF EZRA, NEHEMIAH, ESTHER

Volumes translated by Francis Bolton
THE BOOK OF JOB
THE PSALMS

Volumes translated by M. G. Easton
PROVERBS OF SOLOMON
THE SONG OF SONG AND ECCLESIASTES
THE BOOK OF DANIEL

Volumes translated by David Patrick
THE PROPHECIES OF JEREMIAH, VOL. I

Volumes translated by James Kennedy
THE PROPHECIES OF JEREMIAH, VOL. II

ISBN 0-8028-8038-X
Reprinted, February 1980

TABLE OF CONTENTS

INTRODUCTION.

TRANSLATION AND EXPOSITION OF THE BOOK OF JOB.

FIRST PART.—THE OPENING.—CHAP. I.–III.

INTRODUCTION TO THE BOOK OF JOB.

JOB, maintaining his virtue, and justifying the utterance of the Creator respecting him, sits upon his heap of ashes as the glory and pride of God. God, and with Him the whole celestial host, witnesses the manner in which he bears his misfortune. He conquers, and his conquest is a triumph beyond the stars. Be it history, be it poetry: he who thus wrote was a divine seer.

FRIEDR. HEINR. JACOBI
(*Werke*, iii. 427).

In this Introduction but little has been transferred from the Art. *Hiob*, which the Author has contributed to Herzog's *Real-Encyklopädie*. It presents a new, independent working up of the introductory matter, and contains only so much of it as is required at the commencement of a Commentary. The Author's treatise on the idea of the book of Job in the *Zeitschrift für Protestantismus u. Kirche*, 1851, S. 65–85, is recapitulatory rather than isagogic, and consequently of a totally distinct character.

NOTE.

[This work is enriched by critical notes contributed by Prof. Dr Fleischer, and illustrative notes contributed by Dr Wetzstein, fifteen years Prussian Consul at Damascus.

The second volume will contain an Appendix contributed by Dr Wetzstein on the "Monastery of Job" in Hauran, the tradition concerning Job, and a map of the district.—Tr.]

THE BOOK OF JOB

INTRODUCTION.

§ 1. THE PROBLEM OF THE BOOK OF JOB.

WHY do afflictions upon afflictions befall the righteous man? This is the question, the answering of which is made the theme of the book of Job. Looking to the conclusion of the book, the answer stands: that afflictions are for the righteous man the way to a twofold blessedness. But in itself, this answer cannot satisfy; so much the less, as the twofold blessedness to which Job finally attains is just as earthly and of this world as that which he has lost by affliction. This answer is inadequate, since on the one hand such losses as those of beloved children cannot, as the loss of sheep and camels, really be made good by double the number of other children; on the other hand, it may be objected that many a righteous man deprived of his former prosperity dies in outward poverty. There are numerous deathbeds which protest against this answer. There are many pious sufferers to whom this present material issue of the book of Job could not yield any solace; whom, when in conflict at least, it might the rather bring into danger of despair. With reference to this conclusion, the book of Job is an insufficient theodicy, as in general the truth taught in the Old Testament, that the end, אַחֲרִית, of the righteous, as of the unrighteous, would reveal the hidden divine recompense, could afford no true consolation so long as this אַחֲרִית flowed on with death into the night of Hades, שְׁאוֹל, and had no prospect of eternal life.

But the issue of the history, regarded externally, is by no means the proper answer to the great question of the book. The principal thing is not that Job is doubly blessed, but that God acknowledges him as His servant, which He is able to do, after Job in all his afflictions has remained true to God. Therein lies the important truth, that there is a suffering of the righteous which is not a decree of wrath, into which the love of God has been changed, but a dispensation of that love itself. In fact, this truth is the heart of the book of Job. It has therefore been said—particularly by Hirzel, and recently by Renan—that it aims at destroying the old Mosaic doctrine of retribution. But this old Mosaic doctrine of retribution is a modern phantom. That all suffering is a divine retribution, the Mosaic Thora does not teach. Renan calls this doctrine *la vieille conception patriarcale*. But the patriarchal history, and especially the history of Joseph, gives decided proof against it. The distinction between the suffering of the righteous and the retributive justice of God, brought out in the book of Job, is nothing new. The history before the time of Israel, and the history of Israel even, exhibit it in facts; and the words of the law, as Deut. viii. 16, expressly show that there are sufferings which are the result of God's love; though the book of Job certainly presents this truth, which otherwise had but a scattered and presageful utterance, in a unique manner, and causes it to come forth before us from a calamitous and terrible conflict, as pure gold from a fierce furnace. It comes forth as the result of the controversy with the false doctrine of retribution advanced by the friends; a doctrine which is indeed not Mosaic, for the Mosaic Thora in the whole course of the history of revelation is nowhere impugned and corrected, but ever only augmented, and, consistently with its inherent character, rendered more complete.

But if we now combine both the truths illustrated in the book of Job,—(1) The affliction of the righteous man leads to a so much greater blessedness; (2) The affliction of the righteous is a dispensation of the divine love, which is expressed and verified in the issue of the affliction,—this double answer is still not an adequate solution of the great question of the book. For there ever arises the opposing consideration, wherefore are such afflictions necessary to raise the righteous to blessedness—afflictions which seem so entirely to bear the character of wrath, and are in no way distinguished from judgments of retributive justice?

To this question the book furnishes, as it appears to us, two answers: (1.) The afflictions of the righteous are a means of discipline and purification; they certainly arise from the sins of the righteous man, but still are not the workings of God's wrath, but of His love, which is directed to his purifying and advancement. Such is the view Elihu in the book of Job represents. The writer of the introductory portion of Proverbs has expressed this briefly but beautifully (Prov. iii. 11; cf. Heb. xii.). Oehler, in order that one may perceive its distinction from the view of the three friends, rightly refers to the various theories of punishment. Discipline designed for improvement is properly no punishment, since punishment, according to its true idea, is only satisfaction rendered for the violation of moral order. In how far the speeches of Elihu succeed in conveying this view clear and distinct from the original standpoint of the friends, especially of Eliphaz, matters not to us here; at all events, it is in the mind of the poet as the characteristic of these speeches. (2.) The afflictions of the righteous man are means of proving and testing, which, like chastisements, come from the love of

God. Their object is not, however, the purging away of sin which may still cling to the righteous man, but, on the contrary, the manifestation and testing of his righteousness. This is the point of view from which, apart from Elihu's speeches, the book of Job presents Job's afflictions. Only by this relation of things is the chagrin with which Job takes up the words of Eliphaz, and so begins the controversy, explained and justified or excused. And, indeed, if it should be even impossible for the Christian, especially with regard to his own sufferings, to draw the line between disciplinary and testing sufferings so clearly as it is drawn in the book of Job, there is also for the deeper and more acute New Testament perception of sin, a suffering of the righteous which exists without any causal connection with his sin, viz. confession by suffering, or martyrdom, which the righteous man undergoes, not for his own sake, but for the sake of God.

If we, then, keep in mind these two further answers which the book of Job gives us to the question, "Why through suffering to blessedness?" it is not to be denied that practically they are perfectly sufficient. If I know that God sends afflictions to me because, since sin and evil are come into the world, they are the indispensable means of purifying and testing me, and by both purifying and testing of perfecting me,—these are explanations with which I can and must console myself. But this is still not the final answer of the book of Job to its great question. And its unparalleled magnitude, its high significance in the historical development of revelation, its typical character already recognised in the Old Testament, consists just in its going beyond this answer, and giving us an answer which, going back to the extreme roots of evil, and being deduced from the most intimate connections of the individual life of man with the history and plan of the world in the most comprehensive sense, not only practically, but speculatively, satisfies.

§ 2. THE CHOKMA-CHARACTER OF THE BOOK.

But before we go so far into this final and highest answer as the province of the Introduction permits and requires, in order to assign to the reader the position necessary to be taken for understanding the book, we ask, How comes it that the book of Job presents such a universal and absolute solution of the problem, otherwise unheard of in the Old Testament Scriptures? The reason of it is in the peculiar mental tendency (*Geistesrichtung*) of the Israelitish race from which it proceeded. There was in Israel a bias of a universalistic, humanic, philosophical kind, which, starting from the fear or worship (religion) of Jehovah, was turned to the final causes of things,— the cosmical connections of the earthly, the common human foundations of the Israelitish, the invisible roots of the visible, the universal actual truth of the individual and national historical. The common character of the few works of this Chokma which have been preserved to us is the humanic standpoint, stripped of everything peculiarly Israelitish. In the whole book of Proverbs, which treats of the relations of human life in its most general aspects, the name of the covenant people, יִשְׂרָאֵל, does not once occur. In Ecclesiastes, which treats of the nothingness of all earthly things, and with greater right than the book of Job may be called the canticle of Inquiry,[1] even the covenant name of God, יהוה, does not occur. In the Song of Songs, the groundwork of the picture certainly, but not the picture itself, is Israelitish: it represents a common human primary relation, the love of man and woman; and that if not with allegorical, yet mystical meaning, similar to the Indian *Gitagovinda*,

---

[1] The book of Job, says H. Heine, in his *Vermischte Schriften*, 1854, i., is the canticle of Inquiry (*das Hohelied der Skepsis*), and horrid serpents hiss therein their eternal Wherefore? As man when he suffers must weep his fill, so must he cease to doubt. This poison of doubt must not be wanting in the Bible, that great storehouse of mankind.

and also the third part of the Tamul *Kural*, translated by
Graul.

So the book of Job treats a fundamental question of our
common humanity; and the poet has studiously taken his
hero not from Israelitish history, but from extra-Israelitish
tradition.   From beginning to end he is conscious of relating
an extra-Israelitish history,—a history handed down among
the Arab tribes to the east of Palestine, which has come to
his ears; for none of the proper names contain even a trace of
symbolically intended meaning, and romantic historical poems
were moreover not common among the ancients.   This extra-
Israelitish history from the patriarchal period excited the purpose of his poem, because the thought therein presented lay
also in his own mind.   The Thora from Sinai and prophecy,
the history and worship of Israel, are nowhere introduced;
even indirect references to them nowhere escape him.   He
throws himself with wonderful truthfulness, effect, and vividness, into the extra-Israelitish position.   His own Israelitish
standpoint he certainly does not disavow, as we see from his
calling God יהוה everywhere in the prologue and epilogue; but
the non-Israelitish character of his hero and of his locality he
maintains with strict consistency.   Only twice is יהוה found
in the mouth of Job (i. 21, xii. 9), which is not to be wondered
at, since this name of God, as the names *Morija* and *Jochebed*
show, is not absolutely post-Mosaic, and therefore may have
been known among the Hebrew people beyond Israel.   But
with this exception, Job and his friends everywhere call God
אֱלוֹהַּ, which is more poetic, and for non-Israelitish speakers
(*vid*. Prov. xxx. 5) more appropriate than אֱלֹהִים, which occurs
only three times (xx. 29, xxxii. 2, xxxviii. 7); or they call
Him שַׁדַּי, which is the proper name of God in the patriarchal
time, as it appears everywhere in Genesis, where in the
Elohistic portions the high and turning-points of the self-
manifestation of God occur (xvii. 1, xxxv. 11; cf. Ex.

vi. 3), and when the patriarchs, at special seasons, pronounce the promise which they have received upon their children (xxviii. 3, xlviii. 3, xlix. 25 ; cf. xliii. 14). Even many of the designations of the divine attributes which have become fixed in the Thora, as רַחוּם, חַנּוּן, אֶרֶךְ אַפַּיִם, which one might well expect in the book of Job, are not found in it ; nor טוֹב, often used of Jehovah in Psalms ; nor generally the too (so to speak) dogmatic terminology of the Israelitish religion ;[1] besides which also this characteristic, that only the oldest mode of heathen worship, star-worship (xxxi. 26–28), is mentioned, without even the name of God (אלהים צבאות or יהוה צבאות) occurring, which designates God as Lord of the heavens, which the heathen deified. The writer has also intentionally avoided this name, which is the star of the time of the Israelitish kings ; for he is never unmindful that his subject is an ante- and extra-Israelitish one.

Hengstenberg, in his *Lecture on the Book of Job*, 1856, goes so far as to maintain, that a character like Job cannot possibly have existed in the heathen world, and that revelation would have been unnecessary if heathendom could produce such characters for itself. The poet, however, without doubt, presupposes the opposite ; and if he did not presuppose it, he should have refrained from using all his skill to produce the appearance of the opposite. That he has nevertheless done it, cannot mislead us : for, on the one hand, Job belongs to the patriarchal period, therefore the period before the giving of the law,—a period in which the early revelation was still at work, and the revelation of God, which had not remained

---

[1] קָדוֹשׁ, of God, only occurs once (vi. 10) ; חֶסֶד but twice (x. 12, and with Elihu, xxxvii. 13) ; אָהֵב with its derivatives not at all (gen. only xix. 19). In the speeches of the three, צַדִּיק (only with Elihu, xxxiv. 17), מִשְׁפָּט, and שָׁלֵם, as expressions of the divine *justitia recompensativa*, are not to be found ; נִסָּה and בֹּחַן become nowhere synonymous to designate Job's sufferings by the right name ; מַכָּה appears (ix. 23) only in the general signification of misfortune.

unknown in the side branches of the patriarchal family.   On
the other hand, it is quite consistent with the standpoint of
the Chokma, that it presupposes a preparatory self-manifes-
tation of God even in the extra-Israelitish world ; just as
John's Gospel, which aims at proving in Christianity the
absolute religion which shall satisfy every longing of all mankind, acknowledges τέκνα τοῦ Θεοῦ διεσκορπισμένα also beyond
the people of God, xi. 52, without on this account finding the
incarnation of the Logos, and the possibility of regeneration
by it, to be superfluous.

This parallel between the book of Job and the Gospel by
John is fully authorized ; for the important disclosure which
the prologue of John gives to us of the Logos, is already in
being in the book of Job and the introduction to the book of
Proverbs, especially ch. viii., without requiring the intervening
element of the Alexandrine religious philosophy, which, however, after it is once there, may not be put aside or disavowed.
The Alexandrine doctrine of the Logos is really the genuine
more developed form, though with many imperfections, of that
which is taught of the Chokma in the book of Job and in Proverbs.   Both notions have a universalistic comprehensiveness,
referring not only to Israel, but to mankind.   The חכמה certainly took up its abode in Israel, as it itself proves in the book
Σοφια Σειραχ, ch. xxiv.; but there is also a share of it attainable
by and allotted to all mankind.   This is the view of the writer
of the book of Job.   He is imbued with the conviction, that
even beyond Israel fellowship is possible with the one living
God, who has revealed himself in Israel ; that He also there
continually reveals himself, ordinarily in the conscience, and
extraordinarily in dreams and visions ; that there is also found
there a longing and struggling after that redemption of which
Israel has the clear words of promise.   His wondrous book
soars high above the Old Testament limit ; it is the Melchizedek among the Old Testament books.   The final and highest

solution of the problem with which it grapples, has a quarry extending out even beyond the patriarchal history. The Wisdom of the book of Job originates, as we shall see, from paradise. For this turning also to the primeval histories of Genesis, which are earlier than the rise of the nations, and the investigation of the hieroglyphs in the prelude to the Thora, which are otherwise almost passed over in the Old Testament, belong to the peculiarities of the Chokma.

§ 3. POSITION IN THE CANON.

As a work of the Chokma, the book of Job stands, with the three other works belonging to this class of the Israelitish literature, among the Hagiographa, which are called in He-brew simply כתובים. Thus, by the side of תורה and נביאים, the third division of the canon is styled, in which are included all those writings belonging neither to the province of prophetic history nor prophetic declaration. Among the Hagiographa are writings even of a prophetic character, as Psalms and Daniel; but their writers were not properly נביאים. At present Lamentations stands among them ; but this is not its original place, as also Ruth appears to have stood originally between Judges and Samuel. Both Lamentations and Ruth are placed among the Hagiographa, that there the five so-called מגלות or scrolls may stand together : Schir ha-Schirim the feast-book of the eighth passover-day, Ruth that of the second Schabuoth-day, Kinoth that of the ninth of Ab, Koheleth that of the eighth Succoth-day, Esther that of Purim. The book of Job, which is written neither in prophetico-historical style, nor in the style of prophetic preaching, but is a didactic poem, could stand nowhere else but in the third division of the canon. The position which it occupies is moreover a very shifting one. In the Alexandrine canon, Chronicles, Ezra, Nehemiah, Tobit, Judith, Esther, follow the four books of the Kings. The historical books therefore stand, from the earliest to the latest, side by side; then begins with Job, Psalms, Proverbs, a new row, opened with these three in stricter sense poetical books. Then Melito of Sardis, in the second century, places Chronicles with the books of the Kings, but arranges immediately after them the non-historical Hagiographa in the following order: Psalms, Proverbs, Ecclesiastes, Canticles, Job; here the Salomonic writings are joined to the Davidic Psalter, and the anonymous book of Job stands last. In our editions of the Bible, the Hagiographa division begins with Psalms, Proverbs, Job (the succession peculiar to MSS. of the German class); in the Talmud (*Bathra*, 14b), with Ruth, Psalms, Job, Proverbs; in the Masora, and in MSS. of the Spanish class, with Chronicles, Psalms, Job, Proverbs. All these modes of arrangement are well considered. The Masora connects with the נביאים אחרונים the homogeneous book, the Chronicles; the Talmud places the book of Ruth before the Psalter as an historical prologue, or as a connection between the prophetico-historical books and the Hagiographa.[1] The practice in our editions is to put the Psalms as the first book of the division, which agrees with Luke xxiv. 44, and with Philo, who places ὕμνους next to the prophetical books. Job stands only in the LXX. at the head of the three so-called poetic books, perhaps as a work by its patriarchal contents referring back to the earliest times. Everywhere else the Psalter stands first among the three books. These three are commonly denoted by the *vox memoralis* ספרי א"מת ; but this succession, Job, Proverbs, Psalms, is nowhere found. The Masora styles them after its own, and the Talmudic order ספרי ת"אם.

---

[1] That Job stands after the Psalms is explained by his being contemporary with the Queen of Sheba, or, accepting Moses as the writer of the book (in which case it should stand at the head of the Chethubim), by its not being placed foremost, on account of its terrible contents (according to the maxim לא מתחילין בפרענותא).

§ 4. THE SYSTEM OF ACCENTUATION, MANNER OF WRITING IN VERSES, AND STRUCTURE OF THE STROPHE.

The so-ciphered three books have, as is known, this in common, that they are (with the exception of the prologue and epilogue in the book of Job) punctuated according to a special system, which has been fully discussed in my *Commentary on the Psalms*, and in Baer's edition of the Psalter. This accent system, like the prosaic, is constructed on the fundamental law of dichotomy; but it is determined by better organization, more expressive and melodious utterance. Only the so-called prose accents, however, not the metrical or poetic (with the exception of a few detached fragments), have been preserved in transmission. Nevertheless, we are always still able to discern from these accents how the reading in the synagogue divided the thoughts collected into the form of Masoretic verses, into two chief divisions, and within these again into lesser divisions, and connected or separated the single words; while the musical rhythm accommodated itself as much as possible to the logical, so that the accentuation is on this account an important source for ascertaining the traditional exegesis, and contains an abundance of most valuable hints for the interpreter. Tradition, moreover, requires for the three books a verse-like short line stich-manner of writing; and פסוק, *versus*, meant originally, not the Masoretic verse, but the separate sentence, στίχος, denoted in the accent system by a great distinctive; as *e.g.* Job iii. 3 :

> *Let the day perish wherein I was born,*
> *And the night, which said, There is a man-child con-*
> *ceived,*

is a Masoretic verse divided into two parts by Athnach, and therefore, according to the old order, is to be written as two στίχοι.[1] This also is important. In order to recognise the strophe-structure of Hebrew poems, one must attend to the στίχοι, in which the poetic thoughts follow one another in well-measured flow. Parallelism, which we must likewise acknowledge as the fundamental law of the rhythm of Hebrew poetry, forms the evolutions of thought not always of two members, but often—as *e.g.* iii. 4, 5, 6, 9—also of three. The poetic formation is not, however, confined to this, but even further combines (as is most unmistakeably manifest in the alphabetical psalms,[2] and as recently also Ewald inclines to acknowledge[3]) such distichs and tristichs into a greater whole, forming a complete circle of thought; in other words, into strophes of four, eight, or some higher number of lines, in themselves paragraphs, which, however, show themselves as strophes, inasmuch as they recur and change symmetrically.

---

[1] The meaning of this old order, and the aptness of its execution, has been lost in later copyists, because they break off not according to the sense, but only according to the space, as the στίχοι in numbering the lines, *e.g.* of the Greek orators, are mere lines according to the space (*Raumzeile*), at least according to Ritschl's view (*Die alex. Bibliotheken*, 1838, S. 92-136), which, however, has been disputed by Vömel. The old soferish order intends lines according to the sense, and so also the Greek distinction by πέντε στιχηραὶ (στιχήρεις) βίβλοι, *i.e.* Job, Psalms, Proverbs, Canticles, Ecclesiastes.

[2] That from these we may proceed, the ancients here and there conjectured; as *e.g.* Serpilius says, " It may perhaps occur to some, whether now and then a slight judgment of the Davidic species of verse and poesy may not be in some way formed from his, so to speak, alphabetical psalms."

[3] On strophes in the book of Job, *Jahrb.* iii. 118 : " That the Masoretic division of the verses is not always correct, follows also from a more exact consideration of the strophes. Here comes a further question, whether one must determine the limit of such a strophe only according to the verses, which are often in themselves very irregular, or rather, strictly according to the *members* of the verse ? The latter seems to me, at least in some parts, certainly to be the case, as I have already had opportunity to remark." Nevertheless, he reckons the strophes in *Neue Bemerkungen zum B. Ijob*, ix. 35-37, according to lines = Masoretic verses.

Hupfeld has objected that these strophes, as an aggregate
formed of a symmetrical number of stichs, are opposed to the
nature of the rhythm = parallelism, which cannot stand on one
leg, but needs two ; but this objection is as invalid as if one
should say, Because every soldier has two legs, therefore soldiers
can only march singly, and not in a row and company. It
may be seen, *e.g.*, from xxxvi. 22–25, 26–29, 30–33, where the
poet begins three times with הֵן, and three times the sentences
so beginning are formed of eight lines. Shall we not say
there are three eight-line strophes beginning with הֵן? Never
theless, we are far from maintaining that the book of Job
consists absolutely of speeches in the strophe and poetic form.
It breaks up, however, into paragraphs, which not unfre-
quently become symmetrical strophes. That neither the
symmetrical nor mixed strophe-schema is throughout with
strict unexceptional regularity carried out, arises from the
artistic freedom which the poet was obliged to maintain in
order not to sacrifice the truth as well as the beauty of the
dialogue. Our translation, arranged in paragraphs, and the
schemata of the number of stichs in the paragraph placed
above each speech, will show that the arrangement of the
whole is, after all, far more strophic than its dramatic character allows, according to classic and modern poetic art.[1]   It
is similar in Canticles, with the melodramatic character of
which it better agrees. In both cases it is explained from the

---

[1] What Gottfr. Hermann, in his *diss. de arte poesis Græcorum buco-
licæ*, says respecting the strophe-division in Theocritus, is nevertheless
to be attentively considered : Verendum est ne ipsi nobis somnia fin-
gamus perdamusque operam, si artificiosas stropharum comparationes
comminiscamur, de quibus ipsi poetæ ne cogitaverint quidem.   Videri-
que potest id eo probabilius esse, quod sæpenumero dubitari potest, sic
an aliter constituendæ sint strophæ.   Nam poesis, qualis hæc bucoli-
corum est, quæ maximam partem ex brevibus dictis est composita, ipsa
natura sua talis est ut in partes fere vel pares vel similes dividi possit.
Nihilo tamen minus illam strophicam rationem non negligendam arbi-
tror, ut quæ apud poetas bucolicos in consuetudinem vertisse videatur, etc.

Hebrew poesy being in its fundamental peculiarity lyric, and from the drama not having freed itself from the lyric element, and attained to complete independence. The book of Job is, moreover, not a drama grown to complete development. Prologue and epilogue are treated as history, and the separate speeches are introduced in the narrative style. In the latter respect (with the exception of ch. ii. 10a), Canticles is more directly dramatic than the book of Job.[1] The drama is here in reference to the strophic form in the garb of Canticles, and in respect of the narrative form in the garb of history or epopee. Also the book of Job cannot be regarded as drama, if we consider, with G. Baur,[2] dramatic and scenic to be inseparable ideas; for the Jews first became acquainted with the theatre from the Greeks and Romans.[3] Nevertheless, it is questionable whether the drama everywhere presupposes the existence of the stage, as e.g. A. W. v. Schlegel, in his *Lectures on Dramatic Art and Literature*, maintains. Göthe, at least, more than once asserts, that " drama and a composition for the stage may be separate," and admits a " dramatic plot and execution" in Canticles.[4]

§ 5. THE DRAMATIC ART OF THE PLOT AND EXECUTION.

On the whole, we have as little hesitation as Hupfeld in calling the book of Job a drama; and it is characteristic of

---

[1] Hence there are Greek MSS., in which the names of the speakers (e.g. ἡ νύμφη, αἱ νεανίδες, ὁ νυμφίος) are prefixed to the separate parts of Canticles (vid. *Repertorium für bibl. u. morgenl. Lit.* viii. 1781, S. 180). The Archimandrite Porphyrios, who in his *Travels*, 1856, described the *Codex Sinaiticus* before Tischendorf, though unsatisfactorily, describes there also such διαλογικῶς written MSS. of Canticles.

[2] *Das B. Hiob und Dante's Göttliche Comödie, Studien u. Krit.* 1856, iii.

[3] See my *Geschichte der jüdischen Dramatik* in my edition of the *Migdal Oz* (hebr. handling of the *Pastor fido* of Guarini) by Mose Chajim Luzzatto, Leipz. 1837.

[4] Werke (neue Ausg. in 30 Bden.), xiii. 596 ; xxvi. 513 f.

the Israelitish Chokma, that by Canticles and the book of Job, its two generic manifestations, it has enriched the national poesy with this new form of poetic composition. The book of Job is, though not altogether, yet substantially, a drama, and one consisting of seven divisions : (1) ch. i.–iii., the opening ; (2) ch. iv.–xiv., the first course of the controversy, or the beginning entanglement; (3) ch. xv.–xxi., the second course of the controversy, or the increasing entanglement; (4) ch. xxii.–xxvi., the third course of the controversy, or the increasing entanglement at its highest; (5) ch. xxvii.–xxxi., the transition from the entanglement (δέσις) to the unravelling (λύσις) : Job's monologues ; (6) ch. xxxviii.–xlii. 6, the consciousness of the unravelling ; (7) xlii. 7 sqq., the unravelling in outward reality. In this we have left Elihu's speeches (ch. xxxii.–xxxvii.) out of consideration, because it is very questionable whether they are a part of the original form of the book, and not, on the contrary, the introduction of another poet.   If we include them, the drama has eight divisions. The speeches of Elihu form an interlude in the transition from the δέσις to the λύσις. The book of Job is an audience-chamber, and one can readily suppose that a cotemporary or later poet may have mixed himself up with the speakers. Whether, however, this is really the case, may remain here undecided.   The prologue is narrative, but still partly in dialogue style, and so far not altogether undramatical.   In form it corresponds most to the Euripidean, which also are a kind of epic introduction to the pieces, and it accomplishes what Sophocles in his prologues so thoroughly understands. At the very beginning he excites interest in the occurrences to be brought forward, and makes us acquainted with that which remains concealed from the actors.   After the knot of the puzzle is tied in the prologue, it becomes more and more deeply entangled in the three courses of the controversy. In the monologues of Job it begins to be disentangled, and in the sixth part the unravelling follows, well prepared for, and therefore not ἀπὸ μηχανῆς, and is perfected in the epilogue or exodus : the servant of God, being so far as necessary cleared by penitence, is justified in opposition to his friends ; and the victor, tried in accordance with the divine utterance, is crowned. It is therefore a continually progressing history. The remark of Herder,[1] " Here all is stationary in long conversations," is superficial. It is from beginning to end a stream of the most active life, with external incident only in the opening and in the unravelling ; what Schlegel says of Göthe's *Iphigenie* holds good of the middle of the book, that the ideas are worked into incidents, and brought, as it were, before the eye. Moreover, as in Göthe's *Tasso*, the deficiency of external action is compensated by the richness and precision with which the characters are drawn. Satan, Job's wife, the hero himself, the three friends,—everywhere diversified and minute description. The poet manifests, also, dramatic skill in other directions. He has laid out the controversy with a masterly hand, making the heart of the reader gradually averse to the friends, and in the same degree winning it towards Job. He makes the friends all through give utterance to the most glorious truths, which, however, *in the application to the case before them,* turn out to be untrue. And although the whole of the representation serves one great idea, it is still not represented by any of the persons brought forward, and is by no one expressly uttered. Every person is, as it were, the consonant letter to the word of this idea ; it is throughout the whole book taken up with the realization of itself ; at the end it first comes forth as the resulting product of the whole. Job himself is not less a tragic hero than the Œdipus of both Sophocles' tragedies.[2] What is there an

---

[1] *Geist der Ebräischen Poesie*, 1805, i. S. 137.

[2] Schultens says : Quidquid tragœdia vetus unquam Sophocleo vel Æschyleo molita est cothurno, infra magnitudinem, gravitatem, ardorem,

inevitable fate, expressed by the oracle, is in the book of Job the decree of Jehovah, over whom is no controlling power, decreed in the assembly of angels. As a painful puzzle the lot of affliction comes down on Job. At the beginning he is the victor of an easy battle, until the friends' exhortations to repentance are added to suffering, which in itself is incomprehensible, and make it still harder to be understood. He is thereby involved in a hard conflict, in which at one time, full of arrogant self-confidence, he exalts himself heavenward ; at another time, sinks to the ground in desponding sadness.

The God, however, against which he fights is but a phantom, which the temptation has presented to his saddened eye instead of the true God ; and this phantom is in no way different from the inexorable fate of the Greek tragedy. As in that the hero seeks to maintain his inward freedom against the secret power which crushes him with an iron arm ; so Job maintains his innocence against this God, which has devoted him to destruction as an offender. But in the midst of this terrific conflict with the God of the present, this creation of the temptation, Job's faith gropes after the God of the future, to whom he is ever driven nearer the more mercilessly the enemies pursue him. At length Jehovah really appears, but not at Job's impetuous summons. He appears first after Job has made a beginning of humble self-concession, in order to complete the work begun, by condescendingly going forth to meet him. Jehovah appears, and the fury vanishes. The dualism, which the Greek tragedy leaves unabolished, is here reconciled. Human freedom does not succumb ; but it be-

animositatem horum affectuum infinitum quantum subsidet. Similarly Ewald (*Jahrb.* ix. 27): Neither the Hindoos, nor the Greeks and Romans, have such a lofty and purely perfected poem to produce. One would perhaps compare it with one of Æschylus or Sophocles' tragedies as the nearest ; but we cannot easily find a single one among these approaching its unblemished height and perfection in the midst of the greatest simplicity.

comes evident that not an absolute arbitrary power, but divine wisdom, whose inmost impulse is love, moulds human destiny.

§ 6. TIME OF COMPOSITION.

That this masterpiece of religious reflection and systematic creative art—this, to use Luther's expression, lofty and grand book, in which, as the mountains round an Alpine valley, all the terribly sublime that nature and human history present is ranged one above another—belongs to no other than the Salomonic period, we might almost assume, even if it were not confirmed on all sides. The opinion that Moses wrote the book of Job before the giving of the law, is found in the Talmuds (*jer. Sota V.* 8 ; *b. Bathra,* 15*a*). This view has been recently revived by Ebrard (1858). But how improbable, all but impossible, that the poetical literature of Israel should have taken its rise with such a *non plus ultra* of reflective poetry, and that this poem should have had Moses the lawgiver for its author ! " Moses certainly is not the composer of the book of Job," says Herder rightly,[1] " or Solon might have written the *Iliad* and the *Eumenides* of Æschylus." This opinion, which is also found in Origen, Jerome, Polychronius, and Julian of Halicarnassus, would surely never have suggested itself to any one, had not the studious avoidance in the book of all reference to the law, prophecy, history, religious worship, and even of the religious terminology of Israel, consequent on its design, produced the appearance of a pre-Sinaitic origin. But, first, this absence of such reference is, as we have already seen, the result of the genius and aim which belong to the book ; secondly, the writer distinctly enough betrays his acquaintance with the Thora : for as the Chokma for the most part necessarily presupposes the revelation of God deposited in the Thora,

[1] *Geist der Ebr. Poesie,* 1805, i. S. 130.

and is even at pains to show its universal and eternal ideas, and its imperishable nature full of meaning for all men, so a book like the book of Job could only have been written by an Israelitish author, only have sprung from the spiritual knowledge and experience rendered possible by the Thora.[1] For as insight into the groping of the heathen world after divine truth is only possible in the light of Christianity, so also such a spiritually bold and accurate reproduction of an old patriarchal tradition was only possible in the light of the revelation of Jehovah : not to mention that the middle part of the book is written in the style of the book of Proverbs, the surrounding parts in evident imitation of the style of the primitive histories of the Pentateuch.

But as the supposition of a pre-Salomonic composition is proved invalid, so also are all the grounds on which it has been sought to prove a post-Salomonic. Ewald, whom Heiligstedt and Renan follow, is of opinion that it shows very unsettled and unfortunate times in the background, and from this and other indications was written under Manasseh; Hirzel, that the writer who is so well acquainted with Egypt, seems to have been carried into Egypt with King Jehoahaz; Stickel, that the book presupposes the invasion of the Asiatic conqueror as begun, but not yet so far advanced as the destruction of Jerusalem; Bleek, that it must belong to the post-Salomonic period, because it seems to refer to a previous

---

[1] Reggio indeed maintains (*Kerem Chemed*, vi. 53–60) in favour of the Mosaic pre-Sinaitic composition : " God is only represented as the Almighty, the Ruler of the universe: His love, mercy, forbearance—attributes which the Thora first revealed—are nowhere mentioned ;" and S. D. Luzzatto concludes from this even the non-Israelitish origin of the book : " The God of Job is not the God of Israel, the gracious One: He is the almighty and just, but not the kind and true One ;" but although the book does not once use the words goodness, love, forbearance, compassion of God, it is nevertheless a bright example of them all; and it is the love of God which it manifests as a bright ray in the dark mystery of the affliction of the righteous.

comprehensive diversified literature. But all this rests on invalid grounds, false observation, and deceptive conclusions. Indeed, the assumption that a book which sets forth such a fearful conflict in the depths of affliction must have sprung from a time of gloomy national distress, is untenable : it is sufficient to suppose that the writer himself has experienced the like, and experienced it at a time when all around him were living in great luxury, which must have greatly aggravated his trial. It would be preferable to suppose that the book of Job belongs to the time of the exile (Umbreit and others), and that Job, though not exactly a personification of Israel, is still מֹשֵׁל לְיִשְׂרָאֵל,[1] a pattern for the people of the exile (Bernstein) ; for this view, interesting indeed in itself, has the similarity of several passages of the second part of the book of Isaiah in its favour : comp. ch. xl. 14 with Job xxi. 22, xl. 23 with Job xii. 24, xliv. 25 with Job xii. 17, 20, xliv. 24 with Job ix. 8, lix. 4 with Job xv. 35, Ps. vii. 15. These, however, only prove that the severely tried *ecclesia pressa* of the exiles might certainly recognise itself again in the example of Job, and make it seem far more probable that the book of Job is older than that period of Israel's suffering.

The literature of the Chokma began with Solomon. First in the time of Solomon, whose peculiar gift was worldly wisdom, a time which bears the character of peaceful contemplation resulting from the conflicts of belief of David's time,[2] the external and internal preliminary conditions for

[1] *Vid.* c. 90 of *Ez chajim*, by Ahron b. Elias of Nicomedia, edited by Delitzsch, 1841, which corresponds to *More Nebuchim*, iii. 22–24. The view that the poet himself, by Job intended the Israel of the exile (according to Warburton, the Israel of the restoration after the exile ; according to Grotius, the Edomites carried into exile by the Babylonians), is about the same as the view that the guilty Pericles may be intended by King Œdipus, or the Sophists by the Odysseus of the Philoctetes.

[2] Thus far Gaupp, *Praktische Theol.* ii. 1, 488, is in some degree right, when he considers the book of Job a living testimony of the new spirit of belief which was bursting forth in David's time.

it existed. The chief part of Proverbs and Canticles is by Solomon himself; the introductory passages (Prov. i.-ix.) represent a later period of the Chokma, probably the time of Jehoshaphat; the book of Ecclesiastes, which is rightly assigned by H. G. Bernstein in his *Questiones Kohelethanæ* to the time between Artaxerxes ɪ. Longimanus, and Darius Codomannus, and perhaps belongs to the time of Artaxerxes ɪɪ. Mnemon, represents the latest period. The book of Job is indicated as a work of the first of these three periods, by its classic, grand, and noble fórm. It bears throughout the stamp of that creative, beginning-period of the Chokma,—of that Salomonic age of knowledge and art, of deeper thought respecting revealed religion, and of intelligent, progressive culture of the traditional forms of art,—that unprecedented age, in which the literature corresponded to the summit of glorious magnificence to which the kingdom of the promise had then attained. The heart of Solomon (according to 1 Kings v. 9 sq., Heb.; iv. 29, English version) enclosed within itself a fulness of knowledge, "even as the sand that is on the seashore :" his wisdom was greater than the בני קדם, from whom the traditional matter of the book of Job is borrowed; greater than the wisdom of the מצרים, with whose country and natural marvels the author of the book of Job is intimately acquainted. The extensive knowledge of natural history and general science displayed in the book of Job, is the result of the wide circle of observation which Israel had reached. It was a time when the chasm between Israel and the nations was more than ever bridged over. The entire education of Israel at that time took a so to speak cosmopolitan direction. It was a time introductory to the extension of redemption, and the triumph of the religion of Israel, and the union of all nations in belief on the God of love.

§ 7. SIGNS FROM THE DOCTRINAL CONTENTS.

That the book of Job belongs to this period and no other, is confirmed also by the relation of its doctrinal contents to the other canonical writings. If we compare the doctrine respecting Wisdom—her super-eminence, applicability to worldly matters, and co-operation in the creation of the world—in Prov. i.-ix., especially ch. viii., with Job xxviii., it is there manifestly more advanced, and further developed. If we compare the pointing to the judgment of God, Job xix. 29, with the hint of a future general judgment, which shall decide and adjust all things, in Eccl. xii. 14, we see at once that what comes forward in the former passage only at first as an expression of personal belief, is in the latter already become a settled element of general religious consciousness.

And however we may interpret that brilliant passage of the book of Job, ch. xix. 25–27,—whether it be the beholding of God in the present bodily, future spiritual, or future glorified state,—it is by no means an echo of an already existing revelation of the resurrection of the dead, that acknowledgment of revelation which we see breaking forth and expanding throughout Isa. xxvi. 19, comp. xxv. 8, and Ezek. xxxvii. comp. Hos. vi. 2, until Dan. xii. 2. The prevailing representations of the future in the book of Job are exactly the same as those in the Psalms of the time of David and Solomon, and in the Proverbs of Solomon. The writer speaks as one of the same age in which Heman sighed, Ps. lxxxviii. 11 sq., " *Wilt Thou show wonders to the dead? or shall the shades arise and praise Thee? Shall Thy loving-kindness be declared in the grave, Thy faithfulness in the abyss?*" Besides, the greatest conceivable fulness of allusion to the book of Job, including Elihu's speeches, is found in Ps. lxxxviii. and lxxxix., whose authors, Heman and Ethan, the Ezrahites, are not the same as the chief singers of David of the same name, but the contemporaries of Solomon mentioned in 1 Kings v. 11. These two psalms coincide with the book of Job, both in expressions with which remarkable representations are united, as קדושים of the celestial spirits, רפאים of the shades in Hades, אבדון of Hades itself, and also in expressions which do not occur elsewhere in the Old Testament, as אֵמִים and בְּעֻתִים; and the agreement is manifest, moreover, in the agreement of whole verses either in thought or in expression : comp. Ps. lxxxix. 38 with Job xvi. 19, lxxxix. 48 with Job vii. 7, lxxxix. 49 with Job xiv. 14, lxxxviii. 5 with Job xiv. 10, lxxxviii. 9 with Job xxx. 10, lxxxix. 8 with Job xxxi. 34. In all these passages, however, there is no such similarity as suggests a borrowing, but an agreement which, since it cannot possibly be accidental, may be most easily explained by supposing that the book of Job proceeds from just the same Chokma-fellowship to which, according to 1 Kings v. 11, the two Ezrahites, the writers of Ps. lxxxviii. and lxxxix., belong.

One might go further, and conjecture that the same Heman who composed Ps. lxxxviii., the gloomiest of all the Psalms, and written under circumstances of suffering similar to Job's, may be the author of the book of Job—for which many probable reasons might be advanced; by which also what G. Baur rightly assumes would be confirmed, that the writer of the book of Job has himself passed through the inward spiritual conflict which he describes, and accordingly gives a page from his own religious history. But we are satisfied with the admission, that the book of Job is the work of one of the wise men whose rendezvous was the court of Solomon. Gregory of Nazianzen and Luther have already admitted the origin of the book in Solomon's time; and among later critics, Rosenmüller, Hävernick, Vaihinger, Hahn, Schlottmann, Keil, and Hofmann (though in

his *Weissagung und Erfüllung* he expressed the opinion that
it belongs to the Mosaic period), are agreed in this.[1]

§ 8. ECHOES IN THE LATER SACRED WRITINGS.

It may be readily supposed, that a book like this, which is
occupied with a question of such vital import to every thinking and pious man,—which treats it in such a lively manner,
riveting the attention, and bespeaking sympathy,—which,
apart from its central subject, is so many-sided, so majesti-
cally beautiful in language, and so inexhaustible in imagery,—
will have been one of the most generally read of the national
books of Israel. Such is found to be the case; and also
hereby its origin in the time of Solomon is confirmed : for
at this very period it is to Ps. lxxxviii. lxxxix. only that it
stands in the mutual relation already mentioned. But the
echoes appear as early as in the דברי חכמים, which are appended to the Salomonic משלי in the book of Proverbs: comp.
the teaching from an example in the writer's own experience, Prov. xxiv. 30 sqq. with Job v. 3 sqq. The book of
Job, however, next to the Proverbs of Solomon, was the
favourite source of information for the author of the intro
ductory proverbs (ch. i.–ix.). Here (apart from the doctrine
of wisdom) we find whole passages similar to the book of
Job: comp. Prov. iii. 11 with Job v. 17, viii. 25 with Job
xv. 7, iii. 15 with Job xxviii. 18.

Then, in the prophets of the flourishing period of prophetic literature, which begins with Obadiah and Joel, we
find distinct traces of familiarity with the book of Job.
Amos describes the glory of God the Creator in words
taken from it (ch. iv. 13, v. 8, after Job ix. 8; cf. x. 22,

---

[1] Also Professor Barnwell, in the *Carolina Times*, 1857, No. 785, calls
the book of Job "the most brilliant flower of this brighter than Eliza-
bethan and nobler than Augustan era."

xxxviii. 31).   Isaiah has introduced a whole verse of the
book of Job, almost *verbatim*, into his prophecy against
Egypt (ch. xix. 5 = Job xiv. 11): in the same prophecy, ch.
xix. 13 sq. refer to Job xii. 24 sq., so also ch. xxxv. 3 to Job
iv. 4.   These reminiscences of the book of Job are frequent
in Isaiah (ch. xl.–lxvi.).   This book of solace for the exiles
corresponds to the book of Job not only in words, which
exclusively belong in common to the two (as נֶגַע and צאצאים),
and in surprising similarity of expression (as ch liii. 9, comp.
Job xvi. 17; lx. 6, comp. Job xxii. 11), but also in numerous
passages of similar thought and form (comp. ch. xl. 23 with
Job xii. 24); and in the description of the Servant of Jehovah, one is here and there involuntarily reminded of the book
of Job (as ch. l. 6, comp. with Job xvi. 10).   In Jeremiah,
the short lyric passage, ch. xx. 14–18, in which he curses the
day of his birth, falls back on Job iii.: the form in which
the despondency of the prophet breaks forth is determined by
the book of Job, with which he was familiar.   It requires no
proof that the same prophet follows the book of Job in many
passages of Lamentations, and especially the first part of ch.
iii.: he makes use of confessions, complaints, and imagery from
the affliction of Job, to represent the affliction of Israel.

By the end of the time of the kings, Job was a person
generally known in Israel, a recognised saint; for Ezekiel,
in the year 593–2 B.C. (ch. xiv. 14 sqq.), complains that the
measure of Israel's sin is so great, that if Noah, Daniel, and
Job were in the midst of Israel, though they might save themselves, they would not be able to hold back the arm of divine
justice.   The prophet mentions first Noah, a righteous man
of the old world; then Daniel, a righteous man of contemporary Israel; and last of all Job, a righteous man beyond the
line of the promise.[1]   He would not, however, have been able

---

[1] Hengstenberg (*Beiträge*, i. 72) thinks Job is mentioned last because
less suited to Ezekiel's purpose than Noah and Daniel.   Carpzov (*Introd.*

to mention him, if he had not, by means of the written narrative, been a person well known among the people to whom the prophetical discourse was addressed The literature of the Old Testament has no further reference to the question of the time of the composition of the book of Job ; for, on a comparison of Eccl. v. 14 with Job i. 21, it scarcely remains a question to which the priority belongs.

§ 9. THE CHIEF CRITICAL QUESTIONS.

Whether, however, the whole book, as we now have it, comes from the time of Solomon, as the work of one poet, or of one chief poet,[1] is a question which can be better determined in the course of the exposition. More or less important doubts have been entertained whether some constituent parts of the whole belong to the original setting. By far the most important question of criticism respects the six chapters of Elihu's speeches (ch. xxxii.–xxxvii.), respecting which the suspicion entertained by the fathers, and first decidedly expressed by Stuhlmann (1804), that not only in form are they inferior to the artistic execution of the rest of the work, but also in contents are opposed to its original plan, is not yet set aside, and perhaps never will be altogether satisfactorily settled. Besides this, Kennicot also has suspected the speech of Job, ch. xxvii. 11–xxviii. 28, because there Job seems to yield to the friends' controverted doctrine of retribution. De Wette is more inclined here to suppose a want of connection on the

---

in ll. poet. p. 35) is more ingenious, but too artificial, when he finds an anti-climax in the order : Noachus in clade primi mundi œcumenica, Daniel in clade patriæ ac gentis suæ, Iobus in clade familiæ servatus est.

[1] Compare Böttcher, Æhrenlese, S. 68 : " Respecting the mode of composition, we think there was one chief poet, with several contemporary associates, incited by a conversation on the then (i.e., according to Böttcher's view, in the reign of Manasseh) frequent afflictions of the innocent."

part of the writer than an interpolation. We shall have to prove whether this speech of Job really encroaches upon the province of the unravelling, or renders the transition more complete.

The whole description of *Behemoth* and *Leviathan*, ch. xl. 15–xli. 26, is regarded by Ewald as a later addition : De Wette extends this judgment only to ch. xli. 4–26 : Eichhorn was satisfied at first with changing the order of Jehovah's speeches; but in the last edition of his *Einleitung* ascribed the passage about the two monsters to a later poet. The exposition will have to bring the form of expression of the supposed interpolation, and its relation to the purpose of the second speech of Jehovah, in comparison with the first, under consideration. But we need not defer our judgment of the prologue and epilogue. All the doubts raised by Stuhlmann, Bernstein, Knobel (*diss. de carminis Iobi argumento, fine ac dispositione*, and *Studien u. Kritiken*, 1842, ii.), and others, respecting both these essential parts, are put an end to by the consideration, that the middle part of the book, without them, is a torso without head and feet.

§ 10. THE SATAN OF THE PROLOGUE.

But the Satan in the prologue is a stumbling-block to many, which, if it does not lead them to doubt the authenticity of the prologue, still causes them to question whether the composition of the book belongs to the time of Solomon. For Satan is first definitely named, Zech. iii., and 1 Chron. xxi. 1 ; consequently in writings of the period after the exile. On the other hand, שָׂטָן, Num. xxii. 22, appellatively describes one who comes forward hostilely, or as a hindrance ; and Ps. cix. 6 is at least open to question whether the prince of evil spirits may not be meant, which, according to Zech. iii. 1, seems to be intended. However, in Micaiah's vision, 1 Kings xxii. 19–23,

where one might expect הרוח ,השטן is used. It is even maintained in the present day, that the idea of Satan was first
obtained by the Israelitish race from contact with the East-
Asiatic nations, which began with Israel in the time of
Menahem, with Judah in the time of Ahaz; the view of
Diestel, that it is the copy of the Egyptian *Set-Typhon*, stands
at present alone. When we consider that the redemptive
work of Jesus Christ is regarded by Him and His apostles
from one side as the overthrow of Satan, it were a miserable
thing for the divine truth of Christianity that this Satan
should be nothing more than a copy of the Persian *Ahriman*,
and consequently a mere phantom. However, supposing
there were some such connection, we should then have only
two periods at which the book of Job could possibly have
been composed,—the time after the exile, and the time of
Solomon; for these are the only periods at which not only
collision, but also an interchange of ideas, between Israel and
the profane nations could have taken place. It is also just as
possible for the conception of Satan to have taken possession
of the Israelitish mind under Solomon as during the exile,
especially as it is very questionable whether the religion of
Cyrus, as found in the Zend books, may not have been far
more influenced by Israel, than, contrariwise, have influenced
Israel.

But the conception of Satan is indeed much older in its
existence than the time of Solomon: the serpent of paradise
must surely have appeared to the inquiring mind of Israel as
the disguise of an evil spirit; and nothing further can be
maintained, than that this evil spirit, which in the Mosaic
worship of the great day of atonement is called עזאזל (called
later בעל זבוב, a name borrowed from the goa of Ekron),
appears first in the later literature of Israel under the name
השטן. If now, moreover, the Chokma of the Salomonic
period was specially conversant with the pre-Israelitish his-

tories of Genesis, whence indeed even the chief thought of Canticles and the figure of עץ חיים *e.g.* frequently occurring in Proverbs are drawn, it is difficult to conceive why the evil spirit, that in its guise of a serpent aimed its malice against man, could not have been called השטן so early as the Salomonic period.

The wisdom of the author of the book of Job, we have said above, springs from paradise. Thence he obtains the highest and final solution of his problem. It is now time to give expression to this. At present we need only do so in outline, since it is simply of use to place us from the commencement at the right standpoint for understanding the book of Job.

§ 11. THE FINAL SOLUTION OF THE PROBLEM.

The nature of sin is two-sided. It consists in the creature's setting up himself in opposition to God, who is the essence of the personality of the creature. It consists also, on the other side, in the stirring up of the depth of the nature of the creature, whose essential consistence has its harmony in God; and by this stirring up, falls into a wild confusion. In other words, evil has a personal side and a natural side. And just so, also, is God's wrath which it excites, and which operates against it. For God's wrath is, on the one hand, the personal displeasure or aversion into which His love is changed, since the will of the creature and the will of God are in opposition; on the other hand, an excited condition of the contrary forces of the divine nature, or, as Scripture expresses it, the kindling of the fire of the divine glory, in which sense it is often said of wrath, that God sends it forth, that He pours it forth, and that man has to drink of it (Job xxi. 20, comp. vi. 4).[1]

In reference to the creature, we call evil according to its personal side ἔχθρα, and according to its natural side ἀταξία,

---

[1] *Vid.* my Proleg. to Weber's book on the Wrath of God.

turba.[1] Both personal evil and natural evil have originated in
the spirit world: first of all, in a spirit nearest to God, which
as fallen is called הישׂטן. It has sought its own selfish ends,
and thereby deranged its nature, so that it has become in
every respect the object of the divine wrath, and the material for the burning of the divine wrath: for the *echthra*
and *turba* have the intention and the burning of the wrath
of God in themselves as divine *correlata;* but Satan, after
that he has become entirely possessed of these divine powers
(*Energien*), is also their instrument. The spirit of light and
love is altogether become the spirit of fire and wrath; the
whole sphere of wrath is centred in him. After having given
up his high position in the realm of light, he is become lord
of the realm of wrath.

He has, from the commencement of his fall, the hell within
himself, but is first cast into the lake of fire at the end of the
present dispensation (Matt. xxv. 41; Apoc. xx. 10: comp.
Dan. vii. 11). In the meantime, he is being deprived of his
power by the Son of man, who, in the midst of His own and
His disciples' victories over the demons, beholds him fall as
lightning from heaven (Luke x. 18), and by His death gives
him his deathblow,—a final judgment, which, later on, becomes fully manifest in the continuous degradation of the
vanquished (comp. Apoc. xii. 9, xx. 3, xx. 10). Accordingly,
when Satan, in the book of Job, still appears among the angels
of God in heaven, and indeed as κατήγωρ, it is quite in
accordance with the disclosures which the New Testament
Scriptures give us respecting the invisible angelic side of the
present dispensation.

We will now cast a glance at the relation to the wrath of
God, and to Satan, into which man has fallen through the
temptation of the old serpent. Tempted by Satan, he is himself fallen into the realm of wrath, and become a servant of

[1] *Vid. Biblische Psychologie*, S. 128, 160.

Satan. He is in his grasp. All calamity that befalls him is divine punishment, either proceeding directly from the wrath of God, or worked by the wrath-spirit, Satan. But in prospect of the future atonement, which was to free man from the wrath of God, and from the power of wrath in which Satan holds him, it was possible for man, even under the Old Testament, to realize this deliverance, by virtue of an apprehension of the grace flowing from God's purpose of redemption. Whoever has been made free by this grace is changed from an object of the divine wrath to an object of the divine love, and nothing that befalls him in this condition proceeds from the wrath of God—all from His love. This love cannot, however, manifest itself so brightly as it would, so long as sin remains in the man and in the world; it is only able to manifest itself as loving wrath, *i.e.* as love controlling, and making wrath serviceable to itself.

Thus Job's suffering is a dispensation of love, but brought about by the wrath-spirit, and with every appearance of wrath. It is so with every trial and chastisement of the righteous. And it cannot be otherwise; for *trial* is designed to be for man a means of overcoming the evil that is external to him, and *chastisement* of overcoming the evil that is within him. There is a conflict between evil and good in the world, which can issue in victory to the good only so, that the good proves itself in distinction from the evil, withstands the assault of evil, and destroys the evil that exists bound up with itself : only so, that the good as far as it is still mixed with the evil is refined as by fire, and more and more freed from it.

This is the twofold point of view from which the suffering of Job is to be regarded. It was designed, first of all, that Job should prove himself in opposition to Satan, in order to overcome him ; and since Job does not pass through the trial entirely without sinning, it has the effect at the same time of

purifying and perfecting him.   In both respects, the history
of Job is a passage from the history of God's own conflict
with the evil one, which is the substance of the history of redemption, and ends in the triumph of the divine love.   And
Gaupp[1] well says : In the book of Job, Satan loses a cause
which is intended only as prelude to the greatest of all causes,
since judgment is gone forth over the world, and the prince
of darkness has been cast forth.   Accordingly the church
has always recognised in the passion of Job a type of the
passion of Jesus Christ.   James (v. 11) even compares the
patience of Job and the issue of the Lord's sufferings.   And
according to this indication, it was the custom after the second
century to read the book of Job in the churches during pas-
sion-week.[2]   The final solution of the problem which this
marvellous book sets forth, is then this : the suffering of the
righteous, in its deepest cause, is the conflict of the seed of
the woman with the seed of the serpent, which ends in the
head of the serpent being trampled under foot ; it is the type
or copy of the suffering of Christ, the Holy God, who has
himself borne our sins, and in the constancy of His reconcil-
ing love has withstood, even to the final overthrow, the assault
of wrath and of the angel of wrath.

The real contents of the book of Job is the mystery of the
Cross : the Cross on Golgotha is the solution of the enigma
of every cross ; and the book of Job is a prophecy of this
final solution.

[1] *Praktische Theologie*, ii. 1, S. 488 sqq.

[2] *Vid.* Origen's *Opp.* t. ii. p. 851 : *In conventu ecclesiæ in diébus
sanctis legitur passio Iob, in diebus jejunii, in diebus abstinentiæ, in diebus,
in quibus tanquam compatiuntur ii qui jejunant et abstinent admirabili illo
Iob, in diebus, in quibus in jejunio et abstinentia sanctam Domini nostri
Jesu Christi passionem sectamur.*   Known thus from the public reading
in the churches, Job was called among the Syrians, *Machbono*, the
Beloved, the Friend (Ewald, *Jahrb.* x. 207) ; and among the Arabs,
Es-ssabûr, the patient one.

§ 12. THE HISTORY OF THE EXPOSITION.

Before proceeding to the exposition, we will take a brief review of the *history* of the exposition of the book. The promise of the Spirit to lead into all truth is continually receiving its fulfilment in the history of the church, and especially in the interpretation of Scripture. But nowhere is the progress of the church in accordance with this promise so manifest as in the exposition of the word, and particularly of the Old Testament. In the patristic and middle ages, light was thrown only on detached portions of the Old Testament; they lacked altogether, or had but an inadequate knowledge of, the Hebrew language. They regarded the Old Testament not as the forerunner, but allegory, of the New, and paid less attention to it in proportion as the spiritual perception of the church lost its apostolic purity and freshness. However, so far as inward spiritual feeling and experience could compensate for the almost entire absence of outward conditions, this period has produced and handed down many valuable explanations.

But at the time of the Reformation, the light of the day which had already dawned first spread in all its brightness over the Old Testament. The knowledge of Hebrew, until then the private possession of a few, became the public property of the church: all erroneous interventions which had hitherto separated the church both from Christ and from the living source of the word were put aside; and starting from the central truth of justification by faith and its results, a free but still not unrestricted investigation commenced. Still there was wanting to this period all perception of historical development, and consequently the ability to comprehend the Old Testament as preparing the way for the New by its gradual historical development of the plan of redemption. The exposition of Scripture, moreover, soon fell again under the yoke of an enslaving tradition, of a scholastic systematizing, and of an unhistorical dogmatizing which mistook its peculiar aim ; and this period of bondage, devoid of spirituality, was followed by a period of false freedom, that of rationalism, which cut asunder the mutual relation between the exposition of Scripture and the confession of the church, since it reduced the covenant contents of the church's confession to the most shallow notion of God and the most trivial moral rules, and regarded the Old Testament as historical indeed, but with carnal eyes, which were blind to the work of God that was preparing the way in the history of Israel for the New Testament redemption. The progress of exegesis seemed at that time to have been stayed ; but the Head of the church, who reigns in the midst of His enemies, caused the exposition of His word to come forth again from the dead in a more glorious form. The bias towards the human side of Scripture has taught exegesis that Scripture is neither altogether a divine, nor altogether a human, but a divine-human book. The historical method of regarding it, and the advanced knowledge of language, have taught that the Old Testament presents a divine-human growth tending towards the God-man, a gradual development and declaration of the divine purpose of salvation,—a miraculous history moving onward towards that miracle of all miracles, Jesus Christ. Believing on Him, bearing the seal of His Spirit in himself, and partaking of the true liberty His Spirit imparts, the expositor of Scripture beholds in the Old Testament, with open face, now as never before, the glory of the Lord.

The truth of this sketch is confirmed by the history of the exposition of the book of Job. The Greek fathers, of whom twenty-two (including Ephrem) are quoted in the *Catena*,[1]

---

[1] It contains as basis the Greek text of the book of Job from the *Cod. Alexandrinus*, arranged in stichs.

published by Patricius Junius, 1637, furnish little more than
could be expected. If there be any Old Testament book
whose comprehensive meaning is now first understood according
to the external and internal conditions of its gradual advance
to maturity, it is the book of Job. The Greek fathers were
confined to the LXX., without being in a position to test
that translation by the original text; and it is just the Greek
translation of the book of Job which suffers most seriously
from the flaws which in general affect the LXX. Whole
verses are omitted, others are removed from their original
places, and the omissions are filled up by apocryphal addi-
tions.[1] Origen was well aware of this (*Ep. ad Afric.* § 3
sq.), but he was not sufficiently acquainted with Hebrew to
give a reliable collation of the LXX. with the original text
in his *Tetrapla* and *Hexapla;* and his additions (denoted
by daggers), and the passages restored by him from other
translators, especially Theodotion (by asterisks), deprive the
Septuagint text of its original form, without, however, giving
a correct impression of the original text. And since in the
book of Job the meaning of the whole is dependent upon the
meaning of the most isolated passage, the full meaning of the
book was a perfect impossibility to the Greek fathers. They
occupied themselves much with this mysterious book, but
typical and allegorical could not make up what was wanting
to the fathers, of grammatical and historical interpretation.
The Italic, the next version to the LXX., was still more
defective than this : Jerome calls the book of Job in this
translation, *Decurtatus et laceratus corrosusque.* He revised
it by the text of the *Hexapla,* and according to his own plan
had to supply not less than about 700–800 *versus* (στίχοι).
His own independent translation is far before its age; but he
himself acknowledges its defectiveness, inasmuch as he relates,

---

[1] On this subject *vid.* Gust. Bickel's *De indole ac ratione versionis
Alexandrinæ in interpretando l. Iobi*, just published (1863).

in his *præfatio in l. Iob*, how it was accomplished. He engaged, *non parvis numis*, a Jewish teacher from Lydda, where there was at that time an university, but confesses that, after he had gone through the book of Job with him, he was no wiser than before : *Cujus doctrina an aliquid profecerim nescio; hoc unum scio, non potuisse me interpretari nisi quod antea intellexeram.* On this account he calls it, as though he would complain of the book itself, *obliquus, figuratus, lubricus*, and says it is like an eel—the more tightly one holds it, the faster it glides away. There were then three Latin versions of the book of Job,—the Italic, the Italic improved by Jerome, and the independent translation of Jerome, whose deviations, as Augustine complains, produced no little embarrassment. The Syrians were better off with their *Peschito*, which was made direct from the orignal text;[1] but the *Scholia* of Ephrem (pp. 1–19, t. ii. of the three Syriac *tomi* of his works) contain less that is useful than might be expected.[2] The succeeding age produced nothing better.

Among the expositors of the book of Job we find some illustrious names : Gregory the Great, Beda Venerabilis (whose Commentary has been erroneously circulated as the still undiscovered Commentary of Jerome), Thomas Aquinas, Albertus Magnus,[3] and others ; but no progress was made in the interpretation of the book, as the means were wanting. The principal work of the middle ages was Gregory the Great's *Expositio in beatum Iob seu Moralium*, ll. xxxv., a

---

[1] Perhaps with the use of the Jewish Targum, though not the one extant, for Talmudic literature recognises the existence of a Targum of the book of Job before the destruction of the temple, *b. Sabbath*, 115*a*, etc. Besides, the LXX. was considered of such authority in the East, that the monophysite Bishop Paulus of Tela, 617, formed a new Syriac translation from the LXX. and the text of the *Hexapla* (published by Middeldorff, 1834–35 ; cf. his *Curæ hexaplares in Iobum*, 1817).

[2] Froriep, *Ephræmiana in l. Iobi*, 1769, iv., says much about these *Scholia* to little purpose.

[3] His *Postillæ super Iob* are still unprinted.

gigantic work, which leaves scarcely a dogmatic-ethical theme untouched, though in its own proper sphere it furnishes nothing of importance, for Gregory explained so, *ut super historiæ fundamentum moralitatis construeret ædificium et anagoges imposuerit culmen præstantissimum*,[1] but the linguistic-historical foundation is insufficient, and the exposition, which gives evidence of significant character and talent, accordingly goes off almost constantly into digressions opposed to its object.

It was only towards the end of the middle ages, as the knowledge of the Hebrew language began, through Jewish converts, to come into the church, that a new era commenced. For what advance the Jewish exposition of the book of Job had hitherto made, beyond that of the church, it owed to the knowledge of Hebrew; although, in the absence of any conception of the task of the expositor, and especially the expositor of Scripture, it knew not how fittingly to turn it to account. Saadia's (born 890) Arabic translation of the book of Job, with explanations,[2] does not accomplish much more than that of Jerome, if we may in general say that it surpasses it. Salomo Isaaki of Troyes (Raschi, erroneously called Jarchi), whose *Commentary on the Book of Job* (rendered incomplete by his death, 1105) was completed by his grandson, Samuel b. Meïr (Raschbam, died about 1160),[3] contains a few attempts at grammatical historical exposition, but is in other respects entirely dependent on *Midrash Haggada* (which may be compared with the church system of allegorical interpretation), whose barren material is treasured up in the catena-like compilations, one of which to the collected books of the Old Testa-

---

[1] Notker quoted by Dümmler, *Formelbuch des Bischof's Salomo von Constanz*, 1857, S. 67 f.

[2] *Vid.* Ewald-Duke's *Beiträge zur Gesch. der ältesten Auslegung und Spracherklärung des A. T.* 2 Bdd. 1844.

[3] Respecting this accounts are uncertain: *vid.* Geiger, *Die französische Exegetenschule* (1855), S. 22; and comp. de Rossi, *Catalogus Cod.* 181. Zunz, *Zur Geschichte und Literatur.*

ment bears the name of *Simeon ha-Darschan* (ילקוט שמעוני) ;
the other to the three poetical books, the name of *Machir b.
Todros* (ילקוט מכירי). Abenezra the Spaniard, who wrote his
Commentary on the Book of Job in Rome, 1175, delights in new
bold ideas, and to enshroud himself in a mystifying nimbus.
David Kimchi, who keeps best to the grammatical-historical
course, has not expounded the book of Job; and a commentary
on this book by his brother, Mose Kimchi, is not yet brought to
light. The most important Jewish works on the book of Job
are without doubt the Commentaries of Mose b. Nachman
or Nachmanides (Ramban), born at Gerona 1194, and Levi
b. Gerson, or Gersonides (Ralbag), born at Bagnols 1288.
Both were talented thinkers; the former more of the Pla-
tonic, the latter of the Aristotelic type. Their Commentaries
(taken up in the collective Rabbinical Commentaries), especially that of the latter, were widely circulated in the middle
ages. They have both a philosophical bias.[1] What is to be
found in them that is serviceable on any point, may be pretty
well determined from the compilation of Lyra. Nikolaus de
Lyra, author of *Postillæ perpetuæ in universa Biblia* (completed 1330), possessed, for that age, an excellent knowledge
of the original text, the necessity of which he acknowledged,
and regarded the *sensus literalis* as basis of all other *sensus*.
But, on the one hand, he was not independent of his Jewish
predecessors; on the other, he was fettered by the servile
unevangelical spirit of his age.

The bursting of this fetter was the dawn of a new day for
exegesis. Luther, Brentius, and other reformers, by the
depth of their religious experience, their aversion to the
capriciousness of the system of allegorical interpretation and

---

[1] Other older commentaries bearing on the history of exposition,
as Menahem b. Chelbo, Joseph Kara, Parchon, and others, are not yet
known; also that of the Italian poet Immanuel, a friend of Dante, is
still unprinted. The rabbinical commentaries contain only, in addition,
the Commentary of Abraham Farisol of Avignon (about 1460).

freedom from tradition, were fitted to look into the very heart of the book of Job; and they also possessed sufficient acquaintance with the Hebrew to get an inkling of the carrying out of its chief idea, but no more than an inkling of it. " The book of Job," says Luther in his preface, " treats of the question whether misfortune from God befalls even the godly. Here Job is firm, and maintains that God afflicts even the godly without cause, for His praise alone, as Christ (John ix.) also shows from the man who was born blind." In these words the idea of the book is correctly indicated. But that he had only an approximate conception of the separate parts, he openly confesses. By the help of Melancthon and the Hebraist Aurogallus, he translated the book of Job, and says in his epistle on the translation, that they could sometimes scarcely finish three lines in four days. And while engaged upon the translation, he wrote to Spalatin, in his naïve strong way, that Job seemed to bear his translation less patiently than the consolation of his friends, and would rather remain seated on his dunghill. Jerome Weller, a man who, from inward experience similar to that described in this book, was qualified above many to be its expositor, felt the same unsatisfactoriness. An expositor of Job, says he, must have lain on the same bed of sickness as Job, and have tasted in some measure the bitter experience of Job. Such an expositor was Weller, sorely tried in the school of affliction. But his exposition does not extend beyond the twelfth chapter; and he is glad when at last, by God's grace, he has got through the twelve chapters, as through firm and hard rock; the remaining chapters he commends to another. The most comprehensive work of the Reformation period on the book of Job, is the Sermons (conciones) of Calvin. The exegesis of the pre-rationalistic period advanced beyond these performances of the reformers only in proportion as philological learning extended, particularly Mercier and Cocceius in the

Reformed, Seb. Schmid in the Lutheran, Joannes de Pineda in the Romish Church. The Commentary of the last named (Madrid, 1597), a surprisingly learned compilation, was also used and admired by Protestants, but zealously guards the immaculateness of the Vulgate. The commentaries of the German reformers are to the present day unsurpassed for the comprehension of the fundamental truth of the book.

With the Commentary of Albert Schultens, a Dutchman (2 vols. 1737), a new epoch in the exposition begins. He was the first to bring the Semitic languages, and chiefly the Arabic, to bear on the translation of the book. And rightly so,[1] for the Arabic has retained more that is ancient than any other Semitic dialect; and Jerome, in his preface to Daniel, had before correctly remarked, *Iob cum arabica lingua plurimam habet societatem*. Reiske (*Conjecturæ in Iobum*, 1779) and Schnurrer (*Animadv. ad quædam loca Iobi*, 1781) followed later in the footsteps of Schultens; but in proportion as the Israelitish element was considered in its connection with the Oriental, the divine distinctiveness of the former was forgotten. Nevertheless, the book of Job had far less to suffer than the other biblical books from rationalism, with its frivolous moral judgments and distorted interpretations of Scripture : it reduced the idea of the book to tameness, and Satan, here with more apparent reason than elsewhere, was regarded as a mythical invention ; but there were, however, no miracles and prophecies to be got rid of.

And as, for the first time since the apostolic period, attention was now given to the book as a poetical masterpiece, substantial advantage arose to the exposition itself from the translations and explanations of an Eckermann, Moldenhauer, Stuhlmann, and others. What a High-German rhymster of

---

[1] Though not in due proportion, especially in *Animadversiones philologicæ in Iobum* (*Opp. minora*, 1769), where he seeks to explain the errors of translation in the LXX. from the Arabic.

the fourteenth century, made known by Hennig, and the Florentine national poet Juliano Dati at the beginning of the sixteenth century, accomplished in their poetical reproductions of the book of Job, is here incomparably surpassed. What might not the fathers have accomplished if they had only had at their disposal such a translation of the book of Job as *e.g.* that of Böckel, or of the pious Miss Elizabeth Smith, skilled in the Oriental languages (died, in her twenty-eighth year, 1805),[1] or of a studious Swiss layman (*Notes to the Hebrew Text of the Old Testament, together with a Translation of the Book of Job*, Basel 1841)?

The way to the true and full perception of the divine in Scripture is through the human : hence rationalism—especially after Herder, whose human mode of perception improved and deepened—prepared the way for a new era in the church's exposition of the book of Job. The Commentaries of Samuel Lee (1837), Vaihinger (1842), Welte (1849), Hahn (1850), and Schlottmann (1851),[2] are the first-fruits of this new period, rendered possible by the earlier Commentaries of Umbreit (1824–32), Ewald (1836–51), and Hirzel (1839, second edition, edited by Olshausen, 1852), of whom the first[3] is characterized by enthusiasm for the poetical grandeur of the book, the second by vivid perception of the tragical, and the third by sound tact and good arrangement,—three qualifications which a young Scotch investigator, A. B. Davidson, strives, not unsuccessfully, to unite in his Commentary (vol. i. 1862).[4] Besides these substantially

---

[1] Vid. *Volksblatt für Stadt und Land*, 1859, No. 20.

[2] *Vid.* the review of the last two by Oehler in Reuter's *Repertorium*, Feb. 1852 ; and Kosegarten's *Aufsatz über das B. Hiob in der Kieler Allgem. Monatsschrift*, 1853, S. 761–774.

[3] *Vid.* Ullmann-Riehm's *Blätter der Erinnerung an F. W. C. Umbreit* (1862), S. 54–58.

[4] The author, already known by a *Treatise on the Hebrew Accentuology*, is not to be mistaken for Sam. Davidson. In addition, we would call

progressive works, there is the Commentary of Heiligstedt (1847), which is only a recapitulatory *clavis* after the style of Rosenmüller, but more condensed; and for what modern Jewish commentaries, as those of Blumenfeld, Arnheim (1836), and Löwenthal (1846), contain beyond the standpoint of the earlier פרושים and באורים, they are almost entirely indebted to their Christian predecessors. Also in the more condensed form of translations, with accompanying explanations, the understanding of the book of Job has been in many ways advanced. We may mention here the translations of Köster (1831), who first directed attention to the strophe-structure of Hebrew poetry, but who also, since he regarded the Masoretic verse as the constructive element of the strophe, has introduced an error which has not been removed even to the present day; Stickel (1842), who has, not untastefully, sought to imitate the form of this masterpiece, although his division of the Masoretic verse into strophe lines, according to the accents, like Hirzel's and Meier's in Canticles, is the opposite extreme to the mistake of Köster; Ebrard (1858), who translates in iambic pentameters, as Hosse had previously done;[1] and Renan, who solely determines his arrangement of the *stichs* by the Masoretic division of verses, and moreover haughtily displays his scornful opposition to Christianity in the prefatory *Etude*.[2] Besides, apart from the general commentaries (*Bibelwerke*), among which that of Von Gerlach (Bd. iii. *des A. T.* 1849) may be mentioned as the most noted, and such popular practical expositions as Diedrich's (1858), many—some in the interest of poetry generally (as Spiess,

attention to the Commentary of Carey (1858), in which the archæology and geography of the book of Job is illustrated by eighty woodcuts and a map.

[1] *Vid.* Schneider, *Die neuesten Studien über das B. Hiob, Deutsche Zeitschr. für christl. Wissensch.*, 1859, No. 27.

[2] Against which Abbé Crelier has come forward: *Le livre de Job venge des interprétations fausses et impies de M. Ernest Renan*, 1860.

1852), others in the interest of biblical theology (as Haupt, 1847 ; Hosse, 1849 ; Hayd, 1859 ; Birkholz, 1859 ; and in Sweden, Lindgren, Upsala 1831)—have sought to render the reading of the book of Job easier and more profitable by means of a translation, with a short introduction and occasional explanations.

Even with all these works before us, though they are in part excellent and truly serviceable, it cannot be affirmed that the task of the exposition has been exhaustively performed, so that absolutely no *plus ultra* remains. To adjust the ideal meaning of the book according to its language, its bearing on the history of redemption, and its spiritual character,—and throughout to indicate the relation of the single parts to the idea which animates the whole, is, and remains, a great task worthy of ever-new exertion. We will try to perform it, without presuming that we are able to answer all the claims on the expositor. The right expositor of the book of Job must before everything else bring to it a believing apprehension of the work of Christ, in order that he may be able to comprehend this book from its connection with the historical development of the plan of redemption, whose unity is the work of Christ. Further, he must be able to give himself up freely and cheerfully to the peculiar vein of this (together with Ecclesiastes) most bold of all Old Testament books, in order that he may gather from the very heart its deeply hidden idea. Not less must he possess historical perception, in order that he may be able to appreciate the relativeness with which, since the plan of salvation is actually and confessedly progressive, the development of the idea of the book is burdened, notwithstanding its absolute truth in itself. Then he must not only have a clear perception of the divinely true, but also of the beautiful in human art, in order to be able to appreciate the wonderful blending of the divine and human in the form as in the contents.   Finally, he must stand on the pinnacle of linguistic and antiquarian knowledge, in order to be able to follow the lofty flight of its language, and become familiar with the incomparably rich variety of its matter. This ideal of an expositor of the book of Job we will keep in view, and seek, as near as possible, to attain within the limit assigned to this condensed exegetical handbook.

TRANSLATION AND EXPOSITION
OF THE BOOK OF JOB

Ἐπ᾽ αὐτῶν τῶν λέξεων [τοῦ βιβλίου] γενόμενοι σαφηνίσωμεν τὴν ἔννοιαν,
αὐτοῦ ποδηγοῦντος ἡμᾶς πρὸς τὴν ἑρμηνείαν, τοῦ καὶ τὸν ἅγιον Ἰὼβ
πρὸς τοὺς ἀγῶνας ἐνισχύσαντος.—OLYMPIODOROS.

THE OPENING.

CHAP. I.–III.

JOB'S PIETY IN THE MIDST OF THE GREATEST
PROSPERITY.—CHAP. I. 1–5.

THE book begins in prose style: as Jerome says, *Prosa incipit, versu labitur, pedestri sermone finitur.* Prologue and epilogue are accordingly excepted from the poetical accentuation, and are accented according to the usual system, as the first word shows; for אִישׁ has, in correct editions, Tebir, a smaller distinctive, which does not belong to the poetical accentuation. The writer does not begin with וַיְהִי, as the writers of the historico-prophetical books, who are conscious that they are relating a portion of the connection of the collective Israelitish history, *e.g.* 1 Sam. i. 1, וַיְהִי אִישׁ, but, as the writer of the book of Esther (ii. 5) for similar reasons, with אִישׁ הָיָה, because he is beginning a detached extra-Israelitish history.

Ver. 1. *There was a man in the land of Uz, whose name was Job; and that man was perfect and upright, and one that feared God, and eschewed evil.*

The LXX. translates, ἐν χώρᾳ τῇ Αὐσίτιδι; and adds at

the close of the book, ἐπὶ τοῖς ὁρίοις τῆς Ἰδουμαίας καὶ Ἀραβίας, therefore north-east from Idumea, towards the Arabian desert. There, in the Arabian desert west from Babylon, under the Caucabenes, according to Ptolemy (v. 19, 2), the Αἰσῖται (Αἰσεῖται), i.e. the Uzzites, dwelt. This determination of the position of Uz is the most to be relied on. It tends indirectly to confirm this, that Οὖσος,. in Jos. Ant. i. 6, 4, is described as founder of Trachonitis and Damascus; that the Jakut Hamawi and Moslem tradition generally (as recently Fries, Stud. u. Krit. 1854, ii.) mention the East Haran fertile tract of country north-west of Têmâ and Bûzân, el-Bethenije, the district of Damascus in which Job dwelt;[1] that the Syrian tradition also transfers the dwelling-place of Job to Hauran, where, in the district of Damascus, a monastery to his honour is called Dair Ejjub (vid. Volck, Calendarium Syriacum, p. 29). All these accounts agree that Uz is not to be sought in Idumæa proper (Gebâl). And the early historical genealogies (Gen. x. 23, xxii. 21, xxxvi. 28) are not unfavourable to this, since they place Uz in relation to Seir-Edom on the one hand, and on the other to Aram: the perplexing double occurrence of such names as Têmâ and Dûma, both in Idumæa and East Hauran, perhaps just results from the mixing of the different tribes through migration. But at all events, though Uz did not lie in Gebâl, yet both from Lam. iv. 21, and on account of the reference in the book of Job itself to the Horites (ch. xxiv. 30), a geographical connection between Idumæa and Ausitis is to be held; and from Jer. xxv. 20 one is warranted in supposing, that עוץ, with which the Arabic name of Esau, عيص (العيص), perhaps not accidentally accords, was the collective name of the northern part of the Arabian desert, extending north-east

---

[1] Vid. Abulfeda, Historia anteislam. p. 26 (cf. 207 f.), where it says, " The whole of Bethenije, a part of the province of Damascus, belonged to Job as his possession."

from Idumæa towards Syria. Here, where the aborigines
of Seir were driven back by the Aramaic immigrants, and
to where in later times the territory of Edom extended,
dwelt Job. His name is not symbolic with reference to the
following history. It has been said, אִיּוֹב signifies one hostilely treated, by Satan namely.[1] But the following reasons
are against it : (1) that none of the other names which occur
in the book are symbolically connected with the history ; (2)
that the form קָטוֹל has never a properly passive signification, but
either active, as יִסּוֹר, reprover (as parallel form with קַטָּל), or
neuter, as יִלּוֹד, born, שִׁכּוֹר, drunken, also occasionally infinitive
(vid. Fürst, Concord. p. 1349 s.), so that it may be more
correct, with Ewald, after the Arabic (אוּב, cognate with שׁוּב,
perhaps also בּוֹא), to explain the " one going of himself."
Similar in sound are, יוֹב, the name of one of the sons of Issachar
(Gen. xlvi. 13) ; the name of the Idumæan king, יוֹבָב, Gen.
xxxvi. 33 (which the LXX., Aristeas, Jul. Africanus,[2]
combine with Job) ; and the name of the king of Mauritania,
Juba, which in Greek is written 'Ιόβας (Didymus Chalcenter.
ed. Schmidt, p. 305) : perhaps all these names belong to the
root יב, to shout with joy. The LXX. writes 'Ιώβ with
lenis ; elsewhere the א at the beginning is rendered by asper,
e.g. Αβραάμ, 'Ηλίας. Luther writes Hiob ; he has preferred the latter mode, that it may not be read Job with
consonantal Jod, when it should be Iob, as e.g. it is read by
the English. It had been more correctly Ijob, but Luther
wished to keep to the customary form of the name so far as
he could ; so we, by writing Iob with vowel I, do not wish to

---

[1] Geiger (DMZ, 1858, S. 542 sq.) conjectures that, Sir. xlix. 9 (καὶ γὰρ
ἐμνήσθη τῶν ἐχθρῶν ἐν ὄμβρῳ), τῶν ἐχθρῶν is a false translation of אִיּוֹב.
Renan assents ; but τῶν ἐχθρῶν suits there excellently, and Job would be
unnaturally dragged in.

[2] Vid. Routh, Reliquiæ ii. 154 sq. : 'Εκ τοῦ 'Ησαῦ ἄλλοι τε πολλοὶ καὶ
Ραγουὴλ γεννᾶται, ἀφ' οὗ Ζάρεδ, ἐξ οὗ 'Ιὼβ, ὃς κατὰ συγχώρησιν θεοῦ ὑπὸ
διαβόλου ἐπειράσθη καὶ ἐνίκησε τὸν πειράζοντα.

deviate too much from the mode of writing and pronunciation customary since Luther.[1]

The writer intentionally uses four synonyms together, in order to describe as strongly as possible Job's piety, the reality and purity of which is the fundamental assumption of the history. תָּם, with the whole heart disposed towards God and what is good, and also well-disposed toward mankind; יָשָׁר, in thought and action without deviation conformed to that which is right; יְרֵא אֱלֹהִים, fearing God, and consequently being actuated by the fear of God, which is the beginning (*i.e.* principle) of wisdom; סָר מֵרָע, keeping aloof from evil, which is opposed to God. The first predicate recalls Gen. xxv. 27, the fourth the proverbial Psalms (xxxiv. 15, xxxvii. 27) and Prov. xiv. 16. This mingling of expressions from Genesis and Proverbs is characteristic. First now, after the history has been begun in prætt., aorr. follow.

Vers. 2 sq. *And there were born unto him seven sons and three daughters. His substance also was seven thousand sheep, and three thousand camels, and five hundred yoke of oxen, and five hundred she-asses, and servants in great number; so that this man was the greatest of all the men of the east.*

It is a large, princely household. The numbers are large, but must not on that account be considered an invention. The four animals named include both kinds. With the doubled אַלְפֵי corresponds the also constructive מֵאוֹת, the Tsere of which is never shortened, though in the singular one says מְאַת, from מֵאָה. The aorists, especially of the verb הָיָה (הוה),

---

[1] On the authorizing of the writing Iob, more exactly Îob, also Îjob (not, however, Ijjob, which does not correspond to the real pronunciation, which softens ij into î, and uw into û), vid. Fleischer's *Beiträge zur arab. Sprachkunde* (*Abh. der sächs. Gesellschaft d. Wissenschaften*, 1863), S. 137 f. [The usual English form Job is adopted here, though Dr Delitzsch writes Iob in the original work.—Tr.]

which, according to its root, signifies not so much *esse* as *fieri*, *existere*, are intended to place us at once in the midst of his prosperity. *Ex iis*, says Leo Africanus in reference to flocks, *Arabes suas divitias ac possessiones œstimant.* In fine, Job was without his equal among the בני קדם. So the tribes are called which extend from Arabia Deserta, lying to the east of Palestine, northwards to the countries on the Euphrates, and south over Arabia Petræa and Felix. The wisdom of these tribes, treasured up in proverbs, songs, and traditions, is mentioned in 1 Kings v. 10, side by side with the wisdom of the Egyptians. The writer now takes a very characteristic feature from the life of Job, to show that, even in the height of prosperity, he preserved and manifested the piety affirmed of him.

Vers. 4 sq. *And his sons went and feasted in the house of him whose day it was, and sent and called for their sisters to eat and drink with them. And it happened, when the days of their feasting were gone about, that Job sent and sanctified them, and rose up early in the morning, and offered burnt-offerings according to the number of them all: for Job said, It may be that my sons have sinned, and dismissed God from their hearts. Thus did Job continually.*

The subordinate facts precede, ver. 4, in *perff.*; the chief fact follows, ver. 5, in *fut. consec.* The *perff.* describe, according to Ges. § 126, 3, that which has happened repeatedly in the past, as *e.g.* Ruth iv. 7 ; the *fut. consec.* the customary act of Job, in conjunction with this occurrence. The *consecutio temporum* is exactly like 1 Sam. i. 3 sq.

It is questionable whether בֵּית אִישׁ is a distinct adverbial expression, *in domu uniuscujusque*, and יומו also distinct, *die ejus* (Hirz. and others) ; or whether the three words are only one adverbial expression, *in domo ejus cujus dies erat*, which latter we prefer. At all events, יוֹמוֹ here, in this connection, is not, with Hahn, Schlottm., and others, to be understood of the birthday, as ch. iii. 1. The text, understood simply as it stands, speaks of a weekly round (Oehler and others). The seven sons took it in turn to dine with one another the week round, and did not forget their sisters in the loneliness of the parental home, but added them to their number. There existed among them a family peace and union which had been uninterruptedly cherished ; but early on the morning of every eighth day, Job instituted a solemn service for his family, and offered sacrifices for his ten children, that they might obtain forgiveness for any sins of frivolity into which they might have fallen in the midst of the mirth of their family gatherings.

The writer might have represented this celebration on the evening of every seventh day, but he avoids even the slightest reference to anything Israelitish : for there is no mention in Scripture of any celebration of the Sabbath before the time of Israel. The sacred observance of the Sabbath, which was consecrated by God the Creator, was first expressly enjoined by the Sinaitic Thora. Here the family celebration falls on the morning of the *Sunday*,—a remarkable prelude to the New Testament celebration of Sunday in the age before the giving of the law, which is a type of the New Testament time after the law. The fact that Job, as father of the family, is the *Cohen* of his house,—a right of priesthood which the fathers of Israel exercised at the first passover (פסח מצרים), and from which a relic is still retained in the annual celebration of the passover (פסח הדורות),—is also characteristic of the age prior to the law. The standpoint of this age is also further faithfully preserved in this particular, that עולה here, as also ch. xlii. 8, appears distinctly as an expiatory offering; whilst in the Mosaic ritual, although it still indeed serves לכפר (Lev. i. 4), as does every blood-offering, the idea of expiation as its peculiar intention is transferred to חטאת and אָשָׁם. Neither of these forms of expiatory offering is here mentioned. The blood-offering still bears its most general generic name, עֹלָה, which it received after the flood. This name indicates that the offering is one which, being consumed by fire, is designed to ascend in flames and smoke. הֶעֱלָה refers not so much to bringing it up to the raised altar, as to causing it to rise in flame and smoke, causing it to ascend to God, who is above. קִדֵּשׁ is the outward cleansing and the spiritual preparation for the celebration of the sacred festival, as Ex. xix. 14. It is scarcely necessary to remark, that the masculine suffixes refer also to the daughters. There were ten whole sacrifices offered by Job on each opening day of the weekly round, at the dawn of the Sunday; and one has therefore to imagine this round of entertainment as beginning with the first-born on the first day of the week. "Perhaps," says Job, "my children have sinned, and bidden farewell to God in their hearts." Undoubtedly, בֵּרֵךְ signifies elsewhere (1 Kings xxi. 10; Ps. x. 3), according to a so-called ἀντιφραστικὴ εὐφημία, *maledicere*. This signification also suits ch. ii. 5, but does not at all suit ch. ii. 9. This latter passage supports the signification *valedicere*, which arises from the custom of pronouncing a benediction or benedictory salutation at parting (*e.g.* Gen. xlvii. 10). Job is afraid lest his children may have become somewhat unmindful of God during their mirthful gatherings. In Job's family, therefore, there was an earnest desire for sanctification, which was far from being satisfied with mere outward propriety of conduct. Sacrifice (which is as old as the sin of mankind) was to Job a means of grace, by which he cleansed himself and his family every week from inward blemish. The *futt. consec.* are followed by *perff.*, which are governed by them. כְּכָה, however, is followed by the *fut.*, because in historical connection (cf. on the other hand, Num. viii. 26), in the signification, *faciebat h.e. facere solebat* (Ges. § 127, 4, *b*). Thus Job did every day, *i.e.* continually. As head of the family, he faithfully discharged his priestly vocation, which permitted him to offer sacrifice as an early Gentile servant of God. The writer has now made us acquainted with the chief person of the history which he is about to record, and in ver. 6 begins the history itself.

JEHOVAH'S DETERMINATION TO TRY JOB.—CHAP. I. 6–12.

He transfers us from earth to heaven, where everything that is done on earth has its unseen roots, its final cause.

> Ver. 6. *Now there was a day when the sons of God came to present themselves before Jehovah; and Satan came also in the midst of them.*

The translation " it happened on a day " is rejected in Ges. § 109, rem. 1, *c*.[1] The article, it is there said, refers to what precedes—the day, at the time; but this favourite mode of expression is found at the beginning of a narrative, even when it cannot be considered to have any reference to what has preceded, *e.g.* 2 Kings iv. 18. The article is used in the opposite manner here, because the narrator in thought connects the day with the following occurrence; and this frees it from absolute indefiniteness : the western mode of expression is different. From the writer assigning the earthly measure of time to the place of God and spirits, we see that celestial things are represented by him parabolically. But the assumptions on which he proceeds are everywhere recognised in Scripture ; for (1.) בְּנֵי הָאֱלֹהִים, as the name of the celestial spirits, is also found out of the book of Job (Gen. vi. 2; cf.

---

[1] The references to Gesenius' *Hebrew Grammar* have been carefully verified according to the English edition published by Bagster and Sons, London.—Tr.

Ps. xxix. 1, lxxxix. 7, Dan. iii. 25).   They are so called, as
beings in the likeness of God, which came forth from God in
the earliest beginning of creation, before this material world
and man came into existence (ch. xxxviii. 4–7) : the desig-
nation בְּנֵי points to the particular manner of their creation.
(2.) Further, it is the teaching of Scripture, that these are the
nearest attendants upon God, the nearest created glory, with
which He has surrounded himself in His eternal glory, and
that He uses them as the immediate instruments of His cosmical rule.   This representation underlies Gen. i. 26, which
Philo correctly explains, διαλέγεται ὁ τῶν ὅλων πατὴρ ταῖς
ἑαυτοῦ δυνάμεσιν; and in Ps. lxxxix. 6–8, a psalm which is
closely allied to the book of Job, קְהַל and סוֹד, of the holy
ones, is just the assembly of the heavenly spirits, from which,
as ἄγγελοι of God, they go forth into the universe and among
men.   (3.) It is also further the teaching of Scripture, that
one of these spirits has withdrawn himself from the love of
God, has reversed the truth of his bright existence, and in
sullen ardent self-love is become the enemy of God, and
everything godlike in the creature.   This spirit is called, in
reference to God and the creature, הַשָּׂטָן, from the verb שָׂטַן,
to come in the way, oppose, treat with enmity,—a name which
occurs first here, and except here occurs only in Zech. iii. and
1 Chron. xxi. 1.   Since the Chokma turned, with a decided preference, to the earliest records of the world and mankind before
the rise of nationalities, it must have known the existence
of this God-opposing spirit from Gen. ii. sq.   The frequent
occurrence of the tree of life and the way of life in the Salomonic Proverbs, shows how earnestly the research of that time
was engaged with the history of Paradise : so that it cannot
be surprising that it coined the name הַשָּׂטָן for that evil spirit.
(4.) Finally, it agrees with 1 Kings xxii. 19–22, Zech. iii., on
the one hand, and Apoc. xii. on the other, that Satan here
appears still among the good spirits, resembling Judas Iscariot

among the disciples until his treachery was revealed. The work of redemption, about which his enmity to God overdid itself, and by which his damnation is perfected, is during the whole course of the Old Testament history incomplete.

Herder, Eichhorn, Lutz, Ewald, and Umbreit, see in this distinct placing of Satan in relation to the Deity and good spirits nothing but a change of representations arising from foreign influences; but if Jesus Christ is really the vanquisher of Satan, as He himself says, the realm of spirits must have a history, which is divided into two eras by this triumph. Moreover, both the Old and New Testaments agree herein, that Satan is God's adversary, and consequently altogether evil, and must notwithstanding serve God, since He makes even evil minister to His purpose of salvation, and the working out of His plan in the government of the world. This is the chief thought which underlies the further progress of the scene. The earthly elements of time, space, and dialogue, belong to the poetic drapery.

Instead of הִתְיַצֵּב עַל, לִפְנֵי is used elsewhere (Prov. xxii. 29) : עַל is a usage of language derived from the optical illusion of the one who is in the foreground seeming to surpass the one in the background. It is an assembly day in heaven. All the spirits present themselves to render their account, and expecting to receive commands ; and the following dialogue ensues between Jehovah and Satan :—

Ver. 7. *Then Jehovah said to Satan, Whence comest thou? Satan answered Jehovah, and said, From going to and fro in the earth, and from walking up and down in it.*

The *fut.* follows מֵאַיִן in the signification of the *præs.,* Whence comest thou? the *perf.* would signify, Whence hast thou come? (Ges. § 127, 2.) Cocceius subtly observes : *Notatur Satanas velut Deo nescio h.e. non adprobante res suas agere.* It is implied in the question that his business is selfish, arbitrary, and has no connection with God. In his answer, שׁוּט בְּ, as 2 Sam. xxiv. 2, signifies rapid passing from one end to the other ; הִתְהַלֵּךְ, an observant roaming forth. Peter also says of Satan, περιπατεῖ (1 Pet. v. 8 sq.).[1] He answers at first generally, as expecting a more particular question, which Jehovah now puts to him.

Ver. 8. *Then said Jehovah to Satan, Hast thou considered my servant Job? for there is none like him in the earth, a perfect and an upright man, one that feareth God and escheweth evil.*

By כִּי Jehovah gives the reason of His inquiry. Had Satan been observant of Job, even he must have confessed that there was on the earth real genuine piety. שִׂים לֵב, *animum advertere* (for לֵב is *animus*, נֶפֶשׁ *anima*), is construed with עַל, of the object on which the attention falls, and on which it fixes itself, or אֶל, of the object towards which it is directed (ch. ii. 3). The repetition of the four predicates used of Job (ver. 1) in the mouth of Jehovah (though without the *waw* combining both pairs there) is a skilful touch of the poet. Further on, the narrative is also interwoven with poetic repetitions (as *e.g.* ch. xxxiv. and Gen. i.), to give it architectural symmetry, and to strengthen the meaning and impression of what is said. Jehovah triumphantly displays His servant, the incomparable one, in opposition to Satan ; but this does not disconcert him : he knows how, as on all occasions, so here also, to deny what Jehovah affirms.

Vers. 9–11. *Then Satan answered Jehovah, and said, Doth Job fear God for nought? Hast Thou not made a hedge about him, and about his house, and about all that he hath on every side? Hast Thou not blessed the work of his*

----

[1] Among the Arabs the devil is called الحارث, *el-hharith*—the active, busy, industrious one.

hands, and his substance is increased in the land? But
put forth Thine hand now, and touch all that he hath:
truly he will renounce Thee to Thy face.

Satan is, according to the Apoc. xii. 10, the κατήγωρ who
accuses the servants of God day and night before God. It
is a fact respecting the invisible world, though expressed in
the language and imagery of this world. So long as he is
not finally vanquished and condemned, he has access to God,
and thinks to justify himself by denying the truth of the existence and the possibility of the continuance of all piety. God
permits it; for since everything happening to the creature is
placed under the law of free development, evil in the world
of spirits is also free to maintain and expand itself, until a
spiritual power comes forward against it, by which the
hitherto wavering conflict between the principles of good and
evil is decided. This is the truth contained in the poetic
description of the heavenly scene, sadly mistaken by Umbreit
in his *Essay on Sin*, 1853, in which he explains Satan, according to Ps. cix. 6, as a creation of our author's fancy. The
paucity of the declarations respecting Satan in the Old Testament has misled him. And indeed the historical advance
from the Old Testament to the New, though in itself well
authorized, has in many ways of late induced to the levelling
of the heights and depths of the New Testament. Formerly
Umbreit was of the opinion, as many are still, that the idea
of Satan is derived from Persia; but between Ahriman (*An-
gramainyus*) and Satan there is no striking resemblance;[1]
whereas Diestel, in his *Abh. über Set-Typhon, Asasel und
Satan, Stud. u. Krit.*, 1860, 2, cannot indeed recognise any

[1] Moreover, it is still questionable whether the form of the ancient
doctrine of fire-worship among the Persians did not result from Jewish
influences. *Vid.* Stuhr, *Religionssysteme der heidn. Völker des Orients*, S.
373-75.

connection between עֲזָאזֵל and the Satan of the book of Job, but maintains a more complete harmony in all substantial marks between the latter and the Egyptian Typhon, and infers that " to Satan is therefore to be denied a purely Israelitish originality, the natural outgrowth of the Hebrew mind. It is indeed no special honour for Israel to be able to call him their own. He never has taken firm hold on the Hebrew consciousness." But how should it be no honour for Israel, the people to whom the revelation of redemption was made, and in whose history the plan of redemption was developed, to have traced the poisonous stream of evil up to the fountain of its first free beginning in the spiritual world, and to have more than superficially understood the history of the fall of mankind by sin, which points to a disguised superhuman power, opposed to the divine will? This perception undoubtedly only begins gradually to dawn in the Old Testament; but in the New Testament, the abyss of evil is fully disclosed, and Satan has so far a hold on the consciousness of Jesus, that He regards His life's vocation as a conflict with Satan. And the *Protevangelium* is deciphered in facts, when the promised seed of the woman crushed the serpent's head, but at the same time suffered the bruising of its own heel.

The view (*e.g.* Lutz in his *Biblische Dogmatik*) that Satan as he is represented in the book of Job is not the later evil spirit, is to be rejected : he appears here only first, say Herder and Eichhorn, as impartial executor of judgment, and overseer of morality, commissioned by God. But he denies what God affirms, acknowledges no love towards God in the world which is not rooted in self-love, and is determined to destroy this love as a mere semblance. Where piety is dulled, he rejoices in its obscurity; where it is not, he dims its lustre by reflecting his own egotistical nature therein. Thus it is in Zech. iii., and so here. Genuine love loves God חִנָּם

(adverb from חֵן, like *gratis* from *gratia*): it loves Him for His own sake; it is a relation of person to person, without any actual stipulations and claim. But Job does not thus fear God; יָרֵא is here *præt.*, whereas in vers. 1 and 8 it is the adjective. God has indeed hitherto screened him from all evil; שַׂכְתָּ from שׂוּך, *sepire*, and בְּעַד (בַּעַד) composed of בְּ and עַד, in the primary signification *circum*, since עַד expresses that the one joins itself to the other, and בְּ that it covers it, or covers itself with it. By the addition of מִסָּבִיב, the idea of the triple בְּעַד is still strengthened. מַעֲשֵׂה, LXX., Vulg., have translated by the plural, which is not false according to the thought; for מַעֲשֵׂה יָדַיִם is, especially in Deuteronomy, a favourite collective expression for human enterprise. פָּרַץ, a word, with the Sanskrito-Sem. *frangere*, related to פָּרַק, signifying to break through the bounds, multiply and increase one's self unboundedly (Gen. xxx. 30, and freq.). The particle אוּלָם, proper only to the oldest and classic period, and very commonly used in the first four books of the Pentateuch, and in our book, generally וְאוּלָם, is an emphatic "nevertheless;" Lat. (suited to this passage at least) *verum enim vero.* אִם־לֹא is either, as frequently, a shortened formula of asseveration: May such and such happen to me if he do not, etc., = forsooth he will (LXX. ἦ μήν); or it is half a question: Attempt only this and this, whether he will not deny thee, = *annon*, as ch. xvii. 2, xxii. 20. The first perhaps suits the character of Satan better: he affirms that God is mistaken. בֵּרֵךְ signifies here also, *valedicere*: he will say farewell to thee, and indeed עַל־פָּנֶיךָ (as Isa. lxv. 3), meeting thee arrogantly and shamelessly: it signifies, properly, upon thy countenance, *i.e.* say it to thee, to the very face, that he will have nothing more to do with thee (comp. on ch. ii. 5). In order now that the truth of His testimony to Job's piety, and this piety itself, may be tried, Jehovah surrenders all Job's possessions, all that is his, except himself, to Satan.

Ver. 12. *Then Jehovah said to Satan, Behold, all that he hath is in thy hand; only upon himself put not forth thy hand. And Satan went forth from the presence of Jehovah.*

Notice well : The divine permission appears at the same time as a divine command, for in general there is not a permission by which God remains purely passive; wherefore God is even called in Scripture *creator mali* (the evil act as such only excepted), Isa. xlv. 7. Further, the divine arrangement has not its foundation in the sin which still clings to Job. For in the praise conferred upon Job, it is not said that he is absolutely without sin : universal liability to sin is assumed not only of all the unrighteousness, but even of all the righteousness, of Adam's race. Thirdly, the permission proceeds, on the contrary, from God's purpose to maintain, in opposition to Satan, the righteousness which, in spite of the universal liability to sin, is peculiar to Job; and if we place this single instance in historical connection with the development of the plan of redemption, it is a part of the conflict of the woman's seed with the serpent, and of the gradual degradation of Satan to the lake of fire. After Jehovah's permission, Satan retires forthwith. The licence is welcome to him, for he delights in the work of destruction. And he hopes to conquer. For after he has experienced the unlimited power of evil over himself, he has lost all faith in the power of good, and is indeed become himself the self-deceived father of lies.

THE FOUR MESSENGERS OF MISFORTUNE.—CHAP. I. 13 SQQ.

Satan now accomplishes to the utmost of his power, by repeated blows, that which Jehovah had granted to him : first on Job's oxen, and asses, and herdsmen.

Vers. 13–15. *And it came to pass one day, when his sons and his daughters were eating and drinking wine in the house of their eldest brother, that a messenger came to Job, and said, The oxen were ploughing, and the asses feeding beside them, when the Sabeans fell upon them, and carried them away, and smote the servants with the edge of the sword; and I only am escaped alone to tell thee.*

The principal clause, וַיְהִי הַיּוֹם, in which the art. of הַיּוֹם has no more reference to anything preceding than in ver. 6, is immediately followed by an adverbial clause, which may be expressed by participles, Lat. *filiis ejus filiabusque convivantibus.* The details which follow are important. Job had celebrated the usual weekly worship early in the morning with his children, and knew that they were met together in the house of his eldest son, with whom the order of mutual entertainment came round again, when the messengers of misfortune began to break in upon him: it is therefore on the very day when, by reason of the sacrifice offered, he was quite sure of Jehovah's favour. The participial construction, the oxen were ploughing (*vid.* Ges. § 134, 2, *c*), describes the condition which was disturbed by the calamity that befell them. The verb הָיוּ stands here because the clause is a principal one, not as ver. 13, adverbial. עַל־יְדֵי, properly "at hand," losing its radical meaning, signifies (as Judg. xi. 26) "close by." The interpretation "in their places," after Num. ii. 17, is untenable, as this signification of יָד is only supported in the *sing.* שְׁבָא is construed as *fem.*, since the name of the country is used as the name of the people. In Genesis three races of this name are mentioned: Cushite (x. 7), Joktanish (x. 28), and Abrahamic (xxv. 3). Here the nomadic portion of this mixed race in North Arabia from the Persian Gulf to Idumæa is intended. Luther, for the sake of clearness, translates here, and 1 Kings x. 1, *Arabia.* In וָאִמָּלְטָה, the *waw*, as is seen from the Kametz, is *waw convertens*, and the paragogic *ah*, which otherwise indicates the cohortative, is either without significance, or simply adds intensity to the verbal idea : I have saved myself with great difficulty.   For this common form of the 1 *fut. consec.*, occurring four times in the Pentateuch, *vid.* Ges. § 49, 2.   The clause לְהַגִּיד לָךְ is objective : in order that—so it was intended by the calamity—I might tell thee.

THE SECOND MESSENGER : Ver. 16. *While he was yet speaking, another came, and said, The fire of God fell from heaven, and set fire to the sheep and servants, and consumed them; and I only am escaped alone to tell thee.*

The fire of God, which descends, is not a suitable expression for *Samûm* (Schlottm.), that wind of the desert which often so suddenly destroys man and beast, although indeed it is indicated by certain atmospheric phenomena, appearing first of a yellow colour, which changes to a leaden hue and spreads through the atmosphere, so that the sun when at the brightest becomes a dark red.   The writer, also, can scarcely have intended lightning (Rosenm., Hirz., Hahn), but rain of fire or brimstone, as with Sodom and Gomorrha, and as 1 Kings xviii. 38, 2 Kings i. 12.

THE THIRD MESSENGER : Ver. 17. *While he was yet speaking, there came also another, and said, The Chaldeans ranged themselves in three bands, and rushed upon the camels, and carried them away, and slew the servants with the edge of the sword; and I only am escaped alone to tell thee.*

Without any authority, Ewald sees in this mention of the Chaldeans an indication of the composition of the book in the seventh century B.C., when the Chaldeans under Nabopolassar began to inherit the Assyrian power.   Following Ewald, Renan

observes that the Chaldeans first appear as such marauders
about the time of Uzziah. But in Genesis we find mention
of early Semitic Chaldeans among the mountain ranges lying
to the north of Assyria and Mesopotamia ; and later, Nahor
Chaldeans of Mesopotamia, whose existence is traced back to
the patriarchal times (*vid.* Genesis, p. 422[1]), and who were
powerful enough at any time to make a raid into Idumæa.
To make an attack divided into several רָאשִׁים, heads, multi-
tudes, bands (two—Gen. xiv. 15 ; three—Judg. vii. 16, 1
Sam. xi. 11 ; or four—Judg. ix. 34), is an ancient military
stratagem ; and פָּשַׁט, *e.g.* Judg. ix. 33, is the proper word
for attacks of such bands, either for plunder or revenge. In
לְפִי־חֶרֶב, at the edge of the sword, *à l'epée*, לְ is like the usual
acc. of manner.

THE FOURTH MESSENGER : Ver. 18. *While he was yet
speaking, another also came, and said, Thy sons and thy
daughters were eating and drinking wine in their eldest
brother's house : and, behold, a great wind came across
from the desert, and smote the four corners of the house,
and it fell upon the young people, and they are dead ; and
I only am escaped alone to tell thee.*

Instead of עוֹד, we have עַד here : the former denotes continuity in time, the latter continuity in space, and they may
be interchanged. עַד in the signif. "while" is here construed
with the participle, as Neh. vii. 3 ; comp. other construc-
tions, ch. viii. 21, 1 Sam. xiv. 19, Jonah iv. 2. "From the
other side of the desert" is equivalent to, from its farthest
end. הַנְּעָרִים are the youthful sons and daughters of Job,
according to the epicene use of נַעַר in the Pentateuch (youths
and maidens). In one day Job is now bereft of everything
which he accounted the gift of Jehovah,—his herds, and with

---

[1] This reference is to Delitzsch's *Commentar über die Genesis*, 1860,
a separate work from the Keil and Delitzsch series.—TR.

these his servants, which he not only prizes as property, but for whom he has also a tender heart (ch. xxxi.) ; last of all, even his dearest ones, his children. Satan has summoned the elements and men for the destruction of Job's possessions by repeated strokes. That men and nations can be excited by Satan to hostile enterprises, is nothing surprising (cf. Apoc. xx. 8) ; but here, even the fire of God and the hurricane are attributed to him. Is this poetry or truth? Luther, in the *Larger Catechism*, question iv., says the same : " The devil causes strife, murder, rebellion, and war, also thunder and lightning, and hail, to destroy corn and cattle, to poison the atmosphere," etc.,—a passage of our creed often ridiculed by rationalism ; but it is correct if understood in accordance with Scripture, and not superstitiously. As among men, so in nature, since the Fall two different powers of divine anger and divine love are in operation : the mingling of these is the essence of the present Kosmos. Everything destructive to nature, and everything arising therefrom which is dangerous and fatal to the life of man, is the outward manifestation of the power of anger. In this power Satan has fortified himself ; and this, which underlies the whole course of nature, he is able to make use of, so far as God may permit it as being subservient to His chief design (comp. Apoc. xiii. 13 with 2 Thess. ii. 9). He has no creative power. Fire and storm, by means of which he works, are of God ; but he is allowed to excite these forces to hostility against man, just as he himself is become an instrument of evil. It is similar with human demonocracy, whose very being consists in placing itself *en rapport* with the hidden powers of nature. Satan is the great juggler, and has already manifested himself as such, even in paradise and in the temptation of Jesus Christ. There is in nature, as among men, an entanglement of contrary forces which he knows how to unloose, because it is the sphere of his special dominion ; for the whole course of nature, in the change of its phenomena, is subject not only to abstract laws, but also to concrete supernatural powers, both bad and good.

THE CONDUCT OF JOB : Vers. 20 sq. *Then Job arose, and rent his mantle, and shaved his head, and fell down upon the ground, and worshipped, and said, Naked came I out of my mother's womb, and naked shall I return thither : Jehovah gave, and Jehovah hath taken away ; blessed be the name of Jehovah.*

The first three messengers Job has heard, sitting, and in silence ; but at the news of the death of his children, brought by the fourth, he can no longer overcome his grief. The intensity of his feeling is indicated by rising up (cf. Jonah iii. 6) ; his torn heart, by the rending of his mantle ; the conscious loss of his dearest ones, by cutting off the hair of his head. He does not, however, act like one in despair, but, humbling himself under the mighty hand of God, falls to the ground and prostrates himself, *i.e.* worshipping God, so that his face touches the earth. הִשְׁתַּחֲוָה, *se prosternere*, this is the gesture of adoration, προσκύνησις.[1] יָצָתִי is defectively written, as Num. xi. 11; cf. *infra*, ch. xxxii. 18. The occurrence of שָׁמָּה here is remarkable, and may have given rise to the question of Nicodemus, John iii. 4 : μὴ δύναται ἄνθρωπος εἰς τὴν κοιλίαν τῆς μητρὸς αὐτοῦ δεύτερον εἰσελθεῖν. The writer of Ecclesiastes (ch. v. 14) has left out this difficult שמה. It means either being put back into a state of unconsciousness and seclusion from the light and turmoil of this world, similar to his former state in his mother's womb, which Hupfeld, in his *Commentatio in quosdam Iobeidos locos*, 1853, favours ; or, since the idea of בֶּטֶן אִמִּי may be extended, return to the bosom of mother earth (Ew., Hirz., Schlottm., *et al.*), so that שמה is not so much retrospective as rather prospective with reference to

[1] *Vid.* Hölemann's *Abh. über die biblische Gestaltung der Anbetung*, in his *Bibelstudien, Abth.* 1 (1859).

the grave (Böttch.), which we prefer; for as the mother's bosom can be compared to the bosom of the earth (Ps. cxxxix. 15), because it is of the earth, and recalls the original forming of man from the earth, so the bosom of the earth is compared to the mother's, Sir. xl. 1 : ἀφ' ἡμέρας ἐξόδου ἐκ γαστρὸς μητρὸς ἕως ἡμέρας ἐπιταφῆς εἰς μητέρα πάντων. The writer here intentionally makes Job call God יהוה. In the dialogue portion, the name יהוה occurs only once in the mouth of Job (ch. xii. 9) ; most frequently the speakers use אלוה and שׁדי. This use of the names of God corresponds to the early use of the same in the Pentateuch, according to which שׁדי is the proper name of God in the patriarchal days, and יהוה in the later days, to which they were preparatory. The traditional view, that Elohim describes God according to the attribute of justice, Jehovah according to the attribute of mercy, is only in part correct; for even when the advent of God to judgment is announced, He is in general named Jehovah. Rather, אֱלֹהִים (plur. of אֱלוֹהַ, fear), the Revered One, describes God as object ; יְהוָה or יַהֲוֶה, on the other hand, as subject. אֱלֹהִים describes Him in the fulness of His glorious majesty, including also the spirits, which are round about Him; יהוה as the Absolute One. Accordingly, Job, when he says יהוה, thinks of God not only as the absolute cause of his fate, but as the Being ordering his life according to His own counsel, who is ever worthy of praise, whether in His infinite wisdom He gives or takes away. Job was not driven from God, but praised Him in the midst of suffering, even when, to human understanding and feeling, there was only occasion for anguish : he destroyed the suspicion of Satan, that he only feared God for the sake of His gifts, not for His own sake; and remained, in the midst of *a fourfold temptation, the conqueror.*[1] Throughout the whole book he does not

---

[1] In Oliver Goldsmith's *Vicar of Wakefield* (*vid.* Jul. Hamberger, *Gott und seine Offenbarung,* S. 71), there is much that reminds one of the

go so far as to deny God (בֵּרֵךְ אֱלֹהִים), and thus far he does not fall into any unworthy utterances concerning His rule.

> Ver. 22. *In all this Job sinned not, nor attributed folly to God.*

In all this, *i.e.* as the LXX. correctly renders it : which thus far had befallen him ; Ewald *et al.* translate incorrectly : he gave God no provocation. תִּפְלָה signifies, according to ch. xxiv. 12, comp. ch. vi. 6, saltlessness and tastelessness, dealing devoid of meaning and purpose, and is to be translated either, he uttered not, *non edidit*, anything absurd against God, as Jerome translates, *neque stultum quid contra Deum locutus est;* or, he did not attribute folly to God : so that נתן ל are connected, as Ps. lxviii. 35, Jer. xiii. 16. Since נָתַן by itself nowhere signifies to express, we side with Hirzel and Schlottm. against Rödiger (in his *Thes.*) and Oehler, in favour of the latter. The writer hints that, later on, Job committed himself by some unwise thoughts of the government of God.

THE FIFTH AND SIXTH TEMPTATION.—CHAP. II. 1–10.

Satan has now exhausted his utmost power, but without success.

> Ver. 1. *Again there was a day when the sons of God came to present themselves before Jehovah, and Satan came also among them, to present himself before Jehovah.*

The clause expressive of the purpose of their appearing is here repeated in connection with Satan (comp. on the contrary, ch. i. 6), for this time he appears with a most definite

book of Job, especially the repeated misfortunes which befall the worthy clergyman, his submission under all, and the issue which counterbalances his misfortune. But what is copied from the book of Job appears to be only superficial, not to come from the depth of the spiritual life.

object. Jehovah addresses Satan as He had done on the former occasion.

Ver. 2. *And Jehovah said to Satan, Whence comest thou? And Satan answered Jehovah, and said, From going to and fro in the earth, and wandering up and down in it.*

Instead of מֵאַיִן, ch. i. 7, we have here the similar expression אֵי מִזֶּה (Ges. § 150, *extra*). Such slight variations are also frequent in the repetitions in the Psalms, and we have had an example in ch. i. in the interchange of עוֹד and עַד. After the general answer which Satan gives, Jehovah inquires more particularly.

Ver. 3. *Then Jehovah said to Satan, Hast thou considered my servant Job? for there is none like him in the earth, a perfect and an upright man, fearing God and eschewing evil; and still he holdeth fast his integrity, although thou hast moved me against him, to injure him without cause.*

From the foregoing fact, that amidst all his sufferings hitherto Job has preserved and proved his תֻּמָּה (except in the book of Job, only Prov. xi. 3), the *fut. consec.* draws the conclusion : there was no previous reason for the injury which Satan had urged God to decree for Job. הֵסִית does not signify, as Umbreit thinks, to lead astray, in which case it were an almost blasphemous anthropomorphism : it signifies *instigare*, and indeed generally, to evil, as *e.g.* 1 Chron. xxi. 1 ; but not always, *e.g.* Josh. xv. 18 : here it is certainly in a strongly anthropopathical sense of the impulse given by Satan to Jehovah to prove Job in so hurtful a manner. The writer purposely chooses these strong expressions, הֵסִית and בַּלֵּעַ. Satan's aim, since he suspected Job still, went beyond the limited power which was given him over Job. Satan even now again denies what Jehovah affirms.

Vers. 4 sq. *And Satan answered Jehovah, and said, Skin for skin, and all that man hath will he give for his life : stretch forth yet once Thy hand, and touch his bone, and his flesh, truly he will renounce Thee to Thy face.*

Olshausen refers עוֹר בְּעַד עוֹר to Job in relation to Jehovah : So long as Thou leavest his skin untouched, he will also leave Thee untouched; which, though it is the devil who speaks, were nevertheless too unbecomingly expressed. Hupfeld understands by the skin, that skin which is here given for the other,—the skin of his cattle, of his servants and children, which Job had gladly given up, that for such a price he might get off with his own skin sound; but בְּעַד cannot be used as *Beth pretii :* even in Prov. vi. 26 this is not the case. For the same reason, we must not, with Hirz., Ew., and most, translate, Skin for skin = like for like, which Ewald bases on the strange assertion, that one skin is like another, as one dead piece is like another. The meaning of the words of Satan (rightly understood by Schlottm. and the Jewish expositors) is this : One gives up one's skin to preserve one's skin ; one endures pain on a sickly part of the skin, for the sake of saving the whole skin ; one holds up the arm, as Raschi suggests, to avert the fatal blow from the head. The second clause is climacteric : a man gives skin for skin ; but for his life, his highest good, he willingly gives up everything, without exception, that can be given up, and life itself still retained. This principle derived from experience, applied to Job, may be expressed thus : Just so, Job has gladly given up everything, and is content to have escaped with his life. וְאוּלָם, *verum enim vero,* is connected with this suppressed because self-evident application. The verb נָגַע, above, ch. i. 11, with בְּ, is construed here with אֶל, and expresses increased malignity : Stretch forth Thy hand but once to his very bones, etc. Instead of עַל־פָּנֶיךָ, ch. i. 11,

אֵל־פּ is used here with the same force : forthwith, fearlessly and regardlessly (comp. ch. xiii. 15 ; Deut. vii. 10), he will bid Thee farewell.

THE GRANT OF NEW POWER : Ver. 6. *And Jehovah said to Satan, Behold, he is in thy hand; only take care of his life.*

Job has not forfeited his life; permission is given to place it in extreme peril, and nothing more, in order to see whether or not, in the face of death, he will deny the God who has decreed such heavy affliction for him. נֶפֶשׁ does not signify the same as חַיִּים ; it is the soul producing the spirit-life of man. We must, however, translate "life," because we do not use "soul" in the sense of ψυχή, *anima*.

THE WORKING OUT OF THE COMMISSION : Vers. 7 et seq. *Then Satan went forth from the presence of Jehovah, and smote Job with sore boils, from the sole of his foot to his crown. And he took him a potsherd to scrape himself with, and sat in the midst of ashes.*

The description of this disease calls to mind Deut. xxviii. 35 with 27, and is, according to the symptoms mentioned further on in the book, *elephantiasis* (so called because the limbs become jointless lumps like elephants' legs), Arab. جذام, 'gudhâm, Lat. *lepra nodosa*, the most fearful form of *lepra*, which sometimes seizes persons even of the higher ranks. Artapan (C. Müller, *Fragm.* iii. 222) says, that an Egyptian king was the first man who died of elephantiasis. Baldwin, king of Jerusalem, was afflicted with it in a very dangerous form.[1] The disease begins with the rising of

[1] *Vid.* the history in Heer, *De elephantiasi Græcorum et Arabum*, Breslau, 1842, and coloured plates in *Traité de la Spédalskhed ou Elephantiasis des Grecs par Danielssen et Boeck*, Paris, 1848, translated from the Norwegian ; and in Hecker, *Elephantiasis oder Lepra Arabica*,

tubercular boils, and at length resembles a cancer spreading itself over the whole body, by which the body is so affected, that some of the limbs fall completely away. Scraping with a potsherd will not only relieve the intolerable itching of the skin, but also remove the matter. Sitting among ashes is on account of the deep sorrow (comp. Jonah iii. 6) into which Job is brought by his heavy losses, especially the loss of his children. The LXX. adds that he sat on a dunghill outside the city: the dunghill is taken from the passage Ps. cxiii. 7, and the " outside the city" from the law of the מְצֹרָע. In addition to the four losses, a fifth temptation, in the form of a disease incurable in the eye of man, is now come upon Job: a natural disease, but brought on by Satan, permitted, and therefore decreed, by God. Satan does not appear again throughout the whole book. Evil has not only a personal existence in the invisible world, but also its agents and instruments in this; and by these it is henceforth manifested.

FIRST JOB'S WIFE (who is only mentioned in one other passage (ch. xix. 17), where Job complains that his breath is offensive to her) COMES TO HIM: Ver. 9. *Then his wife said to him, Dost thou still hold fast thine integrity? renounce God, and die.*

In the LXX. the words of his wife are unskilfully extended. The few words as they stand are sufficiently charac-

Lahr, 1858 (with lithographs). " The means of cure," says Aretäus the Cappadocian (*vid.* his writings translated by Mann, 1858, S. 221), "must be more powerful than the disease, if it is to be removed. But what cure can be successfully applied to the fearful evil of elephantiasis? It is not confined to one part, either internally or externally, but takes possession of the entire system. It is terrible and hideous to behold, for it gives a man the appearance of an animal. Every one dreads to live, and have any intercourse, with such invalids; they flee from them as from the plague, for infection is easily communicated by the breath. Where, in the whole range of pharmacy, can such a powerful remedy be found?"

teristic. They are not to be explained, Call on God for the last time, and then die (von Gerl.) ; or, Call on Him that thou die (according to Ges. § 130, 2) ; but בָּרֵךְ signifies, as Job's answer shows, to take leave of. She therefore counsels Job to do that which Satan has boasted to accomplish. And notwithstanding, Hengstenberg, in his *Lecture on the Book of Job* (1860),[1] defends her against the too severe judgment of expositors. Her desperation, says he, proceeds from her strong love for her husband ; and if she had to suffer the same herself, she would probably have struggled against despair. But love hopeth all things ; love keeps its despondency hidden even when it desponds ; love has no such godless utterance, as to say, Renounce God ; and none so unloving, as to say, Die. No, indeed! this woman is truly *diaboli adjutrix* (August.) ; a tool of the tempter (Ebrard) ; *impiæ carnis præco* (Brentius). And though Calvin goes too far when he calls her not only *organum Satanæ,* but even *Proserpinam et Furiam infernalem,* the title of another Xantippe, against which Hengstenberg defends her, is indeed rather flattery than slander. Tobias' Anna is her copy.[2] What experience of life and insight the writer manifests in introducing Job's wife as the mocking opposer of his constant piety! Job has lost his children, but this wife he has retained, for he needed not to be tried by losing her : he was proved sufficiently by having her. She is further on once referred to, but even

---

[1] Clark's Foreign Theological Library.

[2] She says to the blind Tobias, when she is obliged to work for the support of the family, and does not act straightforwardly towards him : ποῦ εἰσιν αἱ ἐλεημοσύναι σου καὶ αἱ δικαιοσύναι σου, ἰδοὺ γνωστὰ πάντα μετὰ σοῦ, i.e. (as Sengelmann, *Book of Tobit,* 1857, and O. F. Fritzsche, *Handbuch zu d. Apokr. Lief.* ii. S. 36, correctly explain) one sees from thy misfortunes that thy virtue is not of much avail to thee. She appears still more like Job in the revised text : *manifeste vana facta est spes tua et eleemosynæ tuæ modo apparuerunt, i.e.* thy benevolence has obviously brought us to poverty. In the text of Jerome a parallel between Tobias and Job precedes this utterance of Tobias' wife.

then not to her advantage. Why, asks Chrysostom, did the
devil leave him this wife? Because he thought her a good
scourge, by which to plague him more acutely than by any
other means. Moreover, the thought is not far distant, that
God left her to him in order that when, in the glorious issue
of his sufferings, he receives everything doubled, he might
not have this thorn in the flesh also doubled.[1] What enmity
towards God, what uncharitableness towards her husband, is
there in her sarcastic words, which, if they are more than
mockery, counsel him to suicide! (Ebrard). But he repels
them in a manner becoming himself.

> Ver. 10. *But he said to her, As one of the ungodly would
> speak, thou speakest. Shall we receive good from God,
> and shall we not also receive evil?*

The answer of Job is strong but not harsh, for the אחת
(comp. 2 Sam. xiii. 13) is somewhat soothing. The translation
" as one of the foolish women" does not correspond to the
Hebrew; נָבָל is one who thinks madly and acts impiously.
What follows is a double question, גַּם for הֲגַם. The גַּם stands
at the beginning of the sentence, but logically belongs to the
second part, towards which pronunciation and reading must
hurry over the first,—a frequent occurrence after interrogative
particles, *e.g.* Num. xvi. 22, Isa. v. 4*b*; after causal particles,
e.g. Isa. xii. 1, Prov. i. 24; after the negative פֶּן, Deut. viii.
12 sqq., and often. Hupfeld renders the thought expressed in
the double question very correctly: *bonum quidem hucusque a
Deo accepimus, malum vero jam non item accipiemus?* גַּם is
found also elsewhere at the beginning of a sentence, although

---

[1] The delicate design of the writer here must not be overlooked: it
has something of the tragi-comic about it, and has furnished acceptable
material for epigrammatic writers not first from Kästner, but from early
times (*vid. das Epigramm vom J.* 1696, in Serpilius' *Personalia Iobi*).
Vid. a Jewish proverb relating thereto in Tendlau, *Sprüchw. u. Redens-
arten deutsch-jüd. Vorzeit* (1860), S. 11.

belonging to a later clause, and that indeed not always the one immediately following, e.g. Hos. vi. 11, Zech. ix. 11 ; the same syntax is to be found with אַף, אַךְ, and רַק. קִבֵּל, like תִּמָּה, is a word common to the book of Job and Proverbs (xix. 20) ; besides these, it is found only in books written after the exile, and is more Aramaic than Hebraic. By this answer which Job gives to his wife, he has repelled the sixth temptation. For

Ver. 10b. *In all this Job sinned not with his lips.*

The Targum adds : but in his thoughts he already cherished sinful words. בִּשְׂפָתָיו is certainly not undesignedly introduced here and omitted in ch. i. 22. The temptation to murmur was now already at work within him, but he was its master, so that no murmur escaped him.

THE SILENT VISIT.—CHAP. II. 11 SQQ.

After the sixth temptation there comes a seventh ; and now the real conflict begins, through which the hero of the book passes, not indeed without sinning, but still triumphantly.

Ver. 11. *When Job's three friends heard of all this evil that was come upon him, they came every one from his own place ; Eliphaz from Teman, and Bildad from Shuach, and Zophar from Naama : for they had made an appointment to come together to go and sympathize with him, and comfort him.*

אֱלִיפַז is, according to Gen. xxxvi., an old Idumæan name (transposed = *Phasaël* in the history of the Herodeans ; according to Michaelis, *Suppl.* p. 87 : *cui Deus aurum est*, comp. ch. xxii. 25), and תֵּימָן a district of Idumæa, celebrated for its native wisdom (Jer. xlix. 7 ; Bar. iii. 22 sq.). But also in East-Hauran a *Têmâ* is still found (described by Wetzstein

in his *Bericht über seine Reise in den beiden Trachonen und um
das Hauran-Gebirge, Zeitschr. für allg. Erdkunde,* 1859), and
about fifteen miles south of *Têmâ,* a *Bûzân* suggestive of
Elihu's surname (comp. Jer. xxv. 23). שׁוּחַ we know only
from Gen. xxv. as the son of Abraham and Keturah, who
settled in the east country. Accordingly it must be a district of Arabia lying not very far from Idumæa : it might
be compared with trans-Hauran *Schakka,* though the sound,
however, of the word makes it scarcely admissible, which is
undoubtedly one and the same with Σακκαία, east from
Batanæa, mentioned in Ptolem. v. 15. נַעֲמָה is a name frequent in Syria and Palestine : there is a town of the Jewish
Shephêla (the low ground by the Mediterranean) of this name,
Josh. xv. 41, which, however, can hardly be intended here.
הַבָּאָה is *Milel,* consequently third pers. with the art. instead
of the relative pron. (as, besides here, Gen. xviii. 21, xlvi. 27),
vid. Ges. § 109 *ad init.* The *Niph.* נוֹעַד is wrongly taken by
some expositors as the same meaning with נוֹעַץ, to confer with,
appoint a meeting : it signifies, to assemble themselves, to
meet in an appointed place at an appointed time (Neh. vi. 2).
Reports spread among the mounted tribes of the Arabian
desert with the rapidity of telegraphic despatches.

THEIR ARRIVAL : Ver. 12. *And when they lifted up their
eyes afar off, and knew him not, they lifted up their voice,
and wept ; and they rent every one his mantle, and threw
dust upon their heads toward heaven.*

They saw a form which seemed to be Job, but in which
they were not able to recognise him. Then they weep and
rend their outer garments, and catch up dust to throw up
towards heaven (1 Sam. iv. 12), that it may fall again upon
their heads. The casting up of dust on high is the outward
sign of intense suffering, and, as von Gerlach rightly remarks,
of that which causes him to cry to heaven.

THEIR SILENCE: Ver. 13. *And they sat with him upon the ground seven days and seven nights; and none spake a word unto him: for they saw that his pain was very great.*

Ewald erroneously thinks that custom and propriety prescribed this seven days' silence; it was (as Ezek. iii. 15) the force of the impression produced on them, and the fear of annoying the sufferer. But their long silence shows that they had not fully realized the purpose of their visit. Their feeling is overpowered by reflection, their sympathy by dismay. It is a pity that they let Job utter the first word, which they might have prevented by some word of kindly solace; for, becoming first fully conscious of the difference between his present and former position from their conduct, he breaks forth with curses.

JOB'S DISCONSOLATE UTTERANCE OF GRIEF.—CHAP. III.

Job's first longer utterance now commences, by which he involves himself in the conflict, which is his seventh temptation or trial.

Vers. 1 sq. *After this Job opened his mouth, and cursed his day. And Job spake, and said.*

Ver. 2 consists only of three words, which are separated by *Rebia;* and ויאמר, although *Milel,* is vocalized וַיֹּאמַר, because the usual form וַיֹּאמֶר, which always immediately precedes direct narration, is not well suited to close the verse. עָנָה signifies to begin to speak from some previous incitement, as the New Testament ἀποκρίνεσθαι (not always = הֵשִׁיב) is also sometimes used.[1] The following utterance of Job, with

---

[1] *Vid.* on this use of ἀποκρίνεσθαι, *Quæstio* xxi. of the *Amphilochia* of Photius in *Ang. Maji Collectio,* i. 229 sq.

which the poetic accentuation begins, is analysed by modern critics as follows: vers. 3–10, 11–19, 20–26. Schlottmann calls it three strophes, Hahn three parts, in the first of which delirious cursing of life is expressed; in the second, eager longing for death; in the third, reproachful inquiry after the end of such a life of suffering. In reality they are not strophes. Nevertheless Ebrard is wrong when he maintains that, in general, strophe-structure is as little to be found in the book of Job as in Wallenstein's *Monologue*. The poetical part of the book of Job is throughout strophic, so far as the nature of the drama admits it. So also even this first speech. Stickel has correctly traced out its divisions; but accidentally, for he has reckoned according to the Masoretic verses. That this is false, he is now fully aware; also Ewald, in his *Essay on Strophes in the Book of Job*, is almost misled into this groundless reckoning of the strophes according to the Masoretic verses (*Jahrb*. iii. S. 118, Anm. 3). The strophe-schema of the following speech is as follows: 8. 10. 6. 8. 6. 8. 6. The translation will show how unmistakeably it may be known. In the translation we have followed the complete lines of the original, and their rhythm: the iambic pentameter into which Ebrard, and still earlier Hosse (1849), have translated, disguises the oriental Hebrew poetry of the book with its variegated richness of form in a western uniform, the monotonous impression of which is not, as elsewhere, counterbalanced in the book of Job by the change of external action. After the translation we give the grammatical explanation of each strophe; and at the conclusion of the speech thus translated and explained, its higher exposition, *i.e.* its artistic importance in the connection of the drama, and its theological importance in relation to the Old and New Testament religion and religious life.

3 *Perish the day wherein I was born.*
   And the night which said, A man-child is conceived!
4 *Let that day become darkness ;*
   Let not Eloah ask after it from above,
   And let not the light shine on it.
5 *May darkness and the shadow of death purchase it back;*
   Let a cloud lie upon it ;
   May that which obscures the day terrify it.

The curse is against the day of his birth and the night of his conception as recurring yearly, not against the actual first day (Schlottm.), to which the imprecations which follow are not pertinent. Job wishes his birth-day may become *dies ater,* swallowed up by darkness as into nothing. The elliptical relative clauses, ver. 3 (Ges. § 123, 3 ; cf. 127, 4, *c*), become clear from the translation. Transl. *the night* (לַיְלָה with parag. *He* is *masc.*) *which said,* not: in which they said; the night alone was witness of this beginning of the development of a man-child, and made report of it to the High One, to whom it is subordinate. Day emerges from the darkness as Eloah from above (as ch. xxxi. 2, 28), *i.e.* He who reigns over the changes here below, asks after it; interests Himself in His own (דָּרַשׁ). Job wishes his birth-day may not rejoice in this. The relations of this his birth-day are darkness and the shadow of death. These are to redeem it, as, according to the right of kinsmen, family property is redeemed when it has got into a stranger's hands. This is the meaning of גְּאַל (LXX. ἐκλάβοι), not = גְּעַל, *inquinent* (Targ.). עֲנָנָה is collective, as נְהָרָה, mass of cloud. Instead of כִּמְרִירִי (the *Caph* of which seems pointed as *præpos.*), we must read with Ewald (§ 157, *a*), Olshausen, (§ 187, *b*), and others, כַּמְרִירִי, after the form חַכְלִיל, darkness, dark flashing (*vid.* on Ps. x. 8), שְׁפְרִיר, tapestry, unless we are willing to accept a form of noun without example elsewhere. The word signifies an obscuring, from כָּמַר, to glow with heat, because the greater the glow the deeper the blackness it leaves behind. All that ever obscures a day is to overtake and render terrible that day.[1]

> 6 *That night! let darkness seize upon it;*
> *Let it not rejoice among the days of the year;*
> *Let it not come into the number of the month.*
> 7 *Lo! let that night become barren;*
> *Let no sound of gladness come to it.*
> 8 *Let those who curse the day curse it,*
> *Who are skilled in stirring up leviathan.*
> 9 *Let the stars of its early twilight be darkened;*
> *Let it long for light and there be none;*
> *And let it not refresh itself with the eyelids of the dawn.*

Darkness is so to seize it, and so completely swallow it up, that it shall not be possible for it to pass into the light of day. It is not to become a day, to be reckoned as belonging to the days of the year and rejoice in the light thereof. יֵחַד, for יֵחְדְּ, *fut. Kal* from חָדָה (Ex. xviii. 9), with *Dagesh lene* retained, and a helping *Pathach* (*vid.* Ges. § 75, rem. 3, *d*); the reverse of the passage Gen. xlix. 6, where יַחַד, from יָחַד, *uniat se*, is found. It is to become barren, גַּלְמוּד, so that no human being shall ever be conceived and born, and greeted joyfully in it.[2] "Those who curse days" are magicians who know how to change days into *dies infausti* by their incantations. According to vulgar superstition, from which the imagery of ver. 8 is borrowed, there was a special art of exciting the dragon, which is the enemy of sun and moon, against them both, so that, by its devouring them, total darkness prevails. The dragon is called in Hindu *râhu;* the Chinese, and also the

---

[1] We may compare here, and further on, Constance's outburst of despair in *King John* (iii. 1 and iii. 4). Shakespeare, like Goethe, enriches himself from the book of Job.

[2] Fries understands רְנָנָה, song of the spheres (*concentum coeli*, ch. xxxviii. 37, Vulg.); but this Hellenic conception is without support in holy Scripture.

natives of Algeria, even at the present day make a wild
tumult with drums and copper vessels when an eclipse of the
sun or moon occurs, until the dragon will release his prey.[1]
Job wishes that this monster may swallow up the sun of his
birth-day. If the night in which he was conceived or born
is to become day, then let the stars of its twilight (*i.e.* the
stars which, as messengers of the morning, twinkle through
the twilight of dawn) become dark. It is to remain for
ever dark, never behold with delight the eyelids of the dawn.
רָאָה בְ, to regale one's self with the sight of anything, refresh
one's self. When the first rays of morning shoot up in the
eastern sky, then the dawn raises its eyelids; they are in
Sophocles' *Antigone*, 103, χρυσέης ἡμέρας βλέφαρον, the eye-
lid of the golden day, and therefore of the sun, the great eye.

10 *Because it did not close the doors of my mother's womb,*
   Nor hid sorrow from my eyes.
11 *Why did I not die from the womb,*
   Come forth from the womb and expire?
12 *Why have the knees welcomed me?*
   And why the breasts, that I should suck?

The whole strophe contains strong reason for his cursing
the night of his conception or birth. It should rather have
closed (*i.e.* make the womb barren, to be explained according
to 1 Sam. i. 5, Gen. xvi. 2) the doors of his womb (*i.e.* the
womb that conceived (*concepit*) him), and so have withdrawn
the sorrow he now experiences from his unborn eyes (on the

---

[1] On the dragon *râhu*, that swallows up sun and moon, *vid.* Pott, in
the *Hallische Lit. Zeitschr.* 1849, No. 199 ; on the custom of the Chinese,
Käuffer, *Das chinesische Volk*, S. 123. A similar custom among the
natives of Algeria I have read of in a newspaper (1856). Moreover, the
clouds which conceal the sky the Indians represent as a serpent. It is
ahi, the cloud-serpent, which Indra chases away when he divides the
clouds with his lightning. *Vid.* Westergaard in Weber's *Indischer Zeitschr.*
1855, S. 417.

extended force of the negative, *vid.* Ges. § 152, 3). Then why, *i.e.* to what purpose worth the labour, is he then conceived and born? The four questions, vers. 11 sqq., form a climax: he follows the course of his life from its commencement in embryo (מֵרֶחֶם, to be explained according to Jer. xx. 17, and ch. x. 18, where, however, it is מִן local, not as here, temporal) to the birth, and from the joy of his father who took the new-born child upon his knees (comp. Gen. l. 23) to the first development of the infant, and he curses this growing life in its four phases (Arnh., Schlottm.). Observe the *consecutio temp.* The fut. אָמוּת has the signification *moriebar*, because taken from the thought of the first period of his conception and birth; so also וְאֶגְוַע, governed by the preceding *perf.*, the signification *et exspirabam* (Ges. § 127, 4, *c*). Just so אִינָק, but modal, *ut sugerem ea.*

13 *So should I now have lain and had quiet,*
   I should have slept, then it would have been well with me,
14 *With kings and councillors of the earth,*
   Who built ruins for themselves,
15 *Or with princes possessing gold,*
   Who filled their houses with silver:
16 *Or like a hidden untimely birth I had not been,*
   And as children that have never seen the light.

The *perf.* and interchanging *fut.* have the signification of oriental *imperfecta conjunctivi*, according to Ges. § 126, 5; כִּי עַתָּה is the usual expression after hypothetical clauses, and takes the *perf.* if the preceding clause specifies a condition which has not occurred in the past (Gen. xxxi. 42, xliii. 10; Num. xxii. 29, 33; 1 Sam. xiv. 30), the *fut.* if a condition is not existing in the present (ch. vi. 3, viii. 6, xiii. 19). It is not to be translated: for then; כי rather commences the clause following: so I should now, indeed then I should. Ruins, חֳרָבוֹת, are uninhabited desolate buildings, elsewhere such as have become, here such as are from the first intended to remain, uninhabited and desolate, consequently sepulchres, mausoleums ; probably, since the book has Egyptian allusions, in other passages also, a play upon the pyramids, in whose name (*ΠΙ-ΧΡΑΜ*, according to Coptic glossaries) *ΠΙ* is the Egyptian article (*vid.* Bunsen, *Aeg.* ii. 361); Arab. without the art. *hirâm* or *ahrâm* (*vid. Abdollatîf,* ed. de Sacy, p. 293, s.).[1] Also Renan : *Qui se bâtissent des mausolées.* Böttch. *de inferis,* § 298 (who, however, prefers to read רחבות, wide streets), rightly directs attention to the difference between בנה החרבות (to rebuild the ruins) and בנה ח' לו (to build ruins for one's self). With או like things are then ranged after one another. Builders of the pyramids, millionaires, abortions (*vid.* Eccl. vi. 3), and the still-born : all these are removed from the sufferings of this life in their quiet of the grave, be their grave a "ruin" gazed upon by their descendants, or a hole dug out in the earth, and again filled in as it was before.

17 *There the wicked cease from troubling,*
   And the weary are at rest.
18 *The captives dwell together in tranquillity ;*
   They hear not the voice of the taskmaster.
19 *The small and great,—they are alike there ;*
   And the servant is free from his lord.

There, *i.e.* in the grave, all enjoy the rest they could not find here : the troublers and the troubled ones alike. רֹגֶז corresponds to the radical idea of looseness, broken in pieces, want of restraint, therefore of *Turba* (comp. Isa. lvii. 20, Jer. vi. 7), contained etymologically in רָשָׁע. The *Pilel* שַׁאֲנַן (*vid.* Ges. § 55, 2) signifies perfect freedom from care. In

---

[1] We think that חרבות sounds rather like חרמות, the name of the pyramids, as the Arabic *haram* (instead of *hharam*), derived from ΧΡΑΜ. recalls *harmân* (*e.g. beith harmân,* a house in ruins), the synonym of *hharbân* (חרבאן).

שֵׁם הוּא‎, הוּא‎ is more than the sign of the copula (Hirz., Hahn, Schlottm.); the rendering of the LXX., Vulg., and Luth., *ibi sunt,* is too feeble. As it is said of God, Isa. xli. 4, xliii. 13, Ps. cii. 28, that He is הוּא‎, *i.e.* He who is always the same, ὁ αὐτός; so here, הוּא‎, used purposely instead of הֵמָּה‎, signifies that great and small are like one another in the grave : all distinction has ceased, it has sunk to the equality of their present lot. Correctly Ewald: *Great and small are there the same.* יַחַד‎, ver. 18, refers to this destiny which brings them together.

> 20 *Why is light given to the wretched,*
> *And life to the sorrowful in soul?*
> 21 *Who wait for death, and he comes not,*
> *Who dig after him more than for treasure,*
> 22 *Who rejoice with exceeding joy,*
> *Who are enraptured, when they can find the grave?*
> 23 *To the man whose way is hidden,*
> *And whom Eloah hath hedged round?*

The descriptive *partt.* vers. 21*a*, 22*a*, are continued in predicative clauses, which are virtually relative clauses; ver. 21*b* has the *fut. consec.,* since the sufferers are regarded as now at least dead ; ver. 22*b* the simple *fut.,* since their longing for the grave is placed before the eye (on this transition from the *part.* to the *verb. fin., vid.* Ges. § 134, rem. 2). Schlottm. and Hahn wrongly translate: who would dig (instead of do dig) for him more than for treasure. אֱלֵי־גִיל‎ (with poetical אֱלֵי‎ instead of אֶל‎) might signify, accompanied by rejoicing, *i.e.* the cry and gesture of joy. The translation *usque ad exultationem,* is, however, more appropriate here as well as in Hos. ix. 1. With ver. 23 Job refers to himself: he is the man whose way of suffering is mysterious and prospectless, and whom God has penned in on all sides (a fig. like ch. xix. 8; comp. Lam. iii. 5). סָכַךְ‎, *sepire,* above, ch. i. 10, to hedge round for protection, here : forcibly straiten.

24 *For instead of my food my sighing cometh,*
   And my roarings pour themselves forth as water.
25 *For I fear something terrible, and it cometh upon me,*
   And that before which I shudder cometh to me.
26 *I dwelt not in security, nor rested, nor refreshed myself :*
   Then trouble cometh.

That לִפְנֵי may pass over from the local signification to the substitutionary, like the Lat. *pro* (*e.g. pro præmio est*), is seen from ch. iv. 19 (comp. 1 Sam. i. 16) : the parallelism, which is less favourable to the interpretation, before my bread (Hahn, Schlottm., and others), favours the signification *pro* here. The *fut. consec.* וַיִּתְּכוּ (*Kal* of נָתַךְ) is to be translated, according to Ges. § 129, 3, *a, se effundunt* (not *effuderunt*) : it denotes, by close connection with the preceding, that which has hitherto happened. Just so ver. 25*a:* I fear something terrible ; forthwith it comes over me (this terrible, most dreadful thing). אָתָה is conjugated by the ה passing into the original of the root (*vid.* Ges. § 74, rem. 4). And just so the conclusion : then also forthwith רֹגֶז (*i.e.* suffering which disorders, rages and ransacks furiously) comes again. Schlottm. translates tamely and wrongly : then comes—oppression. Hahn, better : Nevertheless fresh trouble always comes ; but the "nevertheless" is incorrect, for the *fut. consec.* indicates a close connection, not contrast. The *prætt.*, ver. 26, give the details of the principal fact, which follows in the *fut. consec.* : only a short cessation, which is no real cessation ; then the suffering rages afresh.

Why—one is inclined to ask respecting this first speech of Job, which gives rise to the following controversy—why does the writer allow Job, who but a short time before, in opposition to his wife, has manifested such wise submission to God's dealings, all at once to break forth in such despair ? Does it not seem as though the assertion of Satan were about to be confirmed? Much depends upon one's forming a correct and just judgment respecting the state of mind from which this first speech proceeds. To this purpose, consider (1) That the speech contains no trace of what the writer means by ברך את־האלהים : Job nowhere says that he will have nothing more to do with God ; he does not renounce his former faithfulness : (2) That, however, in the mind of the writer, as may be gathered from ch. ii. 10, this speech is to be regarded as the beginning of Job's sinning. If a man, on account of his sufferings, wishes to die early, or not to have been born at all, he has lost his confidence that God, even in the severest suffering, designs his highest good ; and this want of confidence is sin.

There is, however, a great difference between a man who has in general no trust in God, and in whom suffering only makes this manifest in a terrible manner, and the man with whom trust in God is a habit of his soul, and is only momentarily repressed, and, as it were, paralysed. Such interruption of the habitual state may result from the first pressure of unaccustomed suffering ; it may then seem as though trust in God were overwhelmed, whereas it has only given way to rally itself again. It is, however, not the greatness of the affliction in itself which shakes his sincere trust in God, but a change of disposition on the part of God which seems to be at work in the affliction. The sufferer considers himself as forgotten, forsaken, and rejected of God, as many passages in the Psalms and Lamentations show : therefore he sinks into despair ; and in this despair expression is given to the profound truth (although with regard to the individual it is a sinful weakness), that it is better never to have been born, or to be annihilated, than to be rejected of God (comp. Matt. xxvi. 24, καλὸν ἦν αὐτῷ εἰ οὐκ ἐγεννήθη ὁ ἄνθρωπος ἐκεῖνος). In such a condition of spiritual, and, as we know from the prologue, of Satanic temptation (Luke xxii. 31, Eph. vi. 16),

is Job. He does not despair when he contemplates his affliction, but when he looks at God through it, who, as though
He were become his enemy, has surrounded him with this
affliction as with a rampart. He calls himself a man whose
way is hidden, as Zion laments, Isa. xl. 27, "My way is
hidden from Jehovah;" a man whom Eloah has hedged
round, as Jeremiah laments over the ruins of Jerusalem,
Lam. iii. 1–13 (in some measure a comment on Job iii. 23),
"I am the man who has seen affliction by the rod of His
wrath. . . . He has hedged me round that I cannot get out,
and made my chain heavy." In this condition of entire de-
privation of every taste of divine goodness, Job breaks forth
in curses. He has lost wealth and children, and has praised
God; he has even begun to bear an incurable disease with
submission to the providence of God. Now, however, when
not only the affliction, but God himself, seems to him to be
hostile (*nunc autem occultato patre*, as Brentius expresses it),[1]
we hear from his mouth neither words of *praise* (the highest
excellence in affliction) nor words of *resignation* (duty in affliction), but words of *despair*: his trust in God is not destroyed,
but overcast by thick clouds of melancholy and doubt.

It is indeed inconceivable that a New Testament believer,

---

[1] Fries, in his discussion of this portion of the book of Job, *Jahrbb.
für Deutsche Theologie*, 1859, S. 790 ff., is quite right that the real affliction of Job consists in this, that the inward feeling of being forsaken of
God, which was hitherto strange to him, is come upon him. But the
remark directed against me, that the feeling of being forsaken of God
does not always stand in connection with other affliction, but may come
on the favoured of God even in the midst of uninterrupted outward prosperity, does not concern me, since it is manifestly by the dispensations
which deprive him of all his possessions, and at last affect him corpore-
ally and individually, that Job is led to regard himself as one forsaken of
God, and still more than that, one hated by God; and since, on the other
hand also, this view of the tempted does not appear to be absolutely subjective, God has really withdrawn from Job the external proof, and at
the same time the feeling, of His abiding love, in order to try the fidelity
of His servant's love, and prove its absoluteness.

even under the strongest temptation, should utter such imprecations, or especially such a question of doubt as in ver.
20 : Wherefore is light given to the miserable? But that an
Old Testament believer might very easily become involved
in such conflicts of belief, may be accounted for by the
absence of any express divine revelation to carry his mind
beyond the bounds of the present. Concerning the future
at the period when the book of Job was composed, and the
hero of the book lived, there were longings, inferences, and
forebodings of the soul ; but there was no clear, consoling
word of God on which to rely,—no θεῖος λόγος which, to
speak as Plato (*Phædo*, p. 85, D), could serve as a rescuing
plank in the shipwreck of this life. Therefore the πανταχοῦ
θρυλλούμενον extends through all the glory and joy of the
Greek life from the very beginning throughout. The best
thing is never to have been born ; the second best, as soon
as possible thereafter, to die. The truth, that the suffering
of this present time is not worthy of the glory which shall
be revealed in us, was still silent. The proper disposition of
mind, under such veiling of the future, was then indeed more
absolute, as faith committed itself blindfold to the guidance
of God. But how near at hand was the temptation to regard
a troublous life as an indication of the divine anger, and
doubtingly to ask, Why God should send the light of life to
such ! They knew not that the present lot of man forms but
the one half of his history : they saw only in the one scale
misery and wrath, and not in the other the heaven of love
and blessedness to be revealed hereafter, by which these are
outweighed ; they longed for a present solution of the mystery of life, because they knew nothing of the possibility of
a future solution. Thus it is to be explained, that not only
Job in this poem, but also Jeremiah in the book of his prophecy, ch. xx. 14–18, curses the day of his birth. He curses
the man who brought his father the joyous tidings of the

birth of a son, and wishes him the fate of Sodom and
Gomorrha. He wishes for himself that his mother might
have been his grave, and asks, like Job, " Wherefore came I
forth out of the womb to see labour and sorrow, and that my
days should be consumed in shame ?" Hitzig remarks on
this, that it may be inferred from the contents and form of
this passage, there was a certain brief disturbance of spirit, a
result of the general indescribable distress of the troublous
last days of Zedekiah, to which the spirit of the prophet also
succumbed. And it is certainly a kind of delirium in which
Jeremiah so speaks, but there is no physical disorder of mind
with it: the understanding of the prophet is so slightly and
only momentarily disturbed, that he has the rather gained
power over his faith, and is himself become one of its dis-
turbing forces.

Without applying to this lyric piece either the standard
of pedantic moralizing, or of minute criticism as poetry,
the intense melancholy of this extremely plaintive prophet
may have proceeded from the following reasoning: After I
have lived ten long years of fidelity and sacrifice to my prophetic calling, I see that it has totally failed in its aim : all
my hopes are blighted ; all my exhortations to repentance,
and my prayers, have not availed to draw Judah back from
the abyss into which he is now cast, nor to avert the wrath
of Jehovah which is now poured forth : therefore it had
been better for me never to have been born. This thought
affects the prophet so much the more, since in every fibre of
his being he is an Israelite, and identifies the weal and woe of
his people with his own ; just as Moses would rather himself
be blotted out from the book of life than that Israel should
perish, and Paul was willing to be separated from Christ as
anathema if he could thereby save Israel. What wonder
that this thought should disburden itself in such imprecations! Had Jeremiah not been born, he would not have had

occasion to sit on the ruins of Jerusalem. But his outburst
of feeling is notwithstanding a paroxysm of excitement, for,
though reason might drive him to despair, faith would teach
him to hope even in the midst of downfall; and in reality,
this small lyric piece in the collective prophecy of Jeremiah
is only as a detached rock, over which, as a stream of clear
living water, the prophecy flows on more joyous in faith,
more certain of the future. In the book of Job it is otherwise; for what in Jeremiah and several of the psalms is
compressed into a small compass,—the darkness of temptation and its clearing up,—is here the substance of a long
entanglement dramatically presented, which first of all becomes progressively more and more involved, and to which
this outburst of feeling gives the impulse. As Jeremiah,
had he not been born, would not have sat on the ruins of
Jerusalem; so Job, had he not been born, would not have
found himself in this abyss of wrath. Neither of them
knows anything of the future solution of every present mystery of life; they know nothing of the future life and the
heavenly crown. This it is which, while it justifies their
despair, casts greater glory round their struggling faith.

The first speaker among the friends, who now comes forward, is Eliphaz, probably the eldest of them. In the main,
they all represent one view, but each with his individual
peculiarity: Eliphaz with the self-confident pathos of age,
and the mien of a prophet;[1] Bildad with the moderation and
caution befitting one poorer in thought; Zophar with an
excitable vehemence, neither skilled nor disposed for a lasting
contest. The skill of the writer, as we may here at the outset
remark, is manifested in this, that what the friends say, considered in itself, is true: the error lies only in the inadequacy
and inapplicability of what is said to the case before them.

---

[1] A. B. Davidson thinks Eliphaz is characterized as "the oldest, the
most dignified, the calmest, and most considerate of Job's friends."

SECOND PART.—THE ENTANGLEMENT.

CHAP. IV.–XXVI.

THE FIRST COURSE OF THE CONTROVERSY.—CHAP. IV.–XIV.

Eliphaz' First Speech.—Chap. iv. v.

Schema: 8. 12. 11. 11. | 11. 12. 10. 10. 10. 2.

In reply to Sommer, who in his excellent *biblische Ab-handlungen*, 1846, considers the octastich as the extreme limit of the compass of the strophe, it is sufficient to refer to the Syriac strophe-system. It is, however, certainly an impossibility that, as Ewald (*Jahrb.* ix. 37) remarks with reference to the first speech of Jehovah, ch. xxxviii. xxxix., the strophes can sometimes extend to a length of 12 lines = Masoretic verses, consequently consist of 24 στίχοι and more. [Then Eliphaz the Temanite began, and said :]

2 *If one attempts a word with thee, will it grieve thee?*
   And still to restrain himself from words, who is able?
3 *Behold, thou hast instructed many,*
   And the weak hands thou hast strengthened.
4 *The stumbling turned to thy words,*
   And the sinking knees thou hast strengthened.
5 *But now it cometh to thee, thou art grieved;*
   Now it toucheth thee, thou despondest.

The question with which Eliphaz begins, is certainly one of those in which the tone of interrogation falls on the second of the paratactically connected sentences : Wilt thou, if we speak to thee, feel it unbearable? Similar examples are ch. iv. 21, Num. xvi. 22, Jer. viii. 4 ; and with interrogative Wherefore? Isa. v. 4, l. 2 : comp. the similar paratactic union of sentences, ch. ii. 10, iii. 11*b*. The question arises here, whether נִסָּה is an Aramaic form of writing for נִשָּׂא (as the *Masora* in distinction from Deut. iv. 34 takes it), and also either future, Wilt thou, if we raise, *i.e.* utter, etc.; or passive, as Ewald formerly,[1] If a word is raised, *i.e.* uttered, נִשָּׂא דָבָר, like נָשָׂא מָשָׁל, ch. xxvii. 1; or whether it is *third pers.* *Piel,* with the signification, attempt, *tentare,* Eccles. vii. 23. The last is to be preferred, because more admissible and also more expressive. נִסָּה followed by the *fut.* is a hypothetic *prœt.,* Supposing that, etc., wilt thou, etc., as *e.g.* ch. xxiii. 10. מִלִּין is the Aramaic *plur.* of מִלָּה, which is more frequent in the book of Job than the Hebrew *plur.* מִלִּים. The *futt.,* vers. 3 sq., because following the *perf.,* are like *imperfects* in the western languages: the expression is like Isa. xxxv. 3. In כִּי עַתָּה, ver. 5, כִּי has a temporal signification, Now when, Ges. § 155, 1, *e,* (*b*).

6 *Is not thy piety thy confidence,*
   Thy hope? And the uprightness of thy ways?
7 *Think now: who ever perished, being innocent?!*
   And where have the righteous been cut off?!
8 *As often as I saw, those who ploughed evil*
   And sowed sorrow,—they reaped the same.
9 *By the breath of Eloah they perished,*
   By the breath of His anger they vanished away.
10 *The roaring of the lion, and the voice of the shachal,*
   And the teeth of the young lions, are rooted out.
11 *The lion wanders about for want of prey,*
   And the lioness' whelps are scattered.

In ver. 6 all recent expositors take the last *waw* as *waw*

---

[1] In the second edition, comp. *Jahrb.* ix. 37, he explains it otherwise: "If we attempt a word with thee, will it be grievous to thee *quod ægre feras?*" But that, however, must be נִסָּה; the form נִסָּה can only be *third pers. Piel:* If any one attempts, etc., which, according to Ewald's construction, gives no suitable rendering.

apodosis : And thy hope, is not even this the integrity of thy way? According to our punctuation, there is no occasion for supposing such an application of the *waw apodosis,* which is an error in a clause consisting only of substantives, and is not supported by the examples, ch. xv. 17, xxiii. 12, 2 Sam. xxii. 41.[1] תקותך is the permutative of the ambiguous כסלתך, which, from כָּסַל, to be fat, signifies both the awkwardness of stupidity and the boldness of confidence. The addition of הוּא to מִי, ver. 7, like ch. xiii. 19, xvii. 3, makes the question more earnest : *quis tandem,* like מִי זֶה, *quisnam* (Ges. § 122, 2). In ver. 8, כַּאֲשֶׁר is not comparative, but temporal, and yet so that it unites, as usual, what stands in close connection with, and follows directly upon, the preceding : When, so as, as often as I had seen those who planned and worked out evil (comp. Prov. xxii. 8), I also saw that they reaped it. That the ungodly, and they alone, perish, is shown in vers. 10 sq. under the simile of the lions. The Hebrew, like the oriental languages in general, is rich in names for lions ; the reason of which is, that the lion-tribe, although now become rarer in Asia, and of which only a solitary one is found here and there in the valley of the Nile, was more numerous in the early times, and spread over a wider area.[2] שַׁחַל, which the old expositors often understood as the panther, is perhaps the maneless lion, which is still found on the lower Euphrates and Tigris. נָתַע = נָתַץ, Ps. lviii. 7, *evellere, elidere,* by zeugma, applies to the voice also. All recent expositors

---

[1] We will not, however, dispute the possibility, for at least in Arabic one can say, زَيد فَحَكيم; Zeid, he is wise. Grammarians remark that زَيد in this instance is like a hypothetical sentence: If any one asks, etc. 2 Sam. xv. 34 is similar.

[2] *Vid.* Schmarda, *Geographische Verbreitung der Thiere,* i. 210, where, among other things, we read : The lion in Asia is driven back at almost all points, and also in Africa has been greatly diminished ; for hundreds of lions and panthers were used in the Roman amphitheatres, whilst at the present time it would be impossible to procure so large a number.

translate ver. 11 *init.* wrongly : the lion perishes. The participle אֹבֵד is a stereotype expression for wandering about viewless and helpless (Deut. xxvi. 5, Isa. xxvii. 13, Ps. cxix. 176, and freq.). The *part.*, otherwise remarkable here, has its origin in this usage of the language. The parallelism is like Ps. xcii. 10.

12 *And a word reached me stealthily,*
   And my ear heard a whisper thereof.
13 *In the play of thought, in visions of the night,*
   When deep sleep falleth on men,
14 *Fear came upon me, and trembling ;*
   And it caused the multitude of my bones to quake with fear.
15 *And a breathing passed over my face ;*
   The hair of my flesh stood up :
16 *It stood there, and I discerned not its appearance :*
   An image was before my eyes ;
   A gentle murmur, and I heard a voice.

The *fut.* יְגֻנַּב, like Judg. ii. 1, Ps. lxxx. 9, is ruled by the following *fut. consec.*: *ad me furtim delatum est* (not *deferebatur*). Eliphaz does not say וַיְגֻנַּב אֵלַי (although he means a single occurrence), because he desires, with pathos, to put himself prominent. That the word came to him so secretly, and that he heard only as it were a whisper (שֵׁמֶץ, according to Arnheim, in distinction from שֵׁמַע, denotes a faint, indistinct impression on the ear), is designed to show the value of such a solemn communication, and to arouse curiosity. Instead of the prosaic מִמֶּנּוּ, we find here the poetic pausal-form מֶנְהוּ expanded from מֶנּוּ, after the form מִנִּי, ch. xxi. 16, Ps. xviii. 23. מִן is partitive: I heard only a whisper, murmur ; the word was too sacred and holy to come loudly and directly to his ear. It happened, as he lay in the deep sleep of night, in the midst of the confusion of thought resulting from nightly dreams. שְׂעִפִּים (from שָׂעִיף, branched) are thoughts proceeding like

branches from the heart as their root, and intertwining themselves ; the מִן which follows refers to the cause : there were
all manner of dreams which occasioned the thoughts, and to
which they referred (comp. ch. xxxiii. 15) ; תַּרְדֵּמָה, in distinction from שֵׁנָה, sleep, and תְּנוּמָה, slumber, is the deep sleep
related to death and ecstasy, in which man sinks back from
outward life into the remotest ground of his inner life. In ver.
14, קְרָאַנִי, from קָרָא = קָרָה, to meet (Ges. § 75, 22), is equivalent to קְרָנִי (not קַרְנִי, as Hirz., first edition, wrongly points it ;
comp. Gen. xliv. 29). The subject of הִפְחִיד is the undiscerned
ghostlike something.   Eliphaz was stretched upon his bed
when רוּחַ, a breath of wind, passed (חָלַף, similar to Isa. xxi. 1)
over his face. The wind is the element by means of which
the spirit-existence is made manifest ; comp. 1 Kings xix. 12,
where Jehovah appears in a gentle whispering of the wind,
and Acts ii. 2, where the descent of the Holy Spirit is made
known by a mighty rushing. רוּחַ, πνεῦμα, Sanscrit átma,
signifies both the immaterial spirit and the air, which is proportionately the most immaterial of material things.[1] His
hair bristled up, even every hair of his body ; סַמֵּר, not causative, but intensive of *Kal.* יַעֲמֹד has also the ghostlike appearance as subject. Eliphaz could not discern its outline, only
a תְּמוּנָה, *imago quædam* (the most ethereal word for form,
Num. xii. 8, Ps. xvii. 15, of μορφή or δόξα of God), was before
his eyes, and he heard, as it were proceeding from it, דְּמָמָה וָקֹל,
i.e. per hendiadyn : a voice, which spoke to him in a gentle,
whispering tone, as follows :

17 *Is a mortal just before Eloah,*
      Or a man pure before his Maker ?
18 *Behold, He trusteth not His servants !*
      And His angels He chargeth with imperfection.

[1] On wind and spirit, *vid.* Windischmann, *Die Philosophie im Fort-
gang der Weltgesch.* S. 1331 ff.

19 *How much more those who dwell in houses of clay,*
   Whose origin is in the dust!
   They are crushed as though they were moths.
20 *From morning until evening,—so are they broken in pieces:*
   Unobserved they perish for ever.
21 *Is it not so : the cord of their tent in them is torn away,*
   So they die, and not in wisdom?

The question arises whether מִן is comparative: *præ Deo*, on which Mercier with penetration remarks: *justior sit oportet qui immerito affligitur quam qui immerito affligit;* or causal: *a Deo, h.e., ita ut a Deo justificetur.* All modern expositors rightly decide on the latter. Hahn justly maintains that עִם and בְּעֵינֵי are found in a similar connection in other places; and ch. xxxii. 2 is perhaps not to be explained in any other way, at least that does not restrict the present passage. By the servants of God, none but the angels, mentioned in the following line of the verse, are intended. שִׂים with בְּ signifies *imputare* (1 Sam. xxii. 15); in ch. xxiv. 12 (comp. i. 22) we read תִּפְלָה, *absurditatem* (which Hupf. wishes to restore even here), joined with the verb in this signification. The form תְּהֳלָה is certainly not to be taken as *stultitia* from the verb הָלַל; the half vowel, and still less the absence of the *Dagesh*, will not allow this. תֹּרֶן (Olsh. § 213, *c*), itself uncertain in its etymology, presents no available analogy. The form points to a *Lamedh-He* verb, as תָּרְמָה from רָמָה, so perhaps from הָלָה, *Niph.* נַהֲלָא, *remotus*, Micah iv. 7: being distant, being behind the perfect, difference; or even from הָלָה (Targ. הֲלָא, *Pa.* הַלִּי) = לָאָה, weakness, want of strength.[1] Both sig-

---

[1] Schnurrer compares the Arabic *wahila*, which signifies to be relaxed, forgetful, to err, to neglect. Ewald, considering the ת as radical, compares the Arabic ضَلَّ, to err, and ثَالَ, *med. wau*, to be dizzy, unconscious ; but neither from וְהָל nor from תְּהַל can the substantival form be sustained.

nifications will do, for it is not meant that the good spirits positively sin, as if sin were a natural necessary consequence of their creatureship and finite existence, but that even the holiness of the good spirits is never equal to the absolute holiness of God, and that this deficiency is still greater in spirit-corporeal man, who has earthiness as the basis of his original nature. At the same time, it is presupposed that the distance between God and created earth is disproportionately greater than between God and created spirit, since matter is destined to be exalted to the nature of the spirit, but also brings the spirit into the danger of being degraded to its own level.

Ver. 19. אַף signifies, like אַף כִּי, *quanto minus*, or *quanto magis*, according as a negative or positive sentence precedes : since 18*b* is positive, we translate it here *quanto magis*, as 2 Sam. xvi. 11. Men are called dwellers in clay houses : the house of clay is their φθαρτὸν σῶμα, as being taken *de limo terræ* (ch. xxxiii. 6 ; comp. Wisdom ix. 15) ; it is a fragile habitation, formed of inferior materials, and destined to destruction. The explanation which follows—those whose יְסוֹד, *i.e.* foundation of existence, is in dust—shows still more clearly that the poet has Gen. ii. 7, iii. 19, in his mind. It crushes them (subject, everything that operates destructively on the life of man) לִפְנֵי־עָשׁ, *i.e.* not: sooner than the moth is crushed (Hahn), or more rapidly than a moth destroys (Oehler, Fries), or even appointed to the moth for destruction (Schlottm.) ; but לִפְנֵי signifies, as ch. iii. 24 (cf. 1 Sam. i. 16), *ad instar* : as easily as a moth is crushed. They last only from morning until evening : they are broken in pieces (הֻכַּת, from כָּתַת, for הוּכַת) ; they are therefore as ephemeræ. They perish for ever, without any one taking it to heart (*suppl.* עַל־לֵב, Isa. xlii. 25, lvii. 1), or directing the heart towards it, *animum advertit* (*suppl.* לֵב, ch. i. 8).

In ver. 21 the soul is compared to the cord of a tent, which stretches out and holds up the body as a tent, like

Eccl. xii. 6, with a silver cord, which holds the lamp hanging
from the covering of the tent. Olshausen is inclined to read
יְתֵדָם, their tent-pole, instead of יִתְרָם, and at any rate thinks
the accompanying בָּם superfluous and awkward. But (1) the
comparison used here of the soul, and of the life sustained
by it, corresponds to its comparison elsewhere with a thread
or weft, of which death is the cutting through or loosing (ch.
vi. 9, xxvii. 8; Isa. xxxviii. 12); (2) בָּם is neither superfluous nor awkward, since it is intended to say, that their
duration of life falls in all at once like a tent when that
which *in them* (בם) corresponds to the cord of a tent (*i.e.* the
נֶפֶשׁ) is drawn away from it. The relation of the members
of the sentence in ver. 21 is just the same as in ver. 2: Will
they not die when it is torn away, etc. They then die off in
lack of wisdom, *i.e.* without having acted in accordance with
the perishableness of their nature and their distance from
God; therefore, rightly considered: unprepared and suddenly,
comp. ch. xxxvi. 12, Prov. v. 23. Oehler, correctly: without having been made wiser by the afflictions of God. The
utterance of the Spirit, the compass of which is unmistakeably
manifest by the strophic division, ends here. Eliphaz now,
with reference to it, turns to Job.

Ch. v. 1　*Call now,—is there any one who will answer thee?*
　　　　　And to whom of the holy ones wilt thou turn?
　　　2　*For he is a fool who is destroyed by complaining,*
　　　　　And envy slays the simple one.
　　　3　*I, even I, have seen a fool taking root:*
　　　　　Then I had to curse his habitation suddenly.
　　　4　*His children were far from help,*
　　　　　And were crushed in the gate, without a rescuer;
　　　5　*While the hungry ate his harvest,*
　　　　　And even from among thorns they took it away,
　　　　　And the intriguer snatched after his wealth.

The chief thought of the oracle was that God is the absolutely just One, and infinitely exalted above men and angels. Resuming his speech from this point, Eliphaz tells Job that no cry for help can avail him unless he submits to the all-just One as being himself unrighteous; nor can any cry addressed to the angels avail. This thought, although it is rejected, certainly shows that the writer of the book, as of the prologue, is impressed with the fundamental intuition, that good, like evil, spirits are implicated in the affairs of men; for the "holy ones," as in Ps. lxxxix., are the angels. כִּי supports the negation implied in ver. 1 : If God does not help thee, no creature can help thee ; for he who complains and chafes at his lot brings down upon himself the extremest destruction, since he excites the anger of God still more.   Such a surly murmurer against God is here called אֱוִיל.   לְ is the Aramaic sign of the object, having the force of *quod attinet ad, quoad* (Ew. § 310, *a*).

Eliphaz justifies what he has said (ver. 2) by an example. He had seen such a complainer in increasing prosperity; then he cursed his habitation suddenly, *i.e.* not : he uttered forthwith a prophetic curse over it, which, though פִּתְאֹם might have this meaning (not *subito*, but *illico;* cf. Num. xii. 4), the following *futt.*, equivalent to *imperff.*, do not allow, but : I had then, since his discontent had brought on his destruction, suddenly to mark and abhor his habitation as one overtaken by a curse : the cursing is a recognition of the divine curse, as the echo of which it is intended.   This curse of God manifests itself also on his children and his property (vers. 4 sqq.). שַׁעַר is the gate of the city as a court of justice : the phrase, to oppress in the gate, is like Prov. xxii. 22 ; and the form *Hithpa.* is according to the rule given in Ges. § 54, 2, *b*.   The relative אֲשֶׁר, ver. 5, is here *conj. relativa*, according to Ges. § 155, 1, *e*.   In the connection אֶל־מִצִּנִּים, אֶל is equivalent to עַד, *adeo e spinis*, the hungry fall so eagerly upon what the father of those now orphans has reaped, that even the thorny fence does not hold them back. צִנִּים, as Prov. xxii. 5 : the double *præpos.* אֱלֵי־מָן is also found elsewhere, but with another meaning. צַמִּים has only the appearance of being *plur.* : it is *sing.* after the form צַדִּיק, from the verb צָמַם, *nectere,* and signifies, ch. xviii. 9, a snare ; here, however, not *judicii laqueus* (Böttch.), but what, besides the form, comes still nearer— the snaremaker, intriguer. The Targ. translates לְסָטִיסִין, *i.e.* ληστaί. Most modern critics (Rosenm. to Ebr.) translate : the thirsty (needy), as do all the old translations, except the Targ.; this, however, is not possible without changing the form. The meaning is, that intriguing persons catch up (שָׁאַף, as Amos ii. 7) their wealth.

Eliphaz now tells why it thus befell this fool in his own person and his children.

6 *For evil cometh not forth from the dust,*
　And sorrow sprouteth not from the earth ;
7 *For man is born to sorrow,*
　As the sparks fly upward.
8 *On the contrary, I would earnestly approach unto God,*
　And commit my cause to the Godhead;
9 *To Him who doeth great things and unsearchable ;*
　Marvellous things till there is no number :
10 *Who giveth rain over the earth,*
　And causeth water to flow over the fields :
11 *To set the low in high places ;*
　And those that mourn are exalted to prosperity.

As the oracle above, so Eliphaz says here, that a sorrowful life is allotted to man,[1] so that his wisdom consequently consists

---

[1] Fries explains יֻלָּד as *part.*, and refers to Geiger's *Lehrb. zur Sprache der Mischna,* S. 41 f., according to which מְקֻטָּל signifies killed, and קֻטַל (= *Rabb.* מִתְקַטֵּל) being killed (which, however, rests purely on imagination) : not the matter from which mankind originates brings evil with it, but it is man who inclines towards the evil. Böttch. would read יוֹלִד : man is the parent of misery, though he may rise high in anger.

in accommodating himself to his lot: if he does not do that, he is an אֱוִיל, and thereby perishes. Misfortune does not grow out of the ground like weeds ; it is rather established in the divine order of the world, as it is established in the order of nature that sparks of fire should ascend. The old critics understood by בְּנֵי רֶשֶׁף birds of prey, as being swift as lightning (with which the appellation of beasts of prey may be compared, ch. xxviii. 8, xli. 26); but רֶשֶׁף signifies also a flame or blaze (Cant. viii. 6). Children of the flame is an appropriate name for sparks, and flying upwards is naturally peculiar to sparks as to birds of prey; wherefore among modern expositors, Hirz., Ew., Hahn, von Gerl., Ebr., rightly decide in favour of sparks. Schlottmann understands " angels " by children of flame; but the wings, which are given to angels in Scripture, are only a symbol of their freedom of motion. This remarkable interpretation is altogether opposed to the sententious character of ver. 7, which symbolizes a moral truth by an ordinary thing. The *waw* in וּבְנֵי, which we have translated " as," is the so-called *waw adæquationis* proper to the Proverbs, and also to emblems, *e.g.* Prov. xxv. 25.

Eliphaz now says what he would do in Job's place. Ew. and Ebr. translate incorrectly, or at least unnecessarily: Nevertheless I will. We translate, according to Ges. § 127, 5: Nevertheless I would; and indeed with an emphatic *I:* Nevertheless I for my part. דָּרַשׁ with אֶל is *constr. prægnans*, like Deut. xii. 5, *sedulo adire*. דִּבְרָה is not speech, like אִמְרָה, but cause, *causa*, in a judicial sense. אֵל is God as the Mighty One ; אֱלֹהִים is God in the totality of His variously manifested nature. The fecundity of the earth by rain, and of the fields (חוּצוֹת = *rura*) by water-springs (cf. Ps. civ. 10), as the works of God, are intentionally made prominent. He who makes the barren places fruitful, can also change suffering into joy. To His power in nature corresponds His power among men (ver. 11). לָשׂוּם is here only as a variation for הַשָׂם, as Heiligst.

rightly observes : it is equivalent to *collocaturus*, or *qui in eo est ut collocet*, according to the mode of expression discussed in Ges. § 132, rem. 1, and more fully on Hab. i. 17. The construction of ver. 11*b* is still bolder. שָׂגַב signifies to be high and steep, inaccessible. It is here construed with the *acc.* of motion : those who go in dirty, black clothes because they mourn, shall be high in prosperity, *i.e.* come to stand on an unapproachable height of prosperity.

12   *Who bringeth to nought the devices of the crafty,*
     So that their hands cannot accomplish anything ;
13   *Who catcheth the wise in their craftiness ;*
     And the counsel of the cunning is thrown down.
14   *By day they run into darkness,*
     And grope in the noon-day as in the night.
15   *He rescueth from the sword, that from their mouth,*
     And from the hand of the strong, the needy.
16   *Hope ariseth for the weak,*
     And folly shall close its mouth.

All these attributes are chosen designedly : God brings down all haughtiness, and takes compassion on those who need it. The noun תּוּשִׁיָה, coined by the Chokma, and out of Job and Proverbs found only in Mic. vi. 9, Isa. xxviii. 29, and even there in gnomical connection, is formed from יֵשׁ, *essentia*, and signifies as it were *essentialitas, realitas* : it denotes, in relation to all visible things, the truly existing, the real, the objective ; true wisdom (*i.e.* knowledge resting on an objective actual basis), true prosperity, real profiting and accomplishing. It is meant that they accomplish nothing that has actual duration and advantage. Ver. 13*a* cannot be better translated than by Paul, 1 Cor. iii. 19, who here deviates from the LXX. With נמְהָרָה, God's seizure, which prevents the contemplated achievement, is to be thought of. He pours forth over the worldly wise what the prophets call

the spirit of deep sleep (תַּרְדֵּמָה) and of dizziness (עֲוָעִים). On
the other hand, He helps the poor. In מחרב מפיהם the second
מִן is local : from the sword which proceeds from their mouth
(comp. Ps. lxiv. 4, lvii. 5, and other passages). Böttch.
translates : without sword, *i.e.* instrument of power (comp.
ch. ix. 15, xxi. 9) ; but מן with חרב leads one to expect that
that from which one is rescued is to be described (comp. ver.
20). Ewald corrects מֵחֳרָב, which Olsh. thinks acute : it is,
however, unhebraic, according to our present knowledge of
the usage of the language ; for the passives of חָרֵב are used
of cities, countries, and peoples, but not of individual men.
Olsh., in his hesitancy, arrives at no opinion. But the text is
sound and beautiful. עֹלָתָה with pathetic unaccented *ah* (Ges.
§ 80, rem. 2, *f*), from עֹלָה = עַוְלָה, as Ps. xcii. 16 *Chethib*.

17 *Behold, happy is the man whom Eloah correcteth ;*
  So despise not the chastening of the Almighty !
18 *For He woundeth, and He also bindeth up ;*
  He bruiseth, and His hands make whole.
19 *In six troubles He will rescue thee,*
  And in seven no evil shall touch thee.
20 *In famine He will redeem thee from death,*
  And in war from the stroke of the sword.
21 *When the tongue scourgeth, thou shalt be hidden ;*
  And thou shalt not fear destruction when it cometh.

The speech of Eliphaz now becomes persuasive as it turns
towards the conclusion. Since God humbles him who exalts
himself, and since He humbles in order to exalt, it is a happy
thing when He corrects (הוֹכִיחַ) us by afflictive dispensations ;
and His chastisement (מוּסָר) is to be received not with a tur-
bulent spirit, but resignedly, yea joyously : the same thought
as Prov. iii. 11–13, Ps. xciv. 12, in both passages borrowed
from this ; whereas ver. 18 here, like Hos. vi. 1, Lam. iii.
31 sqq., refers to Deut. xxxii. 39. רָפָא, to heal, is here con-

jugated like a לה״ verb (Ges. § 75, rem. 21). Ver. 19 is
formed after the manner of the so-called number-proverbs
(Prov. vi. 16, xxx. 15, 18), as also the roll of the judgment
of the nations in Amos i. ii.: in six troubles, yea in still
more than six. רָע is the extremity that is perhaps to be
feared. In ver. 20, the *præt.* is a kind of prophetic *præt.*
The scourge of the tongue recalls the similar promise, Ps.
xxxi. 21, where, instead of scourge, it is: the disputes of the
tongue. שׁוֹד, from שָׁדַד, violence, disaster, is allied in sound
with שׁוֹט. Isaiah has this passage of the book of Job in his
memory when he writes ch. xxviii. 15. The promises of
Eliphaz now continue to rise higher, and sound more delightful and more glorious.

22 *At destruction and famine thou shalt laugh,*
    And from the beasts of the earth thou hast nothing to fear.
23 *For thou art in league with the stones of the field,*
    And the beasts of the field are at peace with thee.
24 *And thou knowest that peace is thy pavilion;*
    And thou searchest thy household, and findest nothing
    wanting.
25 *Thou knowest also that thy seed shall be numerous,*
    And thy offspring as the herb of the ground.
26 *Thou shalt come to thy grave in a ripe age,*
    As shocks of corn are brought in in their season.

    .   .   .   .

27 *Lo! this we have searched out, so it is:*
    Hear it, and give thou heed to it.

The verb שָׂחַק is construed (ver. 22) with לְ of that which is
despised, as ch. xxxix. 7, 18, xli. 21 [Hebr.]. אַל־תִּירָא is the
form of *subjective* negation [vid. Ges. § 152, 1: Tr.]: only fear
thou not = thou hast no occasion. In ver. 23, בְּרִיתֶךָ is the
shortest substantive form for בְּרִית לָךְ. The whole of nature
will be at peace with thee: the stones of the field, that they

do not injure the fertility of thy fields; the wild beasts of the field, that they do not hurt thee and thy herds. The same promise that Hosea (ch. ii. 20) utters in reference to the last days is here used individually. From this we see how deeply the Chokma had searched into the history of Paradise and the Fall. Since man, the appointed lord of the earth, has been tempted by a reptile, and has fallen by a tree, his relation to nature, and its relation to him, has been reversed: it is an incongruity, which is again as a whole put right (שָׁלוֹם), as the false relation of man to God is put right. In ver. 24, שָׁלוֹם (which might also be *adj.*) is predicate : thou wilt learn (וְיָדַעְתָּ, *præt. consec.* with accented *ultima*, as *e.g.* Deut. iv. 39, here with *Tiphcha initiale s. anterius*, which does not indicate the grammatical tone-syllable) that thy tent is peace, *i.e.* in a condition of contentment and peace on all sides. Ver. 24*b* is to be arranged : And when thou examinest thy household, then thou lackest nothing, goest not astray, *i.e.* thou findest everything, without missing anything, in the place where thou seekest it.

Ver. 25 reminds one of the Salomonic Ps. lxxii. 16. צֶאֱצָאִים in the Old Testament is found only in Isaiah and the book of Job. The meaning of the noun כֶּלַח, which occurs only here and ch. xxx. 2, is clear. Referring to the verb כָּלַח, Arabic قَحِلَ (قَلَحَم), to be shrivelled up, very aged, it signifies the maturity of old age,—an idea which may be gained more easily if we connect כָּלַח with כָּלָה (to be completed), like קָשַׁח with קָשָׁה (to be hard).[1] In the parallel there is the time of the sheaves, when they are brought up to the high threshing-floor, the latest period of harvest. עָלָה, of the raising of the sheaves to the threshing-floor, as elsewhere of the raising, *i.e.* the bringing up of the animals to the altar.

[1] We may also compare the Arabic كهل (from which comes *cuhulije*, mature manhood, *opp. tufulije*, tender childhood).

גָּדִישׁ is here a heap of sheaves, كُدْس, as ch. xxi. 32, a se

pulchral heap, جَدَث, distinct from אֲלֻמָּה, a bundle, a single
sheaf.

The speech of Eliphaz, which we have broken up into
nine strophes, is now ended. Eliphaz concludes it by an epimythionic distich, ver. 27, with an emphatic *nota bene*. He
speaks at the same time in the name of his companions.
These are principles well proved by experience with which he
confronts Job. Job needs to lay them to heart: *tu scito tibi*.

All that Eliphaz says, considered in itself, is blameless.
He censures Job's vehemence, which was certainly not to be
approved. He says that the destroying judgment of God
never touches the innocent, but certainly the wicked; and at
the same time expiesses the same truth as that placed as a
motto to the Psalter in Ps. i., and which is even brilliantly
confirmed in the issue of the history of Job. When we find
Isa. lvii. 1, comp. Ps. xii. 2, in apparent opposition to this,
הַצַּדִּיק אָבַד, it is not meant that the judgment of destruction
comes upon the righteous, but that his generation experiences
the judgment of his loss (*ætati suæ perit*). And these are
eternal truths, that between the Creator and creature, even
an angel, there remains an infinite distance, and that no
creature possesses a righteousness which it can maintain
before God. Not less true is it, that with God murmuring
is death, and that it is appointed to sinful man to pass
through sorrow. Moreover, the counsel of Eliphaz is the
right counsel: I would turn to God, etc. His beautiful concluding exhortation, so rich in promises, crowns his speech.

It has been observed (*e.g.* by Löwenthal), that if it is allowed
that Eliphaz (ch. v. 17 sqq.) expresses a salutary spiritual
design of affliction, all coherence in the book is from the first
destroyed. But in reality it is an effect producing not only

outward happiness, but also an inward holiness, which Eliphaz ascribes to sorrow. It is therefore to be asked, how it
consists with the plan of the book. There is no doctrinal
error to be discovered in the speech of Eliphaz, and yet he
cannot be considered as a representative of the complete
truth of Scripture. Job ought to humble himself under this;
but since he does not, we must side with Eliphaz.

He does not represent the complete truth of Scripture :
for there are, according to Scripture, three kinds of sufferings, which must be carefully distinguished.[1] The godless
one, who has fallen away from God, is visited with suffering
from God; for sin and the punishment of sin (comprehended
even in the language in עָוֹן and חַטָּאת) are necessarily connected as cause and effect. This suffering of the godless is the
effect of the divine justice in punishment; it is chastisement
(מוּסָר) under the disposition of wrath (Ps. vi. 2, xxxviii. 2;
Jer. x. 24 sqq.), though not yet final wrath; it is punitive
suffering (נֶגַע, נֶקֶם, τιμωρία, pœna). On the other hand, the
sufferings of the righteous flow from the divine love, to which
even all that has the appearance of wrath in this suffering
must be subservient, as the means only by which it operates :
for although the righteous man is not excepted from the
weakness and sinfulness of the human race, he can never
become an object of the divine wrath, so long as his inner life
is directed towards God, and his outward life is governed by
the most earnest striving after sanctification. According to
the Old and New Testaments, he stands towards God in the
relation of a child to his father (only the New Testament
idea includes the mystery of the new birth not revealed in
the Old Testament) ; and consequently all sufferings are

---

[1] Our old dogmatists (vid. e.g. Baier, Compendium Theologiæ positivæ,
ii. 1, § 15) and pastoral theologians (e.g. Danhauer) consider them as
separate. Among the oldest expositors of the book of Job with which I
am acquainted, Olympiodorus is comparatively the best.

fatherly chastisements, Deut. viii. 5, Prov. iii. 12, Heb. xii. 6,
Apoc. iii. 19, comp. Tob. xii. 13 (Vulg.).   But this general
distinction between the sufferings of the righteous and of the
ungodly is not sufficient for the book of Job.   The sufferings
of the righteous even are themselves manifold.   God sends
affliction to them more and more to purge away the sin which
still has power over them, and rouse them up from the danger
of carnal security ; to maintain in them the consciousness of
sin as well as of grace, and with it the lowliness of penitence;
to render the world and its pleasures bitter as gall to them ;
to draw them from the creature, and bind them to himself
by prayer and devotion.   This suffering, which has the sin
of the godly as its cause, has, however, not God's wrath, but
God's love directed towards the preservation and advancement of the godly, as its motive : it is the proper disciplinary
suffering (מוּסָר or תּוֹכַחַת, Prov. iii. 11; παιδεία, Heb. xii.).
It is this of which Paul speaks, 1 Cor. xi. 32.   This disciplinary suffering may attain such a high degree as entirely to
overwhelm the consciousness of the relation to God by grace;
and the sufferer, as frequently in the Psalms, considers himself as one rejected of God, over whom the wrath of God is
passing.   The deeper the sufferer's consciousness of sin, the
more dejected is his mood of sorrow ; and still God's thoughts
concerning him are thoughts of peace, and not of evil (Jer.
xxix. 11).   He chastens, not however in wrath, but בְּמִשְׁפָּט,
with moderation (Jer. x. 24).

Nearly allied to this suffering, but yet, as to its cause and
purpose, distinct, is another kind of the suffering of the
godly.   God ordains suffering for them, in order to prove
their fidelity to himself, and their earnestness after sanctification, especially their trust in God, and their patience.   He
also permits Satan, who impeaches them, to tempt them, to
sift them as wheat, in order that he may be confounded, and
the divine choice justified,—in order that it may be manifest

that neither death, nor life, nor angels, nor principalities, nor powers, are able to separate them from the love of God, and to tear away their faith (אמונה) from God, which has remained stedfast on Him, notwithstanding every apparent manifestation of wrath. The godly will recognise his affliction as such suffering when it comes upon him in the very midst of his fellowship with God, his prayer and watching, and his struggling after sanctification. For this kind of suffering—trial—Scripture employs the expressions נִסָּה (Deut. viii. 2, 16) and בָּחַן (Prov. xvii. 3), πειρασμός (Jas. i. 12; 1 Pet. i. 6 sq., iv. 19; comp. Sir. ii. 1 sqq.). Such suffering, according to a common figure, is for the godly what the smelting-furnace or the fining-pot is to precious metals. A rich reward awaits him who is found proof against the trial, temptation, and conflict, and comes forth from it as pure, refined gold. Suffering for trial is nearly allied to that for chastisement, in so far as the chastisement is at the same time trial; but distinct from it, in so far as every trial is not also chastisement (*i.e.* having as its purpose the purging away of still existing sin).

A third kind of the suffering of the righteous is testimony borne by suffering,—reproach, persecution, and perhaps even martyrdom, which are endured for the sake of fidelity to God and His word. While he is blessed who is found proof against trial, he is blessed in himself who endures this suffering (Matt. v. 11 sq., and other passages); for every other suffering comes upon man for his own sake, this for God's. In this case there is not even the remotest connection between the suffering and the sinfulness of the sufferer. Ps. xliv. is a prayer of Israel in the midst of this form of suffering. Σταυρός is the name expressly used for it in the New Testament—suffering for the kingdom of heaven's sake.

Without a knowledge of these different kinds of human suffering, the book of Job cannot be understood. " Whoever sees with spiritual eyes," says Brentius, " does not judge the moral character of a man by his suffering, but his suffering by his moral character." Just the want of this spiritual discernment and inability to distinguish the different kinds of suffering is the mistake of the friends, and likewise, from the very first, the mistake of Eliphaz. Convinced of the sincere piety of his friend, he came to Job believing that his suffering was a salutary chastisement of God, which would at last turn out for his good. Proceeding upon this assumption, he blames Job for his murmuring, and bids him receive his affliction with a recognition of human sinfulness and the divine purpose for good. Thus the controversy begins. The causal connection with sin, in which Eliphaz places Job's suffering, is after all the mildest. He does not go further than to remind Job that he is a sinner, because he is a man.

But even this causal connection, in which Eliphaz connects Job's sufferings, though in the most moderate way, with previous sin deserving of punishment, is his πρῶτον ψεῦδος. In the next place, Job's suffering is indeed not chastisement, but trial. Jehovah has decreed it for His servant, not to chasten him, but to prove him. This it is that Eliphaz mistakes; and we also should not know it but for the prologue and the corresponding epilogue. Accordingly, the prologue and epilogue are organic parts of the form of the book. If these are removed, its spirit is destroyed.

But the speech of Eliphaz, moreover, beautiful and true as it is, when considered in itself, is nevertheless heartless, haughty, stiff, and cold. For (1.) it does not contain a word of sympathy, and yet the suffering which he beholds is so terribly great: his first word to his friend after the seven days of painful silence is not one of comfort, but of moralizing. (2.) He must know that Job's disease is not the first and only suffering which has come upon him, and that he has endured his previous afflictions with heroic submission; but he ignores this, and acts as though sorrow were now first come upon Job. (3.) Instead of recognising therein the reason of Job's despondency, that he thinks that he has fallen from the love of God, and become an object of wrath, he treats him as self-righteous;[1] and to excite his feelings, presents an oracle to him, which contains nothing but what Job might sincerely admit as true. (4.) Instead of considering that Job's despair and murmuring against God is really of a different kind from that of the godless, he classes them together, and instead of gently correcting him, presents to Job the accursed end of the fool, who also murmurs against God, as he has himself seen it. Thus, in consequence of the false application which Eliphaz makes of it, the truth contained in his speech is totally reversed. Thus delicately and profoundly commences the dramatical entanglement. The skill of the poet is proved by the difficulty which the expositor has in detecting that which is false in the speech of Eliphaz. The idea of the book does not float on the surface. It is clothed with flesh and blood. It is submerged in the very action and history.

Job's First Answer.—Chap. vi. vii.

Schema: 7. 6. 7. 6. 8. 6. 6. 8. 6. | 6. 7. 11. 10. 6. 8.

[Then began Job, and said :]

2 *Oh that my vexation were but weighed,*
   And they would put my suffering in the balance against it!
3 *Then it would be heavier than the sand of the sea :*
   Therefore my words are rash.
4 *The arrows of the Almighty are in me,*
   The burning poison whereof drinketh up my spirit ;
   The terrors of Eloah set themselves in array against me.

---

[1] Oetinger: "Eliphaz mentioned the oracle to affect seriously the hidden hypocrisy of Job's heart."

Vexation (כַּעַשׂ) is what Eliphaz has reproached him with (ch. v. 2). Job wishes that his vexation were placed in one scale and his הַיָּה (*Keri* הַוָּה) in the other, and weighed together (יַחַד). The noun הַוָּה הַיָּה (הַוָּה), from הָוָה הָיָה (הָיָה), *flare, hiare,* signifies properly *hiatus,* then *vorago,* a yawning gulf, χάσμα, then some dreadful calamity (*vid.* Hupfeld on Ps. v. 10). נָשָׂא, like נָטַל, Isa. xl. 15, to raise the balance, as *pendĕre,* to let it hang down; *attollant* instead of the passive. This is his desire; and if they but understood the matter, it would then be manifest (כִּי־עַתָּה, as ch. iii. 13, which see), or: indeed then would it be manifest (כִּי certainly in this inferential position has an affirmative signification: *vid.* Gen. xxvi. 22, xxix. 32, and comp. 1 Sam. xxv. 34, 2 Sam. ii. 27) that his suffering is heavier than the unmeasurable weight of the sand of the sea. יִכְבַּד is neuter with reference to וָהַיָּתִי. לָעוּ, with the tone on the *penult.,* which is not to be accounted for by the rhythm as in Ps. xxxvii. 20, cxxxvii. 7, cannot be derived from לָעָה, but only from לוּע, not however in the signification to suck down, but from לוּע = לָעָה, Arab. لغى or also

لغا, *temere loqui, inania effutire,*—a signification which suits excellently here.[1] His words are like those of one in delirium. עֻמְּדִי is to be explained according to Ps. xxxviii. 3; חֲמָתָם, according to Ps. vii. 15. יַעַרְכוּנִי is short for יערכו מלחמה עלי, they make war against me, set themselves in battle array against me. Böttcher, without brachylogy: they cause me to arm myself, put one of necessity on the defensive, which does not suit the subject. The terrors of God strike down all defence. The wrath of God is irresistible. The sting

---

[1] יָלַע, Prov. xx. 25, which is doubly accented, and must be pronounced as oxytone, has also this meaning: the snare of a man who has thoughtlessly uttered what is holy (an interjectional clause = such an one has implicated himself), and after (having made) vows will harbour care (*i.e.* whether he will be able to fulfil them).

of his suffering, however, is the wrath of God which his spirit drinks as a draught of poison (comp. ch. xxi. 20), and consequently wrings from him, even from his deepest soul, the thought that God is become his enemy : therefore his is an endless suffering, and therefore is it that he speaks so despondingly.

> 5 *Doth the wild ass bray at fresh grass?*
> *Or loweth an ox over good fodder?*
> 6 *Is that which is tasteless eaten unsalted?*
> *Or is there flavour in the white of an egg?*
> 7 *That which my soul refused to touch,*
> *The same is as my loathsome food.*

The meaning of the first two figures is : He would not complain, if there were really no cause for it ; of the two others : It is not to be expected that he should smile at his suffering, and enjoy it as delicate food. עַל־בְּלִילוֹ I have translated " over good fodder," for בְּלִיל is mixed fodder of different kinds of grain, *farrago.* " Without salt" is virtually adjective to תָּפֵל, insipid, tasteless. What is without salt one does not relish, and there is no flavour in the slime of the yolk of an egg, *i.e.* the white of an egg (Targ.),[1] or in the slime of purslain (according to *Chalmetho* in the Peschito, Arab. حَمْقَاء *fatua* = purslain), which is less probable on account of רִיר (slime, not : broth) : there is no flavour so that it can be enjoyed. Thus is it with his sufferings. Those things which he before inwardly detested (dirt and dust of leprosy) are now *sicut fastidiosa cibi mei, i.e.* as loathsome food which he must eat. The first clause, ver. 7*a*, must be taken as an elliptic relative clause forming the subject : *vid.*

---

[1] Saadia compares *b. Aboda zara*, 40, *a*, where it is given as a mark of the purity of the eggs in the roe of fish : חלבון מבחוץ וחלמון מבפנים, when the white is outside and the yellow within.

Ges. § 123, 3, *c.* Such disagreeable counsel is now like his unclean, disgusting diet. Eliphaz desires him to take them as agreeable. דְּוֵי in כִּדְוֵי is taken by Ges., Ew., Hahn, Schlottm., Olsh. (§ 165, *b*), as constr. from דְּוַי, sickness, filth ; but דְּוֵי, as *plur.* from דָּוֶה, sick, unclean (especially of female menstruation, Isa. xxx. 22), as Heiligst. among modern commentators explains it, is far more suitable. Hitz. (as anonym. reviewer of Ewald's *Job* in the *liter. Centralblatt*) translates : they (my sufferings) are the morsels of my food ; but the explanation of הֵמָּה is not correct, nor is it necessary to go to the Arabic for an explanation of כִּדְוֵי. It is also unnecessary, with Böttcher, to read כִּדְוַי (such is my food *in accordance with my disease*) ; Job does not here speak of his diet as an invalid.

> 8 *Would that my request were fulfilled,*
> *And that Eloah would grant my expectation,*
> 9 *That Eloah were willing and would crush me,*
> *Let loose His hand and cut me off :*
> 10 *Then I should still have comfort—*
> *(I should exult in unsparing pain)—*
> *That I have not disowned the words of the Holy One.*

His wish refers to the ending of his suffering by death. Hupfeld prefers to read וְתַאֲוָתִי instead of וְתִקְוָתִי (ver. 8*b*) ; but death, which he desires, he even indeed expects. This is just the paradox, that not life, but death, is his expectation. " Cut me off," *i.e.* my soul or my life, my thread of life (ch. xxvii. 8 ; Isa. xxxviii. 12). The optative מִי יִתֵּן (Ges. § 136, 1) is followed by optative *futt.*, partly of the so-called jussive form, as יֹאֵל, *velit* (*Hiph.* from יָאַל, *velle*), and יַתֵּר, *solvat* (*Hiph.* from נָתַר). In the phrase הִתִּיר יָד, the stretching out of the hand is regarded as the loosening of what was hitherto bound. The conclusion begins with וּתְהִי, just like ch. xiii. 5. But it is to be asked whether by consolation speedy death is to be understood, and the clause with כִּי gives the ground of his claim for the granting of the wish,—or whether he means that just this: not having disowned the words of the Holy One (comp. ch. xxiii. 11 sq., and אִמְרֵי־אֵל in the mouth of Balaam, the non-Israelitish prophet, Num. xxiv. 4, 16), would be his consolation in the midst of death. With Hupfeld we decide in favour of the latter, with Ps. cxix. 50 in view: this consciousness of innocence is indeed throughout the whole book Job's shield and defence. If, however, נֶחָמָתִי (with *Kametz impurum*) points towards כִּי, *quod*, etc., the clause וַאֲסַלְּדָה is parenthetical. The cohortative is found thus parenthetical with a conjunctive sense also elsewhere (Ps. xl. 6, li. 18). Accordingly: my comfort—I would exult, etc.—would be that I, etc. The meaning of סָלַד, *tripudiare*, is confirmed by the LXX. ἡλλόμην, in connection with the Arabic صَلَدَ (of a galloping horse which stamps hard with its fore-feet), according to which the Targ. also translates וְאֶבוּעַ (I will rejoice).[1] For לֹא יַחְמֹל, comp. Isa. xxx. 14 sq. (break in pieces unsparingly). לֹא יחמל certainly appears as though it must be referred to God (Ew., Hahn, Schlottm., and others), since חילה sounds feminine; but one can either pronounce חִילָה = חִיל as *Milel* (Hitz.), or take לֹא יחמל adverbially, and not as an elliptical dependent clause (as Ges. § 147, rem. 1), but as virtually an adjective: in pain unsparing.

> 11 *What is my strength, that I should wait,*
> *And my end, that I should be patient?*
> 12 *Is my strength like the strength of stones?*
> *Or is my flesh brazen?*

[1] The primary meaning of סלד, according to the Arabic, is to be hard, then, to tread hard, firm, as in *pulsanda tellus;* whereas the poetry of the synagogue (Pijut) uses סָלַד in the signification to supplicate, and סֶלֶד, litany (not: hymn, as Zunz gives it) ; and the Mishna-talmudic סָלַד signifies to singe, burn one's self, and to draw back affrighted.

13 *Or am I then not utterly helpless,*
   And continuance is driven from me?

The meaning of the question (ver. 11) is: Is not my
strength already so wasted away, and an unfortunate end
so certain to me, that a long calm waiting is as impossible as
it is useless? הַאֲרִיךְ נֶפֶשׁ, to draw out the soul, is to extend and
distribute the intensity of the emotion, to be forbearing, to be
patient. The question (ver. 11) is followed by אִם, usual in
double questions : or is my strength stone, etc. הַאִם, which
is so differently explained by commentators, is after all to be
explained best from Num. xvii. 28, the only other passage in
which it occurs. Here it is the same as הֲ אִם, and in Num.
אִם הֲלֹא : or is it not so : we shall perish quickly altogether?
Thus we explain the passage before us. The interrogative הֲ
is also sometimes used elsewhere for הֲלֹא, ch. xx. 4, xli. 1
(Ges. § 153, 3) ; the additional אם stands *per inversionem* in
the second instead of the first place : *nonne an = an nonne,*
annon: or is it not so : is not my help in me = or am I
not utterly helpless? Ewald explains differently (§ 356, *a*),
according to which אִם, from the formula of an oath, is equivalent to לֹא. The meaning is the same. Continuance, תּוּשִׁיָּה,
i.e. power of endurance, reasonable prospect is driven away,
frightened away from him, is lost for him.

14 *To him who is consumed gentleness is due from his friend,*
   Otherwise he might forsake the fear of the Almighty.
15 *My brothers are become false as a torrent,*
   As the bed of torrents which vanish away—
16 *They were blackish from ice,*
   Snow is hidden in them—
17 *In the time, when warmth cometh to them, they are de-*
   stroyed.
   It becometh hot, they are extinguished from their place.

Ewald supplies between 14*a* and 14*b* two lines which have professedly fallen out ("from a brother sympathy is due to the oppressed of God, in order he may not succumb to excessive grief"). Hitzig strongly characterizes this interpolation as a "pure swindle." There is really nothing wanting; but we need not even take חֶסֶד, with Hitz., in the signification reproach (like Prov. xiv. 34) : if reproach cometh to the sufferer from his friend, he forsaketh the fear of God. מָס (from מָסַס, *liquefieri*) is one who is inwardly melted, the disheartened. Such an one should receive חֶסֶד from his friend, *i.e.* that he should restore him ἐν πνεύματι πραΰτητος (Gal. vi. 1). The *waw* (ver. 14*b*) is equivalent to *alioqui* with the future subjunctive (*vid.* Ges. § 127, 5). Harshness might precipitate him into the abyss from which love will keep him back. So Schnurrer : *Afflicto exhibenda est ab amico ipsius humanitas, alioqui hic reverentiam Dei exuit.* Such harshness instead of charity meets him from his brothers, *i.e.* friends beloved as brothers. In vain he has looked to them for reviving consolation. Theirs is no comfort; it is like the dried-up water of a wady. נַחַל is a mountain or forest brook, which comes down from the height, and in spring is swollen by melting ice and the snow that thaws on the mountain-tops ; χειμάρρους, *i.e.* a torrent swollen by winter water. The melting blocks of ice darken the water of such a wady, and the snow falling together is quickly hidden in its bosom (הִתְעַלֶּם). If they begin to be warmed (*Pual* זֹרַב, cognate to צָרַב, Ezek. xxi. 3, *aduri*, and שָׂרַף, *comburere*), suddenly they are reduced to nothing (נִצְמָת, *exstingui*) ; they vanish away בְּחֻמּוֹ, when it becomes hot. The suffix is, with Ew., Olsh., and others, to be taken as neuter ; not with Hirz., to be referred to a suppressed עֵת: when the season grows hot. Job bewails the disappointment he has experienced, the "decline" of charity[1] still further, by keeping to the figure of the mountain torrent.

[1] Oetinger says that vers. 15–20 describe those who get "consumption"

18 *The paths of their course are turned about,*
    They go up in the waste and perish.
19 *The travelling bands of Têma looked for them,*
    The caravans of Saba hoped for them ;
20 *They were disappointed on account of their trust,*
    They came thus far, and were red with shame.

As the text is pointed, אָרְחוֹת, ver. 18, are the paths of the
torrents.   Hirz., Ew., and Schlottm., however, correct אֹרְחוֹת,
caravans, which Hahn even thinks may be understood without correction, since he translates : the caravans of their way
are turned about (which is intended to mean : aside from the
way that they are pursuing), march into the desert and perish
(*i.e.* because the streams on which they reckoned are dried
up).   So, in reality, all modern commentators understand it ;
but is it likely that the poet would let the caravans perish in
ver. 18, and in vers. 19 sq. still live?   With this explanation, vers. 19 sq. drag along tautologically, and the feebler
figure follows the stronger.   Therefore we explain as follows:
the mountain streams, נְחָלִים, flow off in shallow serpentine
brooks, and the shallow waters completely evaporate by the
heat of the sun.   עָלָה בַתֹּהוּ signifies to go up into nothing
(comp. Isa. xl. 23), after the analogy of כָּלָה בֶעָשָׁן, to pass
away in smoke.   Thus *e.g.* also Mercier : *in auras abeunt,*
in nihilum rediguntur.   What next happens is related as a
history, vers. 19 sq., hence the *prætt.*   Job compares his
friends to the wady swollen by ice and snow water, and even
to the travelling bands themselves languishing for water.
He thirsts for friendly solace, but the seeming comfort which
his friends utter is only as the scattered meandering waters
in which the mountain brook leaks out.   The *sing.* בָּטַח indi-
vidualizes ; it is unnecessary with Olsh. to read בָּטָחוּ.

when they are obliged to extend " the breasts of compassion " to their
neighbour.

21 *For now ye are become nothing;*
    You see misfortune, and are affrighted.
22 *Have I then said, Give unto me,*
    And give a present for me from your substance,
23 *And deliver me from the enemy's hand,*
    And redeem me from the hand of the tyrant?

In ver. 21, the reading wavers between לֹו and לֹא, with the
Keri לֹו; but לֹו, which is consequently the *lectio recepta,* gives
no suitable meaning, only in a slight degree appropriate, as
this : ye are become it, *i.e.* such a mountain brook; for הייתם
is not to be translated, with Stickel and others, *estis,* but *facti
estis.* The Targum, however, translates after the *Chethib:*
ye are become as though ye had never been, *i.e.* nothingness.
Now, since לֹא, Aramaic לָה, can (as Dan. iv. 32 shows) be
used as a substantive (a not = a null), and the thought: ye
are become nothing, your friendship proves itself equal to
null, suits the imagery just used, we decide in favour of the
Chethib; then in the figure the עָלָה בּתֹּהוּ corresponds most to
this, and is also, therefore, not to be explained away. The
LXX., Syr., Vulg., translate לֹי instead of לֹו : ye are become
it (such deceitful brooks) to me. Ewald proposes to read
בן עתה הייתם לי (comp. the explanation, Ges. § 137, rem. 3),—
a conjecture which puts aside all difficulty; but the sentence
with לֹא commends itself as being bolder and more expressive.
All the rest explains itself. It is remarkable that in ver. 21*b*
the reading תִּירָאוּ is also found, instead of תִּרְאוּ : ye dreaded
misfortune, and ye were then affrighted. הָבוּ is here, as an
exception, *properispomenon,* according to Ges. § 29, 3. כֹּחַ,
as Prov. v. 10, Lev. xxvi. 20, what one has obtained by
putting forth one's strength, syn. חַיִל, outward strength.

24 *Teach me, and I will be silent,*
    And cause me to understand wherein I have failed.

25 *How forcible are words in accordance with truth!*
    But what doth reproof from you reprove?
26 *Do you think to reprove words?*
    The words of one in despair belong to the wind.
27 *Ye would even cast lots for the orphan,*
    And traffic about your friend.

נִמְרְצוּ, ver. 25, in the signification of נִמְלְצוּ (Ps. cxix. 103),
would suit very well : how smooth, delicate, sweet, are, etc.
(Hirz., Ew., Schlottm.) ; but this meaning does not suit ch.
xvi. 3.   Hupfeld, by comparison with מַר, bitter, translates :
quantumvis acerba ; but מָה may signify *quidquid,* though not
quantumvis.   Hahn compares the Arabic verb to be sick, and
translates : in what respect are right words bad ; but physical
disease and ethical badness are not such nearly related ideas.
Ebrard : honest words are not taken amiss; but with an
inadmissible application of ch. xvi. 3.   Von Gerl. is best :
how strong or forcible are, etc.   מָרַץ is taken as related to
פָּרַץ, in the signification to penetrate ; *Hiph.* to goad ; *Niph.*
to be furnished with the property of penetrating,—used here
of penetrating speech ; 1 Kings ii. 8, of a curse inevitably
carried out ; Mic. ii. 10, of unsparing destruction.   Words
which keep the straight way of truth, go to the heart ; on
the contrary, what avails the reproving from you, *i.e.* which
proceeds from you?   הוֹכֵחַ, *inf. absol.* as Prov. xxv. 27, and in
but a few other passages as subject ; מִכֶּם, as ch. v. 15, the
sword going forth out of their mouth.   In 26*b* the *waw*
introduces a subordinate adverbial clause : while, however,
the words of one in despair belong to the wind, that they
may be carried away by it, not to the judgment which retains
and analyzes them, without considering the mood of which
they are the hasty expression.   The *futt.* express the extent
to which their want of feeling would go, if the circumstances
for it only existed ; they are subjunctive, as ch. iii. 13, 16.

גּוֹרָל, the lot, is to be supplied to תַּפִּילוּ, as 1 Sam. xiv. 42.
The verb כָּרָה, however, does not here signify to dig, so that
שַׁחַת, a pit, should be supplied (Heiligst.), still less : dig out
earth, and cast it on any one (Ebrard) ; but has the signification of buying and selling with עַל of the object, exactly like
ch. xl. 30.

28 *And now be pleased to observe me keenly,*
   I will not indeed deceive you to your face.
29 *Try it again, then : let there be no injustice ;*
   Try it again, my righteousness still stands.
30 *Is there wrong on my tongue ?*
   Or shall not my palate discern iniquity ?

He begs them to observe him more closely ; פָּנָה בְ, as Eccl.
ii. 11, to observe scrutinizingly. אִם is the sign of negative
asseveration (Ges. § 155, 2, *f*). He will not indeed shamelessly give them the lie, viz. in respect to the greatness and
inexplicableness of his suffering. The challenging שֻׁבוּ we
do not translate : retrace your steps, but : begin afresh, to
which both the following clauses are better suited. So
Schlottm. and von Gerlach. Hahn retains the *Chethib* שׁוּבִי,
in the signification : my answer ; but that is impossible : to
answer is הֵשִׁיב, not שׁוּב. The עוֹד drawn to שׁוּבוּ by *Rebia
mugrasch* is more suitably joined with צִדְקִי־בָה, in which בָּהּ
refers neutrally to the matter of which it treats. They are
to try from the beginning to find that comfort which will
meet the case. Their accusations are עַוְלָה ; his complaints,
on the contrary, are fully justified. He does not grant that
the outburst of his feeling of pain (ch. iii.) is עַוְלָה : he has
not so completely lost his power against temptation, that he
would not restrain himself, if he should fall into הַוּוֹת. Thus
wickedness, which completely contaminates feeling and utterance, is called (Ps. lii. 4).

Job now endeavours anew to justify his complaints by

turning more away from his friends and more towards God, but without penetrating the darkness in which God, the author of his suffering, is veiled from him.

Ch. vii. 1 *Has not man a warfare upon earth,*
           And his days are like the days of a hireling?
        2 *Like a servant who longs for the shade,*
           And like a hireling who waits for his wages,
        3 *So am I made to possess months of disappoint-*
           ment,
           And nights of weariness are appointed to me.

The conclusion is intended to be : thus I wait for death as refreshing and rest after hard labour. He goes, however, beyond this next point of comparison, or rather he remains on this side of it. צָבָא is not service of a labourer in the field, but active military service, then fatigue, toil in general (Isa. xl. 20 ; Dan. x. 1). Ver. 2 Ewald and others translate incorrectly : as a slave longs, etc. כְּ can never introduce a comparative clause, except an infinitive, as *e.g.* Isa. v. 24, which can then under the regimen of this כְּ be continued by a *verb. fin.;* but it never stands directly for בַּאֲשֶׁר, as כְּמוֹ does in rare instances. In ver. 3, שָׁוְא retains its primary signification, nothingness, error, disappointment (ch. xv. 31) : months that one after another disappoint the hope of the sick. By this it seems we ought to imagine the friends as not having come at the very commencement of his disease. Elephantiasis is a disease which often lasts for years, and slowly but inevitably destroys the body. On מִנּוּ, *adnumeraverunt = adnumeratæ sunt, vid.* Ges. § 137, 3*.

        4 *If I lie down, I think :*
           When shall I arise and the evening break away?
           And I become weary with tossing to and fro until the
           morning dawn.

5 *My flesh is clothed with worms and clods of earth ;*
  My skin heals up to fester again.
6 *My days are swifter than a weaver's shuttle,*
  And vanish without hope.

Most modern commentators take מִדַּד as *Piel* from מָדַד :
the night is extended (Renan : *la nuit se prolonge*), which is
possible ; comp. Ges. § 52, 2. But the metre suggests another
rendering : מִדַּד constr. of מִדָּד from נָדַד, to flee away : and when
fleeing away of the evening. The night is described by its
commencement, the late evening, to make the long interval
of the sleeplessness and restlessness of the invalid prominent.
In נדים and מדד there is a play of words (Ebrard). רִמָּה,
worms, in reference to the putrifying ulcers ; and גּוּשׁ (with
נ׳ זעירא), clod of earth, from the cracked, scaly, earth-coloured
skin of one suffering with elephantiasis. The *prætt.* are used
of that which is past and still always present, the *futt. consec.*
of that which follows in and with the other. The skin heals,
רָגַע (which we render with Ges., Ew., *contrahere se*) ; the
result is that it becomes moist again. יִמָּאֵס, according to Ges.
§ 67, rem. 4 = יִמַּס, Ps. lviii. 8. His days pass swiftly away ;
the result is that they come to an end without any hope whatever. אֶרֶג is like κερκίς, *radius*, a weaver's shuttle, by means
of which the weft is shot between the threads of the warp as
they are drawn up and down. His days pass as swiftly by as
the little shuttle passes backwards and forwards in the warp.

Next follows a prayer to God for the termination of his
pain, since there is no second life after the present, and consequently also the possibility of requital ceases with death.

7 *Remember that my life is a breath,*
  That my eye will never again look on prosperity.
8 *The eye that looketh upon me seeth me no more ;*
  Thine eyes look for me,—I am no more !

9 *The clouds are vanished and passed away,*
  So he that goeth down to Sheól cometh not up.

10 *He returneth no more to his house,*
   And his place knoweth him no more.

11 *Therefore I will not curb my mouth;*
   I will speak in the anguish of my spirit;
   I will complain in the bitterness of my soul.

We see good, *i.e.* prosperity and joy, only in the present life. It ends with death. שׁוּב with לְ *infin.* is a synonym of הוֹסִיף, ch. xx. 9. No eye (עַיִן *femin.*) which now sees me (prop. eye of my seer, as Gen. xvi. 13, comp. Job xx. 7, Ps. xxxi. 12, for רֹאִי, Isa. xxix. 15, or רֹאֵנִי, Isa. xlvii. 10; according to another reading, רְאִי : no eye of seeing, *i.e.* no eye with the power of seeing, from רָאִי, vision) sees me again, even if thy eyes should be directed towards me to help me; my life is gone, so that I can no more be the subject of help. For from Sheól there is no return, no resurrection (comp. Ps. ciii. 16 for the expression); therefore will I at least give free course to my thoughts and feelings (comp. Ps. lxxvii. 4, Isa. xxxviii. 15, for the expression). The גַּם, ver. 11, is the so-called גם *talionis;* the parallels cited by Michaelis are to the point, Ezek. xvi. 43, Mal. ii. 9, Ps. lii. 7. Here we first meet with the name of the lower world; and in the book of Job we learn the ancient Israelitish conception of it more exactly than anywhere else. We have here only to do with the name in connection with the grammatical exposition. שְׁאוֹל (usually *gen. fem.*) is now almost universally derived from שָׁאַל = שָׁעַל, to be hollow, to be deepened; and aptly so, for they imagined the *Sheól* as under ground, as Num. xvi. 30, 33 alone shows, on which account even here, as from Gen. xxxvii. 35 onwards, יָרַד שְׁאוֹלָה is everywhere used. It is, however, open to question whether this derivation is correct: at least passages like Isa. v. 14, Hab. ii. 5, Prov. xxx. 15 sq., show that in the later usage of the language, שָׁאַל, to demand, was thought of in connection with it; derived from which *Sheôl* signifies (1) the appointed inevitable and inexorable demanding of everything earthly (an infinitive noun like פְּקוֹד, אֱלוֹהַּ); (2) conceived of as space, the place of shadowy duration whither everything on earth is demanded; (3) conceived of according to its nature, the divinely appointed fury which gathers in and engulfs everything on the earth. Job knows nothing of a demanding back, a redemption from *Sheôl.*

12 *Am I a sea or a sea-monster,*
   That thou settest a watch over me?
13 *For I said, My bed shall comfort me;*
   My couch shall help me to bear my complaint.
14 *Then thou scaredst me with dreams,*
   And thou didst wake me up in terror from visions,
15 *So that my soul chose suffocation,*
   Death rather than this skeleton.
16 *I loathe it, I would not live alway;*
   Let me alone, for my days are breath.

Since a watch on the sea can only be designed to effect the necessary precautions at its coming forth from the shores, it is probable that the poet had the Nile in mind when he used יָם, and consequently the crocodile by תַּנִּין. The Nile is also called יָם in Isa. xix. 5, and in Homer ὠκεανός, Egyptian *oham* (= ὠκεανός), and is even now called (at least by the Bedouins) *bahhr* (بَحْر). The illustrations of the book, says von Gerlach correctly, are chiefly Egyptian. On the contrary, Hahn thinks the illustration is unsuitable of the Nile, because it is not watched on account of its danger, but its utility; and Schlottman thinks it even small and contemptible without assigning a reason. The figure is, however, appropriate. As watches are set to keep the Nile in channels as

soon as it breaks forth, and as men are set to watch that
they may seize the crocodile immediately he moves here or
there ; so Job says all his movements are checked at the
very commencement, and as soon as he desires to be more
cheerful he feels the pang of some fresh pain.   In ver. 13, בּ
after נָשָׂא is partitive, as Num. xi. 17 ; Mercier correctly : *non-
nihil querelam meam levabit*.   If he hopes for such repose, it
forthwith comes to nought, since he starts up affrighted from
his slumber.   Hideous dreams often disturb the sleep of those
suffering with elephantiasis, says Avicenna (in Stickel, S.
170).   Then he desires death ; he wishes that his difficulty
of breathing would increase to suffocation, the usual end of
elephantiasis. מְחַנַק is absolute (without being obliged to point
it מַחֲנָק with Schlottm.), as *e.g.* מִרְמַס, Isa. x. 6 (Ewald, § 160, *c*).
He prefers death to these his bones, *i.e.* this miserable skeleton
or framework of bone to which he is wasted away.   He
despises, *i.e.* his life, ch. ix. 21.   Amid such suffering he
would not live for ever.   הֶבֶל, like רוּחַ, ver. 7.

17 *What is man that Thou magnifiest him,*
       And that Thou turnest Thy heart toward him,
18 *And visitest him every morning,*
       Triest him every moment?
19 *How long dost Thou not look away from me,*
       Nor lettest me alone till I swallow down my spittle?

The questions in ver. 17 sq. are in some degree a parody
on Ps. viii. 5, comp. cxliv. 3, Lam. iii. 23.   There it is said
that God exalts puny man to a kingly and divine position
among His creatures, and distinguishes him continually with
new tokens of His favour ; here, that instead of ignoring
him, He makes too much of him, by selecting him, perishable
as he is, as the object of ever new and ceaseless sufferings.
כַּמָּה, *quamdiu*, ver. 19, is construed with the *prœt.* instead of
the *fut.* : how long will it continue that Thou turnest not

away Thy look of anger from me ? as the synonymous עַד־מָתַי,
quousque, is sometimes construed with the *præt.* instead of the
fut., *e.g.* Ps. lxxx. 5.　" Until I swallow my spittle" is a proverbial expression for the minimum of time.

> 20　*Have I sinned—what could I do to Thee ? !*
> 　　*O Observer of men,*
> 　　*Why dost Thou make me a mark to Thee,*
> 　　*And am I become a burden to Thee?*
> 21　*And why dost Thou not forgive my transgression,*
> 　　*And put away my iniquity?*
> 　　*For now I will lay myself in the dust,*
> 　　*And Thou seekest for me, and I am no more.*

" I have sinned" is hypothetical (Ges.　§ 155, 4, *a*) :
granted that I have sinned.　According to Ewald and Olsh.,
מה אפעל־לך defines it more particularly : I have sinned by
what I have done to Thee, in my behaviour towards Thee ; but
how tame and meaningless such an addition would be !　It is
an inferential question : what could I do to Thee ? *i.e.* what
harm, or also, since the *fut.* may be regulated by the *præt.* :
what injury have I thereby done to Thee ?　The thought
that human sin, however, can detract nothing from the
blessedness and glory of God, underlies this.　With a measure
of sinful bitterness, Job calls God נצר האדם, the strict and
constant observer of men, *per convicium fere*, as Gesenius not
untruly observes, nevertheless without a breach of *decorum
divinum* (Renan : *O Espion de l'homme*), since the appellation, in itself worthy of God (Isa. xxvii. 3), is used here only
somewhat unbecomingly.　מִפְגָּע is not the target for shooting
at, which is rather מַטָּרָה (ch. xvi. 12, Lam. iii. 12), but the
object on which one rushes with hostile violence (פָּגַע בְּ).
Why, says Job, hast Thou made me the mark of hostile
attack, and why am I become a burden to Thee ?　It is not
so in our text ; but according to Jewish tradition, עָלַי, which

we now have, is only a תקן סופרים, *correctio scribarum*,[1] for
עליך, which was removed as bordering on blasphemy : why
am I become a burden to Thee, so that Thou shouldest seek
to get rid of me ?   This reading I should not consider as the
original, in spite of the tradition, if it were not confirmed by
the LXX., εἰμὶ δὲ ἐπὶ σοὶ φορτίον.

Here Job's second speech ends ; it consists of two parts,
which the division of chapters has correctly marked.   The
first part is addressed to the friends (nowhere specially to
Eliphaz), because Job at once considers the address of
Eliphaz as at the same time an expression of the thoughts
and disposition of the two others who remain silent.   In the
second part he turns direct to God with his complaints,
desponding inquiries, and longing for the alleviation of his
sufferings before his approaching end.   The correct estimate
of this second speech of Job depends upon the right understanding of that of Eliphaz.   It is not to be supposed that
Job in this speech makes too much of his dignity and merit,
as that he intends expressly to defend his innocence, or even
enter into the controversy (Ew., Löwenth.) ; for Eliphaz does
not at present go so far as to explain his suffering as the
suffering commonly inflicted as punishment.   When Job (ch.
vi. 10) incidentally says that he does not disown the words of
the Holy One, it does not imply that his sufferings may be
chastisement : on the contrary, Job even allows the possibility
that he should sin ; but since his habitual state is fidelity to
God, this assumption is not sufficient to account for his
suffering, and he does not see why God should so unmerci-
fully visit such sinfulness instead of pardoning it (ch. vii.
20, 21).

It is not to be objected, that he who is fully conscious of
sin cannot consider the strictest divine punishment even of

[1] *Vid.* the *Commentary on Habakkuk*, S. 206–208 ; comp. Geiger,
Urschrift und Uebersetzungen der Bibel, S. 308 ff.

the smallest sin unjust. The suffering of one whose habitual state is pleasing to God, and who is conscious of the divine favour, can never be explained from, and measured according to, his infirmities: the infirmities of one who trusts in God, or the believer, and the severity of the divine justice in the punishment of sin, have no connection with one another. Consequently, when Eliphaz bids Job regard his affliction as chastisement, Job is certainly in the wrong to dispute with God concerning the magnitude of it: he would rather patiently yield, if his faith could apprehend the salutary design of God in his affliction; but after his affliction once seems to him to spring from wrath and enmity, and not from the divine purpose of mercy, after the phantom of a hostile God is come between him and the brightness of the divine countenance, he cannot avoid falling into complaint of un- mercifulness. For this the speech of Eliphaz is in itself not to blame: he had most feelingly described to him God's merciful purpose in this chastisement, but he is to blame for not having taken the right tone.

The speech of Job is directed against the unsympathetic and reproving tone which the friends, after their long silence, have assumed immediately upon his first manifestation of anguish. He justifies to them his complaint (ch. iii.) as the natural and just outburst of his intense suffering, desires speedy death as the highest joy with which God could re- ward his piety, complains of his disappointment in his friends, from whom he had expected affectionate solace, but by whom he sees he is now forsaken, and earnestly exhorts them to acknowledge the justice of his complaint (ch. vi.). But can they? Yes, they might and should. For Job thinks he is no longer an object of divine favour: an inward conflict, which is still more terrible than hell, is added to his outward suffering. For the damned must give glory to God, because they recognise their suffering as just punishment: Job, however, in his suffering sees the wrath of God, and still is at the same time conscious of his innocence. The faith which, in the midst of his exhaustion of body and soul, still knows and feels God to be merciful, and can call him "my God," like Asaph in Ps. lxxiii.,—this faith is well-nigh overwhelmed in Job by the thought that God is his enemy, his pains the arrows of God. The assumption is false, but on this assumption Job's complaints (ch. iii.) are relatively just, including, what he himself says, that they are mistaken, thoughtless words of one in despair. But that despair is sin, and therefore also those curses and despairing inquiries!

Is not Eliphaz, therefore, in the right? His whole treatment is wrong. Instead of distinguishing between the complaint of his suffering and the complaint of God in Job's outburst of anguish, he puts them together, without recognising the complaint of his suffering to be the natural and unblameable result of its extraordinary magnitude, and as a sympathizing friend falling in with it. But with regard to the complaints of God, Eliphaz, acting as though careful for his spiritual welfare, ought not to have met them with his reproofs, especially as the words of one heavily afflicted deserve indulgence and delicate treatment; but he should have combated their false assumption. First, he should have said to Job, "Thy complaints of thy suffering are just, for thy suffering is incomparably great." In the next place, "Thy cursing thy birth, and thy complaint of God who has given thee thy life, might seem just if it were true that God has rejected thee; but that is not true: even in suffering He designs thy good; the greater the suffering, the greater the glory." By this means Eliphaz should have calmed Job's despondency, so as to destroy his false assumption; but he begins wrongly, and consequently what he says at last so truly and beautifully respecting the glorious issue of a patient endurance of chastisement, makes no impression on Job. He has not fanned the faintly burning wick, but his speech is a cold and violent breath which is calculated entirely to extinguish it.

After Job has defended the justice of his complaints against the insensibility of the friends, he gives way anew to lamentation. Starting from the wearisomeness of human life in general, he describes the greatness of his own suffering, which has received no such recognition on the part of the friends: it is a restless, torturing death without hope (ch. vii. 1–6). Then he turns to God: O remember that there is no second life after death, and that I am soon gone for ever; therefore I will utter my woe without restraint (vii. 7–11). Thus far (from ch. vi. 1 onwards) I find in Job's speech no trace of blasphemous or sinful despair. When he says (ch. vi. 8–12), How I would rejoice if God, whose word I have never disowned, would grant me my request, and end my life, for I can no longer bear my suffering,—I cannot with Ewald see in it despair rising to madness, which (ch. vii. 10) even increases to frantic joy. For Job's disease was indeed really in the eyes of men as hopeless as he describes it. In an incurable disease, however, imploring God to hasten death, and rejoicing at the thought of approaching dissolution, is not a sin, and is not to be called despair, inasmuch as one does not call giving up all hope of recovery despair.

Moreover, it must not be forgotten that the book of Job is an oriental book, and therefore some allowance must be made for the intensity and strength of conception of the oriental nature: then that it is a poetical book, and that frenzy and madness may not be also understood by the intensified expression in which poetry, which idealizes the real, clothes pain and joy: finally, that it is an Old Testament book, and that in the Old Testament the fundamental nature of man is indeed sanctified, but not yet subdued; the spirit shines forth as a light in a dark place, but the day, the ever constant consciousness of favour and life, has not yet dawned. The desire of a speedy termination of life (ch. vi. 8–12) is in ch. vii. 7–11 softened down even to a request for an alleviation of suffering, founded on this, that death terminates life for ever. In the Talmud (*b. Bathra*, 16, *a*) it is observed, on this passage, that Job denies the resurrection of the dead (מכאן שכפר איוב בתחיים המתים) ; but Job knows nothing of a resurrection of the dead, and what one knows not, one cannot deny. He knows only that after death, the end of the present life, there is no second life in this world, only a being in *Sheôl*, which is only an apparent existence = no existence, in which all praise of God is silent, because He no longer reveals himself there as to the living in this world (Ps. vi. 6, xxx. 10, lxxxviii. 11–13, cxv. 17). From this chaotic conception of the other side of the grave, against which even the psalmists still struggle, the doctrine of the resurrection of the dead had not been set forth at the time of Job, and of the author of the book of Job. The restoration of Israel buried in exile (Ezek. xxxvii.) first gave the impulse to it; and the resurrection of the Prince of Life, who was laid in the grave, set the seal upon it. The resurrection of Jesus Christ was first of all the actual overthrow of Hades.

Mortis seu inferni, observes Brentius, in accordance with Scripture, *ea conditio est, ut natura sua quoscunque comprehenderit tantisper teneat nec dimittat, dum Christus, filius Dei, morte ad infernum descenderit, h.e. perierit; per hunc enim devicta morte et inferno liberantur quotquot fide renovati sunt.* This great change in the destiny of the dead was incomplete, and the better hope which became brighter and brighter as the advent of death's Conqueror drew near was not yet in existence. For if after death, or what is the same thing, after the descent into Sheôl, there was only a non-existence for Job, it is evident that on the one hand he can imagine a life after death only as a return to the present world (such a return does, however, not take place), on the other hand that no divine revelation said anything to him of a future life which should infinitely compensate for a return to the present world. And since he knows nothing of a future existence, it can consequently not be said that he denies it : he knows nothing of it, and even his dogmatizing friends have nothing to tell him about it. We shall see by and by, how the more his friends torment him, the more he is urged on in his longing for a future life; but the word of revelation, which could alone change desire into hope, is wanting. The more tragic and heart-rending Job's desire to be freed by death from his unbearable suffering is, the more touching and importunate is his prayer that God may consider that now soon he can no longer be an object of His mercy. Just the same request is found frequently in the Psalms, *e.g.* Ps. lxxxix. 48, comp. ciii. 14–16 : it involves nothing that is opposed to the Old Testament fear of God. Thus far we can trace nothing of frenzy and madness, and of despair only in so far as Job has given up the hope (נואש) of his restoration,—not however of real despair, in which a man impatiently and forcibly snaps asunder the bond of trust which unites him to God. If the poet had anywhere made Job to go to such a length in despair, he would have made Satan to triumph over him.

Now, however, the last two strophes follow in which Job is hurried forward to the use of sinful language, ch. vii. 12–16: Am I a sea or a sea-monster, etc.; and ch. vii. 17–21 : What is man, that thou accountest him so great, etc. We should nevertheless be mistaken if we thought there were sin here in the expressions by which Job describes God's hostility against himself. We may compare *e.g.* Lam. iii. 9, 10 : " He hath enclosed my ways with hewn stone, He hath made my paths crooked; He is to me as a bear lying in wait, a lion in the thicket." It is, moreover, not Job's peculiar sin that he thinks God has changed to an enemy against him ; that is the

view which comes from his vision being beclouded by the
conflict through which he is passing, as is frequently the case
in the Psalms.   His sin does not even consist in the inquiries,
How long? and Wherefore? The Psalms in that case would
abound in sin.   But the sin is that he dwells upon these
doubting questions, and thus attributes apparent mercilessness
and injustice to God.   And the friends constantly urge him
on still deeper in this sin, the more persistently they attribute
his suffering to his own unrighteousness.   Jeremiah (in ch.
iii. of the Lamentations), after similar complaints, adds : Then
I repeated this to my heart, and took courage from it : the
mercies of Jehovah, they have no end ; His compassions do
not cease, etc.   Many of the Psalms that begin sorrowfully,
end in the same way ; faith at length breaks through the
clouds of doubt.   But it should be remembered that the
change of spiritual condition which, *e.g.* in Ps. vi., is condensed to the narrow limits of a lyric composition of eleven
verses, is here in Job worked out with dramatical detail as a
passage of his life's history : his faith, once so heroic, only
smoulders under ashes ; the friends, instead of fanning it to
a flame, bury it still deeper, until at last it is set free from its
bondage by Jehovah himself, who appears in the whirlwind.

Bildad's First Speech.—Chap. viii.

Schema: 6. 7. 6. 10. 8. 6.[1]

[Then began Bildad the Shuhite, and said :]
  2 *How long wilt thou utter such things,*
     And the words of thy mouth are a boisterous wind?

___

[1] We will give an example here of our and Ewald's computation of
the strophes.   " In the speech of Bildad, ch. viii.," says Ewald, *Jahrb.* ix.
35, " the first part may go to ver. 10, and be divided into three strophes
of three lines each."   This is right ; but that the three strophes consist
of three lines, *i.e.* according to Ewald's use of the word, three (*Masoretic*)

3 *Will God reverse what is right,*
   Or the Almighty reverse what is just?
4 *When thy children sinned against Him,*
   He gave them over to the hand of their wickedness.

Bildad[1] begins harshly and self-confidently with *quousque tandem*, עַד־אָן instead of the usual עַד־אָנָה. אֵלֶּה, not: this, but: of this kind, of such kind, as ch. xii. 3, xvi. 2. רוּחַ כַּבִּיר is poetical, equivalent to רוּחַ גְּדוֹלָה, ch. i. 19 ; רוּחַ is *gen. comm.* in the signification wind as well as spirit, although more frequently *fem.* than *masc.* He means that Job's speeches are like the wind in their nothingness, and like a boisterous wind in their vehemence. Bildad sees the justice of God, the Absolute One, which ought to be universally acknowledged, impugned in them. In order not to say directly that Job's

verses, is accidental. There are three strophes, of which the first consists of six lines = stichs, the second of seven, the third again of six. " Just so then," Ewald proceeds, "the second part, vers. 11–19, is easily broken up into like three strophes," viz. vers. 11–13, 14–16, 17–19. But strophes must first of all be known as being groups of stichs forming a complete sense (*Sinngruppen*). They are, according to their idea, groups of measured compass, as members of a symmetrical whole. Can we, however, take vers. 14–16 together as such a complete group? In his edition of Job of 1854, Ewald places a semicolon after ver. 16 ; and rightly, for vers. 16–19 belong inseparably together. Taking them thus, we have in the second part of the speech three groups. In the first, vers. 11–15, the godless are likened to the reed ; and his house in prosperity to a spider's web, since its perishableness, symbolized by the reed, is proved (אֲשֶׁר, ver. 14). In the second, vers. 16–19, follows the figure of the climbing plant which ver. 19 (יִצְמָחוּ) seems to indicate. In the third, vers. 20–22, the figure is given up, and the strophe is entirely *epimythionic*. Of these three groups, the first consists of ten, the second of eight, and the third of six lines = stichs. The schema is therefore as we have given it above: 6. 7. 6. 10. 8. 6. We are only justified in calling these groups strophes by the predominance of the hexastich, which occurs at the beginning, middle, and close of the speech.

[1] Nothing can be said respecting the signification of the name בִּלְדַּד even as a probable meaning, unless perhaps = בַּל־דַּד, *sine mammis, i.e.* brought up without his mother's milk.

children had died such a sudden death on account of their sin, he speaks conditionally.   If they have sinned, death is just the punishment of their sin.   God has not arbitrarily swept them away, but has justly given them over to the destroying hand of their wickedness,—a reference to the prologue which belongs inseparably to the whole.

5 *If thou seekest unto God,*
And makest supplication to the Almighty,
6 *If thou art pure and upright ;*
Surely ! He will care for thee,
And restore the habitation of thy righteousness ;
7 *And if thy beginning was small,*
Thy end shall be exceeding great.

There is still hope for Job (אַתָּה, in opposition to his children), if, turning humbly to God, he shows that, although not suffering undeservedly, he is nevertheless pure and upright in his inmost mind.   Ver. 6*a* is so intended ; not as Mercier and others explain : *si in posterum puritati et justitiæ studueris.*   שִׁחַר אֶל־אֵל, to turn one's self to God earnestly seeking, *constr. prægnans,* like דָּרַשׁ אֶל־אֵל, ch. v. 8.   Then begins the conclusion with כִּי־עַתָּה, like ch. xiii. 18.   "The habitation of thy righteousness" is Job's household cleansed and justified from sin.   God will restore that; שִׁלַּם might also signify, give peace to, but restore is far more appropriate.   Completely falling back on שָׁלֵם, the *Piel* signifies to recompense, of like being returned for like, and to restore, of a complete covering of the loss sustained.   God will not only restore, but increase beyond measure, what Job was and had.   The *verb. masc.* after אַחֲרִית here is remarkable.   But we need not, with Olsh., read יִשְׂגֶּה : we may suppose, with Ewald, according to 174, *e*, that אחרית is purposely treated as *masc.*   It would be a mistake to refer to Prov. xxiii. 32, xxix. 21, in support of it.

8 *For inquire only of former ages,*
  And attend to the research of their fathers—
9 *For we are of yesterday, without experience,*
  Because our days upon earth are a shadow—
10 *Shall they not teach thee, speak to thee,*
  And bring forth words from their heart?

This challenge calls Deut. xxxii. 7 to mind. לְבָּךְ is to be supplied to כּוֹנֵן; the conjecture of Olshausen, וּבוֹנֵן, is good, but unnecessary. רִישׁוֹן is after the Aramaic form of writing, comp. ch. xv. 7, where this and the ordinary form are combined. The " research of their fathers," *i.e.* which the fathers of former generations have bequeathed to them, is the collective result of their research, the profound wisdom of the ancients gathered from experience. Our ephemeral and shadowy life is not sufficient for passing judgment on the dealings of God ; we must call history and tradition to our aid. We are תְּמוֹל (*per aphœresin,* the same as אֶתְמוֹל), yesterday = of yesterday ; it is not necessary to read, with Olshausen, מִתְּמוֹל. There is no occasion for us to suppose that ver. 9 is an antithesis to the long duration of the life of primeval man. לֵב (ver. 10) is not the antithesis of mouth ; but has the pregnant signification of a feeling, *i.e.* intelligent heart, as we find אִישׁ לֵבָב, a man of heart, *i.e.* understanding, ch. xxxiv. 10, 34. יוֹצִיאוּ, *promunt,* calls to mind Matt. xiii. 52. Now follow familiar sayings of the ancients, not directly quoted, but the wisdom of the fathers, which Bildad endeavours to reproduce.

11 *Doth papyrus grow up without mire?*
  Doth the reed shoot up without water?
12 *It is still in luxuriant verdure, when it is not cut off,*
  Then before all other grass it withereth.
13 *So is the way of all forgetters of God,*

And the hope of the ungodly perisheth,
14 *Because his hope is cut off,*
   And his trust is a spider's house :
15 *He leaneth upon his house and it standeth not,*
   He holdeth fast to it and it endureth not.

Bildad likens the deceitful ground on which the prosperity of the godless stands to the dry ground on which, only for a time, the papyrus or reed finds water, and grows up rapidly : shooting up quickly, it withers as quickly ; as the papyrus plant,[1] if it has no perpetual water, though the finest of grasses, withers off when most luxuriantly green, before it attains maturity. גֹּמֶא, which, excepting here, is found only in connection with Egypt (Ex. ii. 3, Isa. xviii. 2; and Isa. xxxv. 7, with the general קָנֶה as specific name for reed), is the proper papyrus plant (Cypērus papȳrus, L.) : this name for it is suitably derived in the Hebrew from גָּמָא, to suck up (comp. Lucan, iv. 136 : *conseritur bibulâ Memphytis cymba papyro*) ; but is at the same time Egyptian, since Coptic *kam, cham,* signifies the reed, and *'gôm, 'gōme,* a book (like *liber,* from the bark of a tree).[2] אָחוּ, occurring only in the book of Job and in the history of Joseph, as Jerome (*Opp. ed. Vallarsi,* iv. 291) learned from the Egyptians, signifies in their language, *omne quod in palude virem nascitur :* the word is trans-

---

[1] *Vid.* Champollion-Figeac, *Aegypten,* German translation, pp. 47 sq.

[2] Comp. the *Book of the Dead* (Todtenbuch), ch. 162 : "Chapter on the creation of warmth at the back of the head of the deceased. Words over a young cow finished in pure gold. Put them on the neck of the dead, and paint them also on a new papyrus," etc. Papyrus is here *cama :* the word is determined by papyrus-roll, fastening and writing, and its first consonant corresponds to the Coptic aspirated *g.* Moreover, we cannot omit to mention that this *cama* = *gôme* also signifies a garment, as in a prayer : "O my mother Isis, come and veil me in thy *cama.*" Perhaps both ideas are represented in *volumen, involucrum ;* it is, however, also possible that *gōme* is to be etymologically separated from *kam, cham* = גָּמָא.

ferred by the LXX. into their translation in the form ἄχι (ἄχει), and became really incorporated into the Alexandrian Greek, as is evident from Isa. xix. 7 (ערות, LXX. καὶ τὸ ἄχι τὸ χλωρόν) and Sir. xl. 16 (ἄχι ἐπὶ παντὸς ὕδατος καὶ χείλους ποταμοῦ πρὸ παντὸς χόρτου ἐκτιλήσεται) ; the Coptic translates pi-akhi, and moreover ake, oke signify in Coptic calamus, juncus.[1] לֹא יִקָּטֵף describes its condition : in a condition in which it is not ready for being gathered. By אֲשֶׁר, quippe, quoniam, this end of the man who forgets God, and of the חָנֵף, i.e. the secretly wicked, is more particularly described. His hope יָקוֹט, from קָטַט, or from קוֹט, med. o,[2] in neuter signification succiditur. One would indeed expect a figure corresponding to the spider's web earlier ; and accordingly Hahn, after Reiske, translates : whose hope is a gourd,—an absurd figure, and linguistically impossible, since the gourd or cucumber is קִשּׁוּא, which has its cognates in Arabic and Syriac. Saadia[3] translates : whose hope is the thread of the sun. The "thread of the sun" is what we call the *fliegender Sommer* or *Altweibersommer*, [i.e. the sunny days in the latter months of the year] : certainly a suitable figure, but unsupportable by any parallel in language.[4] We must therefore

---

[1] The tradition of Jerome, that אחו originally signifies *viride*, is supported by the corresponding use of the verb in the signification to be green. So in the *Papyr. Anastas.* No. 3 (in Brugsch, *Aeg. Geographie*, S. 20, No. 115) : *naif hesbu achach em sim*, his fields are green with herbs ; and in a passage in Young, *Hieroglyphics*, ii. 69 : *achechut uoi ās em senem·t*, the beautiful field is green with senem. The second radical is doubled in *achech*, as in *uot-uet*, which certainly signifies *viriditas*. The substantive is also found represented by three leaf-stalks on one basis ; its radical form is *ah*, plural, weaker or stronger aspirated, *ahu* or *akhu*, greenness : comp. Salvolini, *Campagne de Rhamsès le Grand*, p. 117 ; and Brugsch, above, S. 25.

[2] Both are possible; for even from קָטַט, the mode of writing, יָקוֹט, is not without numerous examples, as Dan. xi. 12, Ps. xciv. 21, cvii. 27.

[3] *Vid.* Ewald-Dukes' *Beiträge zur Gesch. der ältesten Auslegung*, i. 89.

[4] Saadia's interpretation cannot be supported from the Arabic, for the Arabs call the "*Altweibersommer*" the deceitful thread (*el-chaitt el-*

suppose that יָקוֹט, *succiditur*, first gave rise to the figure which follows : as easily as a spider's web is cut through, without offering any resistance, by the lightest touch, or a breath of wind, so that on which he depends and trusts is cut asunder. The name for spider's web, בֵּית עַכָּבִישׁ,[1] leads to the description of the prosperity of the ungodly by בַּיִת (ver. 15) : His house, the spider's house, is not firm to him. Another figure follows : the wicked in his prosperity is like a climbing plant, which grows luxuriantly for a time, but suddenly perishes.

> 16 *He swells with sap in the sunshine,*
> *And his branch spreads itself over his garden.*
> 17 *His roots intertwine over heaps of stone,*
> *He looks upon a house of stones.*
> 18 *If He casts him away from his place,*
> *It shall deny him : I have not seen thee.*
> 19 *Behold, thus endeth his blissful course,*
> *And others spring forth from the dust.*

The subject throughout is not the creeping-plant directly, but the ungodly, who is likened to it. Accordingly the ex-

bâttil), or "sunslime or spittle " (*lu'âb es-schems*), or خَيْتَعُور (a word which Ewald, *Jahrb.* ix. 38, derives from خَيْت = יָקוֹט, a word which does not exist, and عور , chaff, a word which is not Arabic), from خَتَع , to roam about, to be dispersed, to perish, vanish. From this radical signification, *chaita'ûr*, like many similar old Arabic words with a fulness of figurative and related meaning, is become an expression for a number of different things, which may be referred to the notion of roaming about and dispersion. Among others, as the Turkish Kamus says, " That thing which on extremely hot days, in the form of a spider's web, looks as though single threads came down from the atmosphere, which is caused by the thickness of the air," etc. The form brought forward by Ew., written with ﺕ or ﺙ, is, moreover, a fabrication of our lexicons (Fl.).

[1] The spider is called עַכָּבִישׁ, for עַנְכָּבִישׁ, Arabic 'ancabuth, for which they say 'accabuth in *Saida*, on ancient Phœnician ground, as *atta* (thou) for *anta* (communicated by Wetzstein).

pression of the thought is in part figurative and in part literal, בֵּית אֲבָנִים יֶחֱזֶה (ver. 17*b*). As the creeper has stones before it, and by its interwindings, as it were, so rules them that it may call them its own (v. Gerlach : the exuberant growth twines itself about the walls, and looks proudly down upon the stony structure) ; so the ungodly regards his fortune as a solid structure, which he has quickly caused to spring up, and which seems to him imperishable. Ewald translates: he separates one stone from another ; בֵּית, according to § 217, *g*, he considers equivalent to בֵּינַת, and signifies apart from one another ; but although חָזַו = חָזָה, according to its radical idea, may signify to split, pierce through, still בֵּית, when used as a preposition, can signify nothing else but, within. Others, *e.g.* Rosenmüller, translate : he marks a place of stones, *i.e.* meets with a layer of stones, against which he strikes himself ; for this also בֵּית will not do. He who casts away (ver. 18) is not the house of stone, but God. He who has been hitherto prosperous, becomes now as strange to the place in which he flourished so luxuriantly, as if it had never seen him. Behold, that is the delight of his way (course of life), *i.e.* so fashioned, so perishable is it, so it ends. From the ground above which he sprouts forth, others grow up whose fate, when they have no better ground of confidence than he, is the same. After he has placed before Job both the blessed gain of him who trusts, and the sudden destruction of him who forgets, God, as the result of the whole, Bildad recapitulates :

20 *Behold! God despiseth not the perfect man,*
    And taketh not evil-doers by the hand.
21 *While He shall fill thy mouth with laughing,*
    And thy lips with rejoicing,
22 *They who hate thee shall be clothed with shame,*
    And the tent of the ungodly is no more.

" To take by the hand," *i.e.* ready to help as His own, as Isa.

xli. 13, xlii. 6. Instead of עַד (ver. 21), there is no great difficulty in reading עוֹד: again (as *e.g.* Ps. xlii. 6) He will fill;
but even עַד is supportable; it signifies, like ch. i. 18, Ps. cxli.
10, while. On the form יְמַלֶּה, *vid.* Ges. § 75, 21, *b.* This
close of Bildad's speech sounds quite like the Psalms (comp.
Ps. cxxvi. 2 with ver. 21; Ps. xxxv. 26, cix. 29, cxxxii. 18,
with ver. 22). Bildad does all he can to win Job over. He
calls the ungodly שֹׂנְאֶיךָ, to show that he tries to think and
expect the best of Job.

We have seen that Job in his second speech charges God
with the appearance of injustice and want of compassion.
The friends act as friends, by not allowing this to pass without admonition. After Job has exhausted himself with his
plaints, Bildad enters into the discussion in the above speech.
He defends the justice of God against Job's unbecoming
words. His assertion that God does not swerve from the right,
is so true that it would be blasphemy to maintain against him
that God sometimes perverts the right. And Bildad seems
also to make the right use of this truth when he promises
a glorious issue to his suffering, as a substantial proof that
God does not deal unjustly towards him; for Job's suffering
does actually come to such an issue, and this issue in its accomplishment destroys the false appearance that God had
been unjust or unmerciful towards him. Bildad expresses
his main point still more prudently, and more in accordance
with the case before him, when he says, "Behold! God does
not act hostilely towards the godly, neither does He make
common cause with the evil-doer" (ver. 20),—a confession
which he must allow is on both sides the most absolute truth.
By the most telling figures he portrays the perishableness of
the prosperity of those who forget God, and paints in glowing
colours on this dark background the future which awaits Job.
What is there in this speech of Bildad to censure, and how is
it that it does not produce the desired cheering effect on Job?

It is true that nothing that God sends to man proceeds from injustice, but it is not true that everything that He sends to him comes from His justice. As God does not ordain suffering for the hardened sinner in order to *improve* him, because He is *merciful*, so He does not ordain suffering for the truly godly in order to *punish* him, because He is *just*. What we call God's attributes are only separate phases of His indivisible holy being,—*ad extra*, separate modes of His operation in which they all share,—of which, when in operation, one does not act in opposition to another ; they are not, however, all engaged upon the same object at one time. One cannot say that God's love manifests itself in action in hell, nor His anger in heaven ; nor His justice in the afflictions of the godly, and His mercy in the sufferings of the godless.

Herein is Bildad's mistake, that he thinks his common-place utterance is sufficient to explain all the mysteries of human life. We see from his judgment of Job's children how unjust he becomes, since he regards the matter as the working out of divine justice. He certainly speaks hypothetically, but in such a way that he might as well have said directly, that their sudden death was the punishment of their sin. If he had found Job dead, he would have considered him as a sinner, whom God had carried off in His anger. Even now he has no pleasure in promising Job help and blessing ; accordingly from his point of view he expresses himself very conditionally : If thou art pure and upright. We see from this that his belief in Job's uprightness is shaken, for how could the All-just One visit Job with such severe suffering, if he had not deserved it ! Nevertheless אם זך וישר אתה (ver. 6) shows that Bildad thinks it possible that Job's heart may be pure and upright, and consequently his present affliction may not be peremptory punishment, but only disciplinary chastisement. Job must—such is Bildad's counsel—give God glory, and acknowledge that he deserves nothing better ;

and thus humbling himself beneath the just hand of God, he will be again made righteous, and exalted.

Job cannot, however, comprehend his suffering as an act of divine justice. His own fidelity is a fact, his consciousness of which cannot be shaken : it is therefore impossible for him to deny it, for the sake of affirming the justice of God ; for truth is not to be supported by falsehood. Hence Bildad's glorious promises afford Job no comfort. Apart from their being awkwardly introduced, they depend upon an assumption, the truth of which Job cannot admit without being untrue to himself. Consequently Bildad, though with the best intention, only urges Job still further forward and deeper into the conflict.

But does, then, the confession of sin on the part of constantly sinful man admit of his regarding the suffering thus appointed to him not merely not as punishment, but also not as chastisement ? If a sufferer acknowledges the excessive hideousness of sin, how can he, when a friend bids him regard his affliction as a wholesome chastisement designed to mortify sin more and more,—how can he receive the counsel with such impatience as we see in the case of Job ? The utterances of Job are, in fact, so wild, inconsiderate, and unworthy of God, and the first speeches of Eliphaz and Bildad on the contrary so winning and appropriate, that if Job's affliction ought really to be regarded from the standpoint of chastisement, their tone could not be more to the purpose, nor exhortation and comfort more beautifully blended. Even when one knows the point of the book, one will still be constantly liable to be misled by the speeches of the friends ; it requires the closest attention to detect what is false in them. The poet's mastery of his subject, and the skill with which he exercises it, manifests itself in his allowing the opposition of the friends to Job, though existing in the germ from the very beginning, to become first of all in the course of the controversy so harsh that they look upon Job as a sinner undergoing punishment from God, while in opposition to them he affirms his innocence, and challenges a decision from God.

The poet, however, allows Bildad to make one declaration, from which we clearly see that his address, beautiful as it is, rests on a false basis, and loses its effect. Bildad explains the sudden death of Job's children as a divine judgment. He could not have sent a more wounding dart into Job's already broken heart; for is it possible to tell a man anything more heart-rending than that his father, his mother, or his children have died as the direct punishment of their sins? One would not say so, even if it should seem to be an obvious fact, and least of all to a father already sorely tried and brought almost to the grave with sorrow. Bildad, however, does not rely upon facts, he reasons only à priori. He does not know that Job's children were godless; the only ground of his judgment is the syllogism: Whoever dies a fearful, sudden death must be a great sinner; God has brought Job's children to such a death; ergo, etc. Bildad is zealously affected for God, but without understanding. He is blind to the truth of experience, in order not to be drawn away from the truth of his premiss. He does not like to acknowledge anything that furnishes a contradiction to it. It is this same rationalism of superstition or credulity which has originated the false doctrine of the decretum absolutum. With the same icy and unfeeling rigorism with which Calvinism refers the divine rule, and all that happens upon earth, to the one principle of absolute divine will and pleasure, in spite of all the contradictions of Scripture and experience, Bildad refers everything to the principle of the divine justice, and, indeed, divine justice in a judicial sense.

There is also another idea of justice beside this judicial one. Justice, צדקה or צדק, is in general God's dealings as ruled by His holiness. Now there is not only a holy will of God concerning man, which says, Be ye holy, for I am holy;

but also a purpose for the redemption of unholy man springing from the holy love of God to man.   Accordingly justice
is either the agreement of God's dealings with the will of
His holiness manifest in the demands of the law, apart from
redemption, or the agreement of His dealings with the will
of His love as graciously manifested in the gospel; in short,
either retributive or redemptive.   If one, as Bildad, in the first
sense says, God never acts unjustly, and glaringly maintains
it as universally applicable, the mystery of the divine dispensations is not made clear thereby, but destroyed.   Thus also
Job's suffering is no longer a mystery : Job suffers what he
deserves; and if it cannot be demonstrated, it is to be assumed
in contradiction to all experience.   This view of his affliction
does not suffice to pacify Job, in spite of the glorious promises by which it is set off.   His conscience bears him witness
that he has not merited such incomparably heavy affliction;
and if we indeed suppose, what we must suppose, that Job was
in favour with God when this suffering came upon him, then
the thought that God deals with him according to his works,
perhaps according to his unacknowledged sins, must be altogether rejected.

God does not punish His own; and when He chastises
them, it is not an act of His retributive justice, but of His
disciplinary love.   This motive of love, indeed, belongs to
chastisement in common with trial ; and the believer who
clearly discerns this love will be able to look upon even the
severest affliction as chastisement without being led astray,
because he knows that sin has still great power in him ; and
the medicine, if it is designed to heal him, must be bitter.   If,
therefore, Bildad had represented Job's affliction as the chastisement of divine love, which would humble him in order the
more to exalt him, then Job would have humbled himself,
although Bildad might not be altogether in the right.   But
Bildad, still further than Eliphaz from weakening the erro-

neous supposition of a hostile God which had taken possession of Job's mind, represents God's justice, to which he attributes the death of his children, instead of His love, as the hand under which Job is to humble himself. Thereby the comfort which Job's friend offers becomes to him a torture, and his trial is made still greater ; for his conscience does not accuse him of any sins for which he should now have an angry instead of a gracious God.

But we cannot even here withhold the confession that the composition of such a drama would not be possible under the New Testament. The sight of the suffering of Christ and the future crown has a power in calming the mind, which makes such an outburst of sorrow as that of Job impossible even under the strongest temptation. " If the flesh should murmur and cry out, as Christ even cried out and was feeble," says Luther in one of his consolatory letters (Rambach, *Kleine Schriften Luthers*, S. 627), " the spirit nevertheless is ready and willing, and with sighings that cannot be uttered will cry : Abba, Father, it is Thou; Thy rod is hard, but Thou art still Father ; I know that of a truth." And since the consciousness of sin is as deep as the consciousness of grace, the Christian will not consider any suffering so severe but that he may have deserved severer on account of his sins, even though in the midst of his cross he be unable clearly to recognise the divine love. Even such uncharitable, cold-hearted consolation as that of Eliphaz and Bildad, which bids him regard the divine trial as divine chastisement, cannot exasperate him, since he is conscious of the need for even severer divine chastisement; he need not therefore allow the uncharitableness of the friend to pass without loving counter-exhortations.

Hengstenberg observes, in the *Excursus* to his *Commentary on the Psalms*, that the righteousness on which the plea to be heard is based in the Psalms, like Ps. xvii., xviii. 21 sqq., xliv. 18-23, is indeed a righteousness of conduct resting on righteousness by faith, and also this again is only to be considered as the righteousness of endeavour; that moreover their strong tone does not sound altogether becoming, according to our consciousness. We should expect each time, as it happens sometimes urgently (*e.g.* Ps. cxliii. 2), the other side,—that human infirmity which still clings to the righteous should be made prominent, and divine forgiveness for it implored, instead of the plea for deliverance being based on the incongruity of the affliction with the sufferer's consciousness of righteousness towards God. We cannot altogether adopt such psalms and passages of the Psalms as expressive of our Christian feeling; and we are scarcely able to read them in public without hesitation when we attempt it. Whence is this? Hengstenberg replies, "The Old Testament wanted the most effectual means for producing the knowledge of sin —the contemplation of the sufferings of Christ. The New Testament, moreover, possesses a more powerful agency of the Spirit, which does not search more into the depths of the divine nature than it lays open the depths of sin. Hence in Christian songs the sense of sin, as it is more independent of outward occasions than formerly, so it is also more openly disclosed and more delicate in itself; its ground is felt to lie deeper, and also the particular manifestations. It was good that under the Old Covenant the cords of sinful conviction were not strung too tightly, as the full consolation was still not to be found. The gulph closed up again when the sufferings were gone."[1] Such is the actual connection. And this development of the work of redemption in the history of mankind is repeated in the individual experience of every believer. As the individual, the further he progresses in the divine life, becomes the more deeply conscious of the natural

[1] *Vid.* Hengstenberg's *Commentary on the Psalms*, iii., Appendix, p. lxiii. Clark's Foreign Theological Library. 1854.

depravity of man, and acquires a keener and still keener perception of its most subtle working ; so in the New Testament, with the disclosure of actual salvation, a deeper insight into sin is also given.   When the infinite depth and extent of the kingdom of light is unveiled, the veil is for the first time removed from the abyss of the kingdom of darkness.   Had the latter been revealed without the former in the dispensation before Christ, the Old Testament would have been not only what it actually was in connection with the then painful consciousness of sin and death,—a school of severe discipline preparatory to the New Testament, a school of ardent longing for redemption,—but would have become an abyss of despair.

Job's Second Answer.—Chap. ix. x.

Schema: 6. 6. 6. 10. 10. 9. 8. 9. | 9 (ch. ix. 34–x. 2). 11. 10. 12. 11.

[Then Job began, and said :]

2 *Yea, indeed, I know it is thus,*
   And how should a man be just with God !

3 *Should he wish to contend with God,*
   He could not answer Him one of a thousand.

4 *The wise in heart and mighty in strength,*
   Who hath defied Him and remained unhurt ?

Job does not (ver. 2) refer to what Eliphaz said (ch. iv. 17), which is similar, though still not exactly the same ; but "indeed I know it is so" must be supposed to be an assent to that which Bildad had said immediately before. The chief thought of Bildad's speech was, that God does not pervert what is right.   Certainly (אָמְנָם, *scilicet, nimirum,* like ch. xii. 2),—says Job, as he ironically confirms this maxim of Bildad's,—it is so : what God does is always right, because God does it ; how could man maintain that he is in the right in opposition to God !   If God should be willing to enter into controversy with man, he would not be able to give Him information on one of a thousand subjects that might be brought into discussion; he would be so confounded, so disarmed, by reason of the infinite distance of the feeble creature from his Creator. The attributes (ver. 4*a*) belong not to man (Olshausen), but to God, as ch. xxxvi. 5. God is wise of heart (לֵב = νοῦς) in putting one question after another, and mighty in strength in bringing to nought every attempt man may make to maintain his own right; to defy Him (הִקְשָׁה, to harden, *i.e.* עֹרֶף, the neck), therefore, always tends to the discomfiture of him who dares to bid Him defiance.

> 5 *Who removeth mountains without their knowing,*
>   *That He hath overturned them in His wrath;*
> 6 *Who causeth the earth to shake out of its place,*
>   *And its pillars to tremble;*
> 7 *Who commandeth the sun, and it riseth not,*
>   *And sealeth up the stars.*

וְלֹא יָדָעוּ (ver. 5*a*) may also be translated: without one's perceiving it or knowing why; but it is more natural to take the mountains as the subject. אֲשֶׁר, *quod*, that (not " as," Ewald, § 333, *a*), after יָדַע, as Ezek. xx. 26, Eccl. viii. 12. Even the lofty mountains are quite unconscious of the change which He effects on them in a moment. Before they are aware that it is being done, it is over, as the *præt.* implies; the destructive power of His anger is irresistible, and effects its purpose suddenly. He causes the earth to start up from its place (comp. Isa. xiii. 13) which it occupies in space (ch. xxvi. 7); and by being thus set in motion by Him, its pillars tremble, *i.e.* its internal foundations (Ps. civ. 5), which are removed from human perception (ch. xxxviii. 6). It is not the highest mountains, which are rather called the pillars, as it were the supports, of heaven (ch. xxvi. 11), that are meant. By the same almighty will He disposes of the sun and stars. The sun is here called חֶרֶס (as in Judg. xiv. 18 חַרְסָה with

unaccented *ah*, and as Isa. xix. 18 '*Ir ha-Heres* is a play upon
עִיר הַחֶרֶס, ‛Ηλιούπολις), perhaps from the same root as חָרוּץ,
one of the poetical names of gold. At His command the sun
rises not, and He seals up the stars, *i.e.* conceals them behind
thick clouds, so that the day becomes dark, and the night is
not made bright. One may with Schultens think of the
Flood, or with Warburton of the Egyptian darkness, and the
standing still of the sun at the word of Joshua; but these
are only single historical instances of a fact here affirmed as
a universal experience of the divine power.

> 8 *Who alone spreadeth out the heavens,*
>   *And walketh upon the heights of the sea;*
> 9 *Who made the Bear, Orion, and the Pleiades,*
>   *And the chambers of the south;*
> 10 *Who doeth great things past finding out,*
>   *And wondrous things without number.*

Ewald, Hirzel, and others, understand נטה (ver. 8) according
to Ps. xviii. 10 : He letteth down the clouds of heaven, and
walketh on the heights of the sea of clouds, *i.e.* high above
the towering thunder-clouds. But parallel passages, such as
Isa. xl. 22, Ps. civ. 2, and especially Isa. xliv. 24, show that
ver. 8*a* is to be understood as referring to the creation of the
firmament of heaven; and consequently נטה is to be taken in
the sense of *expandere*, and is a form of expression naturally
occurring in connection with the mention of the waters which
are separated by means of the רקיע. The question arises,
whether יָם here means the sea of waters above the firmament
or upon the earth. According to the idea of the ancients,
the waters which descend as rain have their habitation far
away in the infinite expanse of the sky; the ocean of the sky
(Egyptian *Nun-pa*), through which the sun-god *Ra* sails every
day, is there. It is possible that " the heights of the sea "
here, and perhaps also " the roots of the sea " (ch. xxxvi. 30),

may mean this ocean of the sky, as Hahn and Schlottmann suppose. But it is not necessary to adopt such an explanation, and it is moreover hazardous, since this conception of the celestial θάλασσα is not found elsewhere (apart from Apoc. iv. 6, xv. 2, xxii. 1). Why may not בָּמֳתֵי, which is used of the heights of the clouds (Isa. xiv. 14), be used also of the waves of the sea which mount up towards heaven (Ps. cvii. 26)? God walks over them as man walks on level ground (LXX. περιπατῶν ἐπὶ θαλάσσης ὡς ἐπ᾽ ἐδάφους); they rise or lie calmly beneath His feet according to His almighty will (comp. Hab. iii. 15).

Job next describes God as the Creator of the stars, by introducing a constellation of the northern (the Bear), one of the southern (Orion), and one of the eastern sky (the Pleiades). עָיִשׁ, contracted from נַעְיִשׁ, Arabic نعش, a bier, is the constellation of seven stars (*septentrio* or *septentriones*) in the northern sky. The Greater and the Lesser Bear form a square, which the Arabs regarded as a bier; the three other stars, *benâth n'asch, i.e.* daughters of the bier (comp. ch. xxxviii. 32), seem to be the mourners. כְּסִיל is Orion chained to the sky, which the ancients regarded as a powerful giant, and also as an insolent, foolish fellow[1] (K. O. Müller, *Kleine deutsche Schriften*, ii. 125). כִּימָה is the Pleiades, a constellation consisting of seven large and other smaller stars, Arabic ثريّا, which, like the Hebrew (comp.

كومة, *cumulus*), signifies the heap, cluster (*vid.* ch. xxxviii. 31), and is compared by the Persian poets to a bouquet formed of jewels. It is the constellation of seven stars, whose rising

---

[1] The Arabic جاهل is similar, which combines the significations, an ignorant, foolhardy, and passionate man (*vid.* Fleischer, *Ali's hundert Sprüche*, S. 115 f.).

and setting determined the commencement and end of their voyages (πλειάς, probably = constellation of navigation), and is to be distinguished from the northern *septentriones*. חַדְרֵי תֵימָן are, according to the Targ., the chambers of the constellations on the south side of the heavens, as also most expositors explain them (Mercier : *sidera quæ sunt in altero hemisphærio versus alterum polum antarcticum*), according to which תֵּימָן, or written defectively תֵּמָן, would therefore be equivalent to כוכבי תמן; or perhaps, in a more general meaning, the regions of the southern sky (*penetralia*), which are veiled, or altogether lost to view (Hirzel). In ver. 10, Job says, almost *verbatim*, what Eliphaz had said (ch. v. 10). Job agrees with the friends in the recognition of the power of God, and intentionally describes those phases of it which display its terrible majesty. But while the friends deduce from this doctrine the duty of a humble deportment on the part of the sufferer, Job uses it to support the cheerless truth that human right can never be maintained in opposition to the absolute God.

11   *Behold, He goeth by me and I see not,*
     And passeth by and I perceive Him not.
12   *Behold, He taketh away, who will hold Him back?*
     Who will say to Him : What doest Thou?
13   *Eloah restraineth not His anger,*
     The helpers of Rahab stoop under Him—
14   *How much less that I should address Him,*
     That I should choose the right words in answer to Him;
15   *Because, though I were right, I could not answer,—*
     To Him as my Judge I must make supplication.

God works among men, as He works in nature, with a supreme control over all, invisibly, irresistibly, and is not responsible to any being (Isa. xlv. 9). He does not turn or restrain His anger without having accomplished His purpose

This is a proposition which, thus broadly expressed, is only partially true, as is evident from Ps. lxxviii. 38. The helpers of *Rahab* must bow themselves under Him. It is not feasible to understand this in a general sense, as meaning those who are ready with boastful arrogance to yield succour to any against God. The form of expression which follows in ver. 14, "much less I," supports the assumption that עֹזְרֵי רָהַב refers to some well-known extraordinary example of wicked enterprise which had been frustrated, notwithstanding the gigantic strength by which it was supported; and שָׁחֲחוּ may be translated by the present tense, since a familiar fact is used as synonymous with the expression of an universal truth. Elsewhere *Rahab* as a proper name denotes Egypt (Ps. lxxxvii. 4), but it cannot be so understood here, because direct references to events in the history of Israel are contrary to the character of the book, which, with remarkable consistency, avoids everything that is at all Israelitish. But how has Egypt obtained the name of *Rahab?* It is evident from Isa. xxx. 7 that it bears this name with reference to its deeds of prowess; but from Ps. lxxxix. 11, Isa. li. 9, it is evident that *Rahab* properly denotes a sea-monster, which has become the symbol of Egypt, like *tannîn* and *leviathan* elsewhere. This signification of the word is also supported by ch. xxvi. 12, where the LXX. actually translate κῆτος, as here with remarkable freedom, ὑπ᾽ αὐτοῦ ἐκάμφθησαν κήτη τὰ ὑπ᾽ οὐρανόν. It is not clear whether these " sea-monsters" denote rebels cast down into the sea beneath the sky, or chained upon the sky; but at any rate the consciousness of a distinct mythological meaning in עזרי רהב is expressed by this translation (as also in the still freer translation of Jerome, *et sub quo curvantur qui portant orbem*); probably a myth connected with such names of the constellations as Κῆτος and Πρίστις (Ewald, Hirz., Schlottm.). The poesy of the book of Job even in other places does not spurn mythological allusions; and the phrase before us reminds one of the Hindu myth of *Indras'* victory over the dark demon *Vritras*, who tries to delay the descent of rain, and over his helpers. In *Vritras*, as in רהב, there is the idea of hostile resistance.

Job compares himself, the feeble one, to these mythical titanic powers in ver. 14. אַף כִּי (properly: even that), or even אַף alone (ch. iv. 19), signifies, according as the connection introduces a climax or anti-climax, either *quanto magis* or *quanto minus*, as here : how much less can I, the feeble one, dispute with Him! אֲשֶׁר, ver. 15, is best taken, as in ch. v. 5, in the signification *quoniam*. The *part. Poel* מְשֹׁפְטִי we should more correctly translate " my disputant" than " my judge ;" it is *Poel* which Ewald appropriately styles the conjugation of attack: שׁוֹפֵט, *judicando vel litigando aliquem petere;* comp. Ges. § 55, 1. The *part. Kal* denotes a judge, the *part. Poel* one who is accuser and judge at the same time. On such Poel-forms from strong roots, *vid.* on Ps. cix. 10, where *wedŏrschu* is to be read, and therefore it is written וְדָרְשׁוּ in correct Codices.

16 *If when I called He really answered,*
   I could not believe that He would hearken to me ;
17 *He would rather crush me in a tempest,*
   And only multiply my wounds without cause ;
18 *He would not suffer me to take my breath,*
   But would fill me with bitter things.
19 *If it is a question of the strength of the strong—: " Be-*
   hold here ! "
   And if of right—: " Who will challenge me ?"
20 *Were I in the right, my mouth must condemn me ;*
   Were I innocent, He would declare me guilty.

The answer of God when called upon, *i.e.* summoned, is represented in ver. 16a as an actual result (*præt.* followed by *fut. consec.*), therefore ver. 16b cannot be intended to express : I could not believe that He answers me, but : I could not believe that He, the answerer, would hearken to me; His infinite exaltation would not permit such condescension. The אֲשֶׁר which follows, ver. 17*a*, signifies either *quippe qui* or *quoniam;* both shades of meaning are after all blended, as in ver. 15. The question arises here whether שׁוּף signifies *conterere*, or as cognate form with שָׁאַף, *inhiare*,—a question also of importance in the exposition of the *Protevangelium*. There are in all only three passages in which it occurs : here, Gen. iii. 15, and Ps. cxxxix. 11. In Ps. cxxxix. 11 the meaning *conterere* is unsuitable, but even the signification *inhiare* can only be adopted for want of a better : perhaps it may be explained by comparison with צָעַף, in the sense of *obvelare*, or as a denominative from נֶשֶׁף (the verb of which, נשׁף, is kindred to נשׁב, נשׁם, *flare*) in the signification *obtenebrare*. In Gen. iii. 15, if regarded superficially, the meaning *inhiare* and *conterere* are alike suitable, but the meaning *inhiare* deprives that utterance of God of its prophetic character, which has been recognised from the beginning; and the meaning *conterere, contundere*, is strongly supported by the translations. We decide in favour of this meaning also in the present passage, with the ancient translations (LXX. ἐκτρίψῃ, Targ. מְדַקְדִּק, *comminuens*). Moreover, it is the meaning most generally supported by a comparison with the dialects, whereas the signification *inhiare* can only be sustained by comparison with שָׁאַף and the Arabic *sâfa* (to sniff, track by scent, to smell); besides, " to assail angrily" (Hirz., Ewald) is an inadmissible contortion of *inhiare*, which signifies in a hostile sense " to seize abruptly" (Schlottm.), properly to snatch, to desire to seize.

Translate therefore : He would crush me in a tempest and multiply (*multiplicaret*), etc., would not let me take breath (*respirare*), but (כִּי, Ges. § 155, 1, *e. a.*) fill me (יַשְׂבִּעַנִי, with *Pathach* with *Rebia mugrasch*) with bitter things (מַמְּרֹרִים, with *Dag. dirimens*, which gives the word a more pathetic expres sion). The meaning of ver. 19 is that God stifles the attempt to maintain one's right in the very beginning by His being superior to the creature in strength, and not entering into a dispute with him concerning the right. הִנֵּה (for הִנְנִי as אַיֵּה, ch. xv. 23, for אַיּוֹ) : see, here I am, ready for the contest, is the word of God, similar to *quis citare possit me* (in Jer. xlix. 19, l. 44), which sounds as an echo of this passage. The creature must always be in the wrong,—a thought true in itself, in connection with which Job forgets that God's right in opposition to the creature is also always the true objective right. פִּי, with suffix, accented to indicate its logical connection, as ch. xv. 6 : my own mouth.[1] In וַיַעְקְשֵׁנִי the *Chirek* of the *Hiphil* is shortened to a *Sheva*, as 1 Sam. xvii. 25; *vid.* Ges. § 53, rem. 4. The subject is God, not " my mouth" (Schlottm.) : supposing that I were innocent, He would put me down as one morally wrong and to be rejected.

21 *Whether I am innocent, I know not myself,*
  My life is offensive to me.
22 *There is one thing—therefore I maintain—:*
  The innocent and wicked He destroyeth.
23 *If the scourge slay suddenly,*
  He laugheth at the melting away of the innocent.
24 *Countries are given into the hand of the wicked;*
  The countenance of its rulers He veileth—
  Is it not so, who else doeth it?

Ver. 21 is usually considered to be an affirmation of innocence on the part of Job, though without effect, and even at the peril of his own destruction : " I am innocent, I boldly say it even with scorn of my life" (Schnurr., Hirz., Ewald, Schlottm.). But although לֹא אֵדַע נַפְשִׁי may mean : I care

---

[1] Olshausen's conjecture, פִּיו, lessens the difficulty in Isa. xxxiv. 16, but here it destroys the strong expression of the violence done to the moral consciousness.

nothing for my soul, *i.e.* my life (comp. Gen. xxxix. 6), its
first meaning would be : I know not my soul, *i.e.* myself ; and
this sense is also quite in accordance with the context.   He
is innocent, but the contradiction between his lot and his
innocence seems to show that his self-consciousness is deceptive, and makes him a mystery to himself, leads him astray
respecting himself; and having thus become a stranger to
himself, he abhors this life of seeming contradictions, for
which he desires nothing less than its long continuance (*vid.*
ch. vii. 16).   The אַחַת הִיא which follows we do not explain :
" it is all the same to me whether I live or not," but : it is all
one whether man is innocent or not.   He himself is a proof
of this; therefore he maintains, etc.   It is, however, also
possible that this expression, which is similar in meaning to
Eccles. ix. 2 (there is one event, מִקְרֶה אֶחָד, to the righteous
and to the wicked), and is well translated in the Targ. by
חדא מכילא היא (there is one measure of retribution, מכילא =
מִדָּה, μέτρον, Matt. vii. 2), refers to what follows, and that
" therefore I maintain" is parenthetical (like אָמַרְתִּי, Ps. cxix.
57 ; לִי אָמַר, Isa. xlv. 24), and we have translated it accordingly.   There is certainly a kind of suspense, and עַל־כֵּן introduces an assertion of Job, which is founded upon the fact of
the continuance of his own misfortune,—an assertion which
he advances in direct contradiction to the friends, and which
is expressly censured by Elihu.

    In vers. 23 sq., by some striking examples, he completes the
description of that which seems to be supported by the conflict he is called to endure.   שׁוֹט, a scourge, signifies a judgment which passes over a nation (Isa. xxviii. 15).   It sweeps
off the guiltless as well, and therefore Job concludes that
God delights in מַסָּה, πειρασμός, trial (compare above, p. 7,
note), or perhaps more correctly the melting away (from מָסַס,
as ch. vi. 14) of the guiltless, *i.e.* their dissolution in anguish
and dismay, their wearing away and despondency.   Jerome

rightly remarks that in the whole book Job says *nihil asperius* than what he says in ver. 23. Another example in favour of his disconsolate אחת היא is that whole lands are given into the hand of the wicked: the monarch is an evil man, and the countenance of their judges He (God) covers, so that they do not distinguish between right and wrong, nor decide in favour of the former rather than of the latter. God himself is the final cause of the whole : if not, *i.e.* if it is not so, who can it then be that causes it ? אֵפוֹ (four times in the book of Job instead of the usual form אֵפוֹא) is, according to the current opinion, placed *per hyperbaton* in the conditional instead of the interrogative clause; and אפו מי are certainly not, with Hirzel, to be taken together. There is, however, not a proper *hyperbaton*, but אפו here gives intensity to the question; though not directly as ch. xvii. 15 (Ges. § 153, 2), but only indirectly, by giving intensity to that which introduces the question, as ch. xxiv. 25 and Gen. xxvii. 37 ; translate therefore : if it really is not so (comp. the Homeric expression εἰ δ᾽ ἄγε). It is indisputable that God, and no one else, is the final cause of this misery, apparently so full of contradiction, which meets us in the history of mankind, and which Job now experiences for himself.

25 *My days were swifter than a runner,*
   They fled away without seeing prosperity,
26 *They shot by as ships of reeds,*
   As an eagle which dasheth upon its prey.
27 *If my thought is : I will forget my complaint,*
   I will give up my dark looks and look cheerful;
28 *I shudder at all my pains,*
   I feel that Thou dost not pronounce me innocent.

Such, as described in the preceding strophe, is the lot of the innocent in general, and such (this is the connection) is also Job's lot : his swiftly passing life comes to an end

amidst suffering, as that of an evil-doer whom God cuts off
in judgment. In the midst of his present sufferings he has
entirely forgotten his former prosperity ; it is no happiness
to him, because the very enjoyment of it makes the loss of it
more grievous to bear. The days of prosperity are gone,
have passed swiftly away without טובה, *i.e.* without *lasting*
prosperity. They have been swifter מִנִּי רָץ. By reference
to ch. vii. 6, this might be considered as a figure borrowed
from the weaver's loom, since in the Coptic the threads of
the weft (*fila subteminis*) which are wound round the shuttle
are called " runners" (*vid.* Ges. *Thesaurus*); but Rosenmüller
has correctly observed that, in order to describe the fleetness
of his life, Job brings together that which is swiftest on
land (the runners or couriers), in water (fast-sailing ships),
and in the air (the swooping eagle). עִם, ver. 26*a*, signifies,
in comparison with, *æque ac*. But we possess only a rather
uncertain tradition as to the kind of vessels meant by
אֳנִיּוֹת אֵבֶה. Jerome translates, after the Targ. : *naves poma
portantes,* by which one may understand the small vessels,
according to Edrisi, common on the Dead Sea, in which corn
and different kinds of fruits were carried from Zoar to
Jericho and to other regions of the Jordan (Stickel, S. 267) ;
but if אבה were connected with אֵב, we might rather expect
אַבֶּה, after the form אִשֶּׁה (from אֵשׁ), instead of אֵבֶה. Others
derive the word from אָבָה, *avere :* ships of desire, *i.e.* full-
rigged and ready for sea (Gecatilia in Ges. *Thes. suppl.* p.
62), or struggling towards the goal (Kimchi), or steering
towards (Zamora), and consequently hastening to (Symmachus, σπευδούσαις), the harbour; but independently of the
explanation not being suited to the description, it should then
be accented *ébēh,* after the form קֵצֶה, נֶדֶה, instead of *ébēh.*
The explanation, ships of hostility (Syr.[1]), *i.e.* ships belong-

---

[1] Luther also perhaps understood pirate ships, when he translated,
" *wie die starcken Schiff.*"

ing to pirates or freebooters, privateers, which would suit the
subject well, is still less admissible with the present pointing
of the text, as it must then be אֵבָה (אֵיבָה), with which the
Egyptian *uba*, against, and adverse (*contrarius*), may be compared. According to Abulwalid (Parchon, Raschi), אבה is
the name of a large river near the scene of the book of Job;
which may be understood as either the Babylonian name for

river أَبِّى, or the Abyssinian name of the Nile, *abáï;* and אֵבֶה

may be compared with לִבְנֶה in relation to the Arabic, *lubna*.
But a far more satisfactory explanation is the one now generally received, according to the comparison with the Arabic

أَبَّاءٌ, a reed (whence *abaa-t-un*, a reed, a so-called *n. unitatis*):

ships made from reeds, like כְּלֵי גֹמֶא, Isa. xviii. 2, vessels of
papyrus, βαρίδες παπύριναι. In such small ships, with
Egyptian tackling, they used to travel as far as Taprobane.
These canoes were made to fold together, *plicatiles*, so that
they could be carried past the cataracts; Heliodorus describes
them as ὀξυδρομώτατα.[1]

The third figure is the eagle, which swoops down upon its
prey; טוּשׂ, like Chaldee טוּס, by which the Targ. translates
חָשׁ, Hab. i. 8; Grätz' conjecture of יָשׂוּט (which is intended to
mean flutters) is superfluous. Just as unnecessary is it, with
Olshausen, to change אִם אָמְרִי into אם אמרתי: "if my saying
(thinking)" is equivalent to, "as often as I say (think)."
פנים is here (as in the German phrase, *ein Gesicht machen*)

---

[1] There is no Egyptian word which can be compared to אֵבה, whereas
han (*hani*) or *an* (*ana*) in Egyptian, like the Hebrew אֳנִיה, means a
ship (*vid.* Chabas, *Le Papyrus magique Harris*, p. 246, No. 826, cf. pp.
33, 47); it is written with the sign for *set* = downwards, since they
fastened a stone at the front of the vessel, as was even known to
Herodotus, in order to accelerate its speed in descending the river. From
this one might conjecture for the passage before us אֳניות אֵבֶן = swift
sailers.

an ill-humoured, distorted, wry face. When Job desires to give up this look of suffering and be cheerful (הבליג, like ch. x. 20, *hilaritatem præ se ferre, vultum hilarem induere*), the certainty that he is not favoured of God, and consequently that he cannot be delivered from his sufferings, all his anguish in spite of his struggles against it comes ever afresh before his mind. It is scarcely necessary to remark that תנקני is addressed to God, not to Bildad. It is important to notice that Job does not speak of God without at the same time looking up to Him as in prayer. Although he feels rejected of God, he still remains true to God. In the following strophe he continues to complain of God, but without denying Him.

29 *If I am wicked, why do I exert myself in vain?*

30 *If I should wash myself with snow water,*
 And make my hands clean with lye,

31 *Then thou wouldst plunge me into the pit,*
 And my clothes would abhor me.

32 *For He is not a man as I, that I should answer Him,*
 That we should go together to judgment.

33 *There is not an arbitrator between us*
 Who should lay his hand upon us both.

The clause with strongly accented "I" affirms that in relation to God he is from the first, and unchangeably, a wicked, *i.e.* guilty, man (Ps. cix. 7) (רָשַׁע, to be a wicked man, means either to act as such (ch. x. 15), or to appear as such, be accounted as such, as here and ch. x. 7; *Hiph.*, ver. 20, to condemn). Why, therefore, should he vainly (הֶבֶל, *acc. adv.*, like breath, useless) exert himself by crying for help, and basing his plaint on his innocence? In ver. 30a the *Chethib* is בְמוֹ, the *Keri* בְּמֵי, as the reverse in Isa. xxv. 10; *mo* itself appears in the signification water (Egyptian *muau*), in the proper names *Moab* and *Moshe* (according to Jablonsky, *ex aqua servatus*); in במו, however, the *mo* may be understood according to Ges. § 103, 2. This is the meaning—no cleansing, even though he should use snow and בֹּר (a vegetable alkali), *i.e.* not even the best-grounded self-justification can avail him, for God would still bring it to pass, that his clearly proved innocence should change to the most horrible impurity. Ewald, Rödiger, and others translate incorrectly : my clothes would make me disgusting. The idea is tame. The *Piel* תִּעֵב signifies elsewhere in the book (ch. xix. 19, xxx. 10) to abhor, not to make abhorrent; and the causative meaning is indeed questionable, for מְתָעֵב (Isa. xlix. 7) signifies loathing, as מְכַסֶּה (ch. xxiii. 18) covering, and Ezek. xvi. 25 certainly borders on the signification " to make detestable," but תעב may also be in the primary meaning, *abominari,* the strongest expression for that contempt of the beauty bestowed by God which manifests itself by prostitution. Translate : My clothes would abhor me; which does not mean : I should be disgusted with myself (Hirzel) ; Job is rather represented as naked ; him, the naked one, God would—says he—so plunge into the pit that his clothes would conceive a horror of him, *i.e.* start back in terror at the idea of being put on and defiled by such a horrible creature (Schlottm., Oehler). For God is not his equal, standing on the same level with him : He, the Absolute Being, is accuser and judge in one person ; there is between them no arbitrator who (or that he) should lay, etc. Mercier correctly explains : *impositio manus est potestatis signum;* the meaning therefore is : *qui utrumque nostrum velut manu imposita coerceat.*

> 34 *Let Him take away His rod from me,*
> *And let His terrors not stupify me.*
> 35 *Then I would speak and not fear Him,*
> *For not thus do I stand with myself.*
> Ch. x. 1 *My soul is full of disgust with my life,*
> *Therefore I will freely utter my complaint;*

I will speak in the bitterness of my soul.
2 *I will say to Eloah : Condemn me not ;*
  Let me know wherefore Thou contendest with me !

The two Optatives, vers. 34 sq., as is frequently the case
with the Imper., are followed by the Cohortative as the conclusion (אֲדַבְּרָה, therefore will I speak ; whereas ואדברה might
be equivalent to, in order that I may speak) of a conditional
antecedent clause.   שֵׁבֶט is here the rod with which God
smites Job ; comp. ch. xiii. 21.   If God would only remove
his pain from him for a brief space, so that he might recover
himself for self-defence, and if He would not stifle his words
as they come freely forth from his lips by confronting him
with His overwhelming majesty, then he would fearlessly
express himself ; for " not thus am I in myself," *i.e.* I am not
conscious of such a moral condition as compels me to remain
dumb before Him.   However, we must inquire whether,
according to the context, this special reference and shade of
meaning is to be given to לֹא־כֵן.   There is a use of כֵן = nothing, when accompanied by a gesture expressive of contemptuous rejection, Num. xiii. 33 (כְּמוֹ־כֵן, Isa. li. 6, as nothing) ;[1]
and a use of לֹא־כֵן = not only so = not so small, so useless,
2 Sam. xxiii. 5, accompanied by a gesture expressive of the
denial of such contempt, according to which the present
passage may probably be explained : I am in myself, *i.e.*
according to the testimony of my conscience, not so, *i.e.* not
so morally worthless and devoid of right.

His self-consciousness makes him desire that the possibility
of answering for himself might be granted him ; and since he is
weary of life, and has renounced all claim for its continuance,

---

[1] In both these passages (to which Böttcher adds Ps. cxxvii. 2, " so
= without anything further "), כֵּן has been considered to be the sing. of
כַּנִּים, gnats ; but this sing. is an error, as בַּיִץ, formerly considered to be
the sing. of בֵּיצִים.   The respective sing. are בֵּיצָה, כִּנָּה.

he will at least give his complaints free course; and pray the Author of his sufferings that He would not permit him to die the death of the wicked, contrary to the testimony of his own conscience. נְקֹטָה is equivalent to נָקְטָה, Ezek. vi. 9, after the usual manner of the contraction of double *Ayin* verbs (Gen. xi. 6, 7; Isa. xix. 3; Judg. v. 5; Ezek. xli. 7; *vid.* Ges. § 67, rem. 11); it may nevertheless be derived directly from נָקַט, for this secondary verb formed from the *Niph.* נָקֹט is supported by the Aramaic. In like manner, in Gen. xvii. 11 perhaps a secondary verb נָמֵל, and certainly in Gen. ix. 19 and Isa. xxxiii. 3 a secondary verb נָפַץ (1 Sam. xiii. 11), formed from the *Niph.* נָפֹץ (Gen. x. 18), is to be supposed; for the contraction of the *Niphal* form נָקוֹמָה into נְקֹמָה is impossible; and the supposition which has been advanced, of a root פצץ = פוץ in the signification *diffundere, dissipare* is unnecessary. His soul is disgusted (*fastidio affecta est,* or *fastidit*) with his life, therefore he will give free course to his plaint (comp. ch. vii. 11). עָלַי is not *super* or *de me,* but, as ch. xxx. 16, *in me;* it belongs to the Ego, as an expression of spontaneity: I in myself, since the Ego is the subject, ὑποκείμενον, of his individuality (*Psychol.* S. 151 f.). The inner man is meant, which has the Ego over or in itself; from this the complaint shall issue forth as a stream without restraint; not, however, a mere gloomy lamentation over his pain, but a supplicatory complaint directed to God respecting the peculiar pang of his suffering, viz. this stroke which seems to come upon him from his Judge (רִיב, *seq. acc.,* as Isa. xxvii. 8), without his being conscious of that for which he is accounted guilty.

3 *Doth it please Thee when Thou oppressest,*
   That Thou rejectest the work of Thy hands,
   While Thou shinest upon the counsel of the wicked?
4 *Hast Thou eyes of flesh,*

Or seest Thou as a mortal seeth?

5 *Are Thy days as the days of a mortal,*
  Or Thy years as man's days,
6 *That Thou seekest after my iniquity,*
  And searchest after my sin?
7 *Although Thou knowest that I am not a wicked man,*
  And there is none that can deliver out of Thy hand.

There are three questions by which Job seeks to exhaust every possible way of accounting for his sufferings as coming from God. These attempts at explanation, however, are at once destroyed, because they proceed upon conceptions which are unworthy of God, and opposed to His nature. *Firstly,* Whether it gives Him pleasure (טוֹב, agreeable, as ch. xiii. 9) when He oppresses, when He despises, *i.e.* keeps down forcibly or casts from Him as hateful (מָאַס, as Ps. lxxxix. 39, Isa. liv. 6) the work of His hand ; while, on the contrary, He permits light to shine from above upon the design of the wicked, *i.e.* favours it ?　　Man is called the יְגִיעַ of the divine hands, as though he were elaborated by them, because at his origin (Gen. ii. 7), the continuation of which is the development in the womb (Ps. cxxxix. 15), he came into existence in a remarkable manner by the directly personal, careful, and, so to speak, skilful working of God. That it is the morally innocent which is here described, may be seen not only from the contrast (ver. 3c), but also from the fact that he only can be spoken of as oppressed and rejected. Moreover, " the work of Thy hands " involves a negative reply to the question. Such an unloving mood of self-satisfaction is contrary to the bounty and beneficence of that love to which man owes his existence. *Secondly,* Whether God has eyes of flesh, *i.e.* of sense, which regard only the outward appearance, without an insight into the inner nature, or whether He sees as mortals see, *i.e.* judges, κατὰ τὴν σάρκα (John viii. 15) ? Mercier correctly : *num ex facie judicas, ut affectibus ducaris more hominum.* This question also supplies its own negative ; it is based upon the thought that God looketh on the heart (1 Sam. xvi. 7). *Thirdly,* Whether His life is like to the brevity of man's life, so that He is not able to wait until a man's sin manifests itself, but must institute such a painful course of investigation with him, in order to extort from him as quickly as possible a confession of it ? Suffering appears here to be a means of inquisition, which is followed by the final judgment when the guilt is proved. What is added in ver. 7 puts this supposition aside also as inconceivable. Such a mode of proceeding may be conceived of in a mortal ruler, who, on account of his short-sightedness, seeks to bring about by severe measures that which was at first only conjecture, and who, from the apprehension that he may not witness that vengeance in which he delights, hastens forward the criminal process as much as possible, in order that his victim may not escape him. God, however, to whom belongs absolute knowledge and absolute power, would act thus, although, etc. עַל, although, notwithstanding (proceeding from the signification, besides, *insuper*), as ch. xvi. 17 (Isa. liii. 9), xxxiv. 6. God knows even from the first that he (Job) will not appear as a guilty person (רָשַׁע, as in ch. ix. 29) ; and however that may be, He is at all events sure of him, for nothing escapes the hand of God.

That operation of the divine love which is first echoed in " the labour of Thy hands," is taken up in the following strophe, and, as Job contemplates it, his present lot seems to him quite incomprehensible.

8 *Thy hands have formed and perfected me*
  Altogether round about, and Thou hast now swallowed
    me up!

9 *Consider now, that Thou hast perfected me as clay,*
   And wilt Thou turn me again into dust ?
10 *Hast Thou not poured me out as milk,*
    And curdled me as curd ?
11 *With skin and flesh hast Thou clothed me,*
    And Thou hast intertwined me with bones and sinews ;
12 *Life and favour Thou hast shown me,*
    And Thy care hath guarded my breath.

The development of the embryo was regarded by the
Israelitish Chokma as one of the greatest mysteries (Eccles.
xi. 5 ; 2 Macc. vii. 22 sq.). There are two poetical passages
which treat explicitly of this mysterious existence : this
strophe of the book of Job, and the Psalm by David, cxxxix.
13–16 (*Psychol.* S. 210). The assertion of Scheuchzer,
Hoffmann, and Oetinger, that these passages of Scripture
" include, and indeed go beyond, all recent *systemata genera-
tionis,*" attributes to Scripture a design of imparting instruction,—a purpose which is foreign to it. Scripture nowhere
attempts an analysis of the workings of nature, but only
traces them back to their final cause. According to the
view of Scripture, a creative act similar to the creation of
Adam is repeated at the origin of each individual ; and the
continuation of development according to natural laws is not
less the working of God than the creative planting of the
very beginning. Thy hands, says Job, have formed (עָצַב, to
cut, carve, fashion ; cognate are קָצַב, חָצַב, without the accompanying notion of toil, which makes this word specially appropriate, as describing the fashioning of the complicated nature
of man) and perfected me. We do not translate : made ; for
עָשָׂה stands in the same relation to בָּרָא and יָצַר as *perficere* to
creare and *fingere* (Gen. ii. 2 ; Isa. xliii. 7). יַחַד refers to the
members of the body collectively, and סָבִיב to the whole form.
The perfecting as clay implies three things : the earthiness

of the substance, the origin of man without his knowledge
and co-operation, and the moulding of the shapeless substance
by divine power and wisdom.   The primal origin of man, *de
limo terræ* (ch. xxxiii. 6; Ps. cxxxix. 15), is repeated in the
womb.   The figures which follow (ver. 10) describe this origin,
which being obscure is all the more mysterious, and glorifies
the power of God the more.   The *sperma* is likened to milk;
the הִתִּיךְ (used elsewhere of smelting), which Seb. Schmid
rightly explains *rem colliquatam fundere et immittere in for-
mam aliquam*, refers to the *nisus formativus* which dwells in
it.   The embryo which is formed from the *sperma* is likened
to גְּבִינָה, which means in all the Semitic dialects cheese
(curd).   "As whey" (Ewald, Hahn) is not suitable; whey
does not curdle; in making cheese it is allowed to run off
from the curdled milk.   "As cream" (Schlottm.) is not less
incorrect; cream is not *lac coagulatum*, which the word signifies.   The embryo forming itself from the *sperma* is like
milk which is curdled and beaten into shape.

The *consecutio temporum*, moreover, must be observed here.
It is, for example, incorrect to translate, with Ewald: Dost
Thou not let me flow away like milk, etc.   Job looks back
to the beginning of his life; the four clauses, vers. 10, 11,
under the control of the first two verbs (ver. 8), which influence the whole strophe, are also retrospective in meaning.
The *futt.* are consequently like synchronous *imperff.*; as, then,
ver. 12 returns to *perff.*, ver. 11 describes the development
of the embryo to the full-grown infant, on which Grotius
remarks: *Hic ordo est in genitura: primum pellicula fit,
deinde in ea caro, duriora paulatim accedunt*, and by ver. 12,
the manifestations of divine goodness, not only in the womb,
but from the beginning of life and onwards, are intended.
The expression "Life and favour (this combination does not
occur elsewhere) hast Thou done to me" is zeugmatic: He
has given him life, and sustained that life amidst constant

proofs of favour; His care has guarded the spirit (רוּחַ), by which his frame becomes a living and self-conscious being. This grateful retrospect is interspersed with painful reflections, in which Job gives utterance to his feeling of the contrast between the manifestation of the divine goodness which he had hitherto experienced and his present condition. As in ver. 8*b.*, וַתְּבַלְּעֵנִי, which Hirzel wrongly translates : and wilt now destroy me; it is rather : and hast now swallowed me up, *i.e.* drawn me down into destruction, as it were brought me to nought ; or even, if in the *fut. consec.*, as is frequently the case, the consecutive and not the aorist signification preponderates : and now swallowest me up ; and in ver. 9 (where, though not clear from the syntax, it is clear from the substance that תשיבני is not to be understood as an imperfect, like the *futt.* in vers. 10 sq.) : wilt Thou cause me to become dust again ? The same tone is continued in the following strophe. Thus graciously has he been brought into being, and his life sustained, in order that he may come to such a terrible end.

13 *And such Thou hast hidden in Thy heart,*
    I perceive that this was in Thy mind :
14 *If I should sin, Thou wouldst take note of it,*
    And not acquit me of my iniquity.
15 *If I should act wickedly, woe unto me !*
    And were I righteous, I should not lift up my head,
    Being full of shame and conscious of my misery.
16 *And were I to raise it, Thou wouldst hunt me as a lion,*
    And ever display on me Thy wondrous power,
17 *Thou wouldst ever bring fresh witnesses against me,*
    And increase Thy wrath against me,
    I should be compelled to withstand continuously advancing
    troops and a host.

This manifestation of divine goodness which Job has

experienced from the earliest existence seems to him, as he compares his present lot of suffering with it, to have served as a veil to a hidden purpose of a totally opposite character. That purpose—to make this life, which has been so graciously called into existence and guarded thus far, the object of the severest and most condemning visitation—is now manifest. Both אֵלֶּה and זֹאת refer to what is to follow ; זֹאת עִמָּךְ used of the thought conceived, the purpose cherished, as ch. xxiii. 14, xxvii. 11. All that follows receives a future colouring from this principal clause, "This is what Thou hadst designed to do," which rules the strophe. Thus ver. 14*a* is to be rendered : If I had sinned, Thou wouldst have kept me in remembrance, properly *custodies me*, which is here equivalent to *custoditurus eras me.* שָׁמַר, with the acc. of the person, according to Ps. cxxx. 3 (where it is followed by the acc. of the sin), is to be understood : to keep any one in remembrance, *i.e.* to mark him as sinful (Hirzel). This appears more appropriate than *rigide observaturus eras me* (Schlottm.). וּשְׁמַרְתַּנִי, according to Ges. § 121, 4, might be taken for וּשְׁמַרְתָּ לִי (viz. חֲטָאתִי); but this is unnecessary, and we have merely translated it thus for the sake of clearness. His infirmities must not be passed by unpunished ; and if he should act wickedly (רָשַׁע, of malignant sin, in distinction from חטא), woe unto him (comp. οἰαί μοι, 1 Cor. ix. 16). According to the construction referred to above, וְצָדַקְתִּי is *præt. hypotheticum* (Ges. § 155, 4, *a*) ; and the conclusion follows without *waw apodosis* : If I had acted rightly, I should not have raised my head, being full of shame and conscious of my misery. The adjectives are not in apposition to רֹאשִׁי (Böttcher), but describe the condition into which he would be brought, instead of being able (according to the ethical principle, Gen. iv. 7) to raise his head cheerfully. רְאֵה *constr.* of רָאֶה, as שְׂבַע of שָׂבֵעַ. It is needless, with Pisc., Hirz., Böttch., and Ewald, to alter it to רֹאֶה, since רָאֶה is a verbal adjective like קָשֶׁה, נָכֶה, יָפֶה. Moreover, וּרְאֵה

cannot be imperative (Rosenm., De Wette); for although
imperatives, joined by *waw* to sentences of a different construction, do occur (Ps. lxxvii. 2; 2 Sam. xxi. 3), such an
exclamation would destroy the connection and tone of the
strophe in the present case.

Ver. 16. יִגְאֶה is hypothetical, like וְצָדַקְתִּי, but put in the
future form, because referring to a voluntary act (Ewald,
§ 357, *b*) : and if it (the head) would (nevertheless) exalt
itself (גָּאָה, to raise proudly or in joyous self-consciousness),
then (without *waw apod.*, which is found in other passages,
e.g. ch. xxii. 28) Thou wouldst hunt me like a *shachal* (*vid.*
ch. iv. 10),—Job likens God to the lion (as Hos. v. 14, xiii. 7),
and himself to the prey which the lion pursues,—Thou wouldst
ever anew show Thyself wonderful at my expense (תָּשֹׁב, voluntative form, followed by a future with which it is connected
adverbially, Ges. § 142, 3, *b*; תִּתְפַּלָּא, with *â* in the last
syllable, although not in pause, as Num. xix. 12; Ewald,
§ 141, *c*.), *i.e.* wonderful in power, and inventive by ever new
forms of suffering, by which I should be compelled to repent
this haughtiness.   The witnesses (עֵדִים) that God continually
brings forth afresh against him are his sufferings (*vid.* ch. xvi.
8), which, while he is conscious of his innocence, declare him to
be a sinner; for Job, like the friends, cannot think of suffering and sin otherwise than as connected one with the other:
suffering is partly the result of sin, and partly it sets the mark
of sin on the man who is no sinner.   תֶּרֶב (*fut. apoc. Hiph.*
Ges. § 75, rem. 15) is also the voluntative form : Thou wouldst
multiply, increase Thy malignity against me.   עָם, *contra*, as
also in other passages with words denoting strife and war, ch.
xiii. 19, xxiii. 6, xxxi. 13; or where the context implies hostility, Ps. lv. 19, xciv. 16.   The last line is a clause by itself
consisting of nouns.   חֲלִיפוֹת וְצָבָא is considered by all modern
expositors as *hendiadys*, as Mercier translates : *impetor variis
et sibi succedentibus malorum agminibus;* and צָבָא is mostly

taken collectively. Changes and hosts = hosts continuously dispersing themselves, and always coming on afresh to the attack. But is not this form of expression unnatural? By חליפות Job means the advancing troops, and by צבא the main body of the army, from which they are reinforced; the former stands first, because the thought figuratively expressed in תחדש and חרב is continued (comp. ch. xix. 12): the enmity of God is manifested against him by ever fresh sufferings, which are added to the one chief affliction. Böttcher calls attention to the fact that all the lines from ver. 14 end in *i*, a rhythm formed by the inflection, which is also continued in ver. 18. This repetition of the pronominal suffix gives intensity to the impression that these manifestations of the divine wrath have special reference to himself individually.

18 *And wherefore hast Thou brought me forth out of the*
     womb?
     I should have expired, that no eye had seen me,
19 *I should have been as though I had never been,*
     Carried from the womb to the grave.
20 *Are not my days few? then cease*
     And turn from me, that I may become a little cheerful,
21 *Before I go to return no more*
     Into the land of darkness and of the shadow of death,
22 *The land of deep darkness like to midnight,*
     Of the shadow of death and of confusion,
     And which is bright like midnight.

The question Wherefore? ver. 18*a*, is followed by *futt.* as *modi conditionales* (Ges. § 127, 5) of that which would and should have happened, if God had not permitted him to be born alive: I should have expired, prop. I ought to have expired, being put back to the time of birth (comp. ch. iii. 13, where the *præt.* more objectively expressed what would then have happened). These *modi condit.* are continued in ver. 19:

I should have been (*sc.* in the womb) as though I had not
been (comp. the short elliptical[1] expression, Obad. ver. 16),
i.e. as one who had scarcely entered upon existence, and that
only of the earliest (as at conception); I should have been
carried (הוּבַל, as ch. xxi. 32) from the womb (without seeing
the light as one born alive) to the grave. This detestation
of his existence passes into the wish, ver. 20, that God would
be pleased at least somewhat to relieve him ere he is swallowed up by the night of Hades. We must neither with the
Targ. translate: are not my days few, and vanishing away?
nor with Oetinger: will not my fewness of days cease?
Both are contrary to the correct accentuation. Olshausen
thinks it remarkable that there is not a weaker pausal accent
to יָמַי; but such a one is really indirectly there, for *Munach*
is here equivalent to *Dechî*, from which it is formed (*vid.* the
rule in *Comm. über den Psalter*, ii. 504). Accordingly, Seb.
Schmid correctly translates: *nonne parum dies mei? ideo
cessa.* The *Keri* substitutes the precative form of expression
for the optative: cease then, turn away from me then (*imper.
consec.* with *waw* of the result, Ewald, § 235, *a*); comp. the
precative conclusion to the speech, ch. vii. 16 sqq., but there
is no real reason for changing the optative form of the text.
יָשִׁית (voluntative for יָשֵׁת, ch. ix. 33) may be supplemented
by ידו, פניו, עיניו, or לבו (ch. vii. 17) (not, however, with Hirz.,
שׁבטו, after ch. ix. 34, which is too far-fetched for the usage
of the language, or with Böttch., מחנהו, *copias suas*); שׁית can
however, like שׂים, ch. iv. 20, signify to turn one's self to, *se
disponere* = to attend to, consequently שׁית מן, to turn the
attention from, as שׁעה מן, ch. vii. 19, Ps. xxxix. 14 (where,
as here, ואבליגה follows).

He desires a momentary alleviation of his sufferings and

---

[1] כלא is there = לא כאשר, like ללא, Isa. lxv. 1 = לאשר לא [*vid.* Ges.
§ 123, 3], and כְ is used as a conjunction as little as לְ (*vid.* on Ps.
xxxviii. 14).

ease before his descent to Hades, which seems so near at hand. He calls Hades the land of darkness and of the shadow of death. צַלְמָוֶת, which occurs for the first time in the Old Testament in Ps. xxiii. 4, is made into a compound from צַלְמוּת, and is the proper word for the obscurity of the region of the dead, and is accordingly repeated later on. Further, he calls it the land of encircling darkness (עֵפָתָה, defective for עיפתה, from עוּף, *caligare*, and with *He parag.* intensive for עיפה, in Amos iv. 13, who also uses הבליג, ch. v. 9, in common with Job), like midnight darkness. אֹפֶל cannot mean merely the grey of twilight, it is the entire absence of sunlight, ch. iii. 6, xxviii. 3, Ps. xci. 6 ; comp. Ex. x. 22, where the Egyptian darkness is called חשׁך אפלה. Böttch. correctly compares אפל and נפל : *mersa ad imum h.e. profunda nox* (the advancing night). Still further he calls it (the land) of the shadow of death, and devoid of order (סְדָרִים, ἅπ. λεγ. in the Old Testament, but a common word in the later Hebrew), *i.e.* where everything is so encompassed by the shadow of death that it seems a chaos, without any visible or distinct outline. It is difficult to determine whether וַתֹּפַע is to be referred to ארץ : and which lights (*fut. consec.* as the accent on the *penult.* indicates, the syntax like ch. iii. 21, 23, Isa. lvii. 3) ; or is to be taken as neuter : and it shines there (= and where it shines) like midnight darkness. Since הופיע (from יפע = ופע, to rise, shine forth ; *vid.* on Ps. xcv. 4), as also האיר, does not occur elsewhere as neuter, we prefer, with Hirzel, to refer it to ארץ, as being more certain. Moreover, אפל is here evidently the intensest darkness, *ipsum medullitium umbræ mortis ejusque intensissimum*, as Oetinger expresses it. That which is there called light, *i.e.* the faintest degree of darkness, is like the midnight of this world ; " not light, but darkness visible," as Milton says of hell.

In this speech (ch. ix. x.) Job for the first time assents to the principle on which the attack of the friends is founded.

It is primarily directed against Bildad, but applies also to Eliphaz, for the two hold the same opinion. Therefore, because in the first part of the speech Job does not expressly address him or all the friends, it cannot, with Ewald, be said that it bears the characteristics of a soliloquy. To ch. ix. 28 Job inclines towards the friends; and when he afterwards addresses God, all that he says to God is affected by the manner in which the friends have advanced against him.

The maxim of the friends is: God does not pervert right, *i.e.* He deals justly in all that He does. They conclude from this, that no man, no sufferer, dare justify himself: it is his duty to humble himself under the just hand of God. Job assents to all this, but his assent is mere sarcasm at what they say. He admits that everything that God does is right, and must be acknowledged as right; not, however, because it is right in itself, but because it is the act of the absolute God, against whom no protest uttered by the creature, though with the clearest conviction of innocence, can avail. Job separates goodness from God, and regards that which is part of His very being as a product of His arbitrary will. What God says and does must be true and right, even if it be not true and right in itself. The God represented by the friends is a God of absolute justice; the God of Job is a God of absolute power. The former deals according to the objective rule of right; the latter according to a freedom which, because removed from all moral restraint, is pure caprice.

How is it that Job entertains such a cheerless view of the matter? The friends, by the strong view which they have taken up, urge him into another extreme. On their part, they imagine that in the justice of God they have a principle which is sufficient to account for all the misfortunes of mankind, and Job's in particular. They maintain, with respect to mankind in general (Eliphaz by an example from his own observation, and Bildad by calling to his aid the wisdom of the ancients), that the ungodly, though prosperous for a time, come to a fearful end; with respect to Job, that his affliction is a just chastisement from God, although designed for his good. Against the one assertion Job's own experience of life rebels; against the other his consciousness rises up with indignation. Job's observation is really as correct as that of the friends; for the history of the past and of the present furnishes as many illustrations of judgments which have suddenly come upon the godless in the height of their prosperity, as of general visitations in which the innocent have suffered with the guilty, by whom these judgments have been incurred. But with regard to his misfortune, Job cannot and ought not to look at it from the standpoint of the divine justice. For the proposition, which we will give in the words of Brentius, *quidquid post fidei justificationem pio acciderit, innocenti accidit,* is applicable to our present subject.

If, then, Job's suffering were not so severe, and his faith so powerfully shaken, he would comfort himself with the thought that the divine ways are unsearchable; since, on the one hand, he cannot deny the many traces of the justice of the divine government in the world (he does not deny them even here), and on the other hand, is perplexed by the equally numerous incongruities of human destiny with the divine justice. (This thought is rendered more consolatory to us by the revelation which we possess of the future life; although even in the later Old Testament times the last judgment is referred to as the adjustment of all these incongruities; *vid.* the conclusion of Ecclesiastes.) His own lot might have remained always inexplicable to him, without his being obliged on that account to lose the consciousness of the divine love, and that faith like Asaph's, which, as Luther says, struggles towards God through wrath and disfavour, as through thorns, yea, even through spears and swords.

Job is passing through conflict and temptation. He does not perceive the divine motive and purpose of his suffering, nor has he that firm and unshaken faith which will keep him from mistaken views of God, although His dispensations are an enigma to him ; but, as his first speech (ch. iii.) shows, he is tormented by thoughts which form part of the conflict of temptation. The image of the gracious God is hidden from him, he feels only the working of the divine wrath, and asks, Wherefore doth God give light to the suffering ones ?—a question which must not greatly surprise us, for, as Luther says, "There has never been any one so holy that he has not been tormented with this *quare, quare*, Wherefore? wherefore should it be so?" And when the friends, who know as little as Job himself about the right solution of this mystery, censure him for his inquiry, and think that in the propositions : man has no righteousness which he can maintain before God, and God does not pervert the right, they have found the key to the mystery, the conflict becomes fiercer for Job, because the justice of God furnishes him with no satisfactory explanation of his own lot, or of the afflictions of mankind generally. The justice of God, which the friends consider to be sufficient to explain everything that befalls man, Job can only regard as the right of the Supreme Being ; and while it appears to the friends that every act of God is controlled by His justice, it seems to Job that whatever God does *must* be right, by virtue of His absolute power.

This principle, devoid of consolation, drives Job to the utterances so unworthy of him, that, in spite of his conviction of his innocence, he must appear guilty before God, because he must be speechless before His terrible majesty,—that if, however, God would only for once so meet him that he could fearlessly address Him, he would know well enough how to defend himself (ch. ix.). After these utterances of his feeling, from which all consciousness of the divine love is absent, he puts forth the touching prayer : Condemn me not without letting me know why Thou dost condemn me! (ch. x. 1–7.) As he looks back, he is obliged to praise God, as his Creator and Preserver, for what He has hitherto done for him (ch. x. 8–12); but as he thinks of his present condition, he sees that from the very beginning God designed to vent His wrath upon him, to mark his infirmities, and to deprive him of all joy in the consciousness of his innocence (ch. x. 13–17). He is therefore compelled to regard God as his enemy, and this thought overpowers the remembrance of the divine goodness. If, however, God were his enemy, he might well ask, Wherefore then have I come into being? And while he writhes as a worm crushed beneath the almighty power of God, he prays that God would let him alone for a season ere he passes away into the land of darkness, whence there is no return (x. 18–22).

Brentius remarks that this speech of Job contains *inferni blasphemias*, and explains them thus : *non enim in tanto judicii horrore Deum patrem, sed carnificem sentit;* but also adds, that in passages like ch. x. 8–12 faith raises its head even in the midst of judgment; for when he praises the mercies of God, he does so *spiritu fidei*, and these he would not acknowledge were there not a *fidei scintilla* still remaining. This is true. The groundwork of Job's faith remains even in the fiercest conflict of temptation, and is continually manifest; we should be unable to understand the book unless we could see this *fidei scintilla*, the extinction of which would be the accomplishment of Satan's design against him, glimmering everywhere through the speeches of Job. The unworthy thoughts he entertains of God, which Brentius calls *inferni blasphemias*, are nowhere indulged to such a length that Job charges God with being his enemy, although he fancies Him to be an enraged foe. In spite of the imagined enmity of

God against him, Job nowhere goes so far as to declare
enmity on his part against God, so far as ברך אלהים. He
does not turn away from God, but inclines to Him in prayer.
His soul is filled with adoration of God, and with reverence
of His power and majesty; he can clearly discern God's
marvellous works in nature and among men, and His creative
power and gracious providence, the workings of which he has
himself experienced. But that mystery, which the friends
have made still more mysterious, has cast a dark cloud over
his vision, so that he can no longer behold the loving countenance of God. His faith is unable to disperse this cloud,
and so he sees but one side of the divine character—His
Almightiness. Since he consequently looks upon God as the
Almighty and the Wrathful One, his feeling alternately
manifests itself under two equally tragical phases. At one
time he exalts himself in his consciousness of the justice of
his cause, to sink back again before the majesty of God, to
whom he must nevertheless succumb; at another time his
feeling of self-confidence is overpowered by the severity of
his suffering, and he betakes himself to importunate supplication.

It is true that Job, so long as he regards his sufferings as
a dispensation of divine judgment, is as unjust towards God
as he believes God to be unjust towards him; but if we bear
in mind that this state of conflict and temptation does not
preclude the idea of a temporal withdrawal of faith, and
that, as Baumgarten (*Pentat.* i. 209) aptly expresses it, the
profound secret of prayer is this, that man can prevail with
the Divine Being, then we shall understand that this dark
cloud need only be removed, and Job again stands before the
God of love as His saint.

Zophar's First Speech.—Chap. xi.

Schema: 11. 6. 6. 6. 11.

[Then began Zophar the Naamathite, and said:]
2 Shall the torrent of words remain unanswered,
  And shall the prater be in the right?
3 Shall thy vain talking silence the people,
  So that thou mockest without any one putting thee to shame,
4 And sayest: my doctrine is pure,
  And I am guiltless in Thine eyes?
5 But oh that Eloah would speak,
  And open His lips against thee,
6 And make known to thee the secrets of wisdom,
  That she is twofold in her nature—
  Know then that Eloah forgetteth much of thy guilt.

When Job has concluded his long speech, Zophar, the third and most impetuous of the friends, begins. His name, if it is to be explained according to the Arabic Esauitish name *el-assfar*,[1] signifies the yellow one (*flavedo*), and the name of the place whence he comes, pleasantness (*amœnitas*). The very beginning of his speech is impassioned. He calls Job's speech רֹב דְּבָרִים, a multitude of words (besides here, Prov. x. 19, Eccles. v. 2), and asks whether he is to remain unanswered; לֹא יֵעָנֶה, *responsum non feret*, from נַעֲנָה, not in the sense of being humbled, but: to be answered (of the suppliant: to be heard = to receive an answer). He calls Job אִישׁ שְׂפָתַיִם, a prater (distinct from אִישׁ דברים, a ready speaker, Ex. iv. 10), who is not in the right, whom one must not allow to have the last word. The questions, ver. 2, are followed by another which is not denoted by the sign of a question, but is only known by the accent: Shall not thy בַּדִּים, meaningless speeches (from בדד = בטא, βαττολογεῖν),

[1] *Vid.* Abulfeda's *Historia anteislamica* ed. *Fleischer*, p. 168.

put men (מְתִים, like other archaisms, e.g. תֵּבֵל, always without
the article) to silence, so that thou darest mock without any
one making thee ashamed, i.e. leading thee on ad absurdum?
Thou darest mock God (Hirzel) ; better Rosenmüller : nos et
Deum.   The mockery here meant is that which Zophar has
heard in Job's long speech ; mockery at his opponents, in the
belief that he is right because they remain silent.   The futt.
consec., vers. 3 sq., describe the conduct of Job which results
from this absence of contradiction.   Zophar, in ver. 4, does
not take up Job's own words, but means, that one had better
have nothing more to do with Job, as he would some day say
and think so and so, he would consider his doctrine blameless,
and himself in relation to God pure.   לֶקַח occurs only here in
this book ; it is a word peculiar to the book of Proverbs (also
only Deut. xxxii. 2, Isa. xxix. 24), and properly signifies the
act of appropriating, then that which is presented for appro-
priation, i.e. for learning : the doctrine (similar to שמועה, the
hearing, ἀκοή, and then the discourse) ; we see from the
words "my doctrine is pure," which Zophar puts into the
mouth of Job, that the controversy becomes more and more
a controversy respecting known principles.

Ver. 5. With ואולם, verum enim vero, Zophar introduces
his wish that God himself would instruct Job ; this would
most thoroughly refute his utterances.   מי יתן is followed by
the infin., then by futt., vid. Ges. § 136, 1 ; כִּפְלַיִם (only here
and Isa. xl. 2) denotes not only that which is twice as great,
but generally that which far surpasses something else.   The
subject of the clause beginning with כִּי is הִיא understood, i.e.
divine wisdom : that she is the double with respect to (לְ, as
e.g. 1 Kings x. 23) reality (תוּשִׁיה, as ch. v. 12, vi. 13, essentia,
substantia), i.e. in comparison with Job's specious wisdom and
philosophism.   Instead of saying : then thou wouldst perceive,
Zophar, realizing in his mind that which he has just wished,
says imperiously וְדַע (an imper. consec., or, as Ewald, § 345, b,

calls it, *imper. futuri*, similar to Gen. xx. 7, 2 Sam. xxi. 3) : thou must then perceive that God has dealt far more leniently with thee than thou hast deserved. The causative הִשָּׁה (in Old Testament only this passage, and ch. xxxix. 17) denotes here *oblivioni dare*, and the מן of מֵעֲוֹנֶךָ is partitive.

> 7 *Canst thou find out the nature of Eloah,*
>   *And penetrate to the foundation of the existence of the*
>   *Almighty ?*
> 8 *It is as the heights of heaven—what wilt thou do ?*
>   *Deeper than Hades—what canst thou know ?*
> 9 *The measure thereof is longer than the earth,*
>   *And broader than the sea.*

The majority of modern commentators erroneously translate חֵקֶר searching = comprehension, and תַּכְלִית perfection, a meaning which this word never has. The former, indeed, signifies first in an active sense : finding out by search ; and then also objectively : the object sought after : " the hidden ground" (Ewald), the depth (here and ch. xxxviii. 16 ; also, according to Ew., ch. viii. 8, of the deep innermost thought). The latter denotes penetrating to the extreme, and then the extreme, πέρας, itself (ch. xxvi. 10, xxviii. 3). In other words: the nature that underlies that which is visible as an object of search is called חקר; and the extreme of a thing, *i.e.* the end, without which the beginning and middle cannot be understood, is called תכלית. The nature of God may be sought after, but cannot be found out ; and the end of God is unattainable, for He is both : the Perfect One, *absolutus ;* and the Endless One, *infinitus.*

Vers. 8, 9. The feminine form of expression has reference to the divine wisdom (*Chokma*, ver. 6), and amplifies what is there said of its transcendent reality. Its absoluteness is described by four dimensions, like the absoluteness of the love which devised the plan for man's redemption (Eph. iii.

18).   The pronoun הִיא, with reference to this subject of the sentence, must be supplied.   She is as "the heights of heaven" (comp. on *subst. pro adj.* ch. xxii. 12); what wilt or canst thou do in order to scale that which is high as heaven?   In ver. 9*b* we have translated according to the reading מִדָּהּ with *He mappic.*   This feminine construction is a contraction for מִדָּתָהּ, as ch. v. 13, עֲרֹמִם for עֲרֹמֵתֶם; Zech. iv. 2, גֹּלָה for גֻּלָּתָהּ, and more syncopated forms of a like kind (*vid. Comm. über den Psalter,* i. 225, ii. 172).   The reading recorded by the Masora is, however, מִדָּה with *He raph.,* according to which the word seems to be the accusative used adverbially; nevertheless the separation of this *acc. relativus* from its *regens* by the insertion of a word between them (comp. ch. xv. 10) would make a difficulty here where הִיא is wanting, and consequently מדה seems to signify *mensura ejus* whichever way it may be written (since *ah raphe* is also sometimes a softened form of the suffix, ch. xxxi. 22; Ewald, § 94, *b*).   The wisdom of God is in its height altogether inaccessible, in its depth fathomless and beyond research, in its length unbounded, in its breadth incomprehensible, stretching out far beyond all human thought.

> 10 *When He passes by and arrests*
> *And calls to judgment, who will oppose Him?*
> 11 *For He knoweth the men devoid of principle,*
> *And seeth wickedness without observing it.*
> 12 *But before an empty head gaineth understanding,*
> *A wild ass would become a man.*

In יַחֲלֹף God is conceived as one who manifests himself by passing to and fro in the powers of nature (in the whirlwind, Isa. xxi. 1).   Should He meet with one who is guilty, and seize and bring him to judgment, who then (*waw apod.*) will turn Him back, *i.e.* restrain Him?   הקהיל is used of bringing to judgment, with reference to the ancient form of trial which was in public, and in which the carrying out of the sentence was partly incumbent on the people (1 Kings xxi. 9 ; Ezek. xvi. 40, xxiii. 46). One might almost imagine that Zophar looks upon himself and the other two friends as forming such an " assembly :" they cannot justify him in opposition to God, since He accounts him guilty. God's mode of trial is summary, because infallible : He knows altogether מְתֵי שָׁוְא, people who hypocritically disguise their moral nothingness (on this idea, *vid.* on Ps. xxvi. 4) ; and sees (looks through) אָוֶן (from the root *ân*, to breathe), otherwise grief, with which one pants, in a moral sense worthlessness, without any trace whatever of worth or substance. He knows and sees this moral wretchedness at once, and need not first of all reflect upon it : *non opus habet*, as Abenezra has correctly explained, *ut diu consideret* (comp. the like thought, ch. xxxiv. 23).

Ver. 12 has been variously misinterpreted. Gesenius in his *Handwörterbuch*[1] translates : but man is empty and void of understanding ; but this is contrary to the accentuation, according to which אִישׁ נבוב together form the subject. Olshausen translates better : an empty man, on the other hand, is without heart ; but the *fut.* cannot be exactly so used, and if we consider that *Piel* has never properly a privative meaning, though sometimes a privative idea (as *e.g.* סִקֵּל, *operam consumere in lapidos, scil. ejiciendos*), we must regard a privative *Niphal* as likewise inadmissible. Stickel translates peculiarly : the man devoid of understanding is enraged against God ; but this is opposed to the manifest correlation of נבוב and יִלָּבֵב, which does not indicate the antithesis of an empty and sulky person (Böttcher) : the former rather signifies empty, and the latter to acquire heart or marrow (Heidenheim, יקנה לב), so that לב fills up the hollow space. Hirzel's rendering partly bears out the requirement of this correlation : man has under-standing like a hollow pate ; but this explanation, like that of Gesenius, violates the accentuation, and produces an affected witticism. The explanation which regards ver. 12 as descrip-tive of the wholesome effect of the discipline of the divine judgments (comp. Isa. xxvi. 9) is far better; it does not violate the accent, and moreover is more in accordance with the future form : the empty one becomes discerning thereby, the rough, humane (thus recently Ewald, Heiligst., Schlottm.); but according to this explanation, ver. 12 is not connected with what immediately precedes, nor is the peculiarity of the expression fully brought out. Hupfeld opens up another way of interpreting the passage when he remarks, *nil dicto facilius et simplicius;* he understands 12a according to 12b: But man is furnished with an empty heart, *i.e.* receives at his birth an empty undiscerning heart, and man is born as a wild ass's colt, *i.e.* as stupid and obstinate. This thought is satisfac-torily connected with the preceding; but here also נבוב is taken as predicate in violation of the accentuation, nor is justice done to the correlation above referred to, and the whole sen-tence is referred to the portion of man at his birth, in opposi-tion to the impression conveyed by the use of the *fut.* Oehler appears to us to have recognised the right sense : But an empty man is as little endowed with sense, as that a wild ass should ever be born as man—be, so to speak, born again and become a man.[1]

The *waw* in וְעַיִר is just like ch. v. 7, xii. 11, and brings into

[1] Wetzstein explains: " But a man that barks like a dog (*i.e.* rages shamelessly) can become sensible, and a young wild ass (*i.e.* the wildest and roughest creature) be born again as a man (*i.e.* become gentle and civilised)," from נבב = נבח, since נבח is the commoner word for " bark-ing " in the Syrian towns and villages, and נבב, on the other hand, is used among those who dwelt in tents. But we must then point it נָבוּב, and the antithesis יְלֻבַּב is more favourable to the Hebrew meaning, " hollowed out, empty."

close connection the things that are to be compared, as in the form of emblematic proverbs (*vid.* Herzog's *Real Encyklopädie*, xiv. 696) : the one will happen not earlier than, and as little as, the other. The *Niphal* נוֹלָד, which in Prov. xvii. 17 signifies to become manifest, here borders on the notion of *regenerari*; a regeneration would be necessary if the wild ass should become human,—a regeneration which is inconceivable. It is by nature refractory, and especially when young (עַיִר from عار *fut. i* in the signification *vagari, huc illuc discurrere*, of a young, restless, wild, frisking animal). Just so, says Zophar, the vacuum in an empty man is incapable of being filled up,—a side hit at Job, which rebounds on Zophar himself; for the dogma of the friends, which forms the sole contents of their hollowness, can indeed not fill with brightness and peace a heart that is passing through conflict. The peculiarity of the expression is no longer unintelligible; Zophar is the most impassioned of the three friends.

13 *But if thou wilt direct thy heart,*
       And spread out thy hands to Him—
14 *If there is evil in thy hand, put it far away,*
       And let not wickedness dwell in thy tents—
15 *Then indeed canst thou lift up thy face without spot,*
       And shalt be firm without fearing.

The phrase הֵכִין לֵב signifies neither to raise the heart (Ewald), nor to establish it (Hirz.), but to direct it, *i.e.* give it the right direction (Ps. lxxviii. 8) towards God, 1 Sam. vii. 3, 2 Chron. xx. 33; it has an independent meaning, so that there is no need to supply אֶל־אֵל, nor take וּפָרַשְׂתָּ to be for לִפְרֹשׂ (after the construction in 2 Chron. xxx. 19). To spread out the hands in prayer is פָּרַשׂ; (פֵּרֵשׂ) כַּפַּיִם ידים is seldom used instead of the more artistic כַּפִּים, *palmas, h.e. manus supinas.* The conditional antecedent clause is immediately followed, ver. 14, by a similarly conditional parenthetical clause, which inserts the indispensable condition of acceptable prayer; the conclusion might begin with הַרְחִיקֵהוּ : when thou sendest forth thy heart and spreadest out thy hands to Him, if there is wickedness in thy hand, put it far away; but the antecedent requires a promise for its conclusion, and the more so since the *præt.* and *fut.* which follow אִם, ver. 13, have the force of *futt. exact.*: *si disposueris et extenderis*, to which the conclusion: put it far away, is not suited, which rather expresses a preliminary condition of acceptable prayer. The conclusion then begins with כִּי־אָז, then indeed, like ch. viii. 6, xiii. 19, comp. vi. 3, with כִּי עַתָּה, now indeed; the causal signification of כי has in both instances passed into the confirmatory (comp. 1 Sam. xiv. 44, Ps. cxviii. 10–12, cxxviii. 2, and on Gen. xxvi. 22): then verily wilt thou be able to raise thy countenance (without being forced to make any more bitter complaints, as ch. x. 15 sq.), without spot, *i.e.* not: without bodily infirmity, but: without spot of punishable guilt, *sceleris et pœnæ* (Rosenmüller). מִן here signifies without (Targ. דְּלָא), properly: far from, as ch. xxi. 9, 2 Sam. i. 22, Prov. xx. 3. Faultless will he then be able to look up and be firm (מֻצָק from יָצַק, according to Ges. § 71), *quasi ex ære fusus* (1 Kings vii. 16), one whom God can no longer get the better of.

16   *For thou shalt forget thy grief,*
      Shalt remember it as waters that flow by.
17   *And thy path of life shall be brighter than mid-day;*
      If it be dark, it shall become as morning.
18   *And thou shalt take courage, for now there is hope;*
      And thou shalt search, thou shalt lie down in safety.
19   *And thou liest down without any one making thee afraid;*
      And many shall caress thy cheeks.
20   *But the eyes of the wicked languish,*
      And refuge vanisheth from them,
      And their hope is the breathing forth of the soul.

The grief that has been surmounted will then leave no trace in the memory, like water that flows by (not : water that flows away, as Olshausen explains it, which would be differently expressed; comp. ch. xx. 28 with 2 Sam. xiv. 14). It is not necessary to change כִּי אַתָּה into כִּי עַתָּה (Hirzel); אתה, as in ver. 13, strengthens the force of the application of this conclusion of his speech. Life (חֶלֶד, from חָלַד to glide away, slip, *i.e.* pass away unnoticed,[1] as αἰών, both life-time, Ps. xxxix. 6, and the world, Ps. xlix. 2, here in the former sense), at the end of which thou thoughtest thou wert already, and which seemed to thee to run on into dismal darkness, shall be restored to thee (יקום with *Munach* on the *ult.* as ch. xxxi. 14, not on the *penult.*) brighter than noon-day (מִן, more than, *i.e.* here : brighter than, as *e.g.* Mic. vii. 4, more thorny than) ; and be it ever so dark, it shall become like morning. Such must be the interpretation of תָּעֻפָה. It cannot be a substantive, for it has the accent on the *penult. ;* as a substantive it must have been pointed תְּעוּפָה (after the form תְּקוּמָה, תְּעוּדָה, and the like). It is one of the few examples of the paragogic strengthened voluntative in the third pers., like Ps. xx. 4, Isa. v. 19[2] (Ges. § 48, 3) ; the cohortative form of the future is used with or without אִם (*vid.* on Ps. lxxiii. 16) in hypothetical antecedent clauses (Ges. § 128, 1). Translate therefore : should it become dark (accordingly correctly accented with *Rebia mugrasch*), from עוּף, to envelope one's self, to darken

---

[1] *Vid.* Hupfeld on Ps. xvii. 14, and on the other hand Böttcher, *infer.* § 275 s., who, taking חלד in the sense of rooting into, translates : " the mildew springs up more brilliant than mid-day." But whatever judgment one may form of the primary idea of חָלַד, this meaning of חֶלֶד is too imaginary.

[2] In other instances, as תָּרֹנָּה, Prov. i. 20, viii. 3, and וַתַּעְגְּבָה, Ezek. xxiii. 20, the *ah* is not the cohortative form, but either paragogic without special meaning or (so that the *fut.* has a double feminine form) a feminine termination, as is evident in ch. xxii. 21, where the *ah* is combined with the inflection.

(whence עֲפָתָה, ch. x. 22), not : shouldst thou become dark
(Schlottm.).   The feminine forms are instead of the neuter,
like תַּמְטִיר, it rains, Amos iv. 7 ; חָשְׁכָה, it becomes dark, Mic.
iii. 6 (Ges. § 137, 2).

The *fut.* is followed by *perff. consecutiva* in ver. 18 : And
thou shalt take confidence, for there is ground for hope for
thee ; יֵשׁ, with the force of real and lasting existence.   וְחָפַרְתָּ
is also *perf. consec.*, and is rightly accented as such.   If it were
to be interpreted *et si erubueris pudore tranquille cubabis*, it
would require the accent on the *penult.*, since it would be a
perf. hypotheticum.   But although the seeming antithesis of
וחפרת and לבטח (comp. ch. vi. 20) appears to favour this
interpretation, it is nevertheless inadmissible, since it introduces a sadness into the promise: granted that thou shouldest
be put to shame at this or that prospect ; whereas, if חפר be
taken in the sense of *scrutari*, as it is used by our poet (ch.
iii. 21, xxxix. 29) (not with Böttch., who comp. Eccles. v. 11,
in the signification *fodere* = to labour in the field, in which
meaning it is not common), the tone of sadness is removed,
and the accentuation is duly observed : and thou shalt search
about (*i.e.* examine the state of thy household, which is expressed by וּפָקַדְתָּ in ch. v. 24), thou shalt lay thyself down in
peace (*i.e.* because thou findest everything in a prosperous
condition, and hast no anxiety).   This feeling of security
against every harm that may befall one's person or property,
gained from trust in God, is expressed (ver. 19*a*) under the
figure of the peaceful situation of a herd when removed from
danger,—a figure which is borrowed from Lev. xxvi. 6, and
is frequently repeated in the prophets (Isa. xvii. 2 ; Zeph. iii.
13).   The promises of Zophar culminate in a future exaltation which shall command reverence and inspire trust : *et
mulcebunt faciem tuam multi.* חִלָּה פְּנֵי, to approach any one in
humble entreaty, generally used in reference to God ; less
frequently, as here and Ps. xlv. 13, Prov. xix. 6, in reference

to men in high positions. The end of the wicked, on the other hand, is told in ver. 20. Zophar here makes use of the choicest expressions of the style of the prophetic psalms : כָּלָה, otherwise frequently used of those who pine away with longing, here and ch. xvii. 5 of eyes that languish with unsatisfied longing ; מִנְהֶם (Aram. מִנְהֹון), poetic for מֵהֶם ; מַפַּח נֶפֶשׁ, after the phrase נָפַח נֶפֶשׁ, he breathes forth his soul (Jer. xv. 9, comp. Job xxxi. 39). The meaning is not that death is their only hope, but that every expectation remains unfulfilled ; giving up the ghost is that whither all their disappointed hopes tend.

That Zophar, in the mind of the poet, is the youngest of the three speakers, may be concluded from his introducing him last of all, although he is the most impetuous. Zophar manifests a still greater inability than the other two to bring Job to a right state of mind. His standpoint is the same as that of the others; like them, he regards the retributive justice of God as the principle on which alone the divine government in the world is exercised, and to which every act of this government is to be attributed, and it may indeed be assumed to be at work even when the relation of circumstances is mysterious and impenetrably dark to us. This limited view which the friends take of the matter readily accounts for the brevity of their speeches in comparison with Job's. This one *locus communis* is their only theme, which they reiterate constantly in some new and modified form ; while the mind of Job is an exhaustless fountain of thought, suggested by the direct experiences of the past. Before the present dispensation of suffering came upon Job, he enjoyed the peace of true godliness, and all his thoughts and feelings were under the control of a consciousness, made certain by his experience, that God makes himself known to those who fear Him. Now, however, his nature, hitherto kept in subjection by divine grace, is let loose in him; the powers of doubt, mistrust, impatience, and despondency have risen up; his inner life is fallen into the anarchy of conflict; his mind, hitherto peaceful and well-disciplined, is become a wild chaotic confusion; and hence his speeches, in comparison with those of the friends, are as roaring cataracts to small confined streams. But in this chaos lie the elements of a new creation; the harsh pertinacity with which the friends maintain their one dogma only tends to give an impulse to it. The new truth, the solution of the mystery, springs from this spiritual battle Job has to fight, from which, although not scathless, he still shall come forth as conqueror.

When, therefore, Zophar regards the speeches of Job, which are the involuntary expression of the severity of his conflict, as a torrent of words, he shows that from the haughty elevation of his narrow dogma he does not understand this form of experience; and when he reproaches Job by saying, Whoever can babble so much shows that he is not in the right, he makes use of a maxim which is true enough in itself, but its application to Job proceeds from the most uncharitable misconstruction of his suffering friend. As he looks upon Job, who, in the midst of his fierce conflict, struggles after comfort, but thrusts away all false consolation, he regards him as a cavilling opponent because he cuts the knot instead of untying it. He is so blinded by the idea that he is in possession of the key to the mystery, that he malignantly reproaches Job with being an incorrigible " empty-pate." As though there could be hollowness where there is a heart that seethes like metal in the refiner's crucible; and as though the dogma of the friends, which forms the sole contents of their hollowness, could possibly impart light and peace to a heart so sorely troubled!

Is the dogma of the friends, then, so pure a doctrine (לקח זך) as that which, according to Zophar's words, Job claims for himself? On Zophar's side it is maintained that

God always acts in accordance with justice, and Job maintains that God does not always so act. The maxim of the friends is false in the exclusiveness with which they maintain it ; the conclusion to which they are urged gives evidence of the fallacy of the premises : they must condemn Job, and consequently become unjust, in order to rescue the justice of God. Job's maxim, on the other hand, is true ; but it is so unconnected as it stands, that it may be turned over any moment and changed into a falsehood. For that God does not act everywhere as the Just One is a truth, but that He sometimes acts unjustly is blasphemy. Between these two Job hangs in suspense. For the stedfast consciousness of his innocence proves to him that God does not always act as the Just One ; shall he therefore suppose that God deals unjustly with him? From this blasphemous inversion of his maxim, Job seeks refuge in the absolute power of God, which makes that just which is unjust according to the clearest *human* consciousness. This is the feeble thread on which Job's piety hangs. Should this be cut, it would be all over with him. The friends do their best to cut it in twain. Zophar's speech is like a sword-thrust at it.

For while Eliphaz and Bildad with cautious gentleness describe suffering more as chastisement than as punishment, Zophar proceeds more boldly, and demands of Job that he should humble himself, as one who has incurred punishment from God. Of sin on Job's part which may have called down the divine judgment, Zophar knows as little as Job himself. But he wishes that God would grant Job some revelation of His infinite wisdom, since he refuses to humble himself. Then he would confess his folly, and see that God not only does not punish him unjustly, but even allows much of his guilt to go unpunished. Job is therefore to turn penitently to God, and to put away that evil which is the cause of his suffering, in order that he may be heard. Then

shall his hopeless condition become bright with hope ; whereas,
on the other hand, the downfall of the wicked is beyond
recovery.   Ewald aptly remarks that thus even the concluding words of the speeches of the friends are always somewhat
equivocal.   " Eliphaz just adds a slight caution, Bildad introduces the contrast in a few words, and Zophar adds but a
word ; all these seem to be as the forerunners of a multitude
of similar harsh threatenings, ch. xv. xviii. xx."

What impression will this harsh treatment of Zophar's
produce on Job ?   Job is to humble himself as a sinner who
is undergoing the punishment of his sin, though the measure
of it is far below the degree of his guilt ; and while he does
not deny his sinful weaknesses, he is nevertheless convinced
that he is righteous, and having as such experienced the
favour of God, cannot become an object of punishment.
Brentius discriminatingly observes here : *Videntur et Sophar et
reliqui amici Hiob prorsus ignorare quid sit aut efficiat Evan-
gelion et fides in promissionem Dei; sic argumentantur contra
Hiobem, quasi nullus unquam possit coram Deo fide justificari.*
The language is rather too much in accordance with the light
of the New Testament ; but it is true that the friends know
nothing whatever of the condition of a truly righteous man,
over whom the law with its curse, or the retributive justice
of God, has no power.   The interpretation of affliction in
accordance with the recognition of this principle is strange to
them ; and this is just the issue which is developed by the
drama in the case of Job—the idea which comes to light in
the working out of the plot.   Even Job does not perceive
the solution of the mystery, but, in the midst of the conflict,
is in a state of ignorance which excites compassion ; the
ignorance of the friends arising from their shallowness of
understanding, on the contrary, creates aversion.   When
Zophar, therefore, wishes that God would grant Job some
revelation of His infinite wisdom, it is indeed true that Job

is greatly in need of it; but it is self-deceiving pride which leads Zophar to imagine that he has no need of it himself. For this Wisdom which has decreed the suffering of Job is hidden from him also; and yet he does not treat the suffering of his friend as a divine mystery. He explains it as the working of the retributive justice of God; but since he endeavours thus to explain the mystery, he injures his cause, and if possible injures also the slender thread by which Job's faith hangs. For should Job regard his sufferings as a *just* divine retribution, he could then no longer believe on God as the Just One.

Job's Third Answer.—Chap. xii.–xiv.

Schema : 5. 8. 8. 6. 6. 10. 8. | 4. 8. 10. 10. 6. 6. 6. 7. | 6. 7. 7. 7. 10. 7. 6.

[Then Job began, and said :]

Ch. xii. 2 *Truly then ye are the people,*
　　　And wisdom shall die with you !
　3 *I also have a heart as well as you ;*
　　　I do not stand behind you ;
　　　And to whom should not such things be known?

The admission, which is strengthened by אָמְנָם כִּי, truly then (distinct from כִּי אָמְנָם, for truly, ch. xxxvi. 4, similar to הִנֵּה כִי, behold indeed, Ps. cxxviii. 4), is intended as irony : ye are not merely single individuals, but the people = race of men (עָם, as Isa. xl. 7, xlii. 5), so that all human understanding is confined to you, and there is none other to be found ; and when once you die, it will seem to have died out. The LXX. correctly renders : μὴ ὑμεῖς ἐστὲ ἄνθρωποι μόνοι (according to the reading of the *Cod. Alex.*) ; he also has a heart like them, he is therefore not empty, נבוב, ch. xi. 12. Heart is, like ch. xxxiv. 10, comp. נלבב, ch. xi. 12, equivalent to νοῦς, διάνοια ; Ewald's translation, " I also have a head even as

you " (" brains " would better accord with the connection), is
a western form of expression, and modern and unbiblical (vid.
Division " Herz und Haupt," Psychol. iv. § 12). He is not
second to them ; נָפֵל מִן, like ch. xiii. 2, properly to slip from,
to be below any one ; מִן is not the comparative (Ewald).
Oetinger's translation is not bad : I cannot slink away at
your presence. Who has not a knowledge of such things as
those which they, by setting themselves up as defenders of
God, have presented to him ! הָיָה אִתִּי is equivalent to יָדַעְתִּי,
σύνοιδα, Isa. lix. 12.

4 *I must be a mockery to my own friend,*
   I who called on Eloah and He heard me ;
   A mockery—the just, the godly man.
5 *Contempt belongs to misfortune, according to the ideas of*
   the prosperous ;
   It awaits those who are ready to slip.
6 *The tents of the destroyer remain in peace,*
   And those that defy God are prosperous,
   Who taketh Eloah into his hand.

The synallage of לְרֵעֵהוּ for לְרֵעִי is not nearly so difficult as
many others : a laughing-stock to his own friend ; comp. Isa.
ii. 8, they worship the work of their (his) own hands (יָדָיו).
" One who called on Eloah (לֶאֱלוֹהַּ, for which לֵאלוֹהַּ is found
in MSS. at ch. xxxvi. 2) and He heard him " is in apposition
to the subject ; likewise צַדִּיק תָּמִים, which is to be explained
according to Prov. xi. 5, צַדִּיק (from צדק, صدق, to be hard,
firm, stiff, straight), is one who in his conduct rules himself
strictly according to the will of God ; תמים, one whose thoughts
are in all respects and without disguise what they should be,
—in one word : pure. Most old translators (Targ., Vulg.,
Luther) give לַפִּיד the signification, a torch. Thus e.g. Levi
v. Gerson explains : " According to the view of the prosperous
and carnally secure, he who is ready for falterings of the feet,

i.e. likely to fall, is like a lighted torch which burns away and destroys whatever comes in contact with it, and therefore one keeps aloof from him ; but it is also more than this : he is an object of contempt in their eyes." Job might not inappropriately say, that in the eyes of the prosperous he is like a despised, cast-away torch (comp. the similar figure, Isa. xiv. 19, like a branch that is rejected with contempt) ; and ver. 5*b* would be suitably connected with this if לְמוֹעֲדֵי could be derived from a substantive מֹעַד, *vacillatio*, but neither the usage of the language nor the *scriptio plena* (after which Jerome translates *tempus statutum*, and consequently has in mind the מוֹעֲדִים, times of festal pilgrimages, which are also called רְגָלִים in later times), nor the vowel pointing (instead of which מֵעֲדֵי would be expected), is favourable to this. מוֹעֲדֵי רֶגֶל signifies *vacillantes pede*, those whose prosperity is shaken, and who are in danger of destruction that is near at hand. We therefore, like Abenezra and modern expositors, who are here happily agreed, take לפיד as composed of ל and פִּיד, a word common to the books of Job (ch. xxx. 24, xxxi. 29) and Proverbs (ch. xxiv. 22), which is compared by the Jewish lexicographers, according both to form and meaning, to כִּיד (ch. xxi. 20) and אֵיד, and perhaps signifies originally dissolution (comp. פרה), decease (Syr. *f'jodo*, escape ; Arab. *faid*, dying), fall, then generally calamity, misfortune : contempt (befits) misfortune, according to the thoughts (or thinking), idea of the prosperous. The pointing wavers between לְעַשְׁתּוֹת and the more authorized לְעַשְׁתּוּת, with which Parchon compares the nouns עַבְדּוּת and מַרְדּוּת ; the ת, like ד in the latter word, has *Dag. lene*, since the punctuation is in this respect not quite consistent, or follows laws at present unknown (comp. Ges. § 21, rem. 2). Ver. 5*b* is now suitably connected : ready (with reference to בון) for those who stumble, *i.e.* contempt certainly awaits such, it is ready and waiting for them, נָכוֹן, ἕτοιμος, like Ex. xxxiv. 2.

While the unfortunate, in spite of his innocence, has thus
only to expect contempt, the tents, *i.e.* dwellings and possessions, of the oppressor and the marauder remain in prosperity ; יִשְׁלָיוּ for יִשְׁלוּ, an intensive form used not only in
pause (Ps. xxxvi. 8 ; comp. Deut. xxxii. 37) and with greater
distinctives (Num. xxiv. 6 ; Ps. cxxii. 6), but also in passages
where it receives no such accent (Ps. xxxvi. 9, lvii. 2, lxxiii.
2). On אֹהָלִים, instead of אֳהָלִים, *vid.* Ges. § 93, 6, 3. The
verbal clause (ver. 6*a*) is followed by a substantival clause (6*b*).
בַּטֻּחוֹת is an abstract plural from בַּטּוּחַ, perfectly secure ; therefore : the most care-less security is the portion of those who
provoke God (LXX. παροργίζουσι) ;[1] and this is continued
in an individualizing form : him who causes Eloah to go into
his hand.   Seb. Schmid explains this passage in the main
correctly : *qui Deum in manu fert h.e. qui manum aut poten-
tiam suam pro Deo habet et licitum sibi putat quodlibet;* comp.
Hab. i. 11 : "this his strength becomes God to him," *i.e.* he
deifies his own power, and puts it in the place of God.   But
הֵבִיא signifies, in this connection with לְיָדוֹ (not בְיָדוֹ), neither
to carry, nor to lead (Gesenius, who compares Ps. lxxiv. 5,
where, however, it signifies to cause to go into = to strike
into) ; it must be translated : he who causes Eloah to enter into
his hand ; from which translation it is clear that not the deifi-
cation of the hand, but of that which is taken into the hand,
is meant.   This which is taken into the hand is not, however,
an idol (Abenezra), but the sword; therefore : him who thinks
after the manner of Lamech,[2] as he takes the iron weapon of
attack and defence into his hand, that he needs no other
God.

[1] Luther takes בטחות as the adverb to מרגיזי : *und toben wider Gott
thürstiglich* (*vid.* Vilmar, *Pastoraltheolog. Blätter*, 1861, S. 110–112);
according to the Vulg., *et audacter provocant Deum.*

[2] [Comp. *Pentateuch*, vol. i. p. 119, Clark's Foreign Theological
Library.—Tr.]

7 *But ask now even the beasts—they shall teach it thee ;*
And the birds of heaven—they shall declare it to thee :
8 *Or look thoughtfully to the ground—it shall teach it thee;*
And the fish of the sea shall tell it thee.
9 *Who would not recognise in all this*
That the hand of Jehovah hath wrought this,
10 *In whose hand is the soul of every living thing,*
And the breath of all mankind ? !

The meaning of the whole strophe is perverted if זאת (ver.
9) is, with Ewald, referred to " the destiny of severe suffering and pain," and if that which precedes is accordingly
referred to the testimony of creation to God as its author.
Since, as a glance at what follows shows, Job further on
praises God as the governor of the universe, it may be
expected that the reference is here to God as the creator
and preserver of the world, which seems to be the meaning
of the words. Job himself expresses the purpose of this
hymn of confession, vers. 2 sq., xiii. 1 sq. : he will show the
friends that the majesty of God, before which he ought,
according to their demands, to humble himself in penitence,
is not less known to him than to them; and with ואולם, *verum*
enim vero, he passes over to this subject when he begins his
third answer with the following thought : The perception
in which you pride yourselves I also possess ; true, I am
an object of scornful contempt to you, who are as little able
to understand the suffering of the godly as the prosperity
of the godless, nevertheless what you know I also know :
ask now, etc. Bildad had appealed to the sayings of the
ancients, which have the long experience of the past in their
favour, to support the justice of the divine government ;
Job here appeals to the absoluteness of the divine rule over
creation. In form, this strophe is the counterpart of ch. viii.
8–10 in the speech of Bildad, and somewhat also of ch. xi.

7-9 in that of Zophar. The working of God, which infinitely transcends human power and knowledge, is the sermon
which is continuously preached by all created things; they
all proclaim the omnipotence and wisdom of the Creator.

The plural בְּהֵמוֹת is followed by the verb that refers to it,
in the singular, in favour of which Gen. xlix. 22 is the
favourite example among old expositors (Ges. § 146, 3). On
the other hand, the verb might follow the collective עוֹף in the
plural, according to Ges. § 146, 1. The plural, however, is
used only in ver. 8*b*, because there the verb precedes instead
of following its subject. According to the rule Ges. §
128, 2, the jussive form of the fut. follows the imperative.
In the midst of this enumeration of created things, שִׂיחַ, as a
substantive, seems to signify the plants—and especially as
شِيح even now, in the neighbourhood of Job's ancient habitation, is the name of a well-known mountain-plant—under
whose shade a meagre vegetation is preserved even in the hot
season (*vid.* on ch. xxx. 4 sqq.). But (1) שִׂיחַ as subst. is
gen. masc. (Gen. ii. 5); (2) instead of לְאָרֶץ, in order to
describe a plant that is found on the ground, or one rooted
in the ground, it must be עַל־הָאָרֶץ or בָאָרֶץ; (3) the mention
of plants between the birds and fishes would be strange. It
may therefore be taken as the imperative: speak to the earth
(LXX., Targ., Vulg., and most others); or, which I prefer,
since the Aramaic construction סָח לֹ, *narravit ei*, does not
occur elsewhere in Hebrew (although perhaps *implicite*, Prov.
vi. 22, תְּשִׂיחַ לְךָ = תְשִׂיחֶךָ, *fabulabitur*, or *confabulabitur tibi*),
as a pregnant expression: think, *i.e.* look meditatively to the
earth (Ewald), since שׂוּחַ (שִׂיחַ), like הָגָה, combines the significations of quiet or articulate meditation on a subject. The
exhortation directs attention not to the earth in itself, but to
the small living things which move about on the ground,
comprehended in the collective name רֶמֶשׂ, syn. שֶׁרֶץ (creeping
things), in the record of creation. All these creatures, thoug¹

without reason and speech, still utter a language which is heard by every intelligent man. Renan, after Ewald, translates erroneously: *qui ne sait parmi tous ces êtres.* They do not even possess knowledge, but they offer instruction, and are a means of knowledge; בְּ with יָדַע, like Gen. xv. 8, xlii. 33, and freq. All the creatures named declare that the hand of Jehovah has made "this," whatever we see around us, τὸ βλεπόμενον, Heb. xi. 3. In the same manner in Isa. lxvi. 2, Jer. xiv. 22, כָּל־אֵלֶּה is used of the world around us. In the hand of God, *i.e.* in His power, because His workmanship, are the souls of all living things, and the spirit (that which came direct from God) of all men; every order of life, high and low, owes its origin and continuance to Him. אִישׁ is the individual, and in this connection, in which נֶפֶשׁ and רוּחַ (= נְשָׁמָה) are certainly not unintentionally thus separated, the individual man. Creation is the school of knowledge, and man is the learner. And this knowledge forces itself upon one's attention: *quis non cognoverit?* The *perf.* has this subjunctive force also elsewhere in interrogative clauses, *e.g.* Ps. xi. 3 (*vid.* on Gen. xxi. 7). That the name of God, JEHOVAH, for once escapes the poet here, is to be explained from the phrase "the hand of Jehovah hath made this," being a somewhat proverbial expression (comp. Isa. xli. 20, lxvi. 2).

Job now refers to the sayings of the fathers, the authority of which, as being handed down from past generations, Bildad had maintained in his opposition to Job.

11 *Shall not the ear try sayings,*
    As the palate tasteth food?
12 *Among the ancients is wisdom,*
    And long life is understanding.
13 *With Him is wisdom and strength;*
    Counsel and understanding are His.

The meaning of ver. 11 is, that the sayings (מִלִּין, ch. viii. 10, comp. v. 27) of the ancients are not to be accepted without being proved ; the *waw* in וְחֵךְ is *waw adæquationis*, as ch. v. 7, xi. 12, therefore equivalent to *quemadmodum ;* it places together for comparison things that are analogous : The ear, which is used here like αἰσθητήριον (Heb. v. 14), has the task of searching out and testing weighty sayings, as the palate by tasting has to find out delicious and suitable food ; this is indicated by לֹ, the *dat. commodi.* So far Job recognises the authority of these traditional sayings. At any rate, he adds (ver. 12): wisdom is to be expected from the hoary-headed, and length of life is understanding, *i.e.* it accompanies length of life. "Length of days" may thus be taken as the subject (Ewald, Olsh.) ; but בְּ may also, with the old translations and expositors, be carried forward from the preceding clause : ἐν δὲ πολλῷ βίῳ ἐπιστήμη (LXX.). We prefer, as the most natural : long life is a school of understanding. But—such is the antithesis in ver. 13 which belongs to this strophe—the highest possessor of wisdom, as of might, is God. Ewald inserts two self-made couplets before ver. 12, which in his opinion are required both by the connection and "the structure of the strophe ;" we see as little need for this interpolation here as before, ch. vi. 14*b*. עִמּוֹ and לֹ, which are placed first for the sake of emphasis, manifestly introduce an antithesis; and it is evident from the antithesis, that the One who is placed in contrast to the many men of experience is God. Wisdom is found among the ancients, although their sayings are not to be always implicitly accepted ; but wisdom belongs to God as an attribute of His nature, and indeed absolutely, *i.e.* on every side, and without measure, as the piling up of synonymous expressions implies : חָכְמָה, which perceives the reason of the nature, and the reality of the existence, of things ; עֵצָה, which is never perplexed as to the best way of attaining its purpose ; תְּבוּנָה,

which can penetrate to the bottom of what is true and false, sound and corrupt (comp. 1 Kings iii. 9) ; and also גְּבוּרָה, which is able to carry out the plans, purposes, and decisions of this wisdom against all hindrance and opposition.

In the strophe which follows, from his own observation and from traditional knowledge (ch. xiii. 1), Job describes the working of God, as the unsearchably wise and the irresistibly mighty One, both among men and in nature.

14 *Behold, He breaketh down and it cannot be built again,*
    He shutteth up, and it cannot be opened.
15 *Behold, He restraineth the waters and they dry up,*
    And He letteth them out and they overturn the earth.
16 *With Him is might and existence,*
    The erring and the deceiver are His.

God is almighty, and everything in opposition to Him powerless. If He break down (any structure whatever), it can never be rebuilt ; should He close upon any one (*i.e.* the dungeon, as perhaps a cistern covered with a stone, Lam. iii. 53, comp. Jer. xxxviii. 6 ; עַל with reference to the depth of the dungeon, instead of the usual בְּעַד), it (that which is closed from above) cannot be opened again. In like manner, when He desires to punish a land, He disposes the elements according to His will and pleasure, by bringing upon it drought or flood. יַעְצֹר, *coercet*, according to the correct Masoretic mode of writing יַעְצֹר with dagesh in the Ssade, in order clearly to distinguish in the pronunciation between the forms *j̔a-ssor* and *jaa̔ssor* (יַעֲצֹר) ;[1] וְיִבָשׁוּ (for which Abulwalid writes וְיִבְשׁוּ) is a defective form of writing according to Ges. § 69, 3, 3 ; the form וְיַהַפְכוּ with the similarly pointed *fut. consec.*, 1 Sam. xxv. 12, form a pair (זוּג) noted by the Masora. By תּוּשִׁיָּה, which is ascribed to God, is here to be understood that which

---

[1] *Vid.* my notice of Bär's *Psalter-Ausgabe, Luth. Zeitschr.* 1863, 3 ; and comp. Keil on Lev. iv. 13 (*Pentat.* vol. ii. p. 307, Clark's transl.).

really exists, the real, the objective, knowledge resting on an
objective actual basis, in contrast with what only appears to
be ; so that consequently the idea of vers. 16*a* and 13*a* is
somewhat veiled ; for the primary notion of חָכְמָה is thickness,
solidity, purity, like πυκνότης.[1] This strophe closes like the
preceding, which favours our division. The line with עִמּוֹ is
followed by one with לֹ, which affirms that, in the supremacy
of His rule and the wisdom of His counsels, God makes evil
in every form subservient to His designs.

> 17 *He leadeth away counsellors stripped of their robes,*
> *And maketh judges fools.*
> 18 *The authority of kings He looseth,*
> *Ana bindeth their loins with bands.*
> 19 *He leadeth away priests stripped of their robes,*
> *And overthroweth those who are firmly established.*
> 20 *He removeth the speech of the eloquent,*
> *And taketh away the judgment of the aged.*
> 21 *He poureth contempt upon princes,*
> *And maketh loose the girdle of the mighty.*

In vers. 17, 19, שׁוֹלָל is added to מוֹלִיךְ as a conditional
accusative ; the old expositors vary in the rendering of this
word ; at any rate it does not mean : chained (Targ. on ver.
17), from שׁלל (שׁרר), which is reduplicated in the word שַׁלְשֶׁלֶת,
a chain, a word used in later Hebrew than the language of
the Old Testament (שַׁרְשְׁרָה is the Old Testament word) ; nor
is it : taken as booty, made captive (LXX. αἰχμαλώτους;
Targ. on ver. 19, בְּבִזְתָּא, in the quality of spoil) = מְשׁוֹלָל; but

---

[1] The primary notion of חכם, حَكُمَ, is, to be thick, firm, solid, as the
prim. notion of سَخُفَ (to be foolish, silly) is to be thin, loose, not holding together (as a bad texture). The same fundamental notions are
represented in the expression of moral qualities (in distinction from
intellectual) by צדק, صدق, and רשע, (رسخ ,رسع).

it is a neuter adjective closely allied to the idea of the verb, *exutus*, not however *mente* (deprived of sense), but *vestibus* ; not merely barefooted (Hirz., Oehler, with LXX., Mic. i. 8, ἀνυπόδετος), which is the meaning of יָחֵף, but : stripped of their clothes with violence (*vid.* Isa. xx. 4), stripped in particular of the insignia of their power. He leads them half-naked into captivity, and takes away the judges as fools (יְהוֹלֵל, *vid. Psychol.* S. 292), by destroying not only their power, but the prestige of their position also. We find echoes of this utterance respecting God's paradoxical rule in the world in Isa. xl. 23, xliv. 25 ; and Isaiah's oracle on Egypt, ch. xix. 11–15, furnishes an illustration in the reality.

It is but too natural to translate ver. 18 : the bands of kings He looses (after Ps. cxvi. 16, פתחת למוסרי, Thou hast loosed my bands) ; but the relation of the two parts of the verse can then not be this : He unchains and chains kings (Hirz., Ew., Heiligst., Schlottm.), for the *fut. consec.* וַיֶּאְסֹר requires a contrast that is intimately connected with the context, and not of mere outward form : fetters in which kings have bound others (מלכים, *gen. subjectivus*) He looses, and binds *them* in fetters (Raschi),—an explanation which much commends itself, if מוּסַר could only be justified as the construct of מוֹסֵר by the remark that " the *o* sinks into *u*" (Ewald, § 213, *c*). מוֹסֵר does not once occur in the signification *vinculum* ; but only the *plur.* מוֹסְרִים and מוֹסֵרוֹת, *vincula*, accord with the usage of the language, so that even the pointing מוֹסַר proposed by Hirzel is a venture. מוּסַר, however, as constr. of מוּסָר, correction, discipline, rule (*i.e.* as the domination of punishment, from יסר, *castigare*), is an equally suitable sense, and is probably connected by the poet with פָּתַח (a word very familiar to him, ch. xxx. 11, xxxix. 5, xli. 6) on account of its relation both in sound and sense to מוֹסְרִים (comp. Ps. cv. 22). The English translation is correct : *He looseth the authority of kings.* The antithesis is certainly lost, but the thoughts here moreover flow on in synonymous parallelism.

Ver. 19. It is unnecessary to understand כהנים, after 2 Sam. viii. 18, of high officers of state, perhaps privy councillors; such priest-princes as Melchizedek of Salem and Jethro of Midian are meant. אֵיתָנִים, which denotes inexhaustible, *perennis,* when used of waters, is descriptive of nations as invincible in might, Jer. v. 15, and of persons as firmly-rooted and stedfast. נֶאֱמָנִים, such as are tested, who are able to speak and counsel what is right at the fitting season, consequently the ready in speech and counsel. The derivation, proposed by Kimchi, from נָאַם, in the sense of *diserti,* would require the pointing נַאֲמָנִים. טַעַם is taste, judgment, tact, which knows what is right and appropriate under the different circumstances of life, 1 Sam. xxv. 33. יִקָּח is used exactly as in Hos. iv. 11. Ver. 21*a* is repeated verbatim, Ps. cvii. 40; the trilogy, Ps. cv.–cvii., particularly Ps. cvii., is full of passages similar to the second part of Isaiah and the book of Job (*vid. Psalter,* ii. 117). אֲפִיקִים (only here and ch. xli. 7) are the strong, from אָפַק, to hold together, especially to concentrate strength on anything. מְזִיחַ (only here, instead of מֵזַח, not from מָזַח, which is an imaginary root, but from זָחַח, according to Fürst equivalent to זָקַק, to lace, bind) is the girdle with which the garments were fastened and girded up for any great exertion, especially for desperate conflict (Isa. v. 27). To make him weak or relaxed, is the same as to deprive of the ability of vigorous, powerful action. Every word is here appropriately used. This tottering relaxed condition is the very opposite of the intensity and energy which belongs to "the strong." All temporal and spiritual power is subject to God: He gives or takes it away according to His supreme will and pleasure.

22 *He discovereth deep things out of darkness,*
   And bringeth out to light the shadow of death;
23 *He giveth prosperity to nations and then destroyeth them,*
   Increase of territory to nations and then carrieth them
   away;
24 *He taketh away the understanding of the chief people of*
   the land,
   And maketh them to wander in a trackless wilderness;
25 *They grope in darkness without light,*
   He maketh them to stagger like a drunken man.

The meaning of ver. 22 in this connection can only be,
that there is nothing so finely spun out that God cannot
make it visible. All secret plans of the wicked, all secret
sins, and the deeds of the evil-doer though veiled in deep
darkness, He bringeth before the tribunal of the world. The
form of writing given by the Masora is עֲמֻקוֹת with *koph
raphatum*, consequently plur. from עָמֹק, like עֲרוּמִים
עֲצוּמִים from עָרוּם, עָצוּם, not from עָמֹק.[1] The LXX. translates מַשְׁנִיא
πλανῶν, as it is also explained in several Midrash-passages, but
only by a few Jewish expositors (Jachja, Alschech) by מטעה.
The word, however, is not מַשְׁנִיא, but מַשְׂגִּיא with שׂ *sinistrum*,
after which in Midrash Esther it is explained by מגדיל;
and Hirzel correctly interprets it of upward growth (Jerome
after the Targ. unsuitably, *multiplicat*), and שָׂטַח, on the
other hand, of growth in extent. The latter word is falsely
explained by the Targ. in the sense of *expandere rete*, and
Abenezra also falsely explains : He scatters nations, and
brings them to their original peace. The verb שטח is here
connected with לְ, as הִפְתָּה (Gen. ix. 27); both signify to

[1] Kimchi in his *Wörterbuch* adopts the form עֲמֻקוֹת, but gives Abulwalid as an authority for the lengthened form, which, according to the
Masora on Lev. xiii. 3, 25, is the traditional. The two exceptions where
the form occurs with a long vowel are Prov. xxiii. 27 and this passage.

make a wider and longer space for any one, used here of the ground where they dwell and rule. The opposite, in an unpropitious sense, is הִנִּחַה, which is used here, as 2 Kings xviii. 11, in a similar sense with הִגְלָה (*abducere, i.e. in servitutem*). We have intentionally translated גוים nations, עם people; for גּוֹי, as we shall show elsewhere, is the mass held together by the ties of a common origin, language, and country; (עָם) עַם, the people bound together by unity of government, whose *membra præcipua* are consequently called רָאשֵׁי הָעָם. הארץ is, in this conneetion, the country, although elsewhere, as Isa. xxiv. 4, comp. xlii. 5, עם הארץ signifies also the people of the earth or mankind; for the Hebrew language expresses a country as a portion of the earth, and the earth as a whole, by the same name. Job dwells longer on this tragic picture, how God makes the star of the prosperity of these chiefs to set in mad and blind self-destruction, according to the proverb, *quem Deus perdere vult prius dementat.* This description seems to be echoed in many points in Isaiah, especially in the oracle on Egypt, ch. xix. (*e.g.* בַּשְּׁבּוּר, xix. 14). The connection בתהו לא דרך is not genitival; but לא דרך is either an adverbial clause appended to the verb, as לא חקר, ch. xxxiv. 24, לא בנים, 1 Chron. ii. 30, 32, or, which we prefer as being more natural, and on account of the position of the words, a virtual adjective: in a trackless waste, as לֹא אִישׁ, ch. xxxviii. 26; לא עבות, 2 Sam. xxiii. 4 (Olsh.).

Job here takes up the tone of Eliphaz (comp. ch. v. 13 sq.). Intentionally he is made to excel the friends in a recognition of the absolute majesty of God. He is not less cognizant of it than they.

Ch. xiii. 1 *Lo, mine eye hath seen all,*
  Mine ear hath heard and marked it.
 2 *What ye know do I know also,*
  I do not stand back behind you.

Job has brought forward proof of what he has stated at
the commencement of this speech (ch. xii. 3), that he is not
inferior to them in the knowledge of God and divine things,
and therefore he can now repeat as proved what he maintains.   The plain בֹּל, which in other passages, with the force
of הַכֹּל, signifies *omnes* (Gen. xvi. 12 ; Isa. xxx. 5 ; Jer. xliv.
12) and *omnia* (ch. xlii. 2 ; Ps. viii. 7 ; Isa. xliv. 24), has the
definite sense of *hæc omnia* here.   לָהּ (ver. 1*b*) is not after
the Aramaic manner *dat. pro acc. objecti* : my ear has heard
and comprehended it (*id*) ; but *dat. commodi*, or perhaps only
dat. ethicus : and has made it intelligible to itself (*sibi*) ; בִּין
of the apprehension accompanying perception.   He has a
knowledge of the exalted and glorious majesty of God, acquired partly from his own observation and partly from the
teachings of others.   He also knows equal to (*instar*) their
knowledge, *i.e.* he has a knowledge (יָדַע as the idea implied
in it, *e.g.* like Ps. lxxxii. 5) which will bear comparison with
theirs.   But he will no longer contend with them.

3 *But I would speak to the Almighty,*
    And I long to reason with God.
4 *And ye however are forgers of lies,*
    Physicians of no value are ye all.
5 *Oh that ye would altogether hold your peace,*
    It would be accounted to you as wisdom.
6 *Hear now my instruction,*
    And hearken to the answers of my lips!

He will no longer dispute with the friends ; the more they
oppose him, the more earnestly he desires to be able to argue
his cause before God.   אוּלָם (ver. 3) is disjunctive, like ἀλλά,
and introduces a new range of thoughts ; LXX. οὐ μὴν δὲ
ἀλλά, *verum enim vero*.   True, he has said in ch. ix. that no
one can maintain his cause before God ; but his confidence
in God grows in proportion as his distrust of the friends in-

creases ; and at the same time, the hope is begotten that God will grant him that softening of the terror of His majesty which he has reserved to himself in connection with this declaration (ch. ix. 34, comp. xiii. 20 sq.). The *infin. absol.* הוֹכֵחַ, which in ch. vi. 25 is used almost as a substantive, and indeed as the subject, is here in the place of the object, as *e.g.* Isa. v. 5, lviii. 6 : to prove, *i.e.* my cause, to God (אֶל־אֵל, like ver. 15, אֶל־פָּנָיו) I long. With וְאוּלָם (ver. 4) the antithesis is introduced anew : I will turn to God, you on the contrary (καὶ ὑμεῖς δὲ). Since the verb טָפַל, from its primary meaning to spread on, smear on (whence *e.g.* Talmudic טְפֵלָה, the act of throwing on, as when plastering up the cracks of an oven), cogn. תָּפַל (whence תֶּפֶל, plaster, and perhaps also in the signification tasteless, ch. vi. 6 = sticky, greasy, slimy), does not signify, at least not at first, *consuere,* but *assuere* (without any relation of root with תָּפַר), we explain, not with Olshausen and others, *concinnatores mendacii,* such as sew together lies as patchwork ; but with Hirzel and others, *assutores mendacii,* such as patch on lies, *i.e.* charge falsely, since they desire throughout to make him out to be a sinner punished according to his desert. This explanation is also confirmed by ch. xiv. 17. Another explanation is given by Hupfeld : *sarcinatores falsi* = *inanes, inutiles,* so that שֶׁקֶר signifies what lies = what deceives, as in the parallel member of the verse אֱלִל,[1] nothingness, and also עָמָל (ch. xvi. 2) in a similar connection, is not an objective but attributive genitive ; but Ps. cxix. 69 is decisive against this interpretation of טֹפְלֵי שֶׁקֶר. The parallelism is not so exactly adjusted, as *e.g.* even רֹפְאֵי does not on account of the parallel with טֹפְלֵי signify patchers,

---

[1] In the Talmudic, the jugular vein, the cutting of which produces death, is called אֲלַל (later עצב, عصب), according to which (*b. Chullin* 121*a*) it is explained: healer of the jugular artery, *i.e.* those who try to heal what is incurable, therefore charlatans,—a strange idea, which has arisen from the defective form of writing אֱלִל. The LXX. translates ἰαται κακῶν.

ῥάπται, but: they are not able to heal Job's wounds with the
medicine of consolation; they are *medici nihili*, useless physicians. Prov. xvii. 28, " Even a fool, when he holdeth his
peace, is counted wise," applies to them, *si tacuisses, sapiens
mansisses;* or, as a rabbinical proverb of similar meaning,
quoted by Heidenheim, says, הלאות בהשגה השגה, "the fatigue
of comprehension is comprehension," *i.e.* the silent pause before a problem is half the solution. The jussive form וּתְהִי, it
would be (Ges. § 128, 2), is used in the conclusion of the
wish. Thus he challenges them to hear his תּוֹכַחַת (תּוֹכֵחָה)
and his רְבוֹת. Hirzel is quite right when he says the former
does not mean defence (justification), nor the latter proofs
(counter-evidence); תוכחת is, according to his signification
(*significatus*, in distinction from *sensus*), ἔλεγχος, *correptio*
(LXX., Vulg.), and here not so much refutation and answer,
as correction in an ethical sense, in correspondence with which
רבות is also intended of reproaches, reproofs, or reprimands.

7 *Will ye speak what is wrong for God,*
    And speak what is deceitful for Him?
8 *Will ye be partial for Him,*
    Or will ye play the part of God's advocates?
9 *Would it be pleasant if He should search you out,*
    Or can ye jest with Him, as one jesteth with men?
10 *He will surely expose you*
    If ye secretly act with partiality.
11 *Will not His majesty confound you,*
    And His fear fall upon you?

Their advocacy of God—this is the thought of this strophe
—is an injustice to Job, and an evil service rendered to God,
which cannot escape undisguised punishment from Him.
They set themselves up as God's advocates (רִיב לְאֵל, like
רִיב לַבַּעַל, Judg. vi. 31), and at the same time accept His
person, *accipiunt* (as in *acceptus = gratus*), or lift it up, *i.e.*

favour, or give preference to, His person, viz. at the expense
of the truth : they are partial in His favour, as they are
twice reminded and given to understand by the *fut. energicum*
תִּשָּׂאוּן. The addition of בַּסֵּתֶר (ver. 10*b*) implies that they
conceal their better knowledge by the assumption of an
earnest tone and bearing, expressive of the strongest conviction that they are in the right. They know that Job is not
a flagrant sinner ; nevertheless they deceive themselves with
the idea that he is, and by reason of this delusion they take
up the cause of God against him. Such perversion of the
truth *in majorem Dei gloriam* is an abomination to God.
When He searches them, His advocates, out (חָקַר, as Prov.
xxviii. 11), they will become conscious of it ; or will God be
mocked, as one mocketh mortal men ? Comp. Gal. vi. 7 for
a similar thought. הָתֵל is *inf. absol.* after the form הָסֵב, and
תְּהָתֵלּוּ is also to be derived from תָּלַל, and is *fut. Hiph.*, the
preformative not being syncopated, for תְּתָלֻּ (Ges. § 53,
rem. 7) ; not *Piel*, from הָתֵל (as 1 Kings xviii. 27), with the
doubling of the middle radical resolved (Olsh. in his *Lehrb.*
S. 577).   God is not pleased with λατρεία (John xvi. 2)
which gives the honour to Him, but not to truth, such ζῆλος
Θεοῦ ἀλλ᾽ οὐ κατ᾽ ἐπίγνωσιν (Rom. x. 2), such advocacy
contrary to one's better knowledge and conscience, in which
the end is thought to sanctify the means. Such advocacy
must be put to shame and confounded when He who needs
no concealment of the truth for His justification is manifest
in His שְׂאֵת, *i.e.* not: in the kindling of His wrath (after
Judg. xx. 38, Isa. xxx. 27), but: in His exaltation (correctly
by Ralbag : התנשאותו ורוממותו), and by His direct influence
brings all untruth to light.   It is the boldest thought imaginable, that one dare not have respect even to the person of
God when one is obliged to lie to one's self. And still it is
also self-evident. For God and truth can never be anta-
gonistic.

12 *Your memorable words are proverbs of dust,*
   Your strongholds are become strongholds of clay !
13 *Leave me in peace, and I will speak,*
   And let what will come on me.
14 *Wherefore should I bear my flesh in my teeth ?*
   I take my soul in my hands.
15 *Behold, He slayeth me—I wait for Him :*
   I will only prove my way before Him.
16 *Even this would be my salvation,*
   That a hypocrite dare not appear before Him.

The words by which they exhort and warn him are called
זִכְרֹנִים, not because they recall the experience and teaching of
the ancients (Hirz.), but as sayings to which attention and
thought should be given, with the tone of זְכָר־נָא, ch. iv. 7
(Hahn); as ספר זכרון, Mal. iii. 16, the book of remembrance;
and ספר זכרנות, Esth. vi. 1, the book of memorabilia or memo-
randa. These their *loci communes* are proverbs of ashes, *i.e.*
proverbs which, in respect to the present case, say nothing,
passing away like ashes (אֵפֶר = vanity, Isa. xliv. 20). While
ver. 12*a* says what their speeches, with the weighty *nota bene,*
are, ver. 12*b* says what their גַּבִּים become; for לְ always
denotes a κίνησις = γένεσις, and is never the exponent of
the predicate in a simple clause.[1] Like the Arabic ﻇَﻬﺮ, גַּב
signifies a boss, back, then protection, bulwark, rampart :
their arguments or proofs are called גבים (עֲצֻמוֹת, Isa. xli. 21;
comp. ὀχυρώματα, 2 Cor. x. 4); these ramparts which they
throw up become as ramparts of clay, will be shown to be
such by their being soon broken through and falling in.

---

[1] The Jewish expositors compare 1 Chron. iii. 2 on לנבי, but the לְ
there in לאבשלום is a clerical error (comp. 2 Sam. iii. 3). Reiske conjectures רגבי (lumps of clay), one of the best among his most venture-
some conjectures.

Their reasons will not stand before God, but, like clay that
will not hold together, fall to pieces.

Ver. 13. Be silent therefore from me, he says to them, *i.e.*
stand away from me and leave me in peace (*opp.* הַחֲרִישׁ אֶל,
Isa. xli. 1) : then will I speak, or : in order that I may speak
(the cohortative usual in *apod. imper.*)—he, and he alone,
will defend (*i.e.* against God) his cause, which they have so
uncharitably abandoned in spite of their better knowledge
and conscience, let thereby happen (עבר, similar to Deut.
xxiv. 5) to him מָה, whatever may happen (מה שיעבר); or more
simply : whatever it may be, *quidquid est*, as 2 Sam. xviii. 22
ויהי מה, let happen whatever may happen; or more simply :
whatever it may be, like דְּבַר מָה *quodcunque*, Num. xxiii. 3 ;
מִי occurs also in a similar sense, thus placed last (Ewald, §
104, *d*).

Ver. 14. Wherefore should he carry away his flesh in his
teeth, *i.e.* be intent upon the maintenance of his life, as a wild
beast upon the preservation of its prey, by holding it between
its teeth (*mordicus tenet*) and carrying it away ? This is a
proverbial phrase which does not occur elsewhere; for Jer.
xxxviii. 2 (thy life shall become as spoil, לְשָׁלָל, to thee) is only
similar in outward appearance. It may be asked whether
ver. 14*b* continues the question begun with עַל־מָה (*vid.* on Isa.
i. 5) : and wherefore should I take my soul in my hands,
i.e. carefully protect it as a valuable possession ? (Eichh.,
Umbr., Vaih.) But apart from Ps. cxix. 109 (my soul is
continually in my hand),—where it may be asked, whether the
soul is not there regarded as treasure (according to the current religious phrase: to carry his soul in his hand = to work
out the blessedness of his soul with fear and trembling),—
שִׂים נַפְשׁוֹ בְכַפָּיו signifies everywhere else (Judg. xii. 3; 1 Sam. xix.
5, xxviii. 21) as much as to risk one's life without fear of death,
properly speaking : to fight one's way through with one's fist,
perishing so soon as the strength of one's fist is gone (Ewald) ;

comp. the expression for the impending danger of death, Deut. xxviii. 66. If this sense, which is in accordance with the usage of the language, be adopted, it is unnecessary with Hirz., after Ewald, § 352, *b*, to take וְנַפְשִׁי for נם נפשי: also, even my soul, etc., although it cannot be denied that וְ, like καί and *et*, sometimes signifies: also, *etiam* (Isa. xxxii. 7, 2 Chron. xxvii. 5, Eccles. v. 6, and according to the accents, Hos. viii. 6 also; on the contrary, 2 Sam. i. 23, Ps. xxxi. 12, can at least be explained by the copulative meaning, and Amos iv. 10 by "and indeed "). The *waw* joins the positive to the negative assertion contained in the question of ver. 14*a* (Hahn): I will not eagerly make my flesh safe, and will take my soul in my hand, *i.e.* calmly and bravely expose myself to the danger of death. Thus ver. 15 is most directly connected with what precedes.

Ver. 15. This is one of eighteen passages in which the *Chethib* is לֹא and the *Keri* לוֹ; ch. vi. 21 is another.[1] In the LXX., which moreover changes אִיחַל into הֵחֵל, ἄρχεσθαι, the rendering is doubtful, the *Cod. Vat.* translating ἐάν με χειρώσηται, the *Cod. Alex.* ἐὰν μή με χειρ. The Mishna *b. Sota,* 27, *b*, refers to the passage with reference to the question

---

[1] In Fürst, *Concord.* p. 1367, col. 1, the following passages are wanting: 1 Sam. ii. 3, 2 Kings viii. 10, Ps. c. 3, cxxxix. 16, Prov. xix. 7, xxvi. 2, 1 Chron. xi. 20, which are to be supplied from Aurivillius, *diss.* p. 469, where, however, on the other hand, 2 Sam. xix. 7 is wanting. Ex. xxi. 8 also belongs to these passages. In this last passage Mühlau proposes a transposition of the letters thus: לֹא יְדָעָהּ (if she displease her master, so that he *knows* her not, does not like to make her his concubine, then he shall cause her to be redeemed, etc.). [In his volume on Isaiah just published (1866), Dr Delitzsch appends the following note on ch. lxiii. 9 :—" There are fifteen passages in which the *Keri* substitutes לוֹ for לֹא, *vid. Masora magna* on Lev. xi. 21 (*Psalter*, ii. 60). If we include Isa. xlix. 5, 1 Chron. xi. 20, 1 Sam. ii. 16 also, there are then eighteen (comp. on Job xiii. 15); but the first two of these passages are very doubtful, and are therefore intentionally omitted, and in the third it is לֹא that is substituted for לוֹ (Ges. *Thes.* 735, *b*). 2 Sam. xix. 7 also does not belong here, for in this passage the *Keri* is לֹא."—Tr.]

whether Job had served God from love or fear, and in favour of the former appeals to ch. xxvii. 5, since here the matter is doubtful (הדבר שקול), as the present passage may be explained, " I hope in Him," or " I hope not." The Gemara, *ib.* 31, *a*, observes that the reading לא does not determine the sense, for Isa. lxiii. 9 is written לא, and is not necessarily to be understood as לו, but can be so understood.[1] Among the ancient versions, the Targ., Syr., and Jerome (*etiamsi occiderit me, in ipso sperabo*) are in favour of לו. This translation of the Vulgate is followed by the French, English, Italian, and other versions. This utterance, in this interpretation, has a venerable history. The Electoress Louise Henriette von Oranien (died 1667), the authoress of the immortal hymn, " *Jesus meine Zuversicht* " [the English translation begins, " Jesus Christ, my sure defence "], chose these words, " Though the Lord should slay me, yet will I hope in Him," for the text of her funeral oration. And many in the hour of death have adopted the utterance of Job in this form as the expression of their faith and consolation.[2] Among these we may mention a Jewess. The last movement of the wasted fingers of Grace Aguilar was to spell the words, " Though He slay me, yet will I trust in Him."[3]

The words, so understood, have an historic claim in their favour which we will not dispute. Even the apostles do not spurn the use of the Greek words of the Old Testament, though they do not accord with the proper connection in the original text, provided they are in accordance with sacred Scripture, and give brief and pregnant expression to a truth taught elsewhere in the Scriptures. Thus it is with this utterance, which, understood as the Vulgate understands it,

---

[1] *Vid.* Geiger, *Lesestücke aus der Mischnah* (1845), S. 37 f.
[2] *Vid.* Göschel, *Die Kurfürstinnen zu Brandenburg aus dem Hause Hohenzollern* (1857), S. 28–32.
[3] *Marie Henriquez Morales, bearbeitet von Piza* (1860), S. xii.

is thoroughly Job-like, and in some measure the final solution of the book of Job. It is also, according to its most evident meaning, an expression of perfect resignation. We admit that if it is translated : behold, He will slay me, I hope not, *i.e.* I await no other and happier issue, a thought is obtained that also agrees with the context. But יְחֵל does not properly mean to hope, but to wait for ; and even in ch. vi. 11, xiv. 14, where it stands as much without an object as here, it has no other meaning but that of waiting ; and Luther is true to it when he translates : behold, He will destroy me, and I cannot expect it ; it is, however, strange ; and Böttch. translates : I will not wait to justify myself, which is odd. The proper meaning of יחל, *præstolari,* gives no suitable sense. Thus, therefore, the writer will have written or meant לֹ, since לֹ יְחֵל is also elsewhere a familiar expression with him, ch. xxix. 21, 23, xxx. 26. The meaning, then, which agrees both with the context and with the reality, is : behold, He will slay me, I wait for Him, *i.e.* I wait what He may do, even to smite with death, only I will (אַךְ, as frequently, *e.g.* Ps. xlix. 16, does not belong to the word which immediately follows, but to the whole clause) prove my ways to Him, even before His face. He fears the extreme, but is also prepared for it. Hirzel, Heiligst., Vaihinger, and others, think that Job regards his wish for the appearing of God as the certain way of death, according to the belief that no one can behold God and not die. But יִקְטְלֵנִי has reference to a different form of idea. He fears the risk of disputing with God, and being obliged to forfeit his life ; but, as לֹ אֲיַחֵל implies, he resigns himself even to the worst, he waits for Him to whom he resigns himself, whatever He may do to him ; nevertheless (אַךְ restrictive, or as frequently אָכֵן adversative, which is the same thing here) he cannot and will not keep down the inward testimony of his innocence, he is prepared to render Him an account of the ways in which he has walked (*i.e.* the way of

His will)—he can succumb in all respects but that of his moral guiltlessness. And in ver. 16 he adds what will prove a triumph for him, that a godless person, or (what is suitable, and if it does not correspond to the primary idea,[1] still accords with the use of the word) a hypocrite, one who judges thus of himself in his own heart, would not so come forward to answer for himself before God (Hahn). It can be explained : that a godless person has no access to God; but the other explanation gives a truer thought. הוא is here used as neuter, like ch. xv. 9, xxxi. 28 comp. 11, xli. 3, Ex. xxxiv. 10. Correctly LXX., καὶ τοῦτό μοι ἀποβήσεται εἰς σωτηρίαν. יְשׁוּעָה here (comp. ch. xxx. 15) has not, however, the usual deeper meaning which it has in the prophets and in Psalms. It means here salvation, as victory in a contest for the right. Job means that he has already as good as won the contest, by so urgently desiring to defend himself before God. This excites a feeling in favour of his innocence at the onset, and secures him an acquittal.

> 17 *Hear, O hear my confession,*
>   *And let my declaration echo in your ears.*
> 18 *Behold now ! I have arranged the cause,*
>   *I know that I shall maintain the right.*
> 19 *Who then can contend with me?*
>   *Then, indeed, I would be silent and expire.*

Eager for the accomplishment of his wish that he might himself take his cause before God, and as though in imagina-

---

[1] The verb חנף signifies in the Arabic to deviate, to go on one side (whence *e.g. ahhnaf*, bandy-legged) : *hhanîf*, which is derived from it, is a so-called ضِدّ, ἐναντιόσημον, which may mean both one inclining to the good and true (one who is orthodox), and in this sense it is a surname of Abraham, and one inclining to evil. Beidhâwi explains it by *mâïl*, inclining one's self to ; the synonym, but used only in a good sense, is العادل, *el-'âdil.*

tion it were so, he invites the friends to be present to hear his defence of himself. מִלָּה (in Arabic directly used for confession = religion) is the confession which he will lay down, and אַחֲוֶה the declaration that he will make in evidence, *i.e.* the proof of his innocence. The latter substantive, which signifies brotherly conduct in post-biblical Hebrew, is here an ἅπ. λεγ. from חָוָה, not however with *Aleph prostheticum* from *Kal*, but after the form אַזְכָּרָה = הַזְכָּרָה, from the *Aphêl = Hiphil* of this verb, which, except Ps. xix. 3, occurs only in the book of Job as Hebrew (comp. the *n. actionis*, אַחֲוָיָה, Dan. v. 12), Ewald, § 156, *c*. It is unnecessary to carry the שִׁמְעוּ on to ver. 17*b* (hear now . . . . with your own ears, as *e.g.* Jer. xxvi. 11); ver. 17*b* is an independent substantival clause like ch. xv. 11, Isa. v. 9, which carries in itself the verbal idea of תְּהִי or תָּבֹא (Ps. xviii. 7). They shall hear, for on his part he has arranged, *i.e.* prepared (עָרַךְ מִשְׁפָּט, *causam instruere*, as ch. xxiii. 4, comp. xxxiii. 5) the cause, so that the action can begin forthwith; and he knows that he, he and no one else, will be found in the right. With the conviction of this superiority, he exclaims, Who in all the world could contend with him, *i.e.* advance valid arguments against his defence of himself? Then, indeed, if this impossibility should happen, he would be dumb, and willingly die as one completely overpowered not merely in outward appearance, but in reality vanquished. ירִיב עמדי following מִי הוּא (comp. ch. iv. 7) may be taken as an elliptical relative clause: *qui litigare possit mecum* (comp. Isa. l. 9 with Rom. viii. 34, τίς ὁ κατακρίνων); but since מִי הוּא זֶה is also used in the sense of *quis tandem* or *ecquisnam*, this syntactic connection which certainly did exist (Ewald, § 325, *a*) is obliterated, and הוּא serves like זֶה only to give intensity and vividness to the מִי. On כִּי עַתָּה (in meaning not different to כִּי אָז), *vid.* ch. iii. 13, viii. 6. In ver. 19 that is granted as possible which, according to the declaration of his conscience, Job must consider as absolutely impos-

sible. Therefore he clings to the desire of being able to
bring his cause before God, and becomes more and more
absorbed in the thought.

> 20 *Only two things do not unto me,*
>   *Then will I not hide myself from Thy countenance :*
> 21 *Withdraw Thy hand from me,*
>   *And let Thy fear not terrify me—*
> 22 *Call then and I will answer,*
>   *Or I will speak and answer Thou me !*

He makes only two conditions in his prayer, as he has
already expressed it in ch. ix. 34 : (1) That God would grant
him a cessation of his troubles; (2) That He would not
overwhelm him with His majesty. The chastening hand of
God is generally called יָד elsewhere ; but in spite of this
prevalent usage of the language, כַּף cannot be understood
here (comp. on the contrary ch. xxxiii. 7) otherwise than of
the hand (ch. ix. 34 : the rod) of God, which lies heavily on
Job. The painful pressure of that hand would prevent the
collecting and ordering of his thoughts required for meeting
with God, and the אֵימָה (Codd. defectively אֵמָתְךָ) of God
would completely crush and confound him. But if God
grants these two things : to remove His hand for a time, and
not to turn the terrible side of His majesty to him, then he is
ready whether God should himself open the cause or permit
him to have the first word. Correctly Mercerus : *optionem
ei dat ut aut actoris aut rei personam deligat, sua fretus innocentia, sed interim sui oblitus et immodicus.* In contrast with
God he feels himself to be a poor worm, but his consciousness
of innocence makes him a Titan.

He now says what he would ask God ; or rather, he now
asks Him, since he vividly pictures to himself the action with
God which he desires. His imagination anticipates the
reality of that which is longed for. Modern expositors begin

a new division at ver. 23. But Job's speech does not yet take a new turn; it goes on further continually *uno tenore*.

> 23 *How many are mine iniquities and sins?*
> *Make me to know my transgression and sin!* — —
> 24 *Wherefore dost Thou hide Thy face,*
> *And regard me as Thine enemy?*
> 25 *Wilt Thou frighten away a leaf driven to and fro,*
> *And pursue the dry stubble?*

When עָוֺן and חַטָּאת, פֶּשַׁע and חַטָּאת, are used in close connection, the latter, which describes sin as failing and error, signifies sins of weakness (infirmities, *Schwachheitssünde*); whereas עָוֺן (prop. distorting or bending) signifies misdeed, and פֶּשַׁע (prop. breaking loose, or away from, Arab. فسق) wickedness which designedly estranges itself from God and removes from favour, both therefore malignant sin *(Bosheits-sünde*[1]). The bold self-confidence which is expressed in the question and challenge of ver. 23 is, in ver. 24, changed to grievous astonishment that God does not appear to him, and on the contrary continues to pursue him as an enemy without investigating his cause. Has the Almighty then pleasure in scaring away a leaf that is already blown to and fro? הֶעָלֶה, with *He interrog.*, like הֶחָכָם, ch. xv. 2, according to Ges. § 100, 4. עָרַץ used as transitive here, like Ps. x. 18, to terrify, scare away affrighted. Does it give Him satisfaction to pursue dried-up stubble? By אֵת (before an indeterminate noun, according to Ges. § 117, 2) he points δεικτικῶς to himself: he, the powerless one, completely deprived of strength by sickness and pain, is as dried-up stubble; nevertheless God is after him, as though He would get rid of every trace of a

---

[1] Comp. the development of the idea of the synonyms for sin in von Hofmann, *Schriftbeweis*, i. 483 ff., at the commencement of the fourth *Lehrstück*.

dangerous enemy by summoning His utmost strength against him.

26 *For Thou decreest bitter things against me,*
   And causest me to possess the iniquities of my youth,
27 *And puttest my feet in the stocks,*
   And observest all my ways.
   Thou makest for thyself a circle round the soles of my feet,
28 *Round one who moulders away as worm-eaten,*
   As a garment that the moth gnaweth.

He is conscious of having often prayed : " Remember not the sins of my youth, and my transgressions : according to Thy mercy remember Thou me," Ps. xxv. 7 ; and still he can only regard his affliction as the inheritance (*i.e.* entailed upon him by sins not repented of) of the sins of his youth, since he has no sins of his mature years that would incur wrath, to reproach himself with. He does not know how to reconcile with the justice of God the fact that He again records against him sins, the forgiveness of which he implores soon after their commission, and decrees (כָּתַב, as Ps. cxlix. 9, and as used elsewhere in the book of Job with reference to the recording of judgment) for him on account of them such bitter punishment (מְרֹרוֹת, *amara*, bitter calamities ; comp. Deut. xxxii. 32, " bitter" grapes). And the two could not indeed be harmonized, if it really were thus. So long as a man remains an object of the divine mercy, his sins that have been once forgiven are no more the object of divine judgment. But Job can understand his affliction only as an additional punishment. The conflict of temptation through which he is passing has made God's loving-kindness obscure to him. He appears to himself to be like a prisoner whose feet are forced into the holes of a סַד, *i.e.* the block or log of wood in which the feet of a criminal are fastened, and which he must shuffle about with him when he moves ; perhaps connected with سَدَّ, *occludere*, *opplere* (*foramen*), elsewhere מַהְפֶּכֶת (from

the forcible twisting or fastening), Chald. סַדְנָא, סְדְיָא, Syr.
sado, by which Acts xvi. 24, ξύλον = ποδοκάκη, is rendered ;
Lat. *cippus* (which Ralbag compares), *codex* (in Plautus an
instrument of punishment for slaves), or also *nervus*. The
verb תָּשֵׂם which belongs to it, and is found also in ch. xxxiii.
11 in the same connection, is of the jussive form, but is
neither jussive nor optative in meaning, as also the future
with shortened vowel (*e.g.* ch. xxvii. 22, xl. 19) or apocopated
(ch. xviii. 12, xxiii. 9, 11) is used elsewhere from the preference of poetry for a short pregnant form. He seems to
himself like a criminal whose steps are closely watched (שָׁמַר,
as ch. x. 14), in order that he may not have the undeserved
enjoyment of freedom, and may not avoid the execution for
which he is reserved by effecting an escape by flight. Instead of אָרְחֹתַי, the reading adopted by Ben-Ascher, Ben-
Naphtali writes אָרְחֹתַי, with *Cholem* in the first syllable ; both
modes of punctuation change without any fixed law also in
other respects in the inflexion of אֹרַח, as of אֹרְחָה, a caravan,
the construct is both אָרְחוֹת, ch. vi. 19, and אָרְחוֹת. It is
scarcely necessary to remark that the verbs in ver. 27*bc* are
addressed to God, and are not intended as the *third pers. fem.*
in reference to the stocks (Ralbag). The roots of the feet
are undoubtedly their undermost parts, therefore the soles.
But what is the meaning of תִּתְחַקֶּה ? The Vulg., Syr., and
Parchon explain : Thou fixest thine attention upon . . . ,
but certainly according to mere conjecture ; Ewald, by the
help of the Arabic *tahhakkaka ala :* Thou securest thyself
. . ., but there is not the least necessity to depart from
the ordinary use of the word, as those also do who explain :
Thou makest a law or boundary (Aben-Ezra, Ges., Hahn,
Schlottm.). The verb חָקָה is the usual word (certainly cognate and interchangeable with חָקַק) for carved-out work (in-

taglio), and perhaps with colour rubbed in, or filled up with metal (*vid.* ch. xix. 23, comp. Ezek. xxiii. 14); it signifies to hew into, to carve, to dig a trench. Stickel is in some measure true to this meaning when he explains: Thou scratchest, pressest (producing blood); by which rendering, however, the *Hithpa.* is not duly recognised. Raschi is better, *tu t'affiches*, according to which Mercerus: *velut affixus vestigiis pedum meorum adhæres, ne quâ elabi possim aut effugere.* But a closer connection with the ordinary use of the word is possible. Accordingly Rosenm., Umbreit, and others render: Thou markest a line round my feet (drawest a circle round); Hirz., however, in the strictest sense of the *Hithpa.*: Thou diggest thyself in (layest thyself as a circular line about my feet). But the *Hithpa.* does not necessarily mean *se insculpere*, but, as התפשׁט *sibi exuere*, התפתח *sibi solvere*, התחנן *sibi propitium facere*, it may also mean *sibi in-sculpere*, which does not give so strange a representation: Thou makest to thyself furrows (or also: lines) round the soles of my feet, so that they cannot move beyond the narrow boundaries marked out by thee. With והוא, ver. 28, a circumstantial clause begins: While he whom Thou thus fastenest in as a criminal, etc. Observe the fine rhythmical accentuation *achālo 'asch*. Since God whom he calls upon does not appear, Job's defiance is changed to timidity. The elegiac tone, into which his bold tone has passed, is continued in ch. xiv.

Ch. xiv. 1 *Man that is born of a woman,*
      Short of days and full of unrest,
    2 *Cometh forth as a flower and is cut down;*
      He fleeth as a shadow, and continueth not.
    3 *Moreover, Thou openest Thine eyes upon him,*
      And Thou drawest me before Thy tribunal.

Even if he yields to the restraint which his suffering

imposes on him, to regard himself as a sinner undergoing
punishment, he is not able to satisfy himself by thus persuading himself to this view of God's conduct towards him.
How can God pass so strict a judgment on man, whose life
is so short and full of sorrow, and which cannot possibly be
pure from sin?—Ver. 1. אָדָם is followed by three clauses in
apposition, or rather two, for יְלוּד אִשָּׁה (LXX. γεννητὸς
γυναικός, as Matt. xi. 11; comp. γέννημα γυν. Sir. x. 18)
belongs to the subject as an adjectival clause: woman-born
man, short-lived, and full of unrest, opens out as a flower.
Woman is weak, with pain she brings forth children; she is
impure during her lying-in, therefore weakness, suffering,
and impurity is the portion of man even from the birth (ch.
xv. 14, xxv. 4).   As קְצַר is the constr. of קָצֵר, so שְׂבַע (רְנֵי) is
from שָׂבֵעַ, which here, as ch. x. 15, has the strong signification: endowed (with adversity).   It is questionable whether
וַיִּמָּל, ver. 2, signifies *et marcescit* or *et succiditur*.   We have
decided here as elsewhere (*vid.* on Ps. xxxvii. 2, xc. 6,
Genesis, S. 383) in favour of the latter meaning, and as the
Targ. (אִתְמוֹלֵל), translated "he is mown down."   For this
meaning (prop. to cut off from above or before, to lop off),—
in which the verb מָלַל (מוּל, נָמֵל) is become technical for the
περιτομή,—is most probably favoured by its application in
ch. xxiv. 24; where Jerome however translates, *sicut summi-
tates spicarum conterentur,* since he derives ימלו from מלל in
the signification not found in the Bible (unless perhaps
retained in מְלִילָה, Deut. xxiii. 26), *fricare* (Arab. مل, *frigĕre,*
to parch).   At the same time, the signification *marcescere,*
which certainly cannot be combined with *præcidere,* but may
be with *fricare* (*conterere*), is not unnatural; it is more
appropriate to a flower (comp. נבל ציץ, Isa. xl. 7); it accords
with the parallelism Ps. xxxvii. 2, and must be considered
etymologically possible in comparison with קָמֵל, אָמֵל.   But

it is not supported by any dialect, and none of the old translations furnish any certain evidence in its favour ; יְמוֹלֵל, Ps. xc. 6, which is to be understood impersonally rather than intransitively, does not favour it ; and none of the passages in which יְמַל occurs demand it : least of all ch. xxiv. 24, where *præciduntur* is more suitable than, and ch. xviii. 16, *præciditur*, quite as suitable as, *marcescit*. For these reasons we also take וַיִּמַּל here, not as *fut. Kal* from מלל, or, as Hahn, from נָמַל = נָבֵל, to wither, but as *fut. Niph.* from מָלַל, to cut down. At the same time, we do not deny the possibility of the notion of withering having been connected with ימל, whether it be that it belonged originally and independently to the root מל, or has branched off from some other radical notion, as " to fall in pieces" (LXX. here ἐξέπεσεν, and similarly also ch. xviii. 16, xxiv. 24 ; comp. מְלָחִים, rags, נִמְלַח, to come to pieces, to be dissolved) or " to become soft" (with which the significations in the dialects, to grind and to parch, may be connected). As a flower, which having opened out is soon cut or withered, is man : אַף, *accedit quod, insuper.* This particle, related to ἐπί, adds an enhancing *cumulat.* More than this, God keeps His eye open (not : His eyes, for the correct reading, expressly noted by the Masora, is עֵינֶךָ without *Jod plur.*), עַל־זֶה, *super hoc s. tali,* over this poor child of man, who is a perishable flower, and not a " walking light, but a fleeting shadow" (Gregory the Great), to watch for and punish his sins, and brings Job to judgment before himself, *His* tribunal which puts down every justification. Elsewhere the word is pointed בַּמִּשְׁפָּט, ch. ix. 32, xxii. 4; here it is בְמִשְׁפָּט, because the idea is rendered determinate by the addition of עִמָּךְ.

4 *Would that a pure one could come from an impure !*
   Not a single one— —
5 *His days then are determined,*

The number of his months is known to Thee,
Thou hast appointed bounds for him that he may not
  pass over :
6 *Look away from him then, and let him rest,*
  Until he shall accomplish as a hireling his day.

Would that perfect sinlessness were possible to man; but
since (to use a New Testament expression) that which is
born of the flesh is flesh, there is not a single one pure. The
optative מִי־יִתֵּן seems to be used here with an acc. of the
object, according to its literal meaning, *quis det s. afferat,* as
ch. xxxi. 31, Deut. xxviii. 67, Ps. xiv. 7. Ewald remarks
(and refers to § 358, *b,* of his *Grammar*) that לֹא, ver. 4*b,*
must be the same as לוֹ; but although in 1 Sam. xx. 14,
2 Sam. xiii. 26, 2 Kings v. 17, לֹא might be equivalent to the
optative לוֹ, which is questionable, still לֹא אחד here, as an
echo of אֵין גַּם־אֶחָד, Ps. xiv. 3, is Job's own answer to his
wish, that cannot be fulfilled: not one, *i.e.* is in existence.
Like the friends, he acknowledges an hereditary proneness to
sin; but this proneness to sin affords him no satisfactory explanation of so unmerciful a visitation of punishment as his
seems to him to be. It appears to him that man must the
rather be an object of divine forbearance and compassion,
since absolute purity is impossible to him. If, as is really
the case, man's days are חֲרוּצִים, cut off, *i.e.* ἀποτόμως, determined (distinct from חָרוּצִים with an unchangeable Kametz:
sharp, *i.e.* quick, eager, diligent),—if the number of his months
is with God, *i.e.* known by God, because fixed beforehand by
Him,—if He has set fixed bounds (*Keri* חֻקָּיו) for him, and he
cannot go beyond them, may God then look away from him,
i.e. turn from him His strict watch (שְׁעֵה מִן, as ch. vii. 19 ;
שִׁית מִן, x. 20), that he may have rest (יֶחְדָּל, *cesset*), so that he
may at least as a hireling enjoy his day. Thus ירצה is interpreted by all modern expositors, and most of them consider

the object or reason of his rejoicing to be the rest of evening when his work is done, and thereby miss the meaning.

Hahn appropriately says, " He desires that God would grant man the comparative rest of the hireling, who must toil in sorrow and eat his bread in the sweat of his brow, but still is free from any special suffering, by not laying extraordinary affliction on him in addition to the common infirmities beneath which he sighs. Since the context treats of freedom from special suffering in life, not of the *hope* of being set free from it, comp. ch. xiii. 25–27, xiv. 3, the explanation of Umbreit, Ew., Hirz., and others, is to be entirely rejected, viz. that God would at least permit man the rest of a hireling, who, though he be vexed with heavy toil, cheerfully reconciles himself to it in prospect of the reward he hopes to obtain at evening time. Job does not claim for man the toil which the hireling gladly undergoes in expectation of complete rest, but the toil of the hireling, which seems to him to be rest in comparison with the possibility of having still greater toil to undergo." Such is the true connection.[1] Man's life—this life which is as a handbreadth (Ps. xxxix. 6), and in ch. vii. 1 sq. is compared to a hireling's day, which is sorrowful enough—is not to be overburdened with still more and extraordinary suffering.

It must be asked, however, whether רצה *seq. acc.* here signifies εὐδοκεῖν (τὸν βίον, LXX.), or not rather *persolvere;* for it is undeniable that it has this meaning in Lev. xxvi. 34 (*vid.* however Keil [*Pent.* ii. 476]) and elsewhere (prop. to satisfy, remove, discharge what is due). The *Hiphil* is used in this sense in post-biblical Hebrew, and most Jewish expositors explain ירצה by ישלים. If it signifies to enjoy, עַד ought to be interpreted : that (he at least may, like as a

---

[1] In honour of our departed friend, whose *Commentary on Job* abounds in observations manifesting a delicate appreciation of the writer's purpose and thought, we have quoted his own words.

hireling, enjoy his day). But this signification of עַד (*ut* in the final sense) is strange, and the signification *dum* (ch. i. 18, viii. 21) or *adeo ut* (Isa. xlvii. 7) is not, however, suitable, if ירצה is to be explained in the sense of *persolvere*, and therefore translate *donec persolvat* (*persolverit*). We have translated " until he accomplish," and wish " accomplish " to be understood in the sense of " making complete," as Col. i. 24, Luther (" *vollzählig machen* ") $=$ ἀνταναπληροῦν.

> 7 *For there is hope for a tree :*
> *If it is hewn down, it sprouts again,*
> *And its shoot ceaseth not.*
> 8 *If its root becometh old in the ground,*
> *And its trunk dieth off in the dust :*
> 9 *At the scent of water it buddeth,*
> *And bringeth forth branches like a young plant.*

As the tree falleth so it lieth, says a cheerless proverb. Job, a true child of his age, has a still sadder conception of the destiny of man in death ; and the conflict through which he is passing makes this sad conception still sadder than it otherwise is. The fate of the tree is far from being so hopeless as that of man ; for (1) if a tree is hewn down, it (the stump left in the ground) puts forth new shoots (on הֶחָלִיף, *vid.* on Ps. xc. 6), and young branches (יוֹנֶקֶת, the tender juicy sucker μόσχος) do not cease. This is a fact, which is used by Isaiah (ch. vi.) as an emblem of a fundamental law in operation in the history of Israel : the terebinth and oak there symbolize Israel ; the stump (מַצֶּבֶת) is the remnant that survives the judgment, and this remnant becomes the seed from which a new sanctified Israel springs up after the old is destroyed. Carey is certainly not wrong when he remarks that Job thinks specially of the palm (the date), which is propagated by such suckers; Shaw's expression corresponds exactly to תחדל לֹא : "when the old trunk dies, there is *never wanting* one or other of these offsprings to succeed it." Then (2) if the root of a tree becomes old (הִזְקִין inchoative *Hiphil: senescere*, Ew. § 122, *c*) in the earth, and its trunk (גֶּזַע also of the stem of an undecayed tree, Isa. xl. 24) dies away in the dust, it can nevertheless regain its vitality which had succumbed to the weakness of old age : revived by the scent (רֵיחַ always of scent, which anything exhales, not, perhaps Cant. i. 3 only excepted, *odor = odoratus*) of water, it puts forth buds for both leaves and flowers, and brings forth branches (קָצִיר, prop. cuttings, twigs) again, נָטַע כמו, like a plant, or a young plant (the form of נֶטַע in pause), therefore, as if fresh planted, LXX. ὥσπερ νεόφυτον. One is here at once reminded of the palm which, on the one hand, is preeminently a φίλυδρον φυτόν,[1] on the other hand possesses a wonderful vitality, whence it is become a figure for youthful vigour. The palm and the phœnix have one name, and not without reason. The tree reviving as from the dead at the scent of water, which Job describes, is like that wondrous bird rising again from its own ashes (*vid.* on ch. xxix. 18). Even when centuries have at last destroyed the palm—says Masius, in his beautiful and thoughtful studies of nature— thousands of inextricable fibres of parasites cling about the stem, and delude the traveller with an appearance of life.

10 *But man dieth, he lieth there stretched out,*
   Man giveth up the ghost, and where is he?
11 *The waters flow away from the sea,*
   And a stream decayeth and dryeth up:

[1] When the English army landed in Egypt in 1801, Sir Sydney Smith gave the troops the sure sign, that wherever date-trees grew there must be water; and this is supported by the fact of people digging after it generally, within a certain range round the tree within which the roots of the tree could obtain *moisture from the fluid.*—*Vid.* R. Wilson's *History of the Expedition to Egypt*, p. 18.

12 *So man lieth down and riseth not again ;*
   Till the heavens pass away they wake not,
   And are not aroused from their sleep.

How much less favoured is the final lot of man! He dies,
and then lies there completely broken down and melted away
(חָלַשׁ, in the neuter signification, *confectum esse*, rendered in
the Targum by אִתְּבַר and אִתְמַקְמַק). The *fut. consec.* continues the description of the cheerless results of death: He
who has thus once fallen together is gone without leaving a
trace of life. In vers. 11 sq. this vanishing away without
hope and beyond recovery is contemplated under the figure
of running water, or of water that is dried up and never
returns again to its channel. Instead of אָזְלוּ Isaiah uses
נִשְּׁתוּ (ch. xix. 5) in the oracle on Egypt, a prophecy in which
many passages borrowed from the book of Job are interwoven.
The former means to flow away (related radically with נָזַל),
the latter to dry up (transposed נָתַשׁ, Jer. xviii. 14). But
he also uses יֶחֱרַב, which signifies the drying in, and then וַיִּבַשׁ,
which is the complete drying up which follows upon the
drying in (*vid.* Genesis, S. 264). What is thus figuratively
expressed is introduced by *waw* (ver. 12*a*), similar to the *waw
adæquationis* of the emblematic proverbs mentioned at ch. v.
7, xi. 12 : so there is for man no rising (קוּם), no waking up
(הָקִיץ), no ἐγείρεσθαι (נֵעוֹר), and indeed not for ever; for what
does not happen until the heavens are no more (comp. Ps.
lxxii. 7, till the moon is no more), never happens ; because
God has called the heavens and the stars with their laws into
existence, לעד לעולם (Ps. cxlviii. 6), they never cease (Jer.
xxxi. 35 sq.), the days of heaven are eternal (Ps. lxxxix. 30).
This is not opposed to declarations like Ps. cii. 27, for the
world's history, according to the teaching of Scripture, closes
with a change in all these, but not their annihilation. What
is affirmed in vers. 10–12*b* of mankind in general, is, by

the change to the plural in ver. 12*c*, affirmed of each individual of the race.   Their sleep of death is שְׁנַת עוֹלָם (Jer. li.
39, 57).   What Sheôl summons away from the world, the
world never sees again.   Oh that it were otherwise!   How
would the brighter future have comforted him with respect
to the sorrowful present and the dark night of the grave!

13   *Oh that Thou wouldst hide me in Sheôl,*
       That Thou wouldst conceal me till Thine anger change,
       That Thou wouldst appoint me a time and then remem-
           ber me!
14   *If man dieth, shall he live again?*
       All the days of my warfare would I wait,
       Until my change should come.
15   *Thou wouldst call and I would answer,*
       Thou wouldst have a desire for the work of Thy hands—
16   *For now thou numberest my steps,*
       And dost not restrain thyself over my sins.

The optative מִי יִתֵּן introduces a wish that has reference to
the future, and is therefore, as at ch. vi. 8, followed by *futt.*;
comp. on the other hand, ch. xxiii. 3, *utinam noverim.*   The
language of the wish reminds one of such passages in the
Psalms as xxxi. 21, xxvii. 5 (comp. Isa. xxvi. 20) : " In the
day of trouble He hideth me in His pavilion, and in the
secret of His tabernacle doth He conceal me."   So Job
wishes that Hades, into which the wrath of God now precipi-
tates him for ever, may only be a temporary place of safety
for him, until the wrath of God turn away (שׁוּב, comp. the
causative, ch. ix. 13) ; that God would appoint to him, when
there, a חֹק, *i.e.* a *terminus ad quem* (comp. ver. 5), and when
this limit should be reached, again remember him in mercy.
This is a wish that Job marks out for himself.   The reality
is indeed different: " if (ἐὰν) a man dies, will he live
again?"   The answer which Job's consciousness, ignorant of

anything better, alone can give, is : No, there is no life after death. It is, however, none the less a craving of his heart that gives rise to the wish; it is the most favourable thought, —a desirable possibility,—which, if it were but a reality, would comfort him under all present suffering : " all the days of my warfare would I wait until my change came." צָבָא is the name he gives to the whole of this toilsome and sorrowful interval between the present and the wished-for goal,—the life on earth, which he likens to the service of the soldier or of the hireling (ch. vii. 1), and which is subject to an inevitable destiny (ch. v. 7) of manifold suffering, together with the night of Hades, where this life is continued in its most shadowy and dismal phase. And חֲלִיפָה does not here signify destruction in the sense of death, as the Jewish expositors, by comparing Isa. ii. 18 and Cant. ii. 11, explain it; but (with reference to צבא, comp. ch. x. 17) the following after (Arab. خليفة, succession, successor, i.e. of Mohammed), relief, change (syn. תְּמוּרָה, exchange, barter), here of change of condition, as Ps. lv. 20, of change of mind; Aquila, Theod., ἄλλαγμα. Oh that such a change awaited him! What a blessed future would it be if it should come to pass! Then would God call to him in the depth of Sheôl, and he, imprisoned until the appointed time of release, would answer Him from the deep. After His anger was spent, God would again yearn after the work of His hands (comp. ch. x. 3), the natural loving relation between the Creator and His creature would again prevail, and it would become manifest that wrath is only a waning power (Isa. liv. 8), and love His true and essential attribute. Schlottman well observes : " Job must have had a keen perception of the profound relation between the creature and his Maker in the past, to be able to give utterance to such an imaginative expectation respecting the future."

In ver. 16, Job supports what is cheering in this prospect,

with which he wishes he might be allowed to console himself,
by the contrast of the present.   כִּי עַתָּה is used here as in ch.
vi. 21; כִי is not, as elsewhere, where כי עתה introduces the
conclusion, confirmatory (indeed now = then indeed), but
assigns a reason (for now).   Now God numbers his steps
(ch. xiii. 27), watching him as a criminal, and does not
restrain himself over his sin.   Most modern expositors (Ew.,
Hlgst., Hahn, Schlottm.) translate : Thou observest not my
sins, *i.e.* whether they are to be so severely punished or not ;
but this is poor.   Raschi : Thou waitest not over my sins, *i.e.*
to punish them ; instead of which Ralbag directly : Thou
waitest not for my sins = repentance or punishment ; but שׁמֹר
is not supported in the meaning : to wait, by Gen. xxxvii. 11.
Aben-Ezra : Thou lookest not except on my sins, by supplying רַק, according to Eccles. ii. 24 (where, however, probably
מִשִּׁיאכֹל should be read, and מ after אדם, just as in ch. xxxiii.
17, has fallen away).   The most doubtful is, with Hirzel, to
take the sentence as interrogative, in opposition to the parallelism : and dost Thou not keep watch over my sins ?   It
seems to me that the sense intended must be derived from
the phrase שָׁמַר אַף, which means to keep anger, and consequently to delay the manifestation of it (Amos i. 11).   This
phrase is here so applied, that we obtain the sense : Thou
keepest not Thy wrath to thyself, but pourest it out entirely.
Mercerus is substantially correct : *non reservas nec differs*
peccati mei punitionem.

17 *My transgression is sealed up in a bag,*
   And Thou hast devised additions to my iniquity.
18 *But a falling mountain moveth indeed,*
   And a rock falleth from its place.
19 *Water holloweth out stone,*
   Its overflowings carry away the dust of the earth,
   And the hope of man—Thou destroyest.

The meaning of ver. 17 is, not that the judgment which pronounces him guilty lies in the sealed-up bag of the judge, so that it requires only to be handed over for execution (Hirz., Ew., Renan), for although פֶּשַׁע (though not exactly the punishment of sin, which it does not signify even in Dan. ix. 24) can denote wickedness, as proved and recorded, and therefore metonomically the penal sentence, the figure is, however, taken not from the mode of preserving important documents, but from the mode of preserving collected articles of value in a sealed bag. The passage must be explained according to Hos. xiii. 12, Deut. xxxii. 34, Rom. ii. 5, comp. Jer. xvii. 1. The evil Job had formerly (ch. xiii. 26) committed according to the sentence of God, God has gathered together as in a money bag, and carefully preserved, in order now to bring them home to him. And not this alone, however; He has devised still more against him than his actual misdeeds. Ewald translates : Thou hast sewed up my punishment ; but טָפַל (vid. on ch. xiii. 4) signifies, not to sew up, but : to sew on, patch on, and gen. to add (מָפֵל, Rabb. accidens, a subordinate matter, opp. עָקָּר), after which the LXX. translates ἐπεσημήνω (noted in addition), and Gecatilia حفصت (added to in collecting). It is used here just as in the Aramaic phrase טָפַל שִׁקְרָא (to patch on falsehood, to invent scandal).

The idea of the figures which follow is questionable. Hahn maintains that they do not describe destruction, but change, and that consequently the relation of ver. 19c to what precedes is not similarity, but contrast : stones are not so hard, that they are not at length hollowed out, and the firm land is not so firm that it cannot be carried away by the flood ; but man's prospect is for ever a hopeless one, and only for him is there no prospect of his lot ever being changed. Thus I thought formerly it should be explained : considering the waw, ver. 19c, as indicative not of comparison, but of contrast. But the assumption that the point of comparison is *change*, not destruction, cannot be maintained : the figures represent the slow but inevitable destruction wrought by the elements on the greatest mountains, on rocks, and on the solid earth. And if the poet had intended to contrast the slow but certain changes of nature with the hopelessness of man's lot, how many more appropriate illustrations, in which nature seems to come forth as with new life from the dead, were at his command ! Raschi, who also considers the relation of the clauses to be antithetical, is guided by the right perception when he interprets : even a mountain that is cast down still brings forth fruit, and a rock removed from its place, even these are not without some signs of vitality in them, יְבוֹל = (יְבוּל) יַעֲשֶׂה בּוּל, which is indeed a linguistic impossibility. The majority of expositors are therefore right when they take the *waw*, ver. 19c, similarly to ch. v. 7, xi. 12, xii. 11, as *waw adæquationis*. With this interpretation also, the connection of the clause with what precedes by וְאוּלָם (which is used exactly as in ch. i. 11, xi. 5, xii. 7, where it signifies *verum enim vero* or *attamen*) is unconstrained. The course of thought is as follows : With unsparing severity, and even beyond the measure of my guilt, hast Thou caused me to suffer punishment for my sins, but (nevertheless) Thou shouldst rather be gentle and forbearing towards me, since even that which is firmest, strongest, and most durable cannot withstand ultimate destruction ; and entirely in accordance with the same law, weak, frail man (אֱנוֹשׁ) meets an early certain end, and at the same time Thou cuttest off from him every ground of hope of a continued existence. The *waw*, ver. 19c, is consequently, according to the sense, more *quanto magis* than *sic*, placing the things to be contrasted over against each other. הַר־נוֹפֵל is a falling, not a fallen (Ralbag) mountain; and having once received the impetus, it continues gradually to give way ; Renan : *s'effondre peu à peu.* Carey, better : " will decay," for נָבֵל (cogn. נפל) signifies, decrease from external loss ; specially of the falling off of leaves, Isa. xxxiv. 4. The second figure, like ch. xviii. 4, is to be explained according to ch. ix. 5 : a rock removes (not as Jerome translates, *transfertur*, which would be יֶעְתַּק, and also not as LXX. παλαιωθήσεται, Schlottm.: becomes old and crumbles away, although in itself admissible both as to language and fact ; comp. on ch. xxi. 7) from its place ; it does not stand absolutely, immoveably fast. In the third figure אֲבָנִים is a prominent object, as the accentuation with *Mehupach legarmeh* or (as it is found in correct Codd.) with *Asla legarmeh* rightly indicates. שָׁחַק signifies exactly the same as سحق, *atterere*, *conterere*. In the fourth figure, ספיח must not be interpreted as meaning that which grows up spontaneously without re-sowing, although the Targum translates accordingly : it (the water) washes away its (*i.e.* the dust of the earth's) after-growth (כְּתָהָא), which Symm. follows (τὰ παραλελειμμένα). It is also impossible according to the expression ; for it must have been עֲפַר הָאָרֶץ. Jerome is essentially correct : *et alluvione paullatim terra consumitur.* It is true that ספח in Hebrew does not mean *effundere* in any other passage (on this point, *vid.* on Hab. ii. 15), but here the meaning *effusio* or *alluvio* may be supposed without much hesitation ; and in a book whose language is so closely connected with the Arabic, we may even refer to ספח = سفح (kindred to سفك, שפך), although the word may also (as Ralbag suggests), by comparison with מְטַר סֹחֵף, Prov. xxviii. 3, and سحيقة, a storm of rain, be regarded as transposed from סחיפיה, from סחף in Arab. to tear off, sweep away, Targ. to thrust away (= דחף), Syr., Talm. to overthrow, *subvertere* (whence *s'chifto*, a cancer or cancerous ulcer). The suffix refers to מַיִם, and תִּשְׁטֹף before a plural subject is quite according to rule, Ges. § 146, 3. ספיחיה is mostly marked with *Mercha*, but according to our interpretation *Dechî*, which is found here and there in the Codd., would be more correct.

The point of the four illustrations is not that not one of them is restored to its former condition (Oetinger, Hirz.), but that in spite of their stability they are overwhelmed by destruction, and that irrecoverably. Even the most durable things cannot defy decay, and now even as to mortal man—Thou hast brought his hope utterly to nought (האבדת with *Pathach* in pause as frequently; *vid. Psalter* ii. 468). The *perf.* is *prægnans:* all at once, suddenly—death, the germ of which he carries in him even from his birth, is to him an end without one ray of hope,—it is also the death of his hope.

> 20 *Thou seizest him for ever, then he passeth away;*
> *Thou changest his countenance and castest him forth.*
> 21 *If his sons come to honour, he knoweth it not;*
> *Or to want, he observeth them not.*
> 22 *Only on his own account his flesh suffereth pain,*
> *And on his own account is his soul conscious of grief.*

The old expositors thought that תִּתְקְפֵהוּ must be explained by תתקף ממנו (Thou provest thyself stronger than he, according to Ges. § 121, 4), because תָּקַף is intrans.; but it is also transitive in the sense of seizing forcibly and grasping, ch. xv. 24, Eccles. iv. 12, as Talm. תְּקַף (otherwise commonly אַתְקֵף as החזיק), Arab. ثَقَف, *comprehendere.* The many sufferings which God inflicts on him in the course of his life are not meant; לָנֶצַח does not signify here: continually, without intermission, as most expositors explain, but as ch. iv. 20, xx. 7, and throughout the book: for ever (Rosenm., Hahn, Welte). God gives him the death-stroke which puts an end to his life for ever, he passes away βαίνει, οἴχεται (comp. ch. x. 21); disfiguring his countenance, *i.e.* in the struggle of death and in death by the gradual working of decay, distorting and making him unlike himself, He thrusts him out of this life (שִׁלַּח like Gen. iii. 23). The *waw consec.* is used here as *e.g.* Ps. cxviii. 27.

When he is descended into Hades he knows nothing more of the fortune of his children, for as Eccles. ix. 6 says : the dead have absolutely no portion in anything that happens under the sun. In ver. 21 Job does not think of his own children that have died, nor his grandchildren (Ewald) ; he speaks of mankind in general.   כָּבֵד and צָעַר are not here placed in contrast in the sense of much and little, but, as in Jer. xxx. 19, in the wider sense of an important or a destitute position ; כָּבֵד, to be honoured, to attain to honour, as Isa. lxvi. 5.   בִּין (to observe anything) is joined with לְ of the object, as in Ps. lxxiii. 17 (on the other hand, לָהּ, ch. xiii. 1, was taken as *dat. ethicus*).   He neither knows nor cares anything about the welfare of those who survive him : "Nothing but pain and sadness is the existence of the dead ; and the pain of his own flesh, the sadness of his own soul, alone engage him. He has therefore no room for rejoicing, nor does the joyous or sorrowful estate of others, though his nearest ones, affect him" (Hofmann, *Schriftbeweis*, i. 495). This is certainly, as Ewald and *Psychol.* S. 444, the meaning of ver. 22 ; but עָלָיו is hardly to be translated with Hofmann "in him," so that it gives the intensive force of ἴδιος to the *suff.* For it is improbable that in this connection,—where the indifference of the deceased respecting others, and the absolute reference to himself of the existence of pain on his own account, are contrasted,—עליו, ver. 22*b*, is to be understood according to ch. xxx. 16 (*Psychol.* S. 152), but rather objectively (over him). On the other hand, ver. 22*a* is not to be translated : over himself only does his flesh feel pain (Schlottm., Hirz., and others) ; for the flesh as inanimate may indeed be poetically, so to speak zeugmatically, represented as conscious of pain, but not as referring its pain to another, and consequently as *self*-conscious. On this account, עָלָיו, ver. 22*a*, is to be taken in the signification, over him = upon him, or as ver. 22*b* (beyond him), which is doubtful ; or it signifies, as we have sought to render it in our translation in both cases, *propter eum*. Only on his own account does his flesh suffer, *i.e.* only applying to himself, only on his own account does his soul mourn, *i.e.* only over his own condition. He has no knowledge and interest that extends beyond himself ; only he himself is the object of that which takes place with his flesh in the grave, and of that on which his soul reflects below in the depths of Hades. According to this interpretation אַךְ belongs to עָלָיו, after the hyperbaton described at p. 72 [ch. ii. 10], comp. ch. xiii. 15, Isa. xxxiv. 15. And he עָלָיו, ver. 22, implies the idea (which is clearly expressed in Isa. lxvi. 24, and especially in Judith xvi. 17 : δοῦναι πῦρ καὶ σκώλη-κας εἰς σάρκας αὐτῶν καὶ κλαύσονται ἐν αἰσθήσει ἕως αἰῶνος) that the process of the decomposition of the body is a source of pain and sorrow to the departed spirit,—a conception which proceeds from the supposition, right in itself, that a connection between body and soul is still continued beyond the grave,—a connection which is assumed by the resurrection, but which, as Job viewed it, only made the future still more sorrowful.

This speech of Job (ch. xii.–xiv.), which closes here, falls into three parts, which correspond to the divisions into chapters. In the impassioned speech of Zophar, who treats Job as an empty and conceited babbler, the one-sided dogmatical standpoint of the friends was maintained with such arrogance and assumption, that Job is obliged to put forth all his power in self-defence. The first part of the speech (ch. xii.) triumphantly puts down this arrogance and assumption. Job replies that the wisdom, of which they profess to be the only possessors, is nothing remarkable, and the contempt with which they treat him is the common lot of the innocent, while the prosperity of the ungodly remains undisturbed. In order, however, to prove to them that what they say of the majesty of God, before which he should humble himself, can neither overawe nor help him, he refers them to creation, which in its varied works testifies to this majesty, this creative power of God, and the absolute dependence of every living thing on Him, and proves that he is not wanting in an appreciation of the truth contained in the sayings of the ancients by a description of the absolute majesty of God as it is manifested in the works of nature, and especially in the history of man, which excels everything that the three had said. This description is, however, throughout a gloomy picture of disasters which God brings about in the world, corresponding to the gloomy condition of mind in which Job is, and the disaster which is come upon himself.

As the friends have failed to solace him by their descriptions of God, so his own description is also utterly devoid of comfort. For the wisdom of God, of which he speaks, is not the wisdom that orders the world in which one can confide, and in which one has the surety of seeing every mystery of life sooner or later gloriously solved ; but this wisdom is something purely negative, and repulsive rather than attractive, it is abstract exaltation over all created wisdom, whence it follows that he puts to shame the wisdom of the wise. Of the justice of God he does not speak at all, for in the narrow idea of the friends he cannot recognise its control ; and of the love of God he speaks as little as the friends, for as the sight of the divine love is removed from them by the one-sidedness of their dogma, so is it from him by the feeling of the wrath of God which at present has possession of his whole being. Hegel has called the religion of the Old Testament the religion of sublimity (*die Religion der Erha-benheit*) ; and it is true that, so long as that manifestation of love, the incarnation of the Godhead, was not yet realized, God must have relatively transcended the religious consciousness. From the book of Job, however, this view can be brought back to its right limits; for, according to the tendency of the book, neither the idea of God presented by the friends nor by Job is the pure undimmed notion of God that belongs to the Old Testament. The friends conceive of God as the absolute One, who acts only according to justice; Job conceives of Him as the absolute One, who acts according to the arbitrariness of His absolute power. According to the idea of the book, the former is dogmatic one-sidedness, the latter the conception of one passing through temptation. The God of the Old Testament consequently rules neither according to justice alone, nor according to a "sublime whim."

After having proved his superiority over the friends in perception of the majesty of God, Job tells them his decision, that he shall turn away from them. The sermon they address to him is to no purpose, and in fact produces an effect the reverse of that intended by them. And while it does Job no good, it injures them, because their very defence of the honour of God incriminates themselves in the eyes of God. Their aim is missed by them, for the thought of the absolute majesty of God has no power to impart comfort to any kind of sufferer; nor can the thought of His absolute justice give any solace to a sufferer who is conscious that he suffers innocently. By their confidence that Job's affliction is a decree of the *justice* of God, they certainly seem to defend the honour of God; but this defence is reversed as soon as it is manifest that there exists no such *just* ground for inflicting punishment on him. Job's self-consciousness, however, which cannot be shaken, gives no testimony to its justice; their advocacy of God is therefore an injustice to Job, and a miserable attempt at doing God service, which cannot escape the undisguised punishment of God. It is to be carefully noted that in ch. xiii. 6–12 Job seriously warns the friends that God will punish them for their partiality, *i.e.* that they have endeavoured to defend Him *at the expense of truth.*

We see from this how sound Job's idea of God is, so far as it is not affected by the change which seems, according to the light which his temptation casts upon his affliction, to have taken place in his personal relationship to God. While above, ch. ix., he did not acknowledge an objective right, and the rather evaded the thought, of God's dealing unjustly towards him, by the desperate assertion that what God does is in every case right because God does it, he here recognises an objective truth, which cannot be denied, even in favour of God, and the denial of which, even though it were a *pientissima fraus,* is strictly punished by God. God is the God of truth, and will therefore be neither defended nor honoured by any perverting of the truth. By such pious lies the friends involve themselves in guilt, since in opposition to their better knowledge they regard Job as unrighteous, and blind themselves to the incongruities of daily experience and the justice of God. Job will therefore have nothing more to do with them; and to whom does he now turn? Repelled by men, he feels all the more strongly drawn to God. He desires to carry his cause before God. He certainly considers God to be his enemy, but, like David, he thinks it is better to fall into the hands of God than into the hands of man (2 Sam. xxiv. 14). He will plead his cause with God, and prove to Him his innocence : he will do it, even though he be obliged to expiate his boldness with his life; for he knows that morally he will not be overcome in the contest. He requires compliance with but two conditions : that God would grant a temporary alleviation of his pain, and that He would not overawe him with the display of His majesty. Job's disput-

ing with God is as terrible as it is pitiable. It is terrible,
because he uplifts himself, Titan-like, against God; and
pitiable, because the God against which he fights is not the
God he has known, but a God that he is unable to recognise,
—the phantom which the temptation has presented before his
dim vision instead of the true God. This phantom is still the
real God to him, but in other respects in no way differing
from the inexorable ruling fate of the Greek tragedy. As in
this the hero of the drama seeks to maintain his personal
freedom against the mysterious power that is crushing him
with an iron arm, so Job, even at the risk of sudden destruction, maintains the stedfast conviction of his innocence, in
opposition to a God who has devoted him, as an evil-doer, to
slow but certain destruction. The battle of freedom against
necessity is the same as in the Greek tragedy. Accordingly
one is obliged to regard it as an error, arising from simple ignorance, when it has been recently maintained that the boundless oriental imagination is not equal to such a truly exalted
task as that of representing in art and poetry the power of
the human spirit, and the maintenance of its dignity in the
conflict with hostile powers, because a task that can only be
accomplished by an imagination formed with a perception of
the importance of recognising ascertained phenomena.[1] In
treating this subject, the book of Job not only attains to, but
rises far above, the height attained by the Greek tragedy:
for, on the one hand, it brings this conflict before us in all
the fearful earnestness of a death-struggle; on the other,
however, it does not leave us to the cheerless delusion that
an absolute caprice moulds human destiny. This tragic
conflict with the divine necessity is but the middle, not the
beginning nor the end, of the book; for this god of fate is
not the real God, but a delusion of Job's temptation. Human
freedom does not succumb, but it comes forth from the battle,

[1] *Vid.* Arnold Ruge, *Die Academie*, i. S. 29.

which is a refining fire to it, as conqueror. The dualism, which the Greek tragedy leaves unexplained, is here cleared up. The book certainly presents much which, from its tragic character, suggests this idea of destiny, but it is not its final aim—it goes far beyond : it does not end in the destruction of its hero by fate; but the end is the destruction of the idea of this fate itself.

We have seen in this speech (comp. ch. xiii. 23, 26, xiv. 16 sq.), as often already, that Job is as little able as the friends to disconnect *suffering* from the idea of the *punishment of sin*. If Job were mistaken or were misled by the friends respecting his innocence, the history of his sufferings would be no material for a drama, because there would be no inner development. But it is just Job's stedfast conviction of his innocence, and his maintenance of it in spite of the power which this prejudice exercises over him, that makes the history of his affliction the history of the development of a new and grand idea, and makes him as the subject, on whom it is developed, a tragic character. In conformity with his prepossession, Job sees himself put down by his affliction as a great sinner; and his friends actually draw the conclusion from false premises that he is such. But he asserts the testimony of his conscience to his innocence ; and because this contradicts those premises, the one-sidedness of which he does not discern, God himself appears to him to be unjust and unmerciful. And against this God, whom the temptation has distorted and transformed to the miserable image of a ruler, guided only by an absolute caprice, he struggles on, and places the truth and freedom of his moral self-consciousness over against the restraint of the condemnatory sentence, which seems to be pronounced over him in the suffering he has to endure. Such is the struggle against God which we behold in the second part of the speech (ch. xiii.) : ready to prove his innocence, he challenges God to

trial; but since God does not appear, his confidence gives
place to despondency, and his defiant tone to a tone of lamentation, which is continued in the third part of the speech
(ch. xiv.).

While he has raised his head towards heaven with the
conscious pride of a צדיק תמים, first in opposition to the friends
and then to God, he begins to complain as one who is thrust
back, and yielding to the pressure of his affliction, begins to
regard himself as a sinner. But he is still unable to satisfy
himself respecting God's dealings by any such forcible self-
persuasion. For how can God execute such strict judgment
upon man, whose life is so short and full of care, and who,
because he belongs to a sinful race, cannot possibly be pure
from sin, without allowing him the comparative rest of a
hireling? How can he thus harshly visit man, to whose life
He has set an appointed bound, and who, when he once dies,
returns to life no more for ever? The old expositors cannot
at all understand this absolute denial of a new life after death.
Brentius erroneously observes on *donec cœlum transierit : ergo
resurget;* and Mercerus, whose exposition is free from all
prejudice, cannot persuade himself that the *electus et sanctus
Dei vir* can have denied not merely a second earthly life, but
also the eternal imperishable life after death. And yet it is
so : Job does not indeed mean that man when he dies is
annihilated, but he knows of no other life after death but the
shadowy life in Sheôl, which is no life at all. His laments
really harmonize with those in Moschos iii. 106 sqq.:

Αἲ αἲ, ταὶ μαλάχαι μὲν ἐπὰν κατὰ κᾶπον ὄλωνται,
Ἢ τὰ χλωρὰ σέλινα, τό τ᾽ εὐθαλὲς οὖλον ἄνηθον,
Ὕστερον αὖ ζώοντι καὶ εἰς ἔτος ἄλλο φύοντι·
Ἄμμες δ᾽ οἱ μεγάλοι καὶ καρτεροὶ ἢ σοφοὶ ἄνδρες,
Ὁππότε πρῶτα θάνωμες, ἀνάκοοι ἐν χθονὶ κοίλᾳ
Εὕδομες εὖ μάλα μακρὸν ἀτέρμονα νήγρετον ὕπνον.

Alas! alas! the mallows, after they are withered in the garden,
Or the green parsley and the luxuriant curly dill,
Live again hereafter and sprout in future years ;
But we men, the great and brave, or the wise,
When once we die, senseless in the bosom of the earth
We sleep a long, endless, and eternal sleep.

And with that of Horace, Od. iv. 7, 1 :

Nos ubi decidimus
Quo pius Aeneas, quo dives Tullus et Ancus,
Pulvis et umbra sumus ;

Or with that of the Jagur Weda : " While the tree that has
fallen sprouts again from the root fresher than before, from
what root does mortal man spring forth when he has fallen
by the hand of death ?"[1] These laments echo through the
ancient world from one end to the other, and even Job is
without any superior knowledge respecting the future life.

[1] *Vid.* Carey, *The Book of Job*, p. 447. We append here an extract from
a letter of Consul Wetzstein, as giving an explanation of Job xiv. 7–9,
derived from personal observation : " The practice of cutting down the
trees in order to obtain a now and increased use from them, is an important part of husbandry in the country east of the Jordan. It is, however,
now almost confined to the region round Damascus, in consequence of
the devastation of the country. This operation is called *gemm* (גמם), and
is performed only with the axe, because the stump would decay away if
sawn. When the vine, after bearing from sixty to eighty years, loses its
fruitfulness and begins to decay, it is cut down close to the ground in
the second *kânûn* (January). The first year it bears little or nothing,
but throws out new branches and roots ; and afterwards it bears plen-
teously, for the vine-stock has renewed its youth. The fig-tree (*tîne*)
and the pomegranate (*rummâne*), when old and decayed, are cut down
in like manner. Their shoots are very numerous, and in the following
winter as many as ten young plants may be taken from the pomegranate.
Those that are left on the old stem bear fruit in the fourth year. The
walnut-tree (*gôze*) ceases to bear much after 100 years, and becomes
hollow and decayed. It is then cut down to within two or three yards
from the ground. If the trees are well watered, the new shoots spring
up in a year in uncommon luxuriance, and bear fruit in the second year.
The new shoot is called *darbûne*. From many trees, as the citron
(*lîmûne*), ash (*dardâre*), and mulberry (*tûte*), this new shoot often attains
a length of twelve feet in the first year, provided the tree has the *conditio
sine qua non* which Job styles ריח מים—a plentiful supply of water."

He denies a resurrection and eternal life, not as one who
has a knowledge of them and will not however know anything about them, but he really knows nothing of them :
our earthly life seems to him to flow on into the darkness
of Sheôl, and onward beyond Sheôl man has no further
existence.

We inquire here : Can we say that the poet knew nothing
of a resurrection and judgment after death ?   If we look to
the psalms of the time of David and Solomon, we must reply
in the negative.   Since, however, as the Grecian mysteries
fostered and cherished ἡδυστέρας ἐλπίδας, the Israelitish
Chokma also, by its constant struggles upwards and onwards,
anticipated views of the future world which reached beyond
the present (*Psychol.* S. 410) : it may be assumed, and from
the book of Job directly inferred, that the poet had a perception of the future world which went beyond the dim perception of the people, which was not yet lighted up by any
revelation.   For, on the one hand, he has reproduced for us
a history of the patriarchal period, not merely according to
its external, but also according to its internal working, with
as strict historical faithfulness as delicate psychological tact ;
on the other, he has with a master hand described for us in
the history of Job what was only possible from an advanced
standpoint of knowledge,—how the hope of a life beyond
the present, where there is no express word of promise to
guide it, struggles forth from the heart of man as an un-
defined desire and longing, so that the word of promise is the
fulfilment and seal of this desire and yearning.   For when
Job gives expression to the wish that God would hide him in
Sheôl until His anger turn, and then, at an appointed time,
yearning after the work of His hands, raise him again from
Sheôl (ch. xiv. 13–17), this wish is not to be understood other
than that Sheôl might be only his temporary hiding-place
from the divine anger, instead of being his eternal abode.

He wishes himself in Sheôl, so far as he would thereby be removed for a time from the wrath of God, in order that, after an appointed season, he might again become an object of the divine favour. He cheers himself with the delightful thought, All the days of my warfare would I wait till my change should come, etc.; for then the warfare of suffering would become easy to him, because favour, after wrath and deliverance from suffering and death, would be near at hand. We cannot say that Job here expresses the hope of a life after death; on the contrary, this hope is wanting to him, and all knowledge respecting the reasons that might warrant it. The hope exists only in imagination, as Ewald rightly observes, without becoming a certainty, since it is only the idea, How glorious it would be if it were so, that is followed up. But, on the one side, the poet shows us by this touching utterance of Job how totally different would be his endurance of suffering if he but knew that there was really a release from Hades; on the other side, he shows us, in the wish of Job, the incipient tendency of the growing hope that it might be so, for what a devout mind desires has a spiritual power which presses forward from the subjective to the objective reality. The hope of eternal life is a flower, says one of the old commentators, which grows on the verge of the abyss. The writer of the book of Job supports this. In the midst of this abyss of the feeling of divine wrath in which Job is sunk, this flower springs up to cheer him. In its growth, however, it is not hope, but only at first a longing. And this longing cannot expand into hope, because no light of promise shines forth in that night, by which Job's feeling is controlled, and which makes the conflict darker than it is in itself. Scarcely has Job feasted for a short space upon the idea of that which he would gladly hope for, when the thought of the reality of that which he has to fear overwhelms him. He seems to himself to be an evil-doer who is reserved for the execution of the sentence of death. If it is not possible in nature for mountains, rocks, stones, and the dust of the earth to resist the force of the elements, so is it an easy thing for God to destroy the hope of a mortal all at once. He forcibly thrust him hence from this life; and when he is descended to Hades, he knows nothing whatever of the lot of his own family in the world above. Of the life and knowledge of the living, nothing remains to him but the senseless pain of his dead body, which is gnawed away, and the dull sorrow of his soul, which continues but a shadowy life in Sheôl.

Thus the poet shows us, in the third part of Job's speech, a grand idea, which tries to force its way, but cannot. In the second part, Job desired to maintain his conviction of innocence before God: his confidence is repulsed by the idea of the God who is conceived of by him as an enemy and a capricious ruler, and changes to despair. In the third part, the desire for a life after death is maintained; but he is at once overwhelmed by the imagined inevitable and eternal darkness of Sheôl, but overwhelmed soon to appear again above the billows of temptation, until, in ch. xix., the utterance of faith respecting a future life rises as a certain confidence over death and the grave: the γνῶσις which comes forth from the conflict of the πίστις anticipates that better hope which in the New Testament is established and ratified by the act of redemption wrought by the Conqueror of Hades.

THE SECOND COURSE OF THE CONTROVERSY.—
CHAP. XV.–XXI.

Eliphaz' Second Speech.—Chap. xv.

Schema: 10. 8. 6. 6. 6. 10. 14. 10.

[Then began Eliphaz the Temanite, and said :]
2 *Doth a wise man utter vain knowledge,*
   And fill his breast with the east wind?
3 *Contending with words, that profit not,*
   And speeches, by which no good is done?
4 *Moreover, thou makest void the fear of God,*
   And thou restrainest devotion before God;
5 *For thy mouth exposeth thy misdeeds,*
   And thou choosest the language of the crafty.
6 *Thine own mouth condemneth thee and not I,*
   And thine own lips testify against thee.

The second course of the controversy is again opened by Eliphaz, the most respectable, most influential, and perhaps oldest of the friends. Job's detailed and bitter answers seem to him as empty words and impassioned tirades, which ill become a wise man, such as he claims to be in assertions like ch. xii. 3, xiii. 2. הֶחָכָם with *He interr.*, like הַעֲלֶה, ch. xiii. 25. רוּחַ, wind, is the opposite of what is solid and sure; and קָדִים in the parallel (like Hos. xii. 2) signifies what is worthless, with the additional notion of vehement action. If we translate בֶּטֶן by "belly," the meaning is apt to be misunderstood; it is not intended as the opposite of לֵב (Ewald), but it means, especially in the book of Job, not only that which feels, but also thinks and wills, the spiritually receptive and active inner nature of man (*Psychol.* S. 266); as also in Arabic, *el-battin* signifies that which is within, in the deepest mystical sense. Hirz. and Renan translate the *inf. abs.* הוֹכֵחַ, which follows in

ver. 3, as *verb. fin.* : *se défend-il par des vaines paroles;* but
though the *inf. abs.* is so used in an historical clause (ch.
xv. 35), it is not in an interrogative. Ewald takes it as the
subject : "to reprove with words—avails not, and speeches—
whereby one does no good;" but though דָּבָר and מִלִּים might
be used without any further defining, as in λογομαχεῖν (2 Tim.
ii. 14) and λογομαχία (1 Tim. vi. 4), the form of ver. 3*b* is
opposed to such an explanation. The *inf. abs.* is connected
as a gerund (*redarguendo s. disputando*) with the verbs in the
question, ver. 2 ; and the elliptical relative clause לֹא יִסְכֹּן is
best, as referring to things, according to ch. xxxv. 3 : *ser-*
mone (דָּבָר from דִּבֵּר, as *sermo* from *serere*) *qui non prodest;*
לֹא יוֹעִיל בָּם, on the other hand, to persons, *verbis quibus nil*
utilitatis affert. Eliphaz does not censure Job for arguing,
but for defending himself by such useless and purposeless
utterances of his feeling. But still more than that : his
speeches are not only unsatisfactory and unbecoming, אַף,
accedit quod (cumulative like ch. xiv. 3), they are moreover
irreligious, since by doubting the justice of God they deprive religion of its fundamental assumption, and diminish
the reverence due to God. יִרְאָה in such an objective sense
as Ps. xix. 10 almost corresponds to the idea of religion.
שִׂיחָה לִפְנֵי־אֵל is to be understood, according to Ps. cii. 1, cxlii. 3
(comp. lxiv. 2, civ. 34) : before God, and consequently customary devotional meditation, here of the disposition of mind
indispensable to prayer, viz. devotion, and especially reveren-
tial awe, which Job depreciates (גָּרַע, *detrahere*). His speeches
are mostly directed towards God ; but they are violent and
reproachful, therefore irreverent in form and substance.

Ver. 5. כִּי is not affirmative : forsooth (Hirz.), but, confirmatory and explicative. This opinion respecting him, which is
so sharply and definitely expressed by אַתָּה, thrusts itself irresistibly forward, for it is not necessary to know his life more
exactly, his own mouth, whence such words escape, reveals

his sad state: *docet* (אֱלֹף only in the book of Job, from אָלַף, *discere*, a word which only occurs once in the *Hebrew*, Prov. xxii. 25) *culpam tuam os tuum*, not as Schlottm. explains, with Raschi: *docet culpa tua os tuum*, which, to avoid being misunderstood, must have been חטאתך תאלף, and is a thought unsuited to the connection. אֱלֹף is certainly not directly equivalent to הגיד, Isa. iii. 9 ; it signifies to teach, to explain, and this verb is just the one in the mouth of the censorious friend. What follows must not be translated : while thou choosest (Hirz.); ותבחר is not a circumstantial clause, but adds a second confirmatory clause to the first : he chooses the language of the crafty, since he pretends to be able to prove his innocence before God; and convinced that he is in the right, assumes the offensive (as ch. xiii. 4 sqq.) against those who exhort him to humble himself. Thus by his evil words he becomes his own judge (ירשיעך) and accuser (יענו בך after the *fem.* שפתיך, like Prov. v. 2, xxvi. 23). The knot of the controversy becomes constantly more entangled since Job strengthens the friends more and more in their false view by his speeches, which certainly are sinful in some parts (as ch. ix. 22).

7 *Wast thou as the first one born as a man,*
  And hast thou been brought forth before the hills ?
8 *Hast thou attended to the counsel of Eloah,*
  And hast thou kept wisdom to thyself?
9 *What dost thou know that we have not known ?*
  Doest thou understand what we have not been acquainted
     with ?
10 *Both grey-haired and aged are among us,*
   Older in days than thy father.

The question in ver. 7*a* assumes that the first created man, because coming direct from the hand of God, had the most direct and profoundest insight into the mysteries of the world which came into existence at the same time as himself.

Schlottman calls to mind an ironical proverbial expression of the Hindus : "Yea, indeed, he is the first man ; no wonder that he is so wise" (Roberts, *Orient. Illustr.* p. 276). It is not to be translated : wast thou born as the first man, which is as inadmissible as the translation of אחת מעט, Hag. ii. 6, by "a little" (*vid.* Köhler *in loc.*) ; rather ראישון (*i.e.* רָאִישׁוֹן, as Josh. xxi. 10, formed from רָאשׁ, like the Arabic *rais*, from *ras*, if it is not perhaps a mere incorrect amalgamation of the forms רָאשׁוֹן and רִישׁוֹן, ch. viii. 8) is in apposition with the subject, and אָדָם is to be regarded as predicate, according to Ges. § 139, 2. Raschi's translation is also impossible : wast thou born before Adam ? for this Greek form of expression, πρῶτός μου, John i. 15, 30, xv. 18 (comp. *Odyss.* xi. 481 sq., σεῖο μακάρτατος), is strange to the Hebrew. In the parallel question, ver. 7*b*, Umbr., Schlottm., and Renan (following Ewald) see a play upon Prov. viii. 24 sq.: art thou the demiurgic Wisdom itself ? But the introductory proverbs (Prov. ch. i.–ix.) are more recent than the book of Job (*vid. supra*, p. 24), and indeed probably, as we shall show elsewhere, belong to the time of Jehoshaphat. Consequently the more probable relation is that the writer of Prov. viii. 24 sq. has adopted words from the book of Job in describing the pre-existence of the Chokma. Was Job, a higher spirit-nature, brought forth, *i.e.* as it were amidst the pangs of travail (חוֹלָלְתָּ, *Pulal* from חוּל, חִיל), before the hills ? for the angels, according to Scripture, were created before man, and even before the visible universe (*vid.* ch. xxxviii. 4 sqq.). Hirz., Ew., Schlottm., and others erroneously translate the *futt.* in the questions, ver. 8, as *præs.* All the verbs in vers. 7, 8, are under the control of the retrospective character which is given to the verses by רָאישׁוֹן; comp. x. 10 sq., where זָכְר־נָא has the same influence, and also ch. iii. 3, where the historical sense of אִוָּלֵד depends not upon the syntax, but upon logical necessity. Translate therefore : didst thou attend in the

secret council (סוֹד, like Jer. xxiii. 18, comp. Ps. lxxxix. 8) of
Eloah (according to the correct form of writing in Codd. and

in Kimchi, *Michlol* 54a, הַבְּסוֹד, like ver. 11 הַמְעַט and ch.

xxii. 13 הַבְעַד, with *Beth raph.* and without *Gaja*[1]), and didst
then acquire for thyself (גרע, here *attrahere*, like the Arabic,
sorbere, to suck in) wisdom? by which one is reminded of
Prometheus' fire stolen from heaven. Nay, Job can boast of
no extraordinary wisdom. The friends—as Eliphaz, ver. 9,
says in their name—are his cotemporaries; and if he desires
to appeal to the teaching of his father, and of his ancestors
generally, let him know that there are hoary-headed men
among themselves, whose discernment is deeper by reason
of their more advanced age. גַּם is inverted, like ch. ii. 10
(which see); and at the same time, since it is used twice, it is
correlative: *etiam inter nos et cani et senes.* Most modern
expositors think that Eliphaz, " in modestly concealed language" (Ewald), refers to himself. But the reference would
be obvious enough; and wherefore this modest concealing,
which is so little suited to the character of Eliphaz? Moreover, ver. 10a does not sound as if speaking merely of one,
and in ver. 10b Eliphaz would make himself older than he
appears to be, for it is nowhere implied that Job is a young
man in comparison with him. We therefore with Umbreit
explain בָּנוּ : in our generation. Thus it sounds more like
the Arabic, both in words (*kebîr* Arab., usual in the signif.
grandævus) and in substance. Eliphaz appeals to the source
of reliable tradition, since they have even among their races
and districts mature old men, and since, indeed, according to

---

[1] As a rule, the interrogative *He*, when pointed with *Pathach*, has *Gaja*
against the *Pathach* [2 Sam. vii. 5] ; this, however, falls away (among
other instances) when the syllable immediately following the *He* has the
tone, as in the two examples given above (comp. also הַאָל, ch. viii. 3;
הֲלָאל, xiii. 7), or the usual *Gaja* (*Metheg*) which stands in the *ante-
penultima* (Bär, *Metheg-Setzung*, § 23).

Job's own admission (ch. xii. 12), there is "wisdom among the ancient ones."

11 *Are the consolations of God too small for thee,*
   And a word thus tenderly spoken with thee?
12 *What overpowers thy heart?*
   And why do thine eyes wink,
13 *That thou turnest thy snorting against God,*
   And sendest forth such words from thy mouth?

By the consolations of God, Eliphaz means the promises in accordance with the majesty and will of God, by which he and the other friends have sought to cheer him, of course presupposing a humble resignation to the just hand of God. By "a word (spoken) in gentleness to him," he means the gentle tone which they have maintained, while he has passionately opposed them. לָאַט, elsewhere לְאָט (*e.g.* Isa. viii. 6, of the softly murmuring and gently flowing Siloah), from אַט (declined, אִטִּי), with the neutral, adverbial לְ (as לְבֶטַח), signifies: with a soft step, gently. The word has no connection with לוּט, לָאַט, to cover over, and is not third *præt.* (as it is regarded by Raschi, after Chajug): which he has gently said to you, or that which has gently befallen you; in which, as in Fürst's *Handwörterbuch,* the notions *secrete* (Judg. iv. 21, Targ. בְּרָז, in secret) and *leniter* are referred to one root. Are these divine consolations, and these so gentle addresses, too small for thee (מְעַט מִמְּךָ, *opp.* 1 Kings xix. 7), *i.e.* beneath thy dignity, and unworthy of thy notice? What takes away (לקח, *auferre, abripere,* as frequently) thy heart (here of wounded pride), and why do thine eyes gleam, that thou turnest (הֵשִׁיב, not *revertere,* but *vertere,* as freq.) thy ill-humour towards God, and utterest מִלִּין (so here, not מִלִּים) words, which, because they are without meaning and intelligence, are nothing but words? רָזַם, *ἅπ. γεγρ.,* is transposed from רָמַז, to wink, *i.e.* to make known by gestures and grimaces,—a word which does not occur in biblical, but is very common in post-biblical, Hebrew (*e.g.* חרש רומז ונרמז, a deaf and dumb person expresses himself and is answered by a language of signs). Modern expositors arbitrarily understand a rolling of the eyes; it is more natural to think of the vibration of the eye-lashes or eye-brows. רוּחַ, ver. 13, is as in Judg. viii. 3, Isa. xxv. 4, comp. xiii. 11, and freq. used of passionate excitement, which is thus expressed because it manifests itself in πνέειν (Acts ix. 1), and has its rise in the πνεῦμα (Eccl. vii. 9). Job ought to control this angry spirit, θυμός (*Psychol.* S. 198); but he allows it to burst forth, and makes even God the object on which he vents his anger in impetuous language. How much better it would be for him, if he would search within himself (Lam. iii. 39) for the reason of those sufferings which so deprive him of his self-control!

14 *What is mortal man that he should be pure,*
   And that he who is born of woman should be righteous?
15 *He trusteth not His holy ones,*
   And the heavens are not pure in His eyes:
16 *How much less the abominable and corrupt,*
   Man, who drinketh iniquity as water!

The exclamation in ver. 14 is like the utterance: mortal man and man born flesh of flesh cannot be entirely sinless. Even "the holy ones" and "the heavens" are not. The former are, as in ch. v. 1, according to iv. 18, the angels as beings of light (whether קָדשׁ signifies to be light from the very first, spotlessly pure, or, *vid. Psalter*, i. 588 sq., to be separated, distinct, and hence exalted above what is common); the latter is not another expression for the אַנְגְּלֵי מְרוֹמָא (Targ.), the "angels of the heights," but שָׁמַיִם is the word used for the highest spheres in which they dwell (comp. ch. xxv. 5); for the angels are certainly not corporeal, but, like all created things, in space, and the Scriptures everywhere speak of

angels and the starry heavens together. Hence the angels
are called the morning stars in ch. xxxviii. 7, and hence both
stars and angels are called צְבָא הַשָּׁמִים and צְבָאוֹת (*vid. Genesis*,
S. 128). Even the angels and the heavens are finite, and
consequently are not of a nature absolutely raised above the
possibility of sin and contamination.

Eliphaz repeats here what he has already said, ch. iv. 18
sq.; but he does it intentionally, since he wishes still more
terribly to describe human uncleanness to Job (Oetinger).
In that passage אַף was merely the sign of an anti-climax,
here אַף כִּי is *quanto minus*. Eliphaz refers to the hereditary
infirmity and sin of human nature in ver. 14, here (ver. 16)
to man's own free choice of that which works his destruction.
He uses the strongest imaginable words to describe one
actualiter and *originaliter* corrupted. נִתְעָב denotes one who
is become an abomination, or the abominated = abominable
(Ges. § 134, 1); נֶאֱלָח, one thoroughly corrupted (Arabic
alacha, in the medial VIII. conjugation: to become sour,
which reminds one of ζύμη, Rabb. שְׂאֹר שֶׁבָּעִסָּה, as an image of
evil, and especially of evil desire). It is further said of him
(an expression which Elihu adopts, ch. xxxiv. 7), that he drinks
up evil like water. The figure is like Prov. xxvi. 6, comp.
on Ps. lxxiii. 10, and implies that he lusts after sin, and that
it is become a necessity of his nature, and is to his nature
what water is to the thirsty. Even Job does not deny this
corruption of man (ch. xiv. 4), but the inferences which the
friends draw in reference to him he cannot acknowledge.
The continuation of Eliphaz' speech shows how they render
this acknowledgment impossible to him.

17 *I will inform thee, hear me!*
        And what I have myself seen that I will declare,
18 *Things which wise men declare*
        Without concealment from their fathers—

19 *To them alone was the land given over,*
And no stranger had passed in their midst— :

Eliphaz, as in his first speech, introduces the dogma with
which he confronts Job with a solemn preface : in the former
case it had its rise in a revelation, here it is supported by his
own experience and reliable tradition; for חֲזִיתִי is not intended as meaning ecstatic vision (Schlottm.). The poet uses
חָזָה also of sensuous vision, ch. viii. 17; and of observation
and knowledge by means of the senses, not only the more
exalted, as ch. xix. 26 sq., but of any kind (ch. xxiii. 9, xxiv.
1, xxvii. 12, comp. xxxvi. 25, xxxiv. 32), in the widest sense.
זֶה is used as neuter, Gen. vi. 15, Ex. xiii. 8, xxx. 13, Lev. xi.
4, and freq.[1] (comp. the neuter הוּא, ch. xiii. 16, and often),
and זֶה־חָזִיתִי is a relative clause (Ges. § 122, 2): *quod conspexi*,
as ch. xix. 19 *quos amo*, and Ps. lxxiv. 2 *in quo habitas*, comp.
Ps. civ. 8, 26, Prov. xxiii. 22, where the punctuation throughout proceeds from the correct knowledge of the syntax. The
waw of וַאֲסַפְּרָה is the *waw apodosis*, which is customary
(Nägelsbach, § 111, 1, *b*) after relative clauses (*e.g.* Num.
xxiii. 3), or what is the same thing, participles (*e.g.* Prov.
xxiii. 24) : *et narrabo = ea narrabo.* In ver. 18 וְלֹא כִחֲדוּ is,
logically at least, subordinate to יַגִּידוּ, as in Isa. iii. 9,[2] as the
Targum of the Antwerp Polyglott well translates : " what
wise men declare, without concealing (וְלָא מְכַדְּבִין), from the
tradition of their fathers ;" whereas all the other old translations, including Luther's, have missed the right meaning.
These fathers to whom this doctrine respecting the fate of
evil-doers is referred, lived, as Eliphaz says in ver. 19, in
the land of their birth, and did not mingle themselves with

---

[1] So also Ps. lvi. 10, where I now prefer to translate " This I know,"
זֶה neuter, like Prov. xxiv. 12, and referring forward as above, ver. 17.

[2] Heidenheim refers to Hos. viii. 2 for the position of the words, but
there *Israel* may also be an apposition : we know thee, we Israel.

strangers ; consequently their manner of viewing things, and
their opinions, have in their favour the advantage of independence, of being derived from their own experience, and also of
a healthy development undisturbed by any foreign influences,
and their teaching may be accounted pure and unalloyed.

Eliphaz thus indirectly says, that the present is not free
from such influences, and Ewald is consequently of opinion
that the individuality of the Israelitish poet peeps out here,
and a state of things is indicated like that which came about
after the fall of Samaria in the reign of Manasseh.   Hirzel
also infers from Eliphaz' words, that at the time when the
book was written the poet's fatherland was desecrated by
some foreign rule, and considers it an indication for determining the time at which the book was composed.   But how
groundless and deceptive this is !   The way in which Eliphaz
commends ancient traditional lore is so genuinely Arabian,
that there is but the faintest semblance of a reason for supposing the poet to have thrown his own history and national
peculiarity so vividly into the working up of the *rôle* of
another.   Purity of race was, from the earliest times, considered by "the sons of the East" as the sign of highest
nobility, and hence Eliphaz traces back his teaching to a time
when his race could boast of the greatest freedom from intermixture with any other.   Schlottmann prefers to interpret
ver. 19 as referring to the "nobler primeval races of man"
(without, however, referring to ch. viii. 8), but הָאָרֶץ does not
signify the earth here, but: country, as in ch. xxx. 8, xxii. 8,
and elsewhere, and ver. 19*b* seems to refer to nations : זָר =
barbarus (perhaps Semitic : בַּרְבַּר, ὁ ἔξω).   Nevertheless it is
unnecessary to suppose that Eliphaz' time was one of foreign
domination, as the Assyrian-Chaldean time was for Israel : it
is sufficient to imagine it as a time when the tribes of the
desert were becoming intermixed, from migration, commerce,
and feud.

Now follows the doctrine of the wise men, which springs from a venerable primitive age, an age as yet undisturbed by any strange way of thinking (modern enlightenment and free thinking, as we should say), and is supported by Eliphaz' own experience.[1]

[1] Communication from Consul Wetzstein : If this verse affirms that the freer a people is from intermixture with other races, the purer is its tradition, it gives expression to a principle derived from experience, which needs no proof. Even European races, especially the Scandinavians, furnish proof of this in their customs, language, and traditions, although in this case certain elements of their indigenous character have vanished with the introduction of Christianity. A more complete parallel is furnished by the wandering tribes of the 'Aneze and Sharârât of the Syrian deserts, people who have indeed had their struggles, and have even been weakened by emigration, but have certainly never lost their political and religious autonomy, and have preserved valuable traditions which may be traced to the earliest antiquity. It is unnecessary to prove this by special instances, when the whole outer and inner life of these peoples can be regarded as the best commentary on the biblical accounts of the patriarchal age. It is, however, not so much the *fact* that the evil-doer receives his punishment, in favour of which Eliphaz appeals to the teaching handed down from the fathers, as rather the *belief in it*, consequently in a certain degree the dogma of a moral order in the world. This dogma is an essential element of the ancient Abrahamic religion of the desert tribes—that primitive religion which formed the basis of the Mosaic, and side by side with it was continued among the nomads of the desert; which, shortly before the appearance of Christianity in the country east of Jordan, gave birth to mild doctrines, doctrines which tended to prepare the way for the teaching of the gospel ; which at that very time, according to historical testimony, also prevailed in the towns of the *Higâz*, and was first displaced again by the Jemanic idolatry, and limited to the desert, in the second century after Christ, during the repeated migrations of the southern Arabs ; which gave the most powerful impulse to the rise of *Islam*, and furnished its best elements ; which, towards the end of the last century, brought about the reform of Islamism in the province of *Negd*, and produced the *Wahabee* doctrine ; and which, finally, is continued even to the present day by the name of *Dîn Ibrâhîm*, " Religion of Abraham," as a faithful tradition of the fathers, among the vast Ishmaelitish tribes of the Syrian desert, " to whom alone the land is given over, and into whose midst no stranger has penetrated." Had this *cultus* spread among settled races with a higher education, it might have been taught also in writings : if, however, portions of writings in reference to it, which have been handed

20 *So long as the ungodly liveth he suffereth,*
　And numbered years are reserved for the tyrant.
21 *Terrors sound in his ears;*
　In time of peace the destroyer cometh upon him.
22 *He believeth not in a return from darkness,*
　And he is selected for the sword.
23 *He roameth about after bread: "Ah! where is it?"*
　He knoweth that a dark day is near at hand for him.
24 *Trouble and anguish terrify him;*
　They seize him as a king ready to the battle.

All the days of the ungodly he (the ungodly) is sensible of pain. רָשָׁע stands, like *Elohim* in Gen. ix. 6, by the closer definition; here however so, that this defining ends after the manner of a premiss, and is begun by הוּא after the manner of a conclusion. מִתְחוֹלֵל, he writhes, *i.e.* suffers inward anxiety

down to us by the Arabs, are to be regarded as unauthentic, it may also in ʿ*Irâk* have been mixed with the *Sabian* worship of the stars; but among the nomads it will have always been only oral, taught by the poets in song, and contained in the fine traditions handed down uncorrupted from father to son, and practised in life.

It is a dogma of this religion (of which I shall speak more fully in the introduction to my *Anthologie von Poesien der Wanderstämme*), that the pious will be rewarded by God in his life and in his descendants, the wicked punished in his life and in his descendants; and it may also, in ver. 19, be indirectly said that the land of Eliphaz has preserved this faith, in accordance with tradition, purer than Job's land. If Eliphaz was from the Petræan town of *Têmân* (which we merely suggest as possible here), he might indeed rightly assert that no strange race had become naturalized there; for that hot, sterile land, poorly supplied with water, had nothing inviting to the emigrant or marauder, and its natives remain there only by virtue of the proverb: *lôlâ hhibb el-wattan qat.tâl, lakân dâr es-sû' charâb,* "Did not the love of one's country slay (him who is separated from it), the barren country would be uninhabited." Job certainly could not affirm the same of his native country, if this is, with the Syrian tradition, to be regarded as the *Nukra* (on this point, *vid.* the Appendix). As the richest province of Syria, it has, from the earliest time to the present, always been an apple of contention, and has not only frequently changed its rulers, but even its inhabitants.

and distress in the midst of all outward appearance of happiness. Most expositors translate the next line : and throughout the number of the years, which are reserved to the tyrant. But (1) this parallel definition of time appended by *waw* makes the sense drawling ; (2) the change of עָרִיץ (oppressor, tyrant) for רָשָׁע leads one to expect a fresh affirmation, hence it is translated by the LXX.: ἔτη δὲ ἀριθμητὰ δεδομένα δυνάστῃ. The predicate is, then, like ch. xxxii. 7, comp. xxix. 10, 1 Sam. ii. 4 (Ges. § 148), *per attractionem* in the *plur.* instead of in the *sing.*, and especially with מִסְפַּר followed by *gen. plur.;* this attraction is adopted by our author, ch. xxi. 21, xxxviii. 21. The meaning is not, that numbered, *i.e.* few, years are secretly appointed to the tyrant, which must have been *sh'nôth mispâr*, a reversed position of the words, as ch. xvi. 22, Num. ix. 20 (*vid.* Gesenius' *Thes.*) ; but a (limited, appointed) number of years is reserved to the tyrant (צפן as ch. xxiv. 1, xxi. 19, comp. טמן, ch. xx. 26 ; Mercerus : *occulto decreto definiti*), after the expiration of which his punishment begins. The thought expressed by the Targ., Syr., and Jerome would be suitable: and the number of the years (that he has to live unpunished) is hidden from the tyrant ; but if this were the poet's meaning, he would have written שָׁנָיו, and must have written מִן־הֶעָרִיץ.

With regard to the following vers. 21–24, it is doubtful whether only the evil-doer's anxiety of spirit is described in amplification of הוּא מתחולל, or also how the terrible images from which he suffers in his conscience are realized, and how he at length helplessly succumbs to the destruction which his imagination had long foreboded. A satisfactory and decisive answer to this question is hardly possible ; but considering that the real crisis is brought on by Eliphaz later, and fully described, it seems more probable that what has an objective tone in vers. 21–24 is controlled by what has been affirmed respecting the evil conscience of the ungodly, and is to be

understood accordingly. The sound of terrible things (start-
ling dangers) rings in his ears; the devastator comes upon
him (בוא *seq. acc.* as ch. xx. 22, Prov. xxviii. 22 ; comp. Isa.
xxviii. 15) in the midst of his prosperity. He anticipates it
ere it happens. From the darkness by which he feels himself
menaced, he believes not (הֶאֱמִין *seq. infin.* as Ps. xxvii. 13,
לִרְאוֹת, of confident hope) to return ; *i.e.* overwhelmed with a
consciousness of his guilt, he cannot, in the presence of this
darkness which threatens him, rise to the hope of rescue from
it, and he is really—as his consciousness tells him—צָפוּ (like
עָשׂוּ, ch. xli. 25 ; Ges. § 75, rem. 5 ; *Keri* צָפוּי, which is omitted
in our printed copies, contrary to the testimony of the Masora
and the authority of correct MSS.), spied out for, appointed to
the sword, *i.e.* of God (ch. xix. 29 ; Isa. xxxi. 8), or decreed
by God. In the midst of abundance he is harassed by the
thought of becoming poor; he wanders about in search of
bread, anxiously looking out and asking where? (abrupt, like
הִנֵּה, ch. ix. 19), *i.e.* where is any to be found, whence can I
obtain it? The LXX. translates contrary to the connection,
and with a strange misunderstanding of the passage: κατατέ-
τακται δὲ εἰς σῖτα γυψίν (לֶחֶם אַיֵּה, food for the vulture). He
sees himself in the mirror of the future thus reduced to
beggary; he knows that a day of darkness stands in readiness
(נָכוֹן, like ch. xviii. 12), is at his hand, *i.e.* close upon him
(בְּיָדוֹ, elsewhere in this sense לְיַד, Ps. cxl. 6, 1 Sam. xix. 3,
and עַל־יְדֵי, ch. i. 14). In accordance with the previous exposition, we shall now interpret צַר וּמְצוּקָה, ver. 24, not of
need and distress, but subjectively of fear and oppression.
They come upon him suddenly and irresistibly; it seizes or
overpowers him (תִּתְקְפֵהוּ with neutral subject; an unknown
something, a dismal power) as a king עָתִיד לַכִּידוֹר. LXX.
ὥσπερ στρατηγὸς πρωτοστάτης πίπτων, like a leader falling
in the first line of the battle, which is an imaginary interpretation of the text. The translation of the Targum also,

sicut regem qui paratus est ad scabellum (to serve the conqueror as a footstool), furnishes no explanation. Another Targum translation (in Nachmani and elsewhere) is : *sicut rex qui paratus est circumdare se legionibus.* According to this, כִּידוֹר comes from כָּדַר, to surround, be round (comp. כָּתַר, whence כֶּתֶר, Assyr. *cudur,* κίδαρις, perhaps also חֲזַר, Syr. חדר, whence *ch⁰dor,* a circle, round about); and it is assumed, that as כַּדּוּר signifies a ball (not only in Talmudic, but also in Isa. xxii. 18, which is to be translated : rolling he rolleth thee into a ball, a ball in a spacious land), so כִּידוֹר, a round encampment, an army encamped in a circle, synon. of מַעְגָּל. In this first signification the word certainly furnishes no suitable sense in connection with עָתִיד; but one may, with Kimchi, suppose that כִּידוֹר, like the Italian *torniamento,* denotes the circle as well as the tournament, or the round of conflict, *i.e.* the conflict which moves round about, like tumult of battle, which last is a suitable meaning here. The same appropriate meaning is attained, however, if the root is taken, like the Arabic كدر, in the signification *turbidum esse* (comp. קָדַר, ch. vi. 16), which is adopted of misfortunes as troubled experiences of life (according to which Schultens translates : *destinatus est ad turbulentissimas fortunas,* beginning a new thought with עָתִיד, which is not possible, since כמלך by itself is no complete figure), and may perhaps also be referred to the tumult of battle, *tumultus bellici conturbatio* (Rosenm.); or if, with Fleischer, one starts from another turn of the idea of the root, viz. to be compressed, solid, thick, which in a more certain way gives the meaning of a dense crowd.[1] Since,

---

[1] The verb كدر belongs to the root كد, to smite, thrust, *quatere, percutere, tundere, trudere ;* a root that has many branches. It is I. transitive *cadara* (fut. *jacduru,* inf. *cadr*)—by the non-adoption of which from the original lexicons our lexicographers have deprived the whole etymological development of its groundwork—in the signification to *pour, hurl down, pour out,* e.g. *cadara-l-mâa,* he has spilt, poured out, thrown down the water ; hence in the medial VII. form *incadara* intransitive, to fall, fall

therefore, a suitable meaning is obtained in two ways, the natural conjecture, which is commended by Prov. vi. 11, עָתִיד לַכִּידוֹן, *paratus ad hastam = peritus hastæ* (Hupf.), according to ch. iii. 8 (where עֹרֵר = לְעֹרֵר), may be abandoned. The signification *circuitus* has the most support, according to which Saadia and Parchon also explain, and we have preferred to translate round of battle rather than tumult of conflict; Jerome's translation, *qui præparatur ad prælium*, seems also to be gained in the same manner.

> 25 *Because he stretched out his hand against God,*
>   *And was insolent towards the Almighty ;*
> 26 *He assailed Him with a stiff neck,*
>   *With the thick bosses of his shield ;*
> 27 *Because he covered his face with his fatness,*
>   *And addeth fat to his loins,*

down, chiefly of water and other fluids, as of the rain which pours down from heaven, of a cascade, and the like ; then improperly of a bird of prey which shoots down from the air upon its prey (*e.g.* in the poetry in Beidhâwi on *Sur.* 81, 2 : " The hawk saw some bustards on the plain *f'ancadara*, and rushed down ") ; of a hostile host which rushes upon the enemy [first possible signification for כִּידוֹר] ; of a man, horse, etc., which runs very swiftly, *effuse currit, effuso curru ruit ;* of the stars that shall fall from heaven at the last day (*Sur.* 81, 2). Then also II. intransitive *cadara* (fut. *jacdiru*) with the secondary form *cadira* (fut. *jacdaru*) and *cadura* (fut. *jacduru*), prop. *to be shaken and jolted ;* then also of fluid things, mixed and mingled, made turgid, unclean, *i.e.* by shaking, jolting, stirring, etc., with the dregs (the *cudâre* or *cudâde*) ; then gen. *turbidum, non limpidum esse* (*opp.* صفا), with a similar transition of meaning to that in *turbare* (comp. *deturbare*) and the German *trüben* (comp. *traben* or *trappen, treiben, treffen*). The primary meaning of the root takes another III. turn in the derived adjectives *cudur, cudurr, cundur, cunâdir, compressed, solid, thick ;* the last word with us (Germans) forms a transition from *cadir, cadr, cadîr,* dull, slimy, yeasty, etc., inasmuch as we speak of *dickes Bier* (thick beer), etc., *cerevisia spissa, de la bière épaisse.* Here the point of contact for the word כִּידוֹר, tumult of battle, κλόνος ἀνδρῶν, seems indicated : a dense crowd and tumult, where one is close upon another ; as also מלחמה, נלחם, signify not reciprocal destruction, slaughter, but to press firmly and closely upon one another, a dense crowd.—FL.

28 *And inhabited desolated cities,*
   Houses which should not be inhabited,
   Which were appointed to be ruins.
29 *He shall not be rich, and his substance shall not continue*
   And their substance boweth not to the ground.
30 *He escapeth not darkness ;*
   The flame withereth his shoots;
   And he perisheth in the breath of His mouth.

This strophe has periodic members : vers. 25–28 an antecedent clause with a double beginning (כִּי־נָטָה because he has
stretched out, כִּי־כִסָּה because he has covered ; whereas יָרוּץ may
be taken as more independent, but under the government of
the כִּי that stands at the commencement of the sentence) ;
vers. 29, 30, is the conclusion.   Two chief sins are mentioned
as the cause of the final destiny that comes upon the evil-doer :
(1) his arrogant opposition to God, and (2) his contentment
on the ruins of another's prosperity.   The first of these sins
is described vers. 25–27.   The *fut. consec.* is once used instead
of the *perf.*, and the simple *fut.* is twice used with the signification of an *imperf.* (as ch. iv. 3 and freq.)   The *Hithpa.*
הִתְגַּבֵּר signifies here to maintain a heroic bearing, to play the
hero ; הִתְעַשֵּׁר to make one's self rich, to play the part of a rich
man, Prov. xiii. 7.   And בְּצַוָּאר expresses the special prominence of the neck in his assailing God (רוּץ אֶל, as Dan.
viii. 6, comp. עַל, ch. xvi. 14) ; it is equivalent to *erecto collo*
(Vulg.), and in meaning equivalent to ὕβρει (LXX.).   Also
in Ps. lxxv. 6, בצואר (with *Munach*, which there represents a
distinctive[1]) is absolute, in the sense of stiff-necked or hard-
headed ; for the parallels, as Ps. xxxi. 19, xciv. 4, and especially the primary passage, 1 Sam. ii. 3, show that עתק is to
be taken as an accusative of the object.   The proud defiance
with which he challengingly assails God, and renders himself

[1] *Vid.* Dachselt's *Biblia Accentuata*, p. 816.

insensible to the dispensations of God, which might bring him
to a right way of thinking, is symbolized by the additional
clause: with the thickness (עֲבִי cognate form to עֳבִי) of the
bosses of his shields. גַּב is the back (ظهر) or boss (*umbo*)
of the shield; the plurality of shields has reference to the
diversified means by which he hardens himself.   Ver. 27,
similarly to Ps. lxxiii. 4–7, pictures this impregnable carnal
security against all unrest and pain, to which, on account of
his own sinfulness and the distress of others, the nobler-
minded man is so sensitive: he has covered his face with his
fat, so that by the accumulation of fat, for which he anxiously
labours, it becomes a gross material lump of flesh, devoid of
mind and soul, and made fat, *i.e.* added fat, caused it to accu-
mulate, upon his loins (כֶּסֶל for כְּסָלָיו); עָשָׂה (which has nothing
to do with غشى, to cover) is used as in ch. xiv. 9, and in the
phrase *corpus facere* (in Justin), in the sense of producing outwardly something from within.   פִּימָה reminds one of πιμ-ελή
(as Aquila and Symmachus translate here), *o-pim-us*, and of
the Sanscrit *piai*, to be fat (whence adj. *pîvan, pîvara, πιαρός,*
part. *pîna,* subst. according to Roth *pîvas*); the Arabic renders
it probable that it is a contraction of פְּאִימָה (Olsh. § 171, *b*).
The Jewish expositors explain it according to the misunderstood פִּים, 1 Sam. xiii. 21, of the furrows or wrinkles which
are formed in flabby flesh, as if the *ah* were paragogic.

Ver. 28 describes the second capital sin of the evil-doer.
The desolated cities that he dwells in are not cities that he
himself has laid waste; 28*c* distinctly refers to a divinely
appointed punishment, for הִתְעַתְּדוּ does not signify: which
they (evil-doers) have made ruins (Hahn), which is neither
probable from the change of number, nor accords with the
meaning of the verb, which signifies "to appoint to something
in the future."   Hirzel, by referring to the law, Deut. xiii.
13–19 (comp. 1 Kings xvi. 34), which forbids the rebuilding
of such cities as are laid under the curse, explains it to a

certain extent more correctly. But such a play upon the requirements of the Mosaic law is in itself not probable in the book of Job, and here, as Löwenthal rightly remarks, is the less indicated, since it is not the dwelling in such cities that is forbidden, but only the rebuilding of them, so far as they had been destroyed; here, however, the reference is only to dwelling, not to rebuilding. The expression must therefore be understood more generally thus, that the powerful man settles down carelessly and indolently, without any fear of the judgments of God or respect for the manifestations of His judicial authority, in places in which the marks of a just divine retribution are still visible, and which are appointed to be perpetual monuments of the execution of divine judgments.[1] Only by this rendering is the form of expression of the elliptical clause לֹא־יֵשְׁבוּ לָמוֹ explained. Hirz. refers למו to בָּתִּים: in which they do not dwell; but יָשַׁב לְ does not signify: to dwell in a place, but: to settle down in a place; Schlottm. refers למו to the inhabitants: therein they dwell not themselves, *i.e.* where no one dwelt; but the אֲשֶׁר which would be required in this case as *acc. localis* could not be omitted.

[1] For the elucidation of this interpretation of the passage, Consul Wetzstein has contributed the following: "As one who yields to inordinate passion is without sympathy cast from human society because he is called *muqâtal rabbuh,* 'one who is beaten in the conflict against his God' (since he has sinned against the holy command of chastity), and as no one ventures to pronounce the name of Satan because God has cursed him (Gen. iii. 14), without adding 'alêh el-la'ne, 'God's curse upon him!' so a man may not presume to inhabit places which God has appointed to desolation. Such villages and cities, which, according to tradition, have perished and been frequently overthrown (*maqlûbe, muqêlibe, munqalibe*) by the visitation of divine judgment, are not uncommon on the borders of the desert. They are places, it is said, where the primary commandments of the religion of Abraham (*Dîn Ibrâhîm*) have been impiously transgressed. Thus the city of *Babylon* will never be colonized by a Semitic tribe, because they hold the belief that it has been destroyed on account of *Nimrod's* apostasy from God, and his hostility to His favoured one, *Abraham.* The tradition which has even been transferred by the tribes of Arabia Petræa into Islamism of the desolation of the city of *Higr* (or

One might more readily, with Hahn, explain: those to whom they belong do not inhabit them; but it is linguistically impossible for לָמוֹ to stand alone as the expression of this subject (the possessors). The most natural, and also an admissible explanation, is, that יֵשְׁבוּ refers to the houses, and that לָמוֹ, which can be used not only of persons, but also of things, is *dat. ethicus*. The meaning, however, is not: which are uninhabited, which would not be expressed as future, but rather by אֵין בָּהֶם יֹשֵׁב or similarly, but: which shall not inhabit, *i.e.* shall not be inhabited to them (יָשַׁב, to dwell = to have inhabitants, as Isa. xiii. 10, Jer. l. 13, 39, and freq.), or, as we should express it, which ought to remain uninhabited.

Ver. 29 begins the conclusion: (because he has acted thus) he shall not be rich (with a personal subject as Hos. xii. 9, and יֶעְשַׁר to be written with a sharpened שׁ, like יַעְצֹר above, ch. xii. 15), and his substance shall not endure (קוּם, to take place, Isa. vii. 7; to endure, 1 Sam. xiii. 14; and hold fast, ch. xli. 18), and מִנְלָם shall not incline itself to the earth. The interpretation of the older expositors, *non extendet se in terra*, is impossible—that must be יִנָּטֶה בָאָרֶץ; whereas

Medâin Sâlih) on account of disobedience to God, prevents any one from dwelling in that remarkable city, which consists of thousands of dwellings cut in the rock, some of which are richly ornamented; without looking round, and muttering prayers, the desert ranger hurries through, even as does the great procession of pilgrims to *Mekka*, from fear of incurring the punishment of God by the slightest delay in the accursed city. The destruction of *Sodom*, brought about by the violation of the right of hospitality (Gen. xix. 5, comp. Job xxxi. 32), is to be mentioned here, for this legend certainly belongs originally to the '*Dîn Ibrâhîm*' rather than to the Mosaic. At the source of the *Rakkâd* (the largest river of the Golan region) there are a number of erect and remarkably perforated jasper formations, which are called 'the bridal procession' (*el-fârida*). This bridal procession was turned to stone, because a woman of the party cleaned her child that had made itself dirty with a bread-cake (*qurss*). Near it is its village (*Ufûne*), which in spite of repeated attempts is no more to be inhabited. It remains forsaken, as an eternal witness that ingratitude (*kufrân en-ni''ma*), especially towards God, does not remain unpunished."

Kal is commonly used in the intransitive sense to bow down, bend one's self or incline (Ges. § 53, 2). But what is the meaning of the subject מִנְלָם? We may put out of consideration those interpretations that condemn themselves: מִן לָם, *ex iis* (Targ.), or מַן לָם, *quod iis*, what belongs to them (Saad.), or מִלָּם, their word (Syr. and Gecatilia), and such substitutions as σκιάν (צלם or צללם) of the LXX., and *radicem* of Jerome (which seems only to be a guess). Certainly that which throws most light on the signification of the word is כַּנִּלְתְּךָ (for כְּהַנִלְתְּךָ with *Dag. dirimens*, as ch. xvii. 2), which occurs in Isa. xxxiii. 1. The oldest Jewish lexicographers take this הֵנִלָה (parall. הֵתֵם) as a synonym of כִּלָּה in the signification, to bring to an end ; on the other hand, Ges., Knobel, and others, consider כְּכַלֹּתְךָ to be the original reading, because the meaning *perficere* is not furnished for נלה from the Arab. نال, and because נל, standing thus together, is in Arabic an incompatible root combination (Olsh. § 9, 4). This union of consonants certainly does not occur in any Semitic root, but the Arab. *nâla* (the long *a* of which can in the inflection become a short changeable vowel) furnishes sufficient protection for this one exception ; and the meaning *consequi*, which belongs to the Arab. *nâla*, fut. *janîlu*, is perfectly suited to Isa. xxxiii. 1 : if thou hast fully attained (*Hiph.* as intensive of the transitive *Kal*, like הִקְנָה, הֵזְעִיק) to plundering. If, however, the verb נָלָה is established, there is no need for any conjecture in the passage before us, especially since the improvement nearest at hand, מִכְלָם (Hupf. מִכְלָה), produces a sentence (*non figet in terra caulam*) which could not be flatter and tamer ; whereas the thought that is gained by Olshausen's more sensible conjecture, מַנְּלָם (their sickle does not sink to the earth, is not pressed down by the richness of the produce of the field), goes to the other extreme.[1] Juda b. Karisch (Kureisch)

[1] Carey proposes to take מִנְלָם = נמלם, their cutting, layer for planting; but the verb-group מלל, מול, נמל (*vid. supra*, p. 224) is not favourable

has explained the word correctly by مُنَالَهُمْ: that which they have offered (from *nâla, janûlu*) or attained (*nâla, janîlu*), *i.e.* their possession[1] (not : their perfection, as it is chiefly explained by the Jewish expositors, according to כלה = נלה). When the poet says, "their prosperity inclines not to the ground," he denies to it the likeness to a field of corn, which from the weight of the ears bows itself towards the ground, or to a tree, whose richly laden branches bend to the ground. We may be satisfied with this explanation (Hirz., Ew., Stickel, and most others) : מִנְלָם from מִנְלֶה (with which Kimchi compares מִכְרָם, Num. xx. 19, which however is derived not from מִכְרֶה, but from מֶכֶר), similar in meaning to the post-biblical מָמוֹן, μαμωνᾶς; the suff., according to the same change of number as in ver. 35, ch. xx. 23, and freq., refers to רְשָׁעִים. In ver. 30, also, a figure taken from a plant is interwoven with what is said of the person of the ungodly : the flame withers up his tender branch without its bearing fruit, and he himself does not escape darkness, but rather perishes by the breath of His mouth, *i.e.* God's mouth (ch. iv. 9, not

to the supposition of a substantive נָמֵל in this signification, according to the usual application of the language.

[1] Freytag has erroneously placed the infinitives *nail* and *manâl* under نَال *med. Wau*, instead of under نَال *med. Je*, where he only repeats *nail*, and erroneously gives *manâl* the signification *donum*, citing in support of it a passage from *Fâkihat al-chulafâ*, where ʿ*azîz al-manâl* (a figure borrowed from places difficult of access, and rendered strong and impregnable by nature or art) signifies " one who was hard to get at " (*i.e.* whose position of power is made secure). The true connection is this : نَال *med. Wau* signifies originally to *extend, reach*, to hand anything to any one with outstretched arm or hand, the correlatum نَال *med. Je :* to attain, *i.e.* first to touch or reach anything with outstretched arm or hand, and then really to grasp and take it, gen. *adipisci, consequi, assequi, impetrare*, with the ordinary infinitives *nail* and *manâl*. Therefore *manâl* (from نَال *med. Je*) signifies primarily as abstract, *attainment;* it may then, however, like *nail* and the infinitives generally, pass over to the concrete signification : what one attains to, or what one has attained, gotten, although I can give no special example in support of it.—FL.

of his own, after Isa. xxxiii. 11). The repetition of יָסוּר ("he escapes not," as Prov. xiii. 14; "he must yield to," as 1 Kings xv. 14, and freq.) is an impressive play upon words.

31 *Let him not trust in evil—he is deceived,*
   For evil shall be his possession.
32 *His day is not yet, then it is accomplished,*
   And his palm-branch loseth its freshness.
33 *He teareth off as a vine his young grapes,*
   And He casteth down as an olive-tree his flower.
34 *The company of the hypocrite is rigid,*
   And fire consumeth the tents of bribery.
35 *They conceive sorrow and bring forth iniquity,*
   And their inward part worketh self-deceit.

אַל does not merely introduce a declaration respecting the future (Luther: he will not continue, which moreover must have been expressed by the *Niph.*), but is admonitory: may he only not trust in vanity (*Munach* here instead of *Dechî*, according to the rule of transformation, *Psalter*, ii. 504, § 4)— he falls, so far as he does it, into error, or brings himself into error (נִתְעָה, 3 *præt.*, not *part.*, and *Niph.* like Isa. xix. 14, where it signifies to be thrust backwards and forwards, or to reel about helplessly),—a thought one might expect after the admonition (Olsh. conjectures נִתְעָב, one who is detestable): this trusting in evil is self-delusion, for evil becomes his exchange (תְּמוּרָה not *compensatio*, but *permutatio*, *acquisitio*). We have translated שָׁוְא by "evil" (*Unheil*), by which we have sought elsewhere to render אָוֶן, in order that we might preserve the same word in both members of the verse. In ver. 31*a*, שָׁוְא (in form = שָׁוֵא from שׁוֹא, in the *Chethib* שְׁו, the

Aleph being cast away, like the Arabic سَوْ, wickedness, from the *v. cavum hamzatum s â-'a = sawu'a*) is waste and empty in mind, in 31*b* (comp. Hos. xii. 12) waste and empty in fortune; or, to go further from the primary root, in the former case apparent goodness, in the latter apparent prosperity—delusion, and being undeceived ["evil" in the sense of wickedness, and of calamity]. תִּמָּלֵא, which follows, refers to the exchange, or neutrally to the evil that is exchanged : the one or the other fulfils itself, *i.e.* either : is realized (passive of מִלֵּא, 1 Kings viii. 15), or : becomes complete, which means the measure of the punishment of his immorality becomes full, before his natural day, *i.e.* the day of death, is come (comp. for expression, ch. xxii. 16, Eccles. vii. 17). The translation : then it is over with him (Ges., Schlottm., and others), is contrary to the usage of the language ; and that given by the Jewish expositors, תִּמָּלֵא = תִּמָּלֵל (*absoinditur* or *conteritur*), is a needlessly bold suggestion.—Ver. 32*b*. It is to be observed that רַעֲנָנָה is *Milel*, and consequently 3 *prœt.*, not as in Cant. i. 16 *Milra*, and consequently *adj.* כִּפָּה is not the branches generally (Luzzatto, with Raschi : *branchage*), but, as the proverbial expression for the high and low, Isa. ix. 13, xix. 15 (*vid.* Dietrich, *Abhandlung zur hebr. Gramm.* S. 209), shows, the palm-branch bent downwards (comp. Targ. Esth. i. 5, where כִּפִּין signifies seats and walks covered with foliage). "His palm-branch does not become green, or does not remain green" (which Symm. well renders : οὐκ εὐθαλήσει), means that as he himself, the palm-trunk, so also his family, withers away. In ver. 33 it is represented as בֶּסֶר (= בֹּסֶר), wild grapes, or even unripe grapes of a vine, and as נִצָּה, flowers of an olive.[1] In ver. 32*b* the godless man himself might be the subject: he

[1] In order to appreciate the point of the comparison, it is needful to know that the Syrian olive-tree bears fruit plentifully the first, third, and fifth years, but rests during the second, fourth, and sixth. It blossoms in these years also, but the blossoms fall off almost entirely without any berries being formed. The harvest of the olive is therefore in such years very scanty. With respect to the vine, every year an enormous quantity of grapes are used up before they are ripe. When the berries are only about the size of a pea, the acid from them is used in housekeeping, to

casts down, like an olive-tree, his flowers, but in ver 32*a* this is inadmissible; if we interpret: " he shakes off (Targ. יַתֵּר, *excutiet*), like a vine-stock, his young grapes," this (apart from the far-fetched meaning of יַחְמֹס) is a figure that is untrue to nature, since the grapes sit firmer the more unripe they are; and if one takes the first meaning of חמס, " he acts unjustly, as a vine, to his *omphax*" (*e.g.* Hupf.), whether it means that he does not let it ripen, or that he does not share with it any of the sweet sap, one has not only an indistinct figure, but also (since what God ordains for the godless is described as in operation) an awkward comparison. The subject of both verbs is therefore other than the vine and olive themselves. But why only an impersonal "one"? In ver. 30 רוח פיו was referred to God, who is not expressly mentioned. God is also the subject here, and יחמס, which signifies to act with violence to one's self, is modified here to the sense of tearing away, as Lam. ii. 6 (which Aben-Ezra has compared), of tearing out; כזית, כגפן, prop. as a vine-stock, as an olive-tree, is equivalent to even as such an one.

Ver. 34 declares the lot of the family of the ungodly, which has been thus figuratively described, without figure: the congregation (*i.e.* here: family-circle) of the ungodly (חָנֵף according to its etymon *inclinans, propensus ad malum, vid.* on ch. xiii. 16) is (as it is expressed from the standpoint of the judgment that is executed) גַּלְמוּד, a hard, lifeless, stony mass (in the substantival sense of the Arabic *galmûd* instead of the adject. גלמודה, Isa. xlix. 21), *i.e.* stark dead (LXX.

prepare almost every kind of food. The people are exceedingly fond of things sour, a taste which is caused by the heat of the climate. During the months of June, July, and August, above six hundred horses and asses laden with unripe grapes come daily to the market in *Damascus* alone, and during this season no one uses vinegar; hence the word בסרא signifies in Syriac the acid (vinegar) κατ᾽ ἐξοχήν. In Arabic the unripe grapes are exclusively called *hhossrum* (حصرم), or, with a dialectic distinction, *hissrim.*—WETZST.

θάνατος; Aq., Symm., Theod., ἄκαρπος), and fire has devoured the tents of bribery (after Ralbag: those built by
bribery; or even after the LXX.: οἴκους δωροδεκτῶν). The
ejaculatory conclusion, ver. 35, gives the briefest expression
to that which has been already described. The figurative
language, ver. 35a, is like Ps. vii. 15, Isa. lix. 4 (comp. *supra*,
p. 25); in the latter passage similar vividly descriptive infinitives are found (Ges. § 131, 4, *b*). They hatch the burdens
or sorrow of others, and what comes from it is evil for themselves. What therefore their בֶּטֶן, *i.e.* their inward part, with
the intermingled feelings, thoughts, and strugglings (Olympiodorus: κοιλίαν ὅλον τὸ ἐντὸς χωρίον φησὶ καὶ αὐτὴν τὴν
ψυχήν), prepares or accomplishes (יָכִין similar to ch. xxvii. 17,
xxxviii. 41), that on which it works, is מִרְמָה, deceit, with
which they deceive others, and before all, themselves (New
Test. ἀπάτη).

With the speech of Eliphaz, the eldest among the friends,
who gives a tone to their speeches, the controversy enters
upon a second stage. In his last speech Job has turned
from the friends and called upon them to be silent; he turned
to God, and therein a sure confidence, but at the same time
a challenging tone of irreverent defiance, is manifested. God
does not enter into the controversy which Job desires; and
the consequence is, that that flickering confidence is again
extinguished, and the tone of defiance is changed into despair
and complaint. Instead of listening to the voice of God, Job
is obliged to content himself again with that of the friends,
for they believe the continuance of the contest to be just
as binding upon them as upon Job. They cannot consider
themselves overcome, for their dogma has grown up in such
inseparable connection with their idea of God, and therefore
is so much raised above human contradiction, that nothing
but a divine fact can break through it. And they are too
closely connected with Job by their friendship to leave him

to himself as a heretic ; they regard Job as one who is self-deluded, and have really the good intention of converting their friend.

Eliphaz' speech, however, also shows that they become still more and more incapable of producing a salutary impression on Job. For, on the one hand, in this second stage of the controversy also they turn about everywhere only in the circle of their old syllogism : suffering is the punishment of sin, Job suffers, therefore he is a sinner who has to make atonement for his sin ; on the other hand, instead of being disconcerted by an unconditioned acceptation of this maxim, they are strengthened in it. For while at the beginning the *conclusio* was urged upon them only by premises raised above any proof, so that they take for granted sins of Job which were not otherwise known to them ; now, as they think, Job has himself furnished them with proof that he is a sinner who has merited such severe suffering. For whoever can speak so thoughtlessly and passionately, so vexatiously and irreverently, as Job has done, is, in their opinion, his own accuser and judge. It remains unperceived by them that Job's mind has lost its balance by reason of the fierceness of his temptation, and that in it nature and grace have fallen into a wild, confused conflict. In those speeches they see the true state of Job's spirit revealed. What, before his affliction, was the determining principle of his inner life, seems to them now to be brought to light in the words of the sufferer. Job is a godless one ; and if he does affirm his innocence so solemnly and strongly, and challenges the decision of God, this assurance is only hypocritical, and put on against his better knowledge and conscience, in order to disconcert his accusers, and to evade their admonitions to repentance. It is לְשׁוֹן עֲרוּמִים, a mere stratagem, like that of one who is guilty, who thinks he can overthrow the accusations brought against him by assuming the bold bearing of the accuser. Seb. Schmid counts up *quinque vitia,* with which Eliphaz in the introduction to his speech (ch. xv. 1–13) reproaches Job: vexatious impious words, a crafty perversion of the matter, blind assumption of wisdom, contempt of the divine word, and defiance against God. Of these reproaches the first and last are well-grounded; Job does really sin in his language and attitude towards God. With respect to the reproach of assumed wisdom, Eliphaz pays Job in the same coin; and when he reproaches Job with despising the divine consolations and gentle admonitions they have addressed to him, we must not blame the friends, since their intention is good. If, however, Eliphaz reproaches Job with calculating craftiness, and thus regards his affirmation of his innocence as a mere artifice, the charge cannot be more unjust, and must certainly produce the extremest alienation between them. It is indeed hard that Eliphaz regards the testimony of Job's conscience as self-delusion; he goes still further, and pronounces it a fine-spun lie, and denies not only its objective but also its subjective truth. Thus the breach between Job and the friends widens, the entanglement of the controversy becomes more complicated, and the poet allows the solution of the enigma to ripen, by its becoming increasingly enigmatical and entangled.

In this second round of the friends' speeches we meet with no new thoughts whatever; only "in the second circle of the dispute everything is more fiery than in the first" (Oetinger): the only new thing is the harsher and more decided tone of their maintenance of the doctrine of punishment, with which they confront Job. They cannot go beyond the narrow limits of their dogma of retribution, and confine themselves now to even the half of that narrowness; for since Job contemns the consolations of God with which they have hitherto closed their speeches, they now exclusively bring forward the terrible and gloomy phase of their dogma in opposition to him. After Eliphaz has again given prominence to the universal sinfulness of mankind, which Job does not at all deny, he sketches from his own experience and the tradition of his ancestors, which demands respect by reason of their freedom from all foreign influence, with brilliant lines, a picture of the evil-doer, who, being tortured by the horrors of an evil conscience, is overwhelmed by the wrath of God in the midst of his prosperity; and his possessions, children, and whole household are involved in his ruin. The picture is so drawn, that in it, as in a mirror, Job shall behold himself and his fate, both what he has already endured and what yet awaits him. מרמה is the final word of the admonitory conclusion of his speech : Job is to know that that which satisfies his inward nature is a fearful lie.

But what Job affirms of himself as the righteous one, is not מרמה. He knows that he is טמא מטמא (ch. xiv. 4), but he also knows that he is as צדיק תמים (ch. xii. 4). He is conscious of the righteousness of his endeavour, which rests on the groundwork of a mind turned to the God of salvation, therefore a believing mind,—a righteousness which is also accepted of God. The friends know nothing whatever of this righteousness which is available before God. *Fateor quidem*, says Calvin in his *Institutiones*, iii. 12, *in libro Iob mentionem fieri justitiæ, quæ excelsior est observatione legis ; et hanc distinctionem tenere operæ pretium est, quia etiamsi quis legi satisfaceret, ne sic quidem staret ad examen illius justitiæ, quæ sensus omnes exsuperat.* Mercier rightly observes : *Eliphas perstringit hominis naturam, quæ tamen per fidem pura redditur.* In man Eliphaz sees only the life of nature and not the life of grace, which, because it is the word of God, makes man irreproachable before God. He sees in Job only the rough shell, and not the kernel ; only the hard shell, and not the pearl. We know, however, from the prologue, that Jehovah acknowledged Job as His servant when he decreed suffering for him ; and this sufferer, whom the friends regard as one smitten of God, is and remains, as this truly evangelical book will show to us, the servant of Jehovah.

Job's First Answer.—Chap. xvi. xvii.

Schema : 10. 10. 5. 8. 6. 10 | 5. 6. 8. 7. 8.

[Then began Job, and said :]

Ch. xvi. 2 *I have now heard such things in abundance,*
Troublesome comforters are ye all !

3 *Are windy words now at an end,*
Or what goadeth thee that thou answerest ?

4 *I also would speak like you,*
If only your soul were in my soul's stead.
I would weave words against you,
And shake my head at you ;

5 *I would encourage you with my mouth,*
And the solace of my lips should soothe you.

The speech of Eliphaz, as of the other two, is meant to be comforting. It is, however, primarily an accusation ; it wounds instead of soothing. Of this kind of speech, says Job, one has now heard רַבּוֹת, much, *i.e.* (in a pregnant sense) amply sufficient, although the word might signify elliptically (Ps. cvi. 43 ; comp. Neh. ix. 28) many times (Jer. *frequenter*); *multa* (as ch. xxiii. 14) is, however, equally suitable, and therefore is to be preferred as the more natural. Ver. 2*b* shows how כְּאֵלֶּה is intended ; they are altogether מְנַחֲמֵי עָמָל, *consolatores onerosi* (Jer.), such as, instead of alleviating, only cause עָמָל, *molestiam* (comp. on ch. xiii. 4). In ver. 3*a* Job returns their reproach of being windy, *i.e.* one without any purpose and substance, which they brought against him, ch. xv. 2 sq.: have windy words an end, or (אוֹ *vel* = אִם in a disjunctive question, Ges. § 153, 2 ; comp. § 155, 2, *b*) if not, what goads thee on to reply ?   מרץ has been already discussed

on ch. vi. 25.   The Targ. takes it in the sense of מְלִיץ : what
makes it sweet to thee, etc.; the Jewish interpreters give it,
without any proof, the signification, to be strong; the LXX.
transl. παρενοχλήσει, which is not transparent.   Hirz., Ew.,
Schlottm., and others, call in the help of the Arabic مَرِض
(Aramaic מְרַע), to be sick, the IV. form of which signifies
"to make sick," not "to injure."[1]   We keep to the primary
meaning, to pierce, penetrate;   *Hiph.* to goad, bring out,
lacessere: what incites thee, that (כִּי as ch. vi. 11, *quod* not
quum) thou repliest again?   The collective thought of what
follows is not that he also, if they were in his place, could do
as they have done; that he, however, would not so act (thus
e.g. Blumenfeld : with reasons for comfort I would overwhelm
you, and sympathizingly shake my head over you, etc.).   This
rendering is destroyed by the shaking of the head, which is
never a gesture of pure compassion, but always of malignant
joy, Sir. xii. 18 ; or of mockery at another's fall, Isa. xxxvii.
22; and misfortune, Ps. xxii. 8, Jer. xviii. 16, Matt. xxvii. 39.
Hence Merc. considers the antithesis to begin with ver. 5,
where, however, there is nothing to indicate it : *minime id
facerem, quin potius vos confirmarem ore meo*—rather : that
he also could display the same miserable consolation ; he
represents to them a change of their respective positions, in
order that, as in a mirror, they may recognise the hatefulness
of their conduct.   The negative antecedent clause *si essem*

---

[1] The primary meaning of مَرِض (root مر, *stringere*) is *maceratum esse*,
by pressing, rubbing, beating, to be tender, enervated (Germ. dialectic
and popul. *abmaracht*); comp. the nearest related مرص, then مرز,
مرس, مرش, and further, the development of the meaning of *morbus*
and μαλαχία ;—originally and first, of bodily sickness, then also of
diseased affections and conditions of spirit, as envy, hatred, malice, etc. ;
vid. Sur. 2, v. 9, and Beidhâwi thereon.—FL.

(with לוֹ, according to Ges. § 155, 2, *f*) is surrounded by cohortatives, which (since the interrogative form of interpretation is inadmissible) signify not only *loquerer*, but *loqui possem*, or rather *loqui vellem* (comp. *e.g.* Ps. li. 18, *dare vellem*). When he says: I would range together, etc. (Carey: I would combine), he gives them to understand that their speeches are more artificial than natural, more declamations than the outgushings of the heart; instead of מִלִּים, it is בְּמִלִּים, since the object of the action is thought of as the means, as in ver. 4 בְּמוֹ רֹאשִׁי, *capite meo* (for *caput meum*, Ps. xxii. 8), and בְּפִיהֶם, ver. 10, for פִּיהֶם, comp. Jer. xviii. 16, Lam. i. 17, Ges. § 138†; Ew. takes החביר by comparison of the Arabic خبر, to know (the IV. form of which, *achbara*, however, signifies to cause to know, announce), in a sense that belongs neither to the Heb. nor to the Arab.: to affect wisdom. In ver. 5 the chief stress is upon "with my mouth," without the heart being there, so also on the word "my lips," solace (נִיד ἄπ. λεγ., recalling Isa. lvii. 19, נִיב שְׂפָתִים, offspring or fruit of the lips) of my lips, *i.e.* dwelling only on the lips, and not coming from the heart. In אאמצכם (*Piel*, not *Hiph.*) the *Ssere* is shortened to *Chirek* (Ges. § 60, rem. 4). According to ver. 6, כאבכם is to be supplied to יַחְשֹׂךְ. He also could offer such superficial condolence without the sympathy which places itself in the condition and mood of the sufferer, and desires to afford that relief which it cannot. And yet how urgently did he need right and effectual consolation! He is not able to console himself, as the next strophe says: neither by words nor by silence is his pain assuaged.

6 *If I speak, my pain is not soothed ;*
   And if I forbear, what alleviation do I experience ?
7 *Nevertheless now hath He exhausted me ;*
   Thou hast desolated all my household,
8 *And Thou filledst me with wrinkles—for a witness was it,*

And my leanness rose up against me
Complaining to my face.
9 *His wrath tore me, and made war upon me ;*
He hath gnashed upon me with His teeth,
As mine enemy He sharpeneth His eyes against me.

אִם stands with the cohortative in the hypothetical antecedent clause ver. 6*a*, and in 6*b* the cohortative stands alone as ch. xi. 17, Ps. lxxiii. 16, cxxxix. 8, which is more usual, and more in accordance with the meaning which the cohortative has in itself, Nägelsbach, § 89, 3. The interrogative, What goes from me ? is equivalent to, what (= nothing) of pain forsakes me. The subject of the assertion which follows (ver. 7) is not the pain—Aben-Ezra thinks even that this is addressed in ver. 7*b*—still less Eliphaz, whom some think, particularly on account of the sharp expressions which follow, must be understood (*vid.* on the other hand, p. 133), but God, whose wrath Job regards as the cause of his suffering, and feels as the most intolerable part of it. A strained connection is obtained by taking אַךְ either in an affirmative sense (Ew. : surely), as ch. xviii. 21, or in a restrictive sense : only (= entirely) He has now exhausted me (Hirz., Hahn, also Schlottm. : only I feel myself oppressed, at least to express this), by which interpretation the עַתָּה, which stands between אַךְ and the verb, is in the way. We render it therefore in the adversative signification : nevertheless (*verum tamen*) now he seeks neither by speaking to alleviate his pain, nor by silence to control himself ; God has placed him in a condition in which all his strength is exhausted. He is absolutely incapable of offering any resistance to his pain, and care has also been taken that no solacing word shall come to him from any quarter : Thou hast made all my society desolate (Carey : all my clan); עֵדָה of the household, as in ch. xv. 34. Jerome : *in nihilum redacti sunt omnes artus mei* (כל אברי, as explained by the Jewish expositors, *e.g.* Ralbag), as though the human organism could be called עֵדָה. Hahn : Thou hast destroyed all my testimony, which must have been עֵדָתִי (from עוּד, whereas עֵדָה, from יָעַד, has a changeable *Ssere*). He means to say that he stands entirely alone, and neither sees nor hears anything consolatory, for he does not count his wife. He is therefore completely shut up to himself ; God has shrivelled him up ; and this suffering form to which God has reduced him, is become an evidence, *i.e.* for himself and for others, as the three friends, an accusation *de facto*, which puts him down as a sinner, although his self-consciousness testifies the opposite to him.

Ver. 8. The verb קָמַט (Aram. קְמַט), which occurs only once beside (ch. xxii. 16), has, like قمط (in Gecatilia's transl.), the primary meaning of binding and grasping firmly (LXX. ἐπελάβου, Symm. κατέδησας, Targ. for לָכַד, תָּמַךְ, lengthened to a quadriliteral in قمطر, cogn. קָמַץ[1]), *constringere*, from which the significations *comprehendere* and *corrugare* have branched off ; the signification, to wrinkle (make wrinkled), to shrivel up, is the most common, and the reference which follows, to his emaciation, and the lines which occur further on from the picture of one sick with elephantiasis, show that the poet here has this in his mind. Ewald's conjecture, which changes הָיָה into הַיָּה, ch. vi. 2, xxx. 13 = הַוָּה, as subject to וַתִּקְמְטֵנִי (calamity seizes me as a witness), deprives the thought contained in לְעֵד, which renders the inferential clause לְעֵד הָיָה prominent, of much of its force and emphasis. In ver. 8*bc* this thought is continued : כַּחַשׁ signifies here, according to Ps. cix. 24 (which see), a wasting away ; the verb-group כחש, כחד, جحد, كحط, قحط, etc., has the primary meaning

---

[1] On the other hand, קטם, قطم, *abscindere*, *præmordere*, has no connection with קמט, with which Kimchi and Reiske confuse it. This is readily seen from the opposite primary distinction of the two roots, קם and קט, of which the former expresses union, the latter separation.

of taking away and decrease : he becomes thin from whom the fat begins to fail; to disown is equivalent to holding back recognition and admission ; the metaphor, water that deceives = dries up, is similar. His wasted, emaciated appearance, since God has thus shrivelled him up, came forth against him, told him to his face, *i.e.* accused him not merely behind his back, but boldly and directly, as a convicted criminal. God has changed himself in relation to him into an enraged enemy. Schlottm. wrongly translates : one tears and tortures me fiercely ; Raschi erroneously understands Satan by צָרִי. In general, it is the wrath of God whence Job thinks his suffering proceeds. It was the wrath of God which tore him so (like Hos. vi. 1, comp. Amos i. 11), and pursued him hostilely (as he says with the same word in ch. xxx. 21) ; God has gnashed against him with His teeth ; God drew or sharpened (Aq., Symm., Theod., ὤξυνεν, לָטַשׁ like Ps. vii. 13) His eyes or looks like swords (Targ. as a sharp knife, אִזְמֵל, σμίλη) for him, *i.e.* to pierce him through. Observe the *aorr.* interchanging with *perff.* and *imperff.* He describes the final calamity which has made him such a piteous form with the mark of the criminal. His present suffering is only the continuation of the decree of wrath which is gone forth concerning him.

> 10 *They have gaped against me with their mouth,*
> *In contempt they smite my cheeks ;*
> *They conspire together against me.*
> 11 *God left me to the mercy of the ungodly,*
> *And cast me into the hands of the evil-doer.*

He does not mean the friends by those who mock and vex him with their contemptuous words, but the men around him who envied his prosperity and now rejoice at his misfortune ; those to whom his uprightness was a burden, and who now consider themselves disencumbered of their liege lord, the

over-righteous, censorious, godly man. The perfects here also
have not a present signification; he depicts his suffering
according to the change it has wrought since it came upon
him. The verb פָּעַר is used with the instrumental *Beth* instead
of with the acc., as ch. xxix. 23 (comp. on במלים, ver. 4): they
make an opening with their mouth (similar to Ps. xxii. 8,
they make an opening with the lips, for *diducunt labia*).
Smiting on the cheeks is in itself an insult (Lam. iii. 30); the
additional בְּחֶרְפָּה will therefore refer to insulting words which
accompany the act. The *Hithpa.* הִתְמַלֵּא, which occurs only
here, signifies not only to gather together a מְלֹא in general, Isa.
xxxi. 4, but (after the Arab. *tamâla'a 'ala*, to conspire against
any one[1]) to complete one's self, to strengthen one's self (for
a like hostile purpose); Reiske correctly: *sibi invicem mutuam
et auxiliatricem operam contra me simul omnes ferunt.*[2] The
meaning of עֲוִיל is manifest from ch. xxi. 11; from עוּל, to
suckle, *alere* (Arab. عال *med. Wau*, whence the inf. *'aul, 'uwûl,*
and *'ijâle*), it signifies boys, knaves; and it is as unnecessary
to suppose two forms, עֲוִיל and עֲוִיל, as two meanings, *puer* and
pravus, since the language and particularly the book of Job

---

[1] Wetzstein thinks the signification *conspirare* for יתמלאון poor in this
connection, and prefers to translate: All together *they eat themselves full*
upon me, הִתְמַלֵּא as reflexive of מִלֵּא, ch. xxxviii. 39, synon. of נשבע, as
in "the Lovers of *Amâsiâ*," *Ferhhât*, after the death of his beloved, cries
out: We are not separated! To-morrow (*i.e.* soon) the All-kind One
will unite us in paradise, and we shall satisfy ourselves one with another
(ونتملّا من بعضنا البعض). One would, however, expect מִמֶּנִּי instead
of עָלָי; but perhaps we may refer to the interchange of התענג על, ch.
xxii. 26, xxvii..10, with התענג מִן, Isa. lxvi. 11.

[2] The signification *to help,* which belongs to the I. form آلَ, proceeds
from آلَ, to have abundance, to be well off; prop. to be able to furnish
any one with the means (*opes, copias*) for anything, and thereby to place
him in a position to accomplish it. Comp. the Lat. *ops, opem ferre, opi-
tulari, opes, opulentus* (ملي).—FL.

has coined עֲוִל for the latter signification: it signifies in all three passages (here and ch. xix. 18, xxi. 11) boys, or the boyish, childish, knavish. The Arabic *warratta* leaves no doubt as to the derivation and meaning of יִרְטֵנִי; it signifies to cast down to destruction (*warttah*, a precipice, ruin, danger), and so here the *fut. Kal* יִרְטֵנִי for יִירְטֵנִי (Ges. § 69, rem. 3), *præcipitem me dabat* (LXX. ἔρριψε, Symm. ἐνέβαλε), as the *præt. Kal*, Num. xxii. 32: *præceps = exitiosa est via.* The preformative *Jod* has *Metheg* in correct texts, so that we need not suppose, with Ralbag, a רָטָה, similar in meaning to יָרַט.

12 *I was at ease, but He hath broken me in pieces;*
   And He hath taken me by the neck and shaken me to pieces,
   And set me up for a mark for himself.
13 *His arrows whistled about me;*
   He pierced my reins without sparing;
   He poured out my gall upon the ground.
14 *He brake through me breach upon breach,*
   He ran upon me like a mighty warrior.

He was prosperous and contented, when all at once God began to be enraged against him; the intensive form פִּרְפֵּר (Arab. *farfara*) signifies to break up entirely, crush, crumble in pieces (*Hithpo.* to become fragile, Isa. xxiv. 19); the corresponding intensive form פִּצְפֵּץ (from פָּצַץ, Arab. فصّ, cogn. נָפַץ), to beat in pieces (*Polel* of a hammer, Jer. xxiii. 29), to dash to pieces: taking him by the neck, God raised him on high in order to dash him to the ground with all His might. מַטָּרָה (from נָטַר, τηρεῖν, like σκοπός from σκέπτεσθαι) is the target, as in the similar passage, Lam. iii. 12, distinct from מִפְגָּע, ch. vii. 20, object of attack and point of attack: God has set me up for a target for himself, in order as it were to try what He and His arrows can do. Accordingly רַבָּיו (from רָבַב = רָבָה, רָמָה, *jacere*) signifies not: His archers (although this figure would be admissible after ch. x. 17, xix. 12, and the form after the analogy of רֵע, רַב, etc., is naturally taken as a substantival adj.), but, especially since God appears directly as the actor: His arrows (= חִצָּיו, ch. vi. 4), from רַב, formed after the analogy of זַד, מַס, בַּ, etc., according to which it is translated by LXX., Targ., Jer., while most of the Jewish expositors, referring to Jer. l. 29 (where we need not, with Böttch., point רֹבִים, and here רֹבָיו), interpret by מוֹרי החצים. On all sides, whichever way he might turn himself, the arrows of God flew about him, mercilessly piercing his reins, so that his gall-bladder became empty (comp. Lam. ii. 11, and *vid. Psychol. S.* 268). It is difficult to conceive what is here said;[1] it is, moreover, not meant to be understood strictly according to the sense: the divine arrows, which are only an image for divinely decreed sufferings, pressed into his inward parts, and wounded the noblest organs of his nature. In ver. 14 follows another figure. He was as a wall which was again and again broken through by the missiles or battering-rams of God, and against which He ran after the manner of besiegers when storming. פֶּרֶץ is the proper word for such breaches and holes in a wall generally; here it is connected as obj. with its own verb, according to Ges. § 138, rem. 1. The second פרץ (פָּרֶץ with *Kametz*) has *Ssade minusculum*, for some reason unknown to us.

The next strophe says what change took place in his own conduct in consequence of this incomprehensible wrathful disposition of God which had vented itself on him.

---

[1] The emptying of the gall takes place if the gall-bladder or any of its ducts are torn; but how the gall itself (without assuming some morbid condition) can flow outwardly, even with a severe wound, is a difficult question, with which only those who have no appreciation of the stand-point of imagery and poetry will distress themselves. [On the "spilling of the gall" or "bursting of the gall-bladder" among the Arabs, as the working of violent and painful emotions, *vid. Zeitschr. der deutschen mor-genländ. Gesellsch.* Bd. xvi. S. 586, Z. 16 ff.—FL.]

15 *I sewed sackcloth upon my skin,*
   And defiled my horn with dust.
16 *My face is exceeding red with weeping,*
   And on mine eyelids is the shadow of death,
17 *Although there is no wrong in my hand,*
   And my prayer is pure.

Coarse-haired cloth is the recognised clothing which the deeply sorrowful puts on, ἱμάτιον στενοχωρίας καὶ πένθους, as the Greek expositors remark. Job does not say of it that he put it on or slung it round him, but that he sewed it upon his naked body ; and this is to be attributed to the hideous distortion of the body by elephantiasis, which will not admit of the use of the ordinary form of clothes. For the same reason he also uses, not עוֹרִי, but גִּלְדִּי, which signifies either the scurfy scaly surface (as גֶּלֶד and הִגְלִיד in Talmudic of the scab of a healing wound, but also occurring *e.g.* of the be-daggled edge of clothes when it has become dry), or scornfully describes the skin as already almost dead; for the healthy skin is called עוֹר, גֶּלֶד, on the other hand, βύρσα (LXX.), hide (esp. when removed from the body), Talm. *e.g.* sole-leather. We prefer the former interpretation (adopted by Raschi and others) : The crust in which the terrible *lepra* has clothed his skin (*vid.* on ch. vii. 5, xxx. 18, 19, 30) is intended. עֹלַלְתִּי in ver. 15*b* is referred by Rosenm., Hirz., Ges., and others (as indeed by Saad. and Gecat., who transl. " I digged into "), to

עָלַל (غلّ), to enter, penetrate : " I stuck my horn in the dust;" but this signification of the Hebrew עָלַל is unknown, it signifies rather to inflict pain, or scorn (*e.g.* Lam. iii. 51, mine eye causeth pain to my soul), generally with לְ, here with the accusative : I have misused, *i.e.* injured or defiled (as the Jewish expositors explain), my horn with dust. This is not equivalent to my head (as in the Syr. version), but he calls

everything that was hitherto his power and pride קַרְנִי (LXX.,
Targ.); all this he has together at the same time injured, *i.e.*
represented as come to destruction, by covering his head
with dust and ashes.

Ver. 16*a*. The construction of the *Chethib* is like 1 Sam.
iv. 15, of the *Keri* on the other hand like Lam. i. 20, ii. 11
(where the same is said of מֵעַי, *viscera mea*); חֳמַרְמָר is a passive
intensive form (Ges. § 55, 3), not in the signification : they
are completely kindled (LXX. συγκέκαυται, Jer. *intumuit*,
from the חָמַר, حمر, which signifies to ferment), but : they
are red all over (from חָמַר, حمر, whence the Alhambra, as a
red building, takes its name), reddened, *i.e.* from weeping;
and this has so weakened them, that the shadow of death (*vid.*
on ch. x. 21 sq.) seems to rest upon his eyelids; they are therefore sad even to the deepest gloom. Thus exceedingly miserable is his state and appearance, although he is no disguised
hypocrite, who might need to do penance in sackcloth and
ashes, and shed tears of penitence without any solace. Hirz.
explains עַל as a preposition: by the absence of evil in my
hands; but ver. 17*a* and 17*b* are substantival clauses, and עַל is
therefore just, like Isa. liii. 9, a conjunction (= עַל־אֲשֶׁר). His
hands are clean from wrong-doing, free from violence and
oppression; his prayer is pure, *pura;* as Merc. observes, *ex
puritate cordis et fidei.* From the feeling of the strong contrast between his piety and his being stigmatized as an evil-
doer by such terrible suffering,—from this extreme contrast
which has risen now to its highest in his consciousness of
patient endurance of suffering, the lofty thoughts of the next
strophe take their rise.

18 *Oh earth, cover thou not my blood,*
       And let my cry find no resting-place ! !—
19 *Even now behold in heaven is my Witness,*
       And One who acknowledgeth me is in the heights !

20 *Though the mockers of me are my friends—*
   To Eloah mine eyes pour forth tears,
21 *That He may decide for man against Eloah,*
   And for the son of man against his friend.
22 *For the years that may be numbered are coming on,*
   And I shall go a way without return.

Blood that is not covered up cries for vengeance, Ezek. xxiv. 7 sq. ; so also blood still unavenged is laid bare that it may find vengeance, Isa. xxvi. 21. According to this idea, in the lofty consciousness of his innocence, Job calls upon the earth not to suck in his blood as of one innocently slain, but to let it lie bare, thereby showing that it must be first of all avenged ere the earth can take it up;[1] and for his cry, *i.e.* the cry (זַעֲקָתִי to be explained according to Gen. iv. 10) proceeding from his blood as from his poured-out soul, he desires that it may urge its way unhindered and unstilled towards heaven without finding a place of rest (Symm. στάσις). Therefore, in the very God who appears to him to be a blood-thirsty enemy in pursuit of him, Job nevertheless hopes to find a witness of his innocence : He will acknowledge his blood, like that of Abel, to be the blood of an innocent man. It is an inward irresistible demand made by his faith which here brings together two opposite principles—principles which the understanding cannot unite—with bewildering boldness. Job believes that God will even finally avenge the blood which His wrath has shed, as blood that has been innocently shed. This faith, which sends forth beyond death itself the word of absolute command contained in ver. 18, in ver. 19 brightens and becomes a certain confidence, which draws from the future

---

[1] As, according to the tradition, it is said to have been impossible to remove the stain of the blood of Zachariah the son of Jehoiada, who was murdered in the court of the temple, until it was removed by the destruction of the temple itself.

into the present that acknowledgment which God afterwards
makes of him as innocent.   The thought of what is unmerited
in that decree of wrath which delivers him over to death, is
here forced into the background, and in the front stands only
the thought of the exaltation of the God in heaven above
human short-sightednesss, and the thought that no one else
but He is the final refuge of the oppressed : even now (*i.e.*
this side of death)[1] behold in heaven is my witness (הֵנֵּה an
expression of the *actus directus fidei*) and my confessor (שָׂהֵד a
poetic Aramaism, similar in meaning to עֵד, LXX. ὁ συνίστωρ
μου) in the heights.   To whom should he flee from the
mockery of his friends, who consider his appeal to the testimony of his conscience as the stratagem of a hypocrite! מְלִיצָי
from הֵלִיץ, Ps. cxix. 51, my mockers, *i.e.* those mocking me,
lascivientes in me (*vid. Gesch. der jüd. Poesie*, S. 200).   The
short clause, ver. 20*a*, is, logically at least, like a disjunctive
clause with כִּי or גַּם־כִּי, Ewald, § 362, *b*: if his friends mock him
—to Eloah, who is after all the best of friends, his eyes pour
forth tears (דָּלְפָה *stillat*, comp. דַּלּוּ of languishing, Isa. xxxviii.
14), that He may decide (וְיוֹכַח voluntative in a final signification, as ch. ix. 33) for man (לְ here, as Isa. xi. 4, ii. 4, of the
client) against (עִם, as Ps. lv. 19, xciv. 16, of an opponent)
Eloah, and for the son of man (לְ to be supplied here in a
similar sense to ver. 21*a*, comp. ch. xv. 3) in relation to (לְ as
it is used in לְ . . . בֵּין, *e.g.* Ezek. xxxiv. 22) his friend.   Job
longs and hopes for two things from God: (1) that He would
finally decide in favour of גבר, *i.e.* just himself, the patient
sufferer, in opposition to God, that therefore God would
acknowledge that Job is not a criminal, nor his suffering a
merited punishment ; (2) that He would decide in favour of

---

[1] Comp. 1 Kings xiv. 14, where it is probably to be explained : Jehovah
shall raise up for himself a king over Israel who shall cut off the house
of Jeroboam that day, but what ? even now (גם עתה), *i.e.* He hath raised
him up (= but no, even now).

בֶּן־אָדָם, *i.e.* himself, who is become an *Ecce homo,* in relation to his human opponent (רֵעֵהוּ, not collective, but individualizing or distributive instead of רֵעָיו), who regards him as a sinner undergoing punishment, and preaches to him the penitence that becomes one who has fallen. ויוכח is purposely only used once, and the expression ver. 21*b* is contracted in comparison with 21*a* : the one decision includes the other ; for when God himself destroys the idea of his lot being merited punishment, He also at the same time delivers judgment against the friends who have zealously defended Him against Job as a just judge.

Olsh. approves Ewald's translation : "That He allows man to be in the right rather than God, and that He judges man against his friend ;" but granted even that הוֹכִיחַ, like שָׁפַט followed by an acc., may be used in the signification : to grant any one to be in the right (although, with such a construction, it everywhere signifies ἐλέγχειν), this rendering would still not commend itself, on account of the specific gravity of the hope which is here struggling through the darkness of conflict. Job appeals from God to God ; he hopes that truth and love will finally decide against wrath. The meaning of הוכיח has reference to the duty of an arbitrator, as in ch. ix. 33. Schlottm. aptly recalls the saying of the philosophers, which applies here in a different sense from that in which it is meant, *nemo contra Deum, nisi Deus ipse.* In ver. 22 Job now establishes the fact that the heavenly witness will not allow him to die a death that he and others would regard as the death of a sinner, from the brevity of the term of life yet granted him, and the hopelessness of man when he is once dead. שְׁנוֹת מִסְפָּר are years of number = few years (LXX. ἔτη ἀριθμητά) ; comp. the position of the words as they are to be differently understood, ch. xv. 20. On the inflexion *jeethâju, vid.* on ch. xii. 6. Jerome transl. *transeunt,* but אתה cannot signify this in any Semitic dialect. But even that Job (though certainly the course of elephantiasis can continue for years) is intended to refer to the prospect of some, although few, years of life (Hirz. and others : the few years which I can still look forward to, are drawing on), does not altogether suit the tragic picture. The approach of the years that can be numbered is rather thought of as the approach of their end; and the few years are not those which still remain, but in general the but short span of life allotted to him (Hahn). The arrangement of the words in ver. 22*b* also agrees with this, as not having the form of a conclusion (then shall I go, etc.), but that of an independent co-ordinate clause : and a path, there (whence) I come not back (an attributive relative clause according to Ges. § 123, 3, *b*) I shall go (אֶהֱלֹךְ poetic, and in order to gain a rhythmical fall at the close, for אֵלֵךְ). Now follow, in the next strophe, short ejaculatory clauses : as Oetinger observes, Job chants his own requiem while living.

> Ch. xvii. 1 *My breath is corrupt,*
> *My days are extinct,*
> *The graves are ready for me.*
> 2 *Truly mockery surrounds me,*
> *And mine eye shall loiter over their disputings.*

Hirz., Hlgst., and others, wrongly consider the division of the chapter here to be incorrect. The thought in ch. xvi. 22 is really a concluding thought, like ch. x. 20 sqq., vii. 21. Then in ch. xvii. 1 another strain is taken up; and as ch. xvi. 22 is related, as a confirmation, to the request expressed in xvi. 19–21, so xvii. 1, 2 are related to that expressed in xvii. 3. The connection with the conclusion of ch. xvi. is none the less close : the thoughts move on somewhat crosswise (*chiastisch*). We do not translate with Ewald : " My spirit is destroyed," because חֻבָּל (here and Isa. x. 27) signifies not, to be destroyed, but, to be corrupted, disturbed, troubled ; not the spirit (after

خَبل, usually of disturbance of spirit), but the breath is generally meant, which is become short (ch. vii. 15) and offensive (ch. xix. 17), announcing suffocation and decay as no longer far distant. In ver. 1*b* the ἅπ. γεγρ. נִזְעָכוּ is equivalent to נדעכו, found elsewhere. In ver. 1*c* קְבָרִים is used as if the dead were called, Arab. *ssáchib el-kubûr*, grave-companions. He is indeed one who is dying, from whom the grave is but a step distant, and still the friends promise him long life if he will only repent ! This is the mockery which is with him, *i.e.* surrounds him, as he affirms, ver. 2*a*. A secondary verb, הָתַל, is formed from the *Hiph.* הֵתֵל (of which we had the non-syncopated form of the *fut.* in ch. xiii. 9), the *Piel* of which occurs in 1 Kings xviii. 27 of Elijah's derision of the priests of Baal, and from this is formed the *pluralet.* הַתֻלִים (or, according to another reading, הֲתֻלִים, with the same doubling of the ל as in מְהַתַלּוֹת, deceitful things, Isa. xxx. 10 ; comp. the same thing in ch. xxxiii. 7, אראלם, their lions of God = heroes), which has the meaning foolery,—a meaning questioned by Hirz. without right,—in which the idea of deceit and mockery are united. Gecatilia and Ralbag take it as a *part.*: mockers ; Stick., Wolfson, Hahn : deluded ; but the analogy of שַׁעֲשֻׁעִים, תַעֲלוּלִים, and the like, speaks in favour of taking it as a substantive. אִם־לֹא is affirmative (Ges. § 155, 2, *f*). Ewald renders it as expressive of desire : if only not (Hlgst.: *dummodo ne*) ; but this signification (Ew. § 329, *b*) cannot be supported. On the other hand, it might be intended interrogatively (as ch. xxx. 25) : *annon illusiones mecum* (Rosenm.) ; but this אם־לא, corresponding to the second member of a disjunctive question, has no right connection in the preceding. We therefore prefer the affirmative meaning, and explain it like ch. xxii. 20, xxxi. 36, comp. ii. 5. Truly what he continually hears, *i.e.* from the side of the friends, is only false and delusive utterances, which consequently sound to him like jesting and mockery. The suff. in ver. 2*b* refers to

them. הַמְּרוֹת (with *Dag. dirimens,* which renders the sound of
the word more pathetic, as ch. ix. 18, Joel i. 17, and in the
Hiph. form בנלתך, Isa. xxxiii. 1), elsewhere generally (Josh.
i. 18 only excepted) of rebellion against God, denotes here
the contradictory, quarrelsome bearing of the friends, not the
dispute in itself (comp. مرى, III. to attack, VI. to contend
with another), but coming forward controversially; only to
this is תָּלַן עֵינִי suitable. הֵלִין must not be taken as = הֵלִין
here; Ewald's translation, "only let not mine eye come
against their irritation," forces upon this verb, which always
signifies to murmur, γογγύζειν, a meaning foreign to it, and
one that does not well suit it here. The voluntative form
תָּלַן = תָּלַן (here not the pausal form, as Judg. xix. 20, comp.
2 Sam. xvii. 16) quite accords with the sense: mine eye shall
linger on their janglings; it shall not look on anything that
is cheering, but be held fast by this cheerless spectacle, which
increases his bodily suffering and his inward pain. From
these comforters, who are become his adversaries, Job turns
in supplication to God.

> 3 *Lay down now, be bondsman for me with Thyself;*
>   *Who else should furnish surety to me?!*
> 4 *For Thou hast closed their heart from understanding,*
>   *Therefore wilt Thou not give authority to them.*
> 5 *He who giveth his friends for spoil,*
>   *The eyes of his children shall languish.*

It is unnecessary, with Reiske and Olsh., to read עֲרָבֵנִי
(*pone quæso arrhabonem meum = pro me*) in order that שִׂימָה
may not stand without an object; שׂימה has this meaning
included in it, and the עָרְבֵנִי which follows shows that neither
לבך (Ralbag) nor ידך (Carey) is to be supplied; accordingly
שׂים here, like وضع (واضع), and in the classics both τιθέναι
and *ponere,* signifies alone the laying down of a pledge.
Treated by the friends as a criminal justly undergoing

punishment, he seeks his refuge in God, who has set the mark of a horrible disease upon him contrary to his desert, as though he were guilty, and implores Him to confirm the reality of his innocence in some way or other by laying down a pledge for him (ὑποθήκη). The further prayer is עָרְבֵנִי, a word of entreaty which occurs also in Hezekiah's psalm, Isa. xxxviii. 14, and Ps. cxix. 122; עָרַב seq. acc. signifies, as noted on the latter passage, to furnish surety for any one, and gen. to take the place of a mediator (comp. also on Heb. vii. 22, where ἔγγυος is a synon. of μεσίτης). Here, however, the significant עִמָּךְ is added: furnish security for me with Thyself; elsewhere the form is ערב לְ, to furnish security for (Prov. vi. 1), or לִפְנֵי before, any one, here with עִם of the person by whom the security is to be accepted. The thought already expressed in ch. xvi. 21a receives a still stronger expression here: God is conceived of as two persons, on the one side as a judge who treats Job as one deserving of punishment, on the other side as a bondsman who pledges himself for the innocence of the sufferer before the judge, and stands as it were as surety against the future. In the question, ver. 3b, the representation is again somewhat changed: Job appears here as the one to whom surety is given. נִתְקַע, described by expositors as reciprocal, is rather reflexive: to give one's hand (the only instance of the med. form of תָּקַע כַּף) = to give surety by striking hands, dextera data sponsionem in se recipere (Hlgst.). And לְיָדִי is not to be explained after the analogy of the passive, as the usual לְ of the agent: who would allow himself to be struck by my hand, i.e. who would accept the surety from me (Wolfson), which is unnatural both in representation and expression; but it is, according to Prov. vi. 1 (vid. Bertheau), intended of the hand of him who receives the stroke of the hand of him who gives the pledge. This is therefore the meaning of the question: who else (מִי הוּא), if not God himself, should

strike (his hand) to my hand, *i.e.* should furnish to me a
pledge (viz. of my innocence) by joining hands? There is
none but God alone who can intercede for him, as a guarantee
of his innocence before himself and others. This negative
answer: None but Thou alone, is established in ver. 4. God
has closed the heart of the friends against understanding,
prop. concealed, *i.e.* He has fixed a curtain, a wall of partition,
between their hearts and the right understanding of the
matter; He has smitten them with blindness, therefore He
will not (since they are suffering from a want of perception
which He has ordained, and which is consequently known to
Him) allow them to be exalted, *i.e.* to conquer and triumph.
" The exaltation of the friends," observes Hirzel rightly,
" would be, that God should openly justify their assertion of
Job's guilt." Löwenthal translates : therefore art thou not
honoured ; but it is not pointed תְּתרֹמֵם = תְּרֹמֵם, but תְּרֹמֵם,
whether it be that אַתָּה is to be supplied, or that it is
equivalent to תְּרֹמְמֵם (Ew. § 62, *a*, who, however, prefers to
take it as *n. Hithpa.* like תִּקֹמֵם in the unimproved signification : improvement, since he maintains this affords no right
idea), according to the analogy of similar verb-forms (ch.
xxxi. 15, Isa. lxiv. 6), by a resolving of the two similar
consonants which occur together.

The hope thus expressed Job establishes (ver. 5) by a
principle from general experience, that he who offers his
friends as spoil for distribution will be punished most severely
for the same upon his children : he shall not escape the divine
retribution which visits him, upon his own children, for the
wrong done to his friends. Almost all modern expositors are
agreed in this rendering of לְחֵלֶק as regards ver. 5*a* ; but חלק
must not be translated " lot " (Ewald), which it never means ;
it signifies a share of spoil, as *e.g.* Num. xxxi. 36 (Jerome
prædam), or even with a verbal force : plundering (from חָלַק,
2 Chron. xxviii. 21), or even in antithesis to entering into bond

for a friend with all that one possesses (Stick., Schlottm.), a dividing (of one's property) = distraining, as a result of the surrender to the creditor, to which the verb הִגִּיד is appropriate, which would then denote denouncing before a court of justice, as Jer. xx. 10, not merely proclaiming openly, as Isa. iii. 9. We have translated " spoil," which admits of all these modifications and excludes none ; the general meaning is certainly : one deserts (instead of shielding as an intercessor) his friends and delivers them up ; יַגִּיד with a general subj., as ch. iv. 2 (if any one attempts), xv. 3, xxvii. 23. With respect to the other half of the verse, 5b, the optative rendering : may they languish (Vaih.), to the adoption of which the old expositors have been misled by parallels like Ps. cix. 9 sq., is to be rejected ; it is contrary to the character of Job (ch. xxxi. 30). We agree with Mercerus : *Nequaquam hoc per imprecationem, sed ut consequentis justissimæ pœnæ denunciationem ab Iobo dictum putamus.* For ver. 5b is also not to be taken as a circumstantial clause : even if the eyes of his children languish (Ew., Hlgst., Stick., Hahn, Schl.). It is not רֵעֵהוּ, but רֵעִים ; and before supposing here a *Synallage num.* so liable to be misunderstood, one must try to get over the difficulty without it, which is here easy enough. Hence Job is made, in the intended application of the general principle, to allude to his own children, and Ewald really considers him the father of infant children, which, however, as may be seen from the prologue, is nothing but an invention unsupported by the history. Since it is בניו and not בניהם, we refer the suff. to the subj. of יגיד. The *Waw* of וְעֵינֵי Mich. calls *Waw consecutivum ;* it, however, rather combines things that are inseparable (certainly as cause and effect, sin and punishment). And it is יגיד, not הגיד, because the *perf.* would describe the fact as past, while the *fut.* places us in the midst of this faithless conduct. Job says God cannot possibly allow these, his three friends, the upper hand. One proclaims his friends as spoil (comp. ch. vi. 27), and the eyes of his children languish (comp. ch. xi. 20), *i.e.* he who so faithlessly disowns the claims of affection, is punished for it on that which he holds most dear. But this uncharitableness which he experiences is also a visitation of God. In the next strophe he refers all that he meets with from man to Him as the final cause, but not without a presage of the purpose for which it is designed.

6 *And He hath made me a proverb to the world,*
  And I became as one in whose face they spit.
7 *Then mine eye became dim with grief,*
  And all my members were like a shadow.
8 *The upright were astonished at it,*
  And the innocent is stirred up over the godless ;
9 *Nevertheless the righteous holdeth fast on his way,*
  And he that hath clean hands waxeth stronger and stronger.

Without a question, the subj. of ver. 6*a* is God. It is the same thing whether מִשְׁל is taken as *inf.* followed by the subject in the nominative (Ges. § 133, 2), or as a subst. (LXX. θρύλλημα; Aq., Symm., Theod., παραβολήν), like שְׁחֹק, ch. xii. 4, followed by the *gen. subjectivus.* מִשְׁל is the usual word for ridicule, expressed in parables of a satirical character, *e.g.* Joel ii. 17 (according to which, if מִשְׁל were intended as *inf.*, מִשְׁל-בִּי עַמִּים might have been expected) ; עַמִּים signifies both nations and races, and tribes or people, *i.e.* members of this and that nation, or in gen. of mankind (ch. xii. 2). We have intentionally chosen an ambiguous expression in the translation, for what Job says can be meant of a wide range of people (comp. on ch. ii. 11 *ad fin.*), as well as of those in the immediate neighbourhood ; the friends themselves represent different tribes ; and a perishable gipsy-like troglodyte race, to whom Job is become a derision, is specially described further on (ch. xxiv. xxx.).

Ver. 6b. By תֹּפֶת (translated by Jer. *exemplum*, and consequently mistaken for מוֹפֵת) the older expositors are reminded of the name of the place where the sacrifices were offered to Moloch in the valley of the sons of Hinnom (whence גֵּיהִנֹּם, γέεννα, hell), since they explain it by " the fire of hell," but only from want of a right perception ; the לְפָנִים standing with it, which nowhere signifies *palam*, and cannot here (where אֶהְיֶה, although in the signification ἐγενόμην, follows) signify *a multo tempore*, shows that תפת here is to be derived from תּוּף, to spit out (as נֹפֶת, gum, from נוּף). This verb certainly cannot be supported in Hebr. and Aram. (since רקק is the commoner word), except two passages in the Talmud (*Nidda* 42a, comp. *Sabbath* 99b, and *Chethuboth* 61b) ; but it is confirmed by the Æthiopic and Coptic and an onomatopoetic origin, as the words πτύειν, ψύειν, *spuere*, Germ. *speien*, etc., show.[1] Cognate is the Arabic *taffafa*, to treat with contempt, and the interjection *tuffan*, fie upon thee,[2] *e.g.* in the proverb (quoted by Umbreit) : ʿaini fihi watuffan ʿaleihi, my eye rests on it wishfully, and yet I feel disgust at it. Therefore לפנים (spitting upon the face) is equivalent to בפנים, Num. xii. 14, Deut. xxv. 9 (to spit in the face). In consequence of this deep debasement of the object of scorn and spitting, the brightness and vision of his eye (sense of sight) are become dim (comp. Ps. vi. 8, xxxi. 10) מִפַּעַשׂ (always written with שׂ, not ס, in the book of Job), from grief, and his frames, *i.e.* bodily frame = members (Jer. *membra*, Targ. incorrectly : features), are become like a shadow all of them, as fleshless and powerless as a shadow, which is only appearance without substance.

[1] תוף is related to the Sanskrit root *shttîv*, as τέγη, τρύχνος, τρύζω, and the like, to στέγη, στρύχνος, στρύζω, *vid.* Kuhn's *Zeitschrift*, Bd. iv. Abh. i. (the falling away of *s* before mutes).

[2] Almost all modern expositors repeat the remark here, that this *tuffan* is similar in meaning to ῥακά, Matt. v. 22, while they might learn from Lightfoot that it has nothing to do with רק, to spit, but is equivalent to רִיקָא, κενέ.

His suffering, his miserable form (זֹאת), is of such a kind that the upright are astonished (שָׁמֵם, to become desolate, silent), and the guiltless (like himself and other innocent sufferers) become excited (here with vexation as in Ps. xxxvii. 1, as in ch. xxxi. 29 with joy) over the godless (who is none the less prosperous); but the righteous holds firm (without allowing himself to be disconcerted by this anomalous condition of things, though impenetrably mysterious) on his way (the way of good to which he has pledged himself), and the pure of hands (וּמְהָר־ as Prov. xxii. 11, according to another mode of writing וּמְהָר־ with *Chateph-Kametz* under the מ and *Gaja* under the ו; comp. Isa. liv. 9, where the form of writing וּמִגְּעָר־ *umigg°or* is well authorized) increases (יֹסִיף, of inward increase, as Eccles. i. 18) in strength (אֹמֶץ only here in the book of Job); *i.e.* far from allowing suffering to draw him from God to the side of the godless, he gathers strength thereby only still more perseveringly to pursue righteousness of life and purity of conduct, since suffering, especially in connection with such experiences as Job now has with the three friends, drives him to God and makes his communion with Him closer and firmer. These words of Job (if we may be allowed the figure) are like a rocket which shoots above the tragic darkness of the book, lighting it up suddenly, although only for a short time. The confession which breaks through in lyric form in Ps. lxxiii. here finds expression of a more brief, sententious kind. The point of Eliphaz' reproach (ch. xv. 4), that Job makes void the fear of God, and depreciates communion with God, is destroyed by this confession, and the assurance of Satan (ch. ii. 5) is confronted by a fact of experience, which, if it should also become manifest in the case of Job, puts to shame and makes void the hope of the evil spirit.

> 10 *But only come again all of you!*
> *I shall not find a wise man among you.—*

11 *My days are past,*
   My purposes cut off,
   The cherished thoughts of my heart.—
12 *Ye explain night as day,*
   Light is near when darkness sets in.

The truly righteous man, even if in the midst of his affliction he should see destruction before him, does not however
forsake God.   But (nevertheless) ye—he exclaims to the
friends, who promise him a long and prosperous life if he will
only humble himself as a sinner who is receiving punishment
--repeat again and again your hortatory words on penitence!
a wise man who might be able to see into my real condition, I
shall not find among you.   He means that they deceive themselves concerning the actual state of the case before them;
for in reality he is meeting death without being deceived,
or allowing himself to be deceived, about the matter.   His
appeal is similar to ch. vi. 29.   Carey translates correctly:
Attack me again with another round of arguments, etc.
Instead of וְאוּלָם, as it is written everywhere else (generally
when the speech is drawing to a close), we find וְאֻלָּם (as the
form of writing אֻלָּם, אֵלֶם occurs also in the subst. אוּלָם), perh.
in order to harmonize with כֻּלָּם, which is here according to
rule instead of כֻּלְּכֶם, which corresponds more to our form of a
vocative clause, just as in 1 Kings xxii. 28, Mic. i. 2 (Ewald,
§ 327, *a*).[1]   In תָּשֻׁבוּ וּבֹאוּ the jussive and imper. (for the
Chethib יבֹאוּ, which occurs in some Codd. and editions, is
meaningless) are united, the former being occasioned by the
arrangement of the words, which is unfavourable to the
imper. (comp. Ew. § 229); moreover, the first verb gives the
adverbial notion *iterum, denuo* to the second, according to
Ges. § 142, 3, *a*.

---

[1] Comp. my *Anekdota zur Gesch. der mittelalterlichen Scholastik unter
Juden und Moslemen* (1841), S. 380.

What follows, ver. 11, is the confirmation of the fact that there is no wise man among them who might be able to give him efficient solace by a right estimate of the magnitude and undeservedness of his suffering. His life is indeed run out; and the most cherished plans and hopes which he had hedged in and fostered for the future in his heart, he has utterly and long since given up. The *plur.* (occurring only here) of זִמָּה, which occurs also *sensu malo*, signifies projects, as מְזִמּוֹת, ch. xxi. 27, xlii. 2, from זָמַם, to tie ; Aben-Ezra refers to the Arab. *zamâm* (a thread, band, esp. a rein). These plans which are now become useless, these cherished thoughts, he calls מוֹרָשֵׁי, *peculia* (from יָרַשׁ, to take possession of) of his heart. Thus, after Obad. ver. 17, Gecatilia (in Aben-Ezra) also explains, while, according to Ewald, *Beiträge*, S. 98, he understands the heart-strings, *i.e.* the trunks of the arteries (for thus is نِيَاط to be explained), and consequently, as Ewald himself, and even Farisol, most improbably combines מוֹרָשׁ with מוֹתָר (יֶתֶר). Similarly the LXX. τὰ ἄρθρα τῆς καρδίας, as though the joints (instead of the valves) of the heart were intended ; probably with Middeldorpf, after the Syriac Hexapla, ἄκρα is to be read instead of ἄρθρα ; this, however, rests upon a mistaking of מורשי for ראשי. While he is now almost dead, and his life-plans of the future are torn away (נִתְּקוּ), the friends turn night into day (שִׂים, as Isa. v. 20) ; light is (*i.e.* according to their opinion) nearer than the face of darkness, *i.e.* than the darkness which is in reality turned to him, and which is as though it stared at him from the immediate future. Thus Nolde explains it as comparative, but connecting ver. 12b with יָשִׂימוּ, and considering פְנֵי (which is impossible by this compar. rendering) as meaningless : *lucem magis propinquam quam tenebras.* It is however possible that מִפְּנֵי is used the same as in ch. xxiii. 17 : light is, as they think, near before darkness, *i.e.* while darkness sets in (*ingruentibus tenebris*), according to which we have translated. If we understand ver. 12*b* from Job's standpoint, and not from that of the friends, קרוב מן is to be explained according to the Arab. قَرِيب مِن, *prope abest ab*, as the LXX. even translates: φῶς ἐγγὺς ἀπὸ προσώπου σκότους, which Olympiodorus interprets by οὐ μακρὰν σκότους. But by this rendering פני makes the expression, which really needs investigation, only still lamer. Renderings, however, like Renan's *Ah! votre lumière ressemble aux ténèbres*, are removed from all criticism. The subjective rendering, by which ver. 12*b* is under the government of ישׂימו, is after all the most natural. That he has darkness before him, while the friends present to him the approach of light on condition of penitence, is the thought that is developed in the next strophe.

13 *If I hope, it is for Sheôl as my house,*
In darkness I make my bed.
14 *I cry to corruption: Thou art my father! —*
To the worm : Thou art my mother and sister !
15 *Where now therefore is my hope?*
And my hope, who seeth it ?
16 *To the bars of Sheôl it descends,*
When at the same time there is rest in the dust.

All modern expositors transl.: If I hope (wait) for Sheôl as my house, etc., since they regard vers. 13 sq. as a hypothetical antecedent clause to ver. 15, consisting of four members, where the conclusion should begin with וְאַיֵּה, and should be indicated by *Waw apodosis*. There is no objection to this explanation so far as the syntax is concerned, but there will then be weighty thoughts which are also expressed in the form of fresh thoughts, for which independent clauses seem more appropriate, under the government of אִם, as if they were presuppositions. The transition from the preceding strophe to this becomes also easier, if we take vers. 13 sq. as independent clauses from which, in ver. 15, an inference is

drawn, with *Waw* indicative of the train of thought (Ew.
§ 348). Accordingly, we regard אם־אקוה in ver. 13 as antecedent (denoted by *Dechî, i.e. Tiphcha anterius,* just as Ps.
cxxxix. 8*a*) and שאול ביתי as conclusion ; the *Waw apod.* is
wanting, as *e.g.* ch. ix. 27 sq., and the structure of the sentence
is similar to ch. ix. 19. If I hope, says Job, " Sheôl is my
house " = this is the substance of my hope, that Sheôl will be
my house. In darkness he has (*i.e.* in his consciousness, which
anticipates that which is before him as near and inevitable)
fixed his resting-place (poet. *strata,* as Ps. cxxxii. 3). To corruption and the worm he already cries, father ! and, mother !
sister ! It is, as it seems, that bold figure which is indicated
in the Job-like Ps. lxxxviii. 19 (" my acquaintances are the
realms of darkness"), which is here (comp. ch. xxx. 29) worked
out ; and, differently applied, perhaps Prov. vii. 4 echoes it.
Since the *fem.* רמה is used as the object addressed by אמי and
אחותי, which is besides, on account of its always collective
meaning (in distinction from תולעת), well suited for this double
apostrophe, we may assume that the poet will have used a
masc. object for אבי ; and there is really no reason against
שחת here being, with Ramban, Rosenm., Schlottm., Böttcher
(*de inferis,* § 179), derived not from שוח (as נחת, ver. 16*b*,
from נוח), but from שחת (as נחת, Isa. xxx. 30, from נחת),
especially since the old versions transl. שחת also elsewhere
διαφθορά (*putredo*), and thereby prove that both derivations
accord with the structure of the language. Now already
conscious of his belonging to corruption and the worm as by
the closest ties of relationship, he asks : *Itaque ubi tandem
spes mea?*

The accentuation connects אפו to the following word, instead of uniting it with איה, just as in Isa. xix. 12 ; Luzzatto
(on Isa. xix. 12) considers this as a mistake in the Codd.,
and certainly the accentuation Judg. ix. 38 (איה *Kadma,* אפוא
Mercha) is not according to our model, and even in this

passage another arrangement of the accents is found, *e.g.* in
the edition of Brescia.¹ No other hope, in Job's opinion,
but speedy death is before him ; no human eye is capable of
seeing, *i.e.* of discovering (so *e.g.* Hahn), any other hope than
just this. Somewhat differently Hirz. and others : and my
hope, viz. of my recovery, who will it see in process of fulfilment ? Certainly תקותי is in both instances equivalent to a
hope which he dared to harbour; and the meaning is, that
beside the one hope which he has, and which is a hope only
per antiphrasin, there is no room for another hope ; there is
none such (ver. 15*a*), and no one will attain a sight of such,
be it visible in the distance or experienced as near at hand
(ver. 15*b*). The subj. of ver. 16*a* is not the hope of recovery
which the friends present to him (so *e.g.* Ew.), but his only
real hope : this, avoiding human ken, descends to the lower
world, for it is the hope of death, and consequently the death
of hope. בַּדֵּי signifies bars, bolts, which Hahn denies, although
he says himself that בדים signifies beams of wood among other
things; "bolts" is not here intended to imply such as are
now used in locks, but the cross bars and beams of wood of
any size that serve as a fastening to a door ; *vectis* in exactly
the same manner combines the meanings, a carrying-pole and
a bar, in which signification בַּד is the synon. of בְּרִיחַ.² The
meanings assigned to the word, wastes (Schnurrer and others),
bounds (Hahn), clefts (Böttch.), and the like, are fanciful
and superfluous. On תֵּרַדְנָה, instead of תֵּרַד, *vid.* Caspari on
Obad. ver. 13, Ges. § 47, rem. 3. It is *sing.*, not *plur.*

¹ This accentuates ואיה with *Munach*, אפו with *Munach*, which accords
with the matter, instead of which, according to Luzz., since the *Athnach*-
word תקותי consists of three syllables, it should be more correctly accentuated ואיה with *Munach*, אפו with *Dechî*. Both, also *Munach Munach*,
are admissible ; *vid.* Bär, *Thorath Emeth*, S. 43, § 7, comp. S. 71, *not.*

² Accordingly we also explain Hos. xi. 6 after Lam. ii. 9, and transl. :
The sword moveth round in his (Ephraim's) cities, and destroyeth his
(Ephraim's) bars (*i.e.* the bars of his gates), and devoureth round about,
because of their counsels.

(Böttch.), for ver. 15 does not speak of two hopes, not even
if, as it seems according to the ancient versions, another
word of cognate meaning had stood in the place of the
second תקותי originally. His hope goes down to the regions
of the dead, when altogether there is rest in the dust. This
" together, יַחַד," Hahn explains : to me and it, to this hope ;
but that would be pursuing the figure to an inadmissible
length, extending far beyond ch. xx. 11, and must then be
expressed לָנוּ יַחַד. Others (e.g. Hirz., Ew.) explain : if at the
same time, i.e. simultaneously with this descent of my hope,
there is rest to me in the dust. Considering the use of יחד in
itself, it might be explained : if altogether [entirely] there is
rest in the dust; but this meaning integer, totus quantus, the
word has elsewhere always in connection with a subj. or obj.
to which it is referable, e.g. ch. x. 8, Ps. xxxiii. 15 ; and,
moreover, it may be rendered also in the like passages by
" all together," as ch. iii. 18, xxi. 26, xl. 13, instead of
" altogether, entirely." Since, on the other hand, the signification " at the same time " can at least with probability be
supported by Ps. cxli. 10, and since אם, which is certainly used
temporally, brings cotemporary things together, we prefer
the translation : " when at the same time in the dust there is
rest." The descent of his hope to the bars of Hades is at the
same time his own, who hopes for nothing but this. When
the death of his hope becomes a reality, then at the same
time his turmoil of suffering will pass over to the rest of the
grave.

As from the first speech of Eliphaz, so also from this first
speech of Job, it may be seen that the controversy takes a
fresh turn, which brings it nearer to the maturity of decision.
From Eliphaz' speech Job has seen that no assertion of his
innocence can avail to convince the friends, and that the more
strongly he maintains his innocence, even before God, he
only confirms them in the opinion that he is suffering the

punishment of his godlessness, which now comes to light, like a wrong that has been hitherto concealed. Job thus perceives that he is incapable of convincing the friends; for whatever he may say only tends to confirm them in the false judgment, which they first of all inferred from their false premises, but now from his own words and conduct. He is accounted by them as one who is punished of God, whom they address as the preachers of repentance; now, however, they address him so that the chief point of their sermon is no longer bright promises descriptive of the glorious future of the penitent, but fearful descriptions of the desolating judgment which comes upon the impenitent sinner. This zealous solicitude for his welfare seems to be clever and to the point, according to their view; it is, however, only a vexatious method of treating their friend's case; it is only roughly and superficially moulded according to the order of redemption, but without an insight into the spiritual experience and condition of him with whom they have here to do. Their *prudentia pastoralis* is carnal and legal; they know nothing of a righteousness which avails before God, and nothing of a state of grace which frees from the divine vengeance; they know not how to deal with one who is passing through the fierce conflict of temptation, and understand not the mystery of the cross.

Can we wonder, then, that Job is compelled to regard their words as nothing more than דברי רוח, as they regarded his? In the words of Job they miss their certainly compact dogma, in which they believe they possess the philosopher's stone, by means of which all earthly suffering is to be changed into earthly prosperity. Job, however, can find nothing in their words that reminds him of anything he ought to know in his present position, or that teaches him anything respecting it. He is compelled to regard them as מנחמי עמל, who make the burden of his suffering only more grievous, instead of lightening it for him. For their consolation rests upon an unjust

judgment of himself, against which his moral consciousness
rebels, and upon a one-sided notion of God, which is contradicted by his experience. Their speeches exhibit skill as to
their form, but the sympathy of the heart is wanting. Instead
of plunging with Job into the profound mystery of God's
providence, which appoints such a hard lot for the righteous
man to endure, they shake their heads, and think : What a
great sinner Job must be, that God should visit him with so
severe a punishment ! It is the same shaking of the head of
which David complains Ps. xxii. 8 and cix. 25, and which
the incomparably righteous One experienced from those who
passed by His cross, Matt. xxvii. 39, Mark xv. 29. These
comparisons give us the opportunity of noting the remarkable
coincidence of these pictures of suffering, in outline and
expression ; the agreement of Job xvi. 8 with Ps. cix. 24,
comp. cix. 23 with Job xvii. 7, puts it beyond a doubt, that
there is a mutual relation between Job xvi. 4 and Ps. cix. 25
which is not merely accidental.

By such unjust and uncharitable treatment from the
friends, Job's sufferings stand forth before him in increased
magnitude. He exceeds himself in the most terrible figures,
in order to depict the sudden change which the divine dispensation of suffering has brought upon him. The figures are
so terrible, for Job sees behind his sufferings a hostile hideous
God as their author; they are the outburst of His anger, His
quivering looks, His piercing darts, His shattering missiles.
His sufferings are a witness *de facto* against him, the sufferer;
but they are this not merely in themselves, but also in the
eyes of the people around him. To the sufferings which he
has directly to endure in body and soul there is added, as it
were, as their other equally painful part, misconstruction and
scorn, which he has to suffer from without. Not only does
he experience the wrath of God contrary to the testimony to
his righteousness which his consciousness gives him, but also

the scoff of the ungodly, who now deridingly triumph over
him. Therefore he clothes himself in mourning, and lies with
his former majesty in the dust; his face is red with weeping,
and his eyes are become almost blind, although there is no
wrong in his hand, and his prayer is free from hypocrisy.
Who does not here think of the servant of Jehovah, of
whom Isaiah, ch. liii. 9 (in similar words to those which Job
uses of himself, ch. xvi. 16), says, that he is buried among the
godless על לא־חמס עשׂה ולא מרמה בפיו? All that Job says here
of the scorn that he has to endure by being regarded as one
who is punished of God and tormented, agrees exactly with
the description of the sufferings of the servant of Jehovah
in the Psalms and the second part of Isaiah. Job says: they
gape at me with their mouth; and in Ps. xxii. 8 (comp. xxxv.
21) it is: all they that see me laugh me to scorn, they open
wide the lips, they shake the head. Job says: they smite my
cheeks in contempt; and the servant of Jehovah, Isa. l. 6, is
compelled to confess: I gave my back to the smiters, and my
cheeks to them that pluck off the hair; I hid not my face
from shame and spitting. Like Job, the servant of Jehovah
in the Psalms and in Isaiah II. is delivered over into the hands
of the unrighteous, and reckoned among evil-doers, although he
is the servant of Jehovah, and knows himself to be Jehovah's
servant. The same hope that he expresses in Isa. l. 8 sq. in
the words: he is near who justifieth me, who will condemn
me!—the same hope in Job breaks through the night of conflict, with which his direct and indirect suffering has surrounded him.

Just when Job becomes conscious of his doubled affliction
in all its heaviness, when he feels himself equally rejected of
men as of God, must this hope break forth. For there is
only a twofold possibility for a man who thinks God has
become his enemy, and that he has not a friend among men:
either he sinks into the abyss of despair; or if faith still exists,

he struggles upwards through his desertion by God and man to the love that lies deep in the heart of God, which in spite of hostile manifestation cannot abandon the righteous. Whither shall Job turn when God seems to him as an enemy, and when he nevertheless will not renounce God? He can only turn from the hostile God to the God who is differently disposed towards him, and that is equivalent to saying from the imaginary to the real God, to whom faith, clings throughout every outward manifestation of wrath and wrathful feeling.[1] Since both, however, is one God, who only seems to be other than He is, that bold grasp of faith is the exchange of the phantom-god of the conflict of temptation for the true God. Faith, which in its essence is a perception capable of taking root, seizes the real existence behind the appearance, the heart behind the countenance, that which remains the same behind the change, and defies a thousand contradictions with the saintly Nevertheless: God *nevertheless* does not belie himself.

Job challenges the earth not to hide his blood; unceasingly without restraint shall the cry of his blood rise up. What he says in ch. xvi. 18 is to be taken not so much as the expression of a desire as of a demand, and better still as a command; for even in case he should succumb to his sufferings, and consequently in the eyes of men die the death of a sinner, his clear consciousness of innocence does not allow him to renounce his claim to a public declaration that he has died guiltless. But to whom shall the blood of the slain cry out? To whom else but God; and yet it is God who has slain him? We see distinctly here how Job's idea of God is lighted up by the prospect of a decisive trial of his cause. The God who abandons Job to death as guilty, and the God who

---

[1] Compare the prayer of Juda ha-Levi, אברח ממך אליך (لك اعوذ منك), in Kämpf's *Nichtandalusische Poesien andalusischer Dichter* (1858), ii. 206.

cannot (and though it should be even after death) leave him unvindicated, come forth distinct and separate as darkness from light from the chaos of the conflict of temptation. Since, however, the thought of a vindication after death for Job, which knows only of a seeming life after death, according to the notion that rules him, and which is here not yet broken through, is only the extreme demanded by his moral consciousness, he is compelled to believe in a vindication in this world; and he expresses this faith (ch. xvi. 19) in these words: "Even now, behold, my Witness is in heaven, and One who acknowledgeth me is in the heights." He pours forth tears to this God that He would decide between God and him, between his friends and him. He longs for this decision now, for he will now soon be gone beyond return. Thus Job becomes here the prophet of the issue of his own course of suffering; and over his relation to Eloah and to the friends, of whom the former abandons him to the sinner's death, and the latter declare him to be guilty, hovers the form of the God of the future, which now breaks through the darkness, from whom Job believingly awaits and implores what the God of the present withholds from him.[1]

What Job (ch. xvi. 20 sq.), by reason of that confident "Behold, my Witness is in heaven," had expressed as the end of his longing,—that God would vindicate him both before Himself, and before the friends and the world,—urges him onward, when he reflects upon his twofold affliction, that he is sick unto death and one who is misjudged even to mockery, to the importunate request: Lay down now (a pledge), be surety for me with Thyself; for who else should strike his hand into mine, *i.e.* in order to become bondsman to me, that

---

[1] Ewald very truly says: "This is the true turn of the human controversy, which is favoured by the whole course of Job's life, that he, though in the present utterly despairing of all, even God, still holds fast to the eternal hidden God of the future, and with this faith rises wondrously, when to all human appearance it seemed that he must succumb."

Thou dost not regard me as an unrighteous person? The friends are far from furnishing a guarantee of this; for they, on the contrary, are desirous of persuading him, that, if he would only let his conscience speak, he must regard himself as an unrighteous one, and that he is regarded as such by God. Therefore God cannot give them the victory; on the contrary, he who so uncompassionately abandons his friends, must on his own children experience similar suffering to that which he made heavier for his friend, instead of making it lighter to him. The three have no insight into the affliction of the righteous one; they dispose of him mercilessly, as of spoil or property that has fallen into the hands of the creditor; therefore he cannot hope to obtain justice unless God become surety for him with himself,—a thought so extraordinary and bold, that one cannot wonder that the old expositors were misled by it: God was in Christ, and reconciled the world with Himself, 2 Cor. v. 19. The God of holy love has reconciled the world with himself, the God of righteous anger, as Job here prays that the God of truth may become surety for him with the God of absolute sovereignty.

When Job then complains of the misconstruction of his character, and tracing it to God, says: He hath made me לִמְשֹׁל עַמִּים, one is reminded, in connection with this extravagant expression, of complaints of a like tone in the mouth of the true people of Israel, Ps. xliv. 15, and of the great sufferer, Ps. lxix. 12. When we further read, that, according to Job's affirmation, the godly are scared at his affliction, the parallel Isa. lii. 14 forces itself upon us, where it is said of the servant of Jehovah, "How were many astonied at thee." And when, with reference to himself, Job says that the suffering of the righteous must at length prove a gain to him that hath clean hands, who does not call to mind the fact that the glorious issue of the suffering of the servant of Jehovah which the Old Testament evangelist sets before us,

—that servant of Jehovah who, once himself a prey to oppression and mocking, now divides the spoil among the mighty,— tends to the reviving, strengthening, and exaltation of Israel? All these parallels cannot and are not intended to prove that the book of Job is an allegorical poem; but they prove that the book of Job stands in the closest connection, both retrospective and prospective, with the literature of Israel; that the poet, by the relation to the passion-psalms stamped on the picture of the affliction of Job, has marked Job, whether consciously or unconsciously, as a typical person; that, by taking up, probably not unintentionally, many national traits, he has made it natural to interpret Job as a *Mashal* of Israel; and that Isaiah himself confirms this typical relation, by borrowing some Job-like expressions in the figure of the עבד יהוה, who is a personification of the true Israel. The book of Job has proved itself a mirror of consolation for the people, faithful to God, who had cause to complain, as in Ps. xliv., and a mirror of warning to their scoffers and persecutors, who had neither true sympathy with the miserable state of God's people, nor a true perception of God's dealings. At the same time, however, Job appears in the light which the New Testament history, by the fulfilment of the prophecies of suffering in the Psalms, Isaiah, and also Zechariah, throws upon him, as a type of Him who suffers in like manner, in order that Satan may have his deserts, and thereby be confounded; who also has an affliction to bear which in itself has the nature and form of wrath, but has its motive and end in the love of God; who is just so misjudged and scorned of men, in order at length to be exalted, and to enter in as intercessor for those who despised and rejected Him. At the same time, it must not be forgotten that there remains an infinite distance between the type and antitype, which, however, must be in the very nature of a type, and does not annul the typical relation, which exists only *exceptis excipiendis.* Who could fail to recognise the involuntary picture of the three friends in the penitent ones of Isa. liii., who esteemed the servant of Jehovah as one smitten of God, for whom, however, at last His sacrifice and intercession avail?

Job at last considers his friends as devoid of wisdom, because they try to comfort him with the nearness of light, while darkness is before him; because they give him the hope of a bodily restoration, while he has nothing to expect but death, and earnestly longs for the rest of death. It is surprising that the speech of Job plunges again into complete hopelessness, after he has risen to the prospect of being vindicated in this life. He certainly does not again put forth that prospect, but he does not even venture to hope that it can be realized by a blessing in this life after a seeming curse. It is in this hopelessness that the true greatness of Job's faith becomes manifest. He meets death, and to every appearance is overwhelmed by death, as a sinner, while he is still conscious that he is righteous. Is it not faith in and fidelity to God, then, that, without praying for recovery, he is satisfied with this one thing, that God acknowledges him? The promises of the friends ought to have rested on a different foundation, if he was to have the joy of appropriating them to himself. He feels himself to be inevitably given up as a prey to death, and as from the depth of Hades, into which he is sinking, he stretches out his hands to God, not that He would sustain him in life, but that He would acknowledge him before the world as His. If he is to die even, he desires only that he may not die the death of a criminal. And is this intended at the same time for the rescue of his honour? No, after all, for the honour of God, who cannot possibly destroy as an evil-doer one who is in everything faithful to Him. When, then, the issue of the history is that God acknowledges Job as His servant, and after he is proved and refined by the temptation, preserves to him a doubly rich and

prosperous life, Job receives beyond his prayer and comprehension ; and after he has learned from his own experience
that God brings to Hades and out again, he has for ever con-
quered all fear of death, and the germs of a hope of a future
life, which in the midst of his affliction have broken through
his consciousness, can joyously expand. For Job appears to
himself as one who is risen from the dead, and is a pledge to
himself of the resurrection from the dead.

Bildad's Second Speech.—Chap. xviii.

Schema : 4. 9. 8. 8. 8. 4.

[Then began Bildad the Shuhite, and said :]
2 *How long will ye hunt for words ? !*
   Attend, and afterwards we will speak.
3 *Wherefore are we accounted as beasts,*
   And narrow-minded in your eyes ?

Job's speeches are long, and certainly are a trial of patience
to the three, and the heaviest trial to Bildad, whose turn
now comes on, because he is at pains throughout to be brief.
Hence the reproach of endless babbling with which he begins
here, as at ch. viii. 2, when he at last has an opportunity of
speaking ; in connection with which it must, however, not be
forgotten that Job also, ch. xvi. 3, satirically calls upon them
to cease. He is indeed more entitled than his opponents to the
entreaty not to weary him with long speeches. The question,
ver. 2*a*, if קִנְצֵי is derived from קֵץ, furnishes no sense, unless
perhaps it is, with Ralbag, explained : how long do you make
close upon close in order, when you seem to have come to an
end, to begin continually anew ? For to give the thought :
how long do you make no end of speaking, it must have been
עַד־אָנָה לֹא, as the LXX. (μέχρι τίνος οὐ παύσῃ;) involuntarily inserts the negative. And what should the *plur.* mean

by this rendering? The form קְצֵי = קָצֵי would not cause
doubt; for though קָצִים does not occur elsewhere in the Old
Testament, it is nevertheless sufficient that it is good Aramaic (קִצִּין), and that another Hebr. plural, as קָצֵי, קַצְוֵי, קַצְווֹת,
would have been hardly in accordance with the usage of
the language. But the plural would not be suitable here
generally, the over-delicate explanation of Ralbag perhaps
excepted. Since the book of Job abounds in Arabisms, and
in Arabic قَنَص (as synon. of صاد) signifies *venari, venando*
capere, and قَنَص (مِقْنَص) *cassis, rete venatorium*; since, further,
שִׂים קְנָצִים (comp. שִׂים אֹרֶב, Jer. ix. 7) is an incontrovertible
reading, and all the difficulties in connection with the reference to קֵץ lying in the עַד־אָנה for עַד־אָנה לֹא and in the plur.
vanish, we translate with Castell., Schultens, J. D. Mich., and
most modern expositors: how long (here not different from ch.
viii. 2, xix. 2) will ye lay snares (construction, as also by the
other rendering, like ch. xxiv. 5, xxxvi. 16, according to Ges.
§ 116, 1) for words; which, however, is not equivalent to
hunt for words in order to contradict, but in order to talk on
continually.[1] Job is the person addressed, for Bildad agrees
with the two others. It is remarkable, however, that he
addresses Job with "you." Some say that he thinks of Job
as one of a number; Ewald observes that the controversy
becomes more wide and general; and Schlottm. conjectures
that Bildad fixes his eye on individuals of his hearers, on
whose countenances he believed he saw a certain inclination
to side with Job. This conjecture we will leave to itself; but
the remark which Schlottm. also makes, that Bildad regards

---

[1] In post-bibl. Hebrew, קנצים has become common in the signification,
proofs, arguments, as *e.g.* a Karaitic poet says, ויחוד שמך בקנצים הקימותי,
the oneness of thy name have I upheld with proofs ; *vid.* Pinsker, *Likute*
Kadmoniot. Zur Gesch. des Karaismus und der karäischen Literatur,
1860, S. קסו.

Job as a type of a whole class, is correct, only one must also add, this address in the *plur.* is a reply to Job's sarcasm by a similar one. As Job has told the friends that they act as if they were mankind in general, and all wisdom were concentrated in them, so Bildad has taken it amiss that Job connects himself with the whole of the truly upright, righteous, and pure; and he addresses him in the plural, because he, the unit, has puffed himself up as such a collective whole. This wrangler—he means—with such a train behind him, cannot accomplish anything: Oh that you would understand (הָבִין, as *e.g.* ch. xlii. 3, not causative, as vi. 24), *i.e.* come to your senses, and afterward we will speak, *i.e.* it is only then possible to walk in the way of understanding. That is not now possible, when he, as one who plays the part of their many, treats them, the three who are agreed in opposition to him, as totally void of understanding, and each one of them unwise, in expressions like ch. xvii. 4, 10. Looking to Ps. xlix. 13, 21, one might be tempted to regard נִטְמִינוּ (on the vowel *î* instead of *ê*, *vid.* Ges. § 75, rem. 7) as an interchange of consonants from נדמינו : be silent, make an end, ye *profligati;* but the supposition of this interchange of consonants would be arbitrary. On the other hand, there is no suitable thought in " why are we accounted unclean ? " (Vulg. *sorduimus*), from טָמֵא = טָמָה, Lev. xi. 43 (Ges. § 75, vi.) ; the complaint would have no right connection, except it were a very slight one, with ch. xvii. 9. On the contrary, if we suppose a verb טָמָה in the signification *opplere, obturare,* which is peculiar to this consonant-combination in the whole range of the Semitic languages (comp. אָ־טַם, اطم, *obstruere,* Aram. טַמְטֵם, טִמְטֵם, Arab. طم, *e.g.* Talm. : transgression stoppeth up, מטמטמת, man's heart), and after which this טמה has been explained by the Jewish expositors (Raschi : נחשבנו טמומים), and is interpreted by סתם (Parchon : נסתמה דעתנו), we gain a

sense which corresponds both with previous reproaches of
Job and the parallelism, and we decide in its favour with
the majority of modern expositors. With the interrogative
Wherefore, Bildad appeals to Job's conscience. These in-
vectives proceed from an impassioned self-delusion towards
the truth, which he wards off from himself, but cannot however alter.

> 4 *Thou art he who teareth himself in his anger :*
>   *Shall the earth become desolate for thy sake,*
>   *And a rock remove from its place ?*
> 5 *Notwithstanding, the light of the wicked shall be put out,*
>   *And the glow of his fire shineth not;*
> 6 *The light becometh dark in his tent,*
>   *And his lamp above him is extinguished ;*
> 7 *His vigorous steps are straitened,*
>   *And his own counsel casteth him down.*

The meaning of the strophe is this : Dost thou imagine
that, by thy vehement conduct, by which thou art become
enraged against thyself, thou canst effect any change in the
established divine order of the world ? It is a divine law,
that sufferings are the punishment of sin; thou canst no
more alter this, than that at thy command, or for thy sake,
the earth, which is appointed to be the habitation of man
(Isa. xlv. 18), will become desolate (*têʿâzab* with the tone
drawn back, according to Ges. § 29, 3, *b*, Arab. with similar
signification in intrans. Kal *tʿazibu*), or a rock remove from its
place (on יֶעְתַּק, *vid.* ch. xiv. 18). Bildad here lays to Job's
charge what Job, in ch. xvi. 9, has said of God's anger, that
it tears him : he himself tears himself in his rage at the
inevitable lot under which he ought penitently to bow. The
address, ver. 4*a*, as *apud Arabes ubique fere* (Schult.), is put
objectively (not : Oh thou, who); comp. what is said on כֻּבָּם,
ch. xvii. 10, which is influenced by the same syntactic custom.

The LXX. transl. ver. 4*b* : Why! will Hades be tenant-less if thou diest (ἐὰν σὺ ἀποθάνῃς)? after which Rosenm. explains: *tuâ causâ h. e. te cadente.* But that ought to be הַבְמוּתְךָ. The peopling of the earth is only an example of the arrangements of divine omnipotence and wisdom, the continuance of which is exalted over the human power of volition, and does not in the least yield to human self-will, as (ver. 4*c*) the rock is an example, and at the same time an emblem, of what God has fixed and rendered immoveable. That of which he here treats as fixed by God is the law of retribution. However much Job may rage, this law is and remains the unavoidable power that rules over the evil-doer.

Ver. 5. גַּם is here equivalent to nevertheless, or prop. even, ὅμως, as *e.g.* Ps. cxxix. 2 (Ew. § 354, *a*). The light of the evil-doer goes out, and the comfortable brightness and warmth which the blaze (שְׁבִיב, only here as a Hebr. word ; according to Raschi and others, *étincelle*, a spark ; but according to LXX., Theod., Syr., Jer., a flame ; Targ. the brightness of light) of his fire in his dwelling throws out, comes to an end. In one word, as the *præt.* חָשַׁךְ implies, the light in his tent is changed into darkness ; and his lamp above him, *i.e.* the lamp hanging from the covering of his tent (ch. xxix. 3, comp. xxi. 17), goes out. When misfortune breaks in upon him, the Arab says : *ed-dahru attfaa es-sirâgi,* fate has put out my lamp ; this figure of the decline of prosperity receives here a fourfold application. The figure of straitening one's steps is just as Arabic as it is biblical ; צַעֲדֵי אוֹנוֹ, the steps of his strength (אוֹן synon. of כֹּחַ, ch. xl. 16) become narrow (comp. Prov. iv. 12, Arab. *takâssarat*), by the wide space which he could pass over with a self-confident feeling of power becoming more and more contracted ; and the purpose formed selfishly and without any recognition of God, the success of which he considered infallible, becomes his overthrow.

8 *For he is driven into the net by his own feet,*
   And he walketh over a snare.
9 *The trap holdeth his heel fast,*
   The noose bindeth him.
10 *His snare lieth hidden in the earth,*
   His nets upon the path ;
11 *Terrors affright him on every side,*
   And scare him at every step.

The *Pual* שֻׁלַּח signifies not merely to be betrayed into,
but driven into, like the *Piel*, ch. xxx. 12, to drive away, and
as it is to be translated in the similar passage in the song
of Deborah, Judg. v. 15 : "And as Issachar, Barak was
driven (*i.e.* with desire for fighting) behind him down into
the valley (the place of meeting under Mount Tabor) ;" בְּרַגְלָיו,
which there signifies, according to Judg. iv. 10, viii. 5,
"upon his feet = close behind him," is here intended of the
intermediate cause : by his own feet he is hurried into the
net, *i.e.* against his will, and yet with his own feet he runs
into destruction.   The same thing is said in ver. 8*b* ; the way
on which he complacently wanders up and down (which the
Hithp. signifies here) is שְׂבָכָה, lattice-work, here a snare (Arab.
schabacah, a net, from שָׂבַךְ, *schabaca*, to intertwine, weave),
and consequently will suddenly break in and bring him to
ruin.   This fact of delivering himself over to destruction is
established in apocopated *futt.* (ver. 9) used as *præs.*, and
without the voluntative signification in accordance with the
poetic licence : a trap catches a heel (poetic brevity for : the
trap catches his heel), a noose seizes upon him, עָלָיו (but with
the accompanying notion of overpowering him, which the
translation " bind" is intended to express).   Such is the
meaning of צַמִּים here, which is not *plur.*, but *sing.*, from צָמַם

(ضمّ), to tie, and it unites in itself the meanings of snare-

layer (ch. v. 5) and of snare ; the form (as אַבִּיר, אַדִּיר) corresponds more to the former, but does not, however, exclude
the latter, as תַּנִּין and לַפִּיד (λαμπας) show.

The continuation in ver. 10 of the figure of the fowler
affirms that that issue of his life (ver. 9) has been preparing
long beforehand ; the prosperity of the evil-doer from the
beginning tends towards ruin. Instead of חֶבְלוֹ we have the
pointing חַבְלוֹ, as it would be in Arab. in a similar sense
hhabluhu (from *hhabl*, a cord, a net). The nearer destruction
is now to him, the stronger is the hold which his foreboding
has over him, since, as ver. 11 adds, terrible thoughts (בַּלָּהוֹת)
and terrible apparitions fill him with dismay, and haunt him,
following upon his feet. לְרַגְלָיו, close behind him, as Gen.
xxx. 30, 1 Sam. xxv. 42, Isa. xli. 2, Hab. iii. 5. The best
authorized pointing of the verb is וְהֵפִיצֻהוּ, with *Segol* (Ges. §
104, 2, *c*), *Chateph-Segol*, and *Kibbutz*. Except in Hab. iii. 14,
where the prophet includes himself with his people, הֵפִיץ,
diffundere, dissipare (*vid.* ch. xxxvii. 11, xl. 11), never has a
person as its obj. elsewhere. It would also probably not be
used, but for the idea that the spectres of terror pursue him
at every step, and are now here, now there, and his person is
as it were multiplied.

12 *His calamity looketh hunger-bitten,*
   And misfortune is ready for his fall.
13 *It devoureth the members of his skin ;*
   The first-born of death devoureth his members.
14 *That in which he trusted is torn away out of his tent,*
   And he must march on to the king of terrors.
15 *Beings strange to him dwell in his tent ;*
   Brimstone is strewn over his habitation.

The description of the actual and total destruction of the
evil-doer now begins with יְהִי (as ch. xxiv. 14, after the
manner of the voluntative forms already used in ver. 9).

Step by step it traces his course to the total destruction, which leaves no trace of him, but still bears evident marks of being the fulfilment of the curse pronounced upon him. In opposition to this explanation, Targ., Raschi, and others, explain אֹנוֹ according to Gen. xlix. 3 : the son of his manhood's strength becomes hungry, which sounds comical rather than tragic; another Targ. transl.: he becomes hungry in his mourning, which is indeed inadmissible, because the signif. *planctus*, *luctus*, belongs to the derivatives of אנה, אנן, but not to אֹן. But even the translation recently adopted by Ew., Stick., and Schlottm., "his strength becomes hungry," is unsatisfactory ; for it is in itself no misfortune to be hungry, and רָעֵב does not in itself signify "exhausted with hunger." It is also an odd metaphor, that strength becomes hungry ; we would then rather read with Reiske, רעב באנו, *famelicus in media potentia sua*. But as אֹן signifies strength (ch. xviii. 7), so אָוֶן (root אן, to breathe and pant) signifies both wickedness and evil (the latter either as evil = calamity, or as *anhelitus*, sorrow, Arab. *ain*) ; and the thought that his (*i.e.* appointed to the evil-doer) calamity is hungry to swallow him up (Syr., Hirz., Hahn, and others), suits the parallelism perfectly : "and misfortune stands ready for his fall."[1] אֵיד signifies prop. a weight, burden, then a load of suffering, and gen. calamity (root אד, Arab. *âda*, *e.g.* Sur. 2, 256, *la jaûduhu*, it is not difficult for him, and *adda*, comp. on Ps. xxxi. 12) ; and לְצַלְעוֹ

---

[1] If רעב elsewhere corresponds to the Arabic رغب, to be voraciously hungry, the Arab. رعب, to be paralyzed with fright, might correspond to it in the present passage : "from all sides spectres alarm him (בעתתהו from בעת = بغت, to fall suddenly upon any one; or better : = بعث, to hunt up, *excitare*, to cause to rise, to fill with alarm) and urge him forward, seizing on his heels; then his strength becomes a paralyzing fright (רַעֵב), and destruction is ready to overwhelm him." The *ro'b* (רֹעֵב, thus in Damascus) or *ra'b* (רַעֵב, thus in Hauran and among the

not : at his side (Ges., Ew., Schlottm., Hahn), but, according to Ps. xxxv. 15, xxxviii. 18 : for his fall (LXX. freely, but correctly : ἐξαίσιον); for instead of " at the side" (Arab. *ila ganbi*), they no more say in Hebrew than in Germ. " at the ribs."

Ver. 13 figuratively describes how calamity takes possession of him. The members, which are called יְצֻרִים in ch. xvii. 7, as parts of the form of the body, are here called בַּדִּים, as the parts into which the body branches out, or rather, since the word originally signifies a part, as that which is actually split off (*vid.* on ch. xvii. 16, where it denotes " cross-bars"), or according to appearance that which rises up, and from this primary signification applied to the body and plants, the members (not merely as Farisol interprets : the veins) of which the body consists and into which it is distributed. עוֹר (distinct from גֶּלֶד, ch. xvi. 15, similar in meaning to Arab. *baschar*, but also to the Arab. *gild*, of which the former signifies rather the epidermis, the latter the skin in the widest sense) is the soluble surface of the naked animal body. בְּכוֹר מָוֶת devours this, and indeed, as the repetition implies, gradually, but surely and entirely. " The first-born of the poor," Isa. xiv. 30, are those not merely who belong (בְּנֵי) to the race of the poor, but the poor in the highest sense and first rank. So here diseases are conceived of as children of death, as in the Arabic malignant fevers are called *benât el-*

Beduins) is a state of mind which only occurs among us in a lower degree, but among the Arabs it is worthy of note as a psychological fact. If the *wahm* (الوهم), or idea of some great and inevitable danger or misfortune, overpowers the Arab, all strength of mind and body suddenly forsakes him, so that he breaks down powerless and defenceless. Thus on July 8, 1860, in Damascus, in a few hours, about 6000 Christian men were slain, without any one raising a hand or uttering a cry for mercy. Both European and native doctors have assured me the *ro'b* in Arabia kills, and I have witnessed instances myself. Since it often produces a stiffness of the limbs with chronic paralysis, all kinds of paralysis are called *ro'b*, and the paralytics *mar'ûb*.—WETZST.

menîjeh, daughters of fate or death; that disease which Bildad has in his mind, as the one more terrible and dangerous than all others, he calls the "first-born of death," as that in which the whole destroying power of death is contained, as in the first-born the whole strength of his parent.[1] The Targ. understands the figure similarly, since it transl. מַלְאַךְ מוֹתָא (angel of death); another Targ. has instead שֵׁרוּי מוֹתָא, the firstling of death, which is intended in the sense of the *primogenita* (= *præmatura*) *mors* of Jerome. Least of all is it to be understood with Ewald as an intensive expression for בֶּן־מָוֶת, 1 Sam. xx. 31, of the evil-doer as liable to death. While now disease in the most fearful form consumes the body of the evil-doer, מִבְטַחוֹ (with *Dag. f. impl.*, as ch. viii. 14, xxxi. 24, Olsh. § 198, *b*) (a collective word, which signifies everything in which he trusted) is torn away out of his tent; thus also Rosenm., Ew., and Umbr. explain, while Hirz., Hlgst., Schlottm., and Hahn regard מבטחו as in apposition to אהלו, in favour of which ch. viii. 14 is only a seemingly suitable parallel. It means everything that made the ungodly man

---

[1] In Arabic the positive is expressed in the same metonymies with *abu*, e.g. *abû 'l-chêr*, the benevolent; on the other hand, e.g. *ibn el-hhâge* is much stronger than *abu 'l-hhâge*: the person who is called *ibn* is conceived of as a child of these conditions; they belong to his inmost nature, and have not merely affected him slightly and passed off. The Hebrew בכור represents the superlative, because among Semites the power and dignity of the father is transmitted to the first-born. So far as I know, the Arab does not use this superlative; for what is terrible and revolting he uses "mother," e.g. *umm el-fâritt*, mother of death, a name for the plague (in one of the modern popular poets of Damascus), *umm el-qashshâsh*, mother of the sweeping death, a name for war (in the same); for that which awakens the emotions of joy and grief he frequently uses "daughter." In an Arabian song of victory the fatal arrows are called *benât el-môt*, and the heroes (slayers) in the battle *benî el-môt*, which is similar to the figure used in the book of Job. Moreover, that disease which eats up the limbs could not be described by a more appropriate epithet than בכור מות. Its proper name is shunned in common life; and if it is necessary to mention those who are affected with it, they always say *sâdât el-gudhamâ* to avoid offending the company, or to escape the curse of the thing mentioned.—WETZST.

happy as head of a household, and gave him the brightest hopes of the future. This is torn away (*evellitur*) from his household, so that he, who is dying off, alone survives. Thus, therefore, ver. 14*b* describes how he also himself dies at last. Several modern expositors, especially Stickel, after the example of Jerome (*et calcet super eum quasi rex interitus*), and of the Syr. (*præcipitem eum reddent terrores regis*), take בַּלָּהוֹת as subj., which is syntactically possible (*vid.* ch. xxvii. 20, xxx. 15) : and destruction causes him to march towards itself (Ges. : *fugant eum*) like a military leader ; but since הִצְעִיד signifies to cause to approach, and since no אֵלָיו (to itself) stands with it, לְמֶלֶךְ is to be considered as denoting the goal, especially as לְ never directly signifies *instar*. In the passage advanced in its favour it denotes that which anything becomes, that which one makes a thing by the mode of treatment (ch. xxxix. 16), or whither anything extends (*e.g.* in Schultens on ch. xiii. 12 : they had claws *li-machâlibi, i.e.* "approaching to the claws" of wild beasts).[1] One falls into these strange interpretations when one departs from the accentuation, which unites מלך בלהות quite correctly by *Munach*.

Death itself is called "the king of terrors," in distinction from the terrible disease which is called its first-born. Death is also personified elsewhere, as Isa. xxviii. 15, and esp. Ps. xlix. 15, where it appears as a רֹעֶה, ruler in Hades, as in the Indian mythology the name of the infernal king *Jamas* signifies the tyrant or the tamer. The biblical representation does not recognise a king of Hades, as *Jamas* and Pluto : the judicial power of death is allotted to angels, of whom one, the angel of the abyss, is called *Abaddon* (אבדון), Apoc. ix. 11 ; and the chief possessor of this judicial power, ὁ τὸ κρατος ἔχων τοῦ θανάτου, is, according to Heb. ii. 14, the angel-prince, who, according to the prologue of our book, has also

---

[1] [Comp. a note *infra* on ch. xxi. 4.—TR.]

brought a fatal disease upon Job, without, however, in this
instance being able to go further than to bring him to the
brink of the abyss. It would therefore not be contrary to
the spirit of the book if we were to understand Satan by the
king of terrors, who, among other appellations in Jewish
theology, is called שׂר על־התהו, because he has his existence in
the *Thohu*, and seeks to hurl back every living being into the
Thohu. But since the prologue casts a veil over that which
remains unknown in this world in the midst of tragic woes,
and since a reference to Satan is found nowhere else in the
book—on the contrary, Job himself and the friends trace
back directly to God that mysterious affliction which forms
the dramatic knot—we understand (which is perfectly sufficient) by the king of terrors death itself, and with Hirz., Ew.,
and most expositors, transl.: "and it causes him to march
onward to the king of terrors." The "it" is a secret power,
as also elsewhere the *fem.* is used as *neut.* to denote the "dark
power" (Ewald, § 294, *b*) of natural and supernatural events,
although sometimes, *e.g.* ch. iv. 16, Isa. xiv. 9, the *masc.* is
also so applied. After the evil-doer is tormented for a while
with temporary בלהות, and made tender, and reduced to ripe-
ness for death by the first-born of death, he falls into the
possession of the king of בלהות himself; slowly and solemnly,
but surely and inevitably (as תצעיד implies, with which is combined the idea of the march of a criminal to the place of
execution), he is led to this king by an unseen arm.

In ver. 15 the description advances another step deeper
into the calamity of the evil-doer's habitation, which is now
become completely desolate. Since ver. 15*b* says that brimstone (from heaven, Gen. xix. 24, Ps. xi. 6) is strewn over
the evil-doer's habitation, *i.e.* in order to mark it as a place
that, having been visited with the fulfilment of the curse,
shall not henceforth be rebuilt and inhabited (*vid.* Deut.
xxix. 22 sq., and *supra*, on ch. xv. 28), ver. 15*a* cannot be

intended to affirm that a company of men strange to him take up their abode in his tent. But we shall not, however, on that account take בלהות as the subj. of תִּשְׁכּוֹן. The only natural translation is : what does not belong to him dwells in his tent (Ew. § 294, *b*) ; מִבְּלִי, elsewhere *præpos.* (ch. iv. 11, 20, xxiv. 7 sq.), is here an adverb of negation, as which it is often used as an intensive of אַיִן, *e.g.* Ex. xiv. 11. It is unnecessary to take the מ as partitive (Hirz.), although it can have a special signification, as Deut. xxviii. 55 (because not), by being separated from בלי. The neutral *fem.* תִּשְׁכֹּן refers to such inhabitants as are described in Isa. xiii. 20 sqq., xxvii. 10 sq., xxxiv. 11 sqq., Zeph. ii. 9, and in other descriptions of desolation. Creatures and things which are strange to the deceased rich man, as jackals and nettles, inhabit his domain, which is appointed to eternal unfruitfulness ; neither children nor possessions survive him to keep up his name. What does dwell in his tent serves only to keep up the recollection of the curse which has overtaken him.[1]

16   *His roots wither beneath,*
     And above his branch is lopped off.
17   *His remembrance is vanished from the land,*
     And he hath no name far and wide on the plain ;
18   *They drive him from light into darkness,*
     And chase him out of the world.
19   *He hath neither offspring nor descendant among his people,*
     Nor is there an escaped one in his dwellings.

The evil-doer is represented under the figure of a plant, ver. 16, as we have had similar figures already, ch. viii. 16

---

[1] The desolation of his house is the most terrible calamity for the Semite, *i.e.* when all belonging to his family die or are reduced to poverty, their habitation is desolated, and their ruins are become the byword of future generations. For the Beduin especially, although his hair tent leaves no mark, the thought of the desolation of his house, the extinction of his hospitable hearth, is terrible.—WETZST.

sq., xv. 30, 32 sq. ;[1] his complete extirpation is like the dying off of the root and of the branch, as Amos ii. 9, Isa. v. 24, and "let him not have a root below and a branch above" in the inscription on the sarcophagus of Eschmunazar. Here we again meet with יִמַּל, the proper meaning of which is so disputed ; it is translated by the Targ. (as by us) as *Niph.* יִתְמוֹלָל, but the meaning "to wither" is near at hand, which, as we said on ch. xiv. 2, may be gained as well from the primary notion "to fall to pieces" (whence LXX. ἐπιπεσεῖται), as from the primary notion "to parch, dry." אָמֵל (whence אֻמְלַל, formed after the manner of the Arabic IX. form, usually of failing ; *vid.* Caspari, § 59) offers a third possible explanation ; it signifies originally to be long and lax, to let anything hang down, and thence in Arab. (*amala*) to hope, *i.e.* to look out into the distance. Not the evil-doer's family alone is rooted out, but also his memory. With חוּץ, a very relative notion, both the street outside in front of the house (ch. xxxi. 32), and the pasture beyond the dwelling (ch. v. 10), are described ; here it is to be explained according to Prov. viii. 26 (אֶרֶץ וְחוּצוֹת), where Hitz. remarks : "The LXX. translates correctly ἀοικήτους. The districts beyond each person's land, which also belong to no one else, the desert, whither one goes forth, is meant." So אֶרֶץ seems also here (comp. ch. xxx. 8) to denote the land that is regularly inhabited— Job himself is a large proprietor within the range of a city (ch. xxix. 7)—and חוּץ the steppe traversed by the wandering tribes which lies out beyond. Thus also the Syr. version transl. 'al apai barito, over the plain of the desert, after which

[1] To such biblical figures taken from plants, according to which root and branch are become familiar in the sense of ancestors and descendants (comp. Sir. xxiii. 25, xl. 15 ; Wisd. iv. 3-5 ; Rom. xi. 16), the *arbor consanguineitatis*, which is not Roman, but is become common in the Christian refinement of the Roman right, may be traced back ; the first trace of this is found in Isidorus Hispalensis (as also the Cabbalistic tree אִילָן, which represents the Sephir-genealogy, has its origin in Spain).

the Arabic version is *el-barrîje* (the synon. of *bedw*, *bâdije*, whence the name of the Beduin[1]). What is directly said in ver. 17 is repeated figuratively in ver. 18; as also what has been figuratively expressed in ver. 16 is repeated in ver. 19 without figure. The subj. of the verbs in ver. 18 remains in the background, as ch. iv. 19, Ps. lxiii. 11, Luke xii. 20 : they thrust him out of the light (of life, prosperity, and fame) into the darkness (of misfortune, death, and oblivion) ; so that the *illustris* becomes not merely *ignobilis*, but totally *ignotus*, and they hunt him forth (יְנִדֻּהוּ from the *Hiph.* הֵנֵד of the verb נדד, instead of which it might also be יַנְדּהוּ from נָדָה, they banish him) out of the habitable world (for this is the signification of תֵּבֵל, the earth as built upon and inhabited). There remains to him in his race neither sprout nor shoot ; thus the rhyming alliteration נִין and נֶכֶד (according to Luzzatto on Isa. xiv. 22, used only of the descendants of persons in high rank, and certainly a nobler expression than our rhyming pairs : Germ. *Stumpf und Stiel, Mann und Maus, Kind und Kegel*). And there is no escaped one (as Deut. ii. 34 and freq., Arab. *shârid*, one fleeing; *sharûd*, a fugitive) in his abodes (מָגוּר, as only besides Ps. lv. 16). Thus to die away without descendant and remembrance is still at the present day among the Arab races that profess *Dîn Ibrâhîm* (the religion of Abraham) the most unhappy thought, for the point of gravitation of continuance beyond the grave is transferred by them to the immortality of the righteous in the continuance of his posterity and works in this world (*vid. supra*, p. 260) ; and where else should it be at the time of Job, since no revelation had as yet drawn the curtain aside

[1] The village with its meadow-land is *el-beled wa 'l-berr*. The arable land, in distinction from the steppe, is *el-ardd el-âmira*, and the steppe is *el-berrîje*. If both are intended, *ardd* can be used alone. Used specially, *el-berrîje* is the proper name for the great Syrian desert; hence the proverb : *el-hhurrîje fi 'l-berrîje*, there is freedom in the steppe (not in towns and villages).—WETZST.

from the future world ?   Now follows the declamatory conclusion of the speech.

> 20 *Those who dwell in the west are astonished at his day,*
> *And trembling seizeth those who dwell in the east ;*
> 21 *Surely thus it befalleth the dwellings of the unrighteous,*
> *And thus the place of him that knew not God.*

It is as much in accordance with the usage of Arabic as
it is biblical, to call the day of a man's doom " his day," the
day of a battle at a place " the day of that place."   Who are
the אַחֲרֹנִים who are astonished at it, and the קַדְמֹנִים whom
terror (שַׂעַר as twice besides in this sense in Ezek.) seizes, or
as it is properly, who seize terror, *i.e.* of themselves, without being able to do otherwise than yield to the emotion (as
ch. xxi. 6, Isa. xiii. 8 ; comp. on the contrary Ex. xv. 14 sq.) ?
Hirz., Schlottm., Hahn, and others, understand posterity by
אחרנים, and by קדמנים their ancestors, therefore Job's cotemporaries.   But the return from the posterity to those then
living is strange, and the usage of the language is opposed
to it ; for קדמנים is elsewhere always what belongs to the
previous age in relation to the speaker (*e.g.* 1 Sam. xxiv. 14,
comp. Eccles. iv. 16).   Since, then, קדמני is used in the signification eastern (*e.g.* הים הקדמוני, the eastern sea = the Dead
Sea), and אחרון in the signification western (*e.g.* הים האחרון, the
western sea = the Mediterranean), it is much more suited
both to the order of the words and the usage of the language
to understand, with Schult., Oetinger, Umbr., and Ew., the
former of those dwelling in the west, and the latter of those
dwelling in the east.   In the summarizing ver. 21, the retrospective pronouns are also *prægn.*, like ch. viii. 19, xx. 29,
comp. xxvi. 14 : Thus is it, viz. according to their fate, *i.e.*
thus it befalls them ; and אַךְ here retains its original affirmative signification (as in the concluding verse of Ps. lviii.),
although in Hebrew this is blended with the restrictive.   וְזֶה

has *Rebia mugrasch* instead of great *Schalscheleth*,[1] and מָקוֹם
has in correct texts *Legarme*, which must be followed by
לֹא־יָדַע with *Illuj* on the *penult*. On the relative clause
אֶל לֹא־יָדַע without אֲשֶׁר, comp. *e.g.* ch. xxix. 16 ; and on this
use of the *st. constr.*, *vid.* Ges. § 116, 3. The last verse is as
though those mentioned in ver. 20 pointed with the finger
to the example of punishment in the "desolated" dwellings
which have been visited by the curse.

This second speech of Bildad begins, like the first (ch. viii.
2), with the reproach of endless babbling ; but it does not end
like the first (ch. viii. 22). The first closed with the words :
" Thy haters shall be clothed with shame, and the tent of
the godless is no more ;" the second is only an amplification
of the second half of this conclusion, without taking up again
anywhere the tone of promise, which there also embraces the
threatening.

It is manifest also from this speech, that the friends, to
express it in the words of the old commentators, know nothing
of evangelical but only of legal suffering, and also only of
legal, nothing of evangelical, righteousness. For the righteousness of which Job boasts is not the righteousness of single
works of the law, but of a disposition directed to God, of
conduct proceeding from faith, or (as the Old Testament
generally says) from trust in God's mercy, the weaknesses
of which are forgiven because they are exonerated by the
habitual disposition of the man and the primary aim of his
actions. The fact that the principle, " suffering is the consequence of human unrighteousness," is accounted by Bildad as
the formula of an inviolable law of the moral order of the
world, is closely connected with that outward aspect of human
righteousness. One can only thus judge when one regards
human righteousness and human destiny from the purely

---

[1] *Vid.* Psalter ii. 503, and comp. Davidson, *Outlines of Hebrew Accentuation* (1861), p. 92, note.

legal point of view. A man, as soon as we conceive him in faith, and therefore under grace, is no longer under that supposed exclusive fundamental law of the divine dealing. Brentius is quite right when he observes that the sentence of the law certainly is modified for the sake of the godly who have the word of promise. Bildad knows nothing of the worth and power which a man attains by a righteous heart. By faith he is removed from the domain of God's justice, which recompenses according to the law of works; and before the power of faith even rocks move from their place.

Bildad then goes off into a detailed description of the total destruction into which the evil-doer, after going about for a time oppressed with the terrors of his conscience as one walking over snares, at last sinks beneath a painful sickness. The description is terribly brilliant, solemn, and pathetic, as becomes the stern preacher of repentance with haughty mien and pharisaic self-confidence ; it is none the less beautiful, and, considered in itself, also true—a masterpiece of the poet's skill in poetic idealizing, and in apportioning out the truth in dramatic form. The speech only becomes untrue through the application of the truth advanced, and this untruthfulness the poet has most delicately presented in it. For with a view of terrifying Job, Bildad interweaves distinct references to Job in his description ; he knows, however, also how to conceal them under the rich drapery of diversified figures. The first-born of death, that hands the ungodly over to death itself, the king of terrors, by consuming the limbs of the ungodly, is the Arabian leprosy, which slowly destroys the body. The brimstone indicates the fire of God, which, having fallen from heaven, has burned up one part of the herds and servants of Job ; the withering of the branch, the death of Job's children, whom he himself, as a drying-up root that will also soon die off, has survived. Job is the ungodly man, who, with wealth, children, name, and all that he possessed, is being destroyed as an example of punishment for posterity both far and near.

But, in reality, Job is not an example of punishment, but an example for consolation to posterity; and what posterity has to relate is not Job's ruin, but his wondrous deliverance (Ps. xxii. 31 sq.). He is no עַוָּל, but a righteous man; not one who לֹא יָדַע־אֵל, but he knows God better than the friends, although he contends with Him, and they defend Him. It is with him as with the righteous One, who complains, Ps. lxix. 21: "Contempt hath broken my heart, and I became sick: I hoped for sympathy, but in vain; for comforters, and found none;" and Ps. xxxviii. 12 (comp. xxxi. 12, lv. 13-15, lxix. 9, lxxxviii. 9, 19): "My lovers and my friends stand aloof from my stroke, and my kinsmen stand afar off." Not without a deep purpose does the poet make Bildad to address Job in the plural. The address is first directed to Job alone; nevertheless it is so put, that what Bildad says to Job is also intended to be said to others of a like way of thinking, therefore to a whole party of the opposite opinion to himself. Who are these like-minded? Hirzel rightly refers to ch. xvii. 8 sq. Job is the representative of the suffering and misjudged righteous, in other words: of the "congregation," whose blessedness is hidden beneath an outward form of suffering. One is hereby reminded that in the second part of Isaiah the עבד יהוה is also at one time spoken of in the sing., and at another time in the plur.; since this idea, by a remarkable contraction and expansion of expression (*systole* and *diastole*), at one time describes the one servant of Jehovah, and at another the congregation of the servants of Jehovah, which has its head in Him. Thus we again have a trace of the fact that the poet is narrating a history that is of universal significance, and that, although Job is no mere personification, he has in him brought forth to view an idea connected with the history of redemption. The ancient interpreters were on the track of this idea when they said in their way, that in Job we behold the image of Christ, and the figure of His church. *Christi personam figuraliter gessit*, says Beda; and Gregory, after having stated and explained that there is not in the Old Testament a righteous man who does not typically point to Christ, says: *Beatus Iob venturi cum suo corpore typum redemtoris insinuat.*

Job's Second Answer.—Chap. xix.

Schema: 10. 10. 10. 10. 10. 10.

[Then began Job, and said:]

2 *How long will ye vex my soul,*
  And crush me with your words?

3 *These ten times have ye reproached me;*
  Without being ashamed ye astound me.

4 *And if I have really erred,*
  My error rests with myself.

5 *If ye will really magnify yourselves against me,*
  And prove my reproach to me:

6 *Know then that Eloah hath wronged me,*
  And hath compassed me with His net.

This controversy is torture to Job's spirit; enduring in himself unutterable agony, both bodily and spiritually, and in addition stretched upon the rack by the three friends with their united strength, he begins his answer with a well-justified *quousque tandem.* תּוֹגְיוּן (Norzi: תּוֹגְיוּן) is *fut. energicum* from הוֹנָה (יָנָה), with the retention of the third radical, Ges. § 75, rem. 16. And in וּתְדַכְּאוּנַנִי (Norzi: וּתְדַכְּאוּנַנִי with quiescent *Aleph*) the suff. is attached to the *ûn* of the *fut. energicum*, Ges. § 60, rem. 3; the connecting vowel is *a*, and the suff. is *ani*, without epenthesis, not *anni* or *an⁰ni*, Ges. § 58,

4. In ver. 3 Job establishes his How long? Ten times is not to be taken strictly (Saad.), but it is a round number; ten, from being the number of the fingers on the human hand, is the number of human possibility, and from its position at the end of the row of numbers (in the decimal system) is the number of that which is perfected (vid. Genesis, S. 640 sq.); as not only the Sanskrit daçan is traceable to the radical notion "to seize, embrace," but also the Semitic עשר is traceable to the radical notion "to bind, gather together" (cogn. קשר). They have already exhausted what is possible in reproaches, they have done their utmost. Renan, in accordance with the Hebr. expression, transl.: Voilà (זֶה, as e.g. Gen. xxvii. 36) la dixième fois que vous m'insultez. The ἅπ. γεγρ. תַּהְכְּרוּ is connected by the Targ. with הִפִּיר (of respect of persons = partiality), by the Syr. with כְּרָא (to pain, of crève-cœur), by Raschi and Parchon with נִכַּר (to mistake) or הִתְנַכֵּר (to alienate one's self), by Saadia (vid. Ewald's Beitr. S. 99) with עָכַר (to dim, grieve[1]); he, however, compares the Arab. هكر, stupere (which he erroneously regards as differing only in sound from قهر, to overpower, oppress); and Abulwalid (vid. Rödiger in Thes. p. 84 suppl.) explains تهكرون منّى, ye gaze at me, since at the same time he mentions as possible that הכר may be = كهر, to treat indignantly, insultingly (which is only a different shade in sound of قهر,[2] and therefore refers to Saadia's interpretation). David Kimchi interprets according to Abulwalid, תתמהו לו; he however remarks at the same time, that his father Jos. Kimchi interprets after the Arab. הכר, which also signifies "shamelessness," תעיזו פניכם לי. Since the idea of dark wild looks is connected with هكر, he has un-

---

[1] Reiske interprets according to the Arabic عكر, denso et turbido agmine cum impetu ruitis in me.

[2] In Sur. 93, 9 (oppress not the orphan), the reading تكهر is found alternating with تنهر.

doubtedly this verb in his mind, not that compared by Ewald (who translates, " ye are devoid of feeling towards me"), and especially حكر, to deal unfairly, used of usurious trade in corn (which may also have been thought of by the LXX. ἐπίκεισθέ μοι, and Jerome *opprimentes*), which signifies as intrans. to be obstinate about anything, pertinacious. Gesenius also, *Thes.* p. 84, *suppl.*, suggests whether תַּחְכְּרוּ may not perhaps be the reading. But the comparison with حكر is certainly safer, and gives a perfectly satisfactory meaning, only תַּהְכְּרוּ must not be regarded as *fut. Kal* (as יְהֵלֹם, Ps. lxxiv. 6, according to the received text), but as *fut. Hiph.* for תַּהְכִּירוּ, according to Ges. § 53, rem. 4, 5, after which Schultens transl.: *quod me ad stuporem redigatis.* The connection of the two verbs in ver. 3*b* is to be judged of according to Ges. § 142, 3, *a*: ye shamelessly cause me astonishment (by the assurance of your accusations). One need not hesitate because it is תהכרו־לי instead of תהכרוני; this indication of the obj. by לְ, which is become a rule in Arabic with the inf. and part. (whence *e.g.* it would here be *muhkerina li*), and is still more extended in Aramaic, is also frequent in Hebrew (*e.g.* Isa. liii. 11, Ps. cxvi. 16, cxxix. 3, and 2 Chron. xxxii. 17, חָרֵף לְ, after which Olsh. proposes to read תחרפו־לי in the passage before us).

Much depends upon the correct perception of the structure of the clauses in ver. 4. The rendering, *e.g.*, of Olshausen, gained by taking the two halves of the verse as independent clauses, " yea certainly I have erred, I am fully conscious of my error," puts a confession into Job's mouth, which is at present neither mature nor valid. Hirz., Hahn, Schlottm., rightly take ver. 4*a* as a hypothetical antecedent clause (comp. ch. vii. 20, xi. 18): and if I have really erred (אַף־אָמְנָם, as ch. xxxiv. 12, yea truly; Gen. xviii. 13, and if I should really), my error remains with me, *i.e.* I shall have to expiate it, without your having on this account any right to take upon your-selves the office of God and to treat me uncharitably; or

what still better corresponds with אִתִּי תָּלִין‎ : my transgression
remains with me, without being communicated to another, *i.e.*
without having any influence over you or others to lead you
astray or involve you in participation of the guilt.   Ver. 6
stands in a similar relation to ver. 5.   Hirz., Ew., and Hahn
take ver. 5 as a double question : "or will ye really boast
against me, and prove to me my fault?"   Schlottm., on the
contrary, takes אִם‎ conditionally, and begins the conclusion
with ver. 5*b* : "if ye will really look proudly down upon me,
it rests with you at least, to prove to me by valid reasons,
the contempt which ye attach to me."   But by both of
these interpretations, especially by the latter, ver. 6 comes
in abruptly.   Even אַפוֹ‎ (written thus in three other passages
besides this) indicates in ver. 5 the conditional antecedent
clause (comp. ix. 24, xxiv. 25) of the expressive γνῶτε οὖν
(δή) : if ye really boast yourselves against me (*vid.* Ps. lv. 13
sq., comp. xxxv. 26, xxxviii. 17), and prove upon me, *i.e.* in
a way of punishment (as ye think), my shame, *i.e.* the sins
which put me to shame (not : the right of shame, which has
come upon me on account of my sins, an interpretation which
the conclusion does not justify), therefore : if ye really continue (which is implied by the *futt.*) to do this, then know,
etc.   If they really maintain that he is suffering on account
of flagrant sins, he meets them on the ground of this assumption with the assertion that God has wronged him (עִוְּתָנִי‎ short
for עִוֵּת מִשְׁפָּטִי‎, ch. viii. 3, xxxiv. 12, as Lam. iii. 36), and has
cast His net (מְצוּדוֹ‎, with the change of the *ô* of מָצוֹד‎ from צוּד‎,
to search, hunt, into the deeper *û* in inflexion, as מְנוּסִי‎ from
מָנוֹס‎, מְצוּרֶךְ‎, Ezek. iv. 8, from מָצוֹר‎) over him, together with
his right and his freedom, so that he is indeed obliged to
endure punishment.   In other words : if his suffering is really
not to be regarded otherwise than as the punishment of sin,
as they would uncharitably and censoriously persuade him, it
urges on his self-consciousness, which rebels against it, to the

conclusion which he hurls into their face as one which they
themselves have provoked.

7 *Behold I cry violence, and I am not heard;*
   I cry for help, and there is no justice.
8 *My way He hath fenced round, that I cannot pass over,*
   And He hath set darkness on my paths.
9 *He hath stripped me of mine honour,*
   And taken away the crown from my head.
10 *He destroyed me on every side, then I perished,*
   And lifted out as a tree my hope.
11 *He kindled His wrath against me,*
   And He regarded me as one of His foes.

He cries aloud חָמָס (that which is called out regarded as
accus. or as an interjection, *vid.* on Hab. i. 2), *i.e.* that illegal
force is exercised over him.   He finds, however, neither with
God nor among men any response of sympathy and help; he
cries for help (which שַׁוַּע, perhaps connected with יֵשַׁע, اسع,
from ישׁע, وسع, seems to signify), without justice, *i.e.* the
right of an impartial hearing and verdict, being attainable by
him.   He is like a prisoner who is confined to a narrow space
(comp. ch. iii. 23, xiii. 27) and has no way out, since darkness
is laid upon him wherever he may go.   One is here reminded
of Lam. iii. 7–9; and, in fact, this speech generally stands
in no accidental mutual relation to the lamentations of Jeremiah.   The "crown of my head" has also its parallel in Lam.
v. 16; that which was Job's greatest ornament and most
costly jewel is meant.   According to ch. xxix. 14, צדק and
משפט were his robe and diadem.   These robes of honour
God has stripped from him, this adornment more precious
than a regal diadem He has taken from him since, *i.e.*, his
affliction puts him down as a transgressor, and abandons him
to the insult of those around him.   God destroyed him round
about (*destruxit*), as a house that is broken down on all sides,

and lifted out as a tree his hope. הִפִּיעַ does not in itself signify to root out, but only to lift out (ch. iv. 21, of the tent-cord, and with it the tent-pin) of a plant : to remove it from the ground in which it has grown, either to plant it elsewhere, as Ps. lxxx. 9, or as here, to put it aside. The ground was taken away from his hope, so that its greenness faded away like that of a tree that is rooted up. The *fut. consec.* is here to be translated : then I perished (different from ch. xiv. 20 : and consequently he perishes); he is now already one who is passed away, his existence is only the shadow of life. God has caused, *fut. Hiph. apoc.* וַיַּחַר, His wrath to kindle against him, and regarded him in relation to Himself as His opponents, therefore as one of them. Perhaps, however, the expression is intentionally intensified here, in contrast with ch. xiii. 24 : he, the one, is accounted by God as the host of His foes; He treats him as if all hostility to God were concentrated in him.

12 *His troops came together,*
   And threw up their way against me,
   And encamped round about my tent.
13 *My brethren hath He removed far from me,*
   And my acquaintance are quite estranged from me.
14 *My kinsfolk fail,*
   And those that knew me have forgotten me.
15 *The slaves of my house and my maidens,*
   They regard me as a stranger,
   I am become a perfect stranger in their eyes.

It may seem strange that we do not connect ver. 12 with the preceding strophe or group of verses; but between vers. 7 and 21 there are thirty στίχοι, which, in connection with the arrangement of the rest of this speech in decastichs (accidentally coinciding remarkably with the prominence given to the number ten in ver. 3*a*), seem intended to be divided into

three decastichs, and can be so divided without doing violence
to the connection.   While in ver. 12, in connection with ver.
11, Job describes the course of the wrath, which he has to
withstand as if he were an enemy of God, in vers. 13 sqq. he
refers back to the degradation complained of in ver. 9.   In
ver. 12 he compares himself to a besieged (perhaps on account
of revolt) city.   God's גְּדוּדִים (not : bands of marauders, as
Dietr. interprets, but : troops, *i.e.* of regular soldiers, synon.
of צָבָא, ch. x. 17, comp. xxv. 3, xxix. 25, from the root גד, to
unite, join, therefore prop. the assembled, a heap ; *vid.* Fürst's
Handwörterbuch) are the bands of outward and inward sufferings sent forth against him for a combined attack (יַחַד).
Heaping up a way, *i.e.* by filling up the ramparts, is for the
purpose of making the attack upon the city with battering-
rams (ch. xvi. 14) and javelins, and then the storm, more
effective (on this erection of offensive ramparts (*approches*),
called elsewhere שָׁפַךְ סֹלְלָה, *vid.* Keil's *Archäologie*, § 159).
One result of this condition of siege in which God's wrath
has placed him is that he is avoided and despised as one
smitten of God : neither love and fidelity, nor obedience and
dependence, meet him from any quarter.   What he has said
in ch. xvii. 6, that he is become a byword and an abomination
(an object to spit upon), he here describes in detail.   There
is no ground for understanding אַחַי in the wider sense of
relations ; brethren is meant here, as in Ps. lxix. 9.   He calls
his relations קְרוֹבַי, as Ps. xxxviii. 12.   יֹדְעַי are (in accordance
with the pregnant biblical use of this word in the sense of
nosse cum affectu et effectu) those who know him intimately
(with objective suff. as Ps. lxxxvii. 4), and מְיֻדָּעַי, as Ps. xxxi.
12, and freq., those intimately known to him ; both, therefore, so-called heart- or bosom-friends.   גָּרֵי בֵיתִי Jer. well
translates *inquilini domus meœ ;* they are, in distinction from
those who by birth belong to the nearer and wider circle of
the family, persons who are received into this circle as ser-

vants, as vassals (comp. Ex. iii. 22, and Arabic جار, an associate, one sojourning in a strange country under the protection of its government, a neighbour), here espec. the domestics. The verb תְּחָשְׁבֻנִי (Ges. § 60) is construed with the nearest feminine subject. These people, who ought to thank him for taking them into his house, regard him as one who does not belong to it (זָר) ; he is looked upon by them as a perfect stranger (נָכְרִי), as an intruder from another country.

16 *I call to my servant and he answereth not,*
   I am obliged to entreat him with my mouth.

17 *My breath is offensive to my wife,*
   And my stench to my own brethren.

18 *Even boys act contemptuously towards me;*
   If I will rise up, they speak against me.

19 *All my confidential friends abhor me,*
   And those whom I loved have turned against me.

20 *My bone cleaveth to my skin and flesh,*
   And I am escaped only with the skin of my teeth.

His servant, who otherwise saw every command in his eyes, and was attent upon his wink, now not only does not come at his call, but does not return him any answer. The one of the home-born slaves (*vid.* on Gen. xiv. 14[1]), who stood in the same near connection to Job as Eliezer to Abraham, is intended here, in distinction from גרי ביתי, ver. 15. If he, his master, now in such need of assistance, desires any service from him, he is obliged (*fut.* with the sense of being compelled, as *e.g.* ch. xv. 30*b*, xvii. 2) to entreat him with his mouth. הִתְחַנֵּן, to beg חֵן of any one for one's self (*vid. supra*, p. 222),

---

[1] The (black) slaves born within the tribe itself are in the present day, from their dependence and bravery, accounted as the stay of the tribe, and are called *fadâwîje*, as those who are ready to sacrifice their life for its interest. The body-slave of Job is thought of as such a יְלִיד בַּיִת.

therefore to implore, *supplicare;* and בְּמוֹ־פִי here (as Ps. lxxxix. 2, cix. 30) as a more significant expression of that which is loud and intentional (not as ch. xvi. 5, in contrast to that which proceeds from the heart). In ver. 17*a*, רוּחִי signifies neither my vexation (Hirz.) nor my spirit = I (Umbr., Hahn, with the Syr.), for רוח in the sense of angry humour (as ch. xv. 13) does not properly suit the predicate, and روحى in the signification *ipse* may certainly be used in Arabic, where روح (perhaps under the influence of the philosophical usage of the language) signifies the animal spirit-life (*Psychol.* S. 154), not however in Hebrew, where נפשׁ is the stereotype form in that sense. If one considers that the elephantiasis, although its proper pathological symptom consists in an enormous hypertrophy of the cellular tissue of single distinct portions of the body, still easily, if the bronchia are drawn into sympathy, or if (what is still more natural) putrefaction of the blood with a scorbutic ulcerous formation in the mouth comes on, has difficulty of breathing (ch. vii. 15) and stinking breath as its result, as also a stinking exhalation and the discharge of a stinking fluid from the decaying limbs is connected with it (*vid.* the testimony of the Arabian physicians in Stickel, S. 169 f.), it cannot be doubted that Jer. has lighted upon the correct thing when he transl. *halitum meum exhorruit uxor mea.* רוחי is intended as in ch. xvii. 1, and it is unnecessary to derive זרה from a special verb זיר, although in Arab. the notions which are united in the Hebr. זור, *deflectere* and *abhorrere* (to turn one's self away from what is disgusting or horrible), are divided between زار *med. Wau* and ذار *med. Je* (*vid.* Fürst's *Handwörterbuch*).

In ver. 17 the meaning of חַנּוֹתִי is specially questionable. In Ps. lxxvii. 10, חַנּוֹת is, like שַׁמּוֹת, Ezek. xxxvi. 3, an infinitive from חָנַן, formed after the manner of the *Lamed He* verbs. Ges. and Olsh. indeed prefer to regard these forms as plurals of substantives (חַנָּה, שַׁמָּה), but the respective passages, regarded syntactically and logically, require infinitives. As regards the accentuation, according to which וחנותי is accented by *Rebia mugrasch* on the *ultima*, this does not necessarily decide in favour of its being *infin.*, since in the 1 *præt.* סַבֹּתִי, which, according to rule, has the tone on the *penultima*, the *ultima* is also sometimes (apart from the *perf. consec.*) found accented (on this, *vid.* on Ps. xvii. 3, and Ew. § 197, *a*), as סַבּוּ, קוּמָה, קוּמִי, also admit of both accentuations.[1] If וחנותי is *infin.*, the clause is a nominal clause, or a verbal one, that is to be supplemented by the *v. fin.* זָרָה; if it is first pers. *præt.*, we have a verbal clause. It must be determined from the matter and the connection which of these explanations, both of which are in form and syntax possible, is the correct one. The translation, "I entreat (groan to) the sons of my body," is not a thought that accords with the context, as would be obtained by the infin. explanation : my entreating (is offensive) ; this signif. (prop. to *Hithp.* as above) assigned to *Kal* by von Hofmann (*Schriftbew.* ii. 2, 612) is at least not to be derived from the derivative חֵן ; it might be more easily de-

---

[1] The *ultima*-accentuation of the form סַבֹּתִי is regular, if the *Waw conv. præt. in fut.* is added, as Ex. xxxiii. 19, 22, 2 Kings xix. 34, Isa. lxv. 7, Ezek. xx. 38, Mal. ii. 2, Ps. lxxxix. 24. Besides, the *penultima* has the tone regularly, *e.g.* Josh. v. 9, 1 Sam. xii. 3, xxii. 22, Jer. iv. 28, Ps. xxxv. 14, xxxviii. 7, Job xl. 4, Eccles. ii. 20. There are, however, exceptions, Deut. xxxii. 41 (שַׁנּוֹתִי), Isa. xliv. 16 (חַמּוֹתִי), Ps. xvii. 3 (זַמֹּתִי), xcii. 11 (בַּלֹּתִי), cxvi. 6 (דַּלֹּתִי). Perhaps the *ultima*-accentuation in these exceptional instances is intended to protect the indistinct pronunciation of the consonants *Beth*, *Waw*, or even *Resh*, at the beginning of the following words, which might easily become blended with the final syllable תִי ; certainly the reason lies in the pronunciation or in the rhythm (*vid.* on Ps. cxvi. 6, and comp. the retreating of the tone in the *infin.* חַלּוֹתִי (Ps. lxxvii. 11). Looking at this last exception, which has not yet been cleared up, וחנותי in the present passage will always be able to be regarded on internal grounds either as *infin.* or as 1 *præt.* The *ultima*-accentuation makes the word at first sight appear to be *infin.*, whereas in comparison with זרה, which is accented on the *penult.*, and therefore as 3 *præt.*, וחנותי seems also to be intended as *præt.* The accentuation, therefore, leaves the question in uncertainty.

duced from נֶחֱנָתְ, Jer. xxii. 23, which appears to be a *Niph.*
like נֶאֱנָח, נִחַם from חָנַן, but might also be derived from נֶנְחַת =
נֶאֱנָחְתְ by means of a transposition (*vid.* Hitz.). In the present passage one might certainly compare حَنّ, the usual
word for the utterance and emotion of longing and sympathy,
or also خَنّ, *fut. i* (with the infin. noun *chanîn*), which occurs
in the signifn. of weeping, and transl. : my imploring, groaning, weeping, is offensive, etc. Since, however, the X. form
of the Arab. خَنّ (*istachanna*) signifies to give forth an offensive smell (esp. of the stinking refuse of a well that is dried
up) ; and besides, since the significatn. *fœtere* is supported for
the root חן (comp. צְחַן) by the Syriac *chanîno* (*e.g. meshcho
chanîno*, rancid oil), we may also translate : " My stinking
is offensive," etc., or : " I stink to the children of my body "
(Rosenm., Ew., Hahn, Schlottm.) ; and this translation is not
only not hazardous in a book that so abounds in derivations
from the dialects, but it furnishes a thought that is as closely
as possible connected with ver. 17*a*.[1]

The further question now arises, who are meant by לִבְנֵי בִטְנִי.
Perhaps his children ? But in the prologue these have utterly

---

[1] Supplementary : Instead of *istachanna* (of the stinking of a well,
perhaps *denom.* from خَنّ, prop. to smell like a hen-house), the verb
hhannana (with ܟ) = *'affana*, " to be corrupt, to have a mouldy smell,"
can, with Wetzstein, be better compared with חַנּוֹתִי ; thence comes *zêt
mohhannin* = *mo'affin*, corrupt rancid oil, corresponding to the Syriac
חנינא. Thus ambiguously do the sellers of walnuts in Damascus cry out
their wares with the words : *el-mohhannin maugûd*, " the merciful One
liveth," *i.e.* He will send me buyers, and " there are (among them) corrupt (nuts)," *i.e.* I do not guarantee the quality of my wares. In like
manner, not only can ذَار inf. *dheir* (*dhêr*), to be offensive, be compared
with זָרָה, but, with Wetzstein, also the very common steppe word for
" to be bad, worthless," زَرِي, whence adj. *zarî* (with nunation *zarîjun*).

perished. Are we to suppose, with Eichhorn and Olshausen, that the poet, in the heat of discourse, forgets what he has laid down in the prologue ? When we consider that this poet, within the compass of his work,—a work into which he has thrown his whole soul,—has allowed no anachronism, and no reference to anything Israelitish that is contradictory to its extra-Israelitish character, to escape him, such forgetfulness is very improbable ; and when we, moreover, bear in mind that he often makes the friends refer to the destruction of Job's children (as ch. viii. 4, xv. 30, xviii. 16), it is altogether inconceivable. Hence Schröring has proposed the following explanation : " My soul [a substitution of which Hahn is also guilty] is strange to my wife ; my entreaty does not even penetrate to the sons of my body, it cannot reach their ear, for they are long since in Sheôl." But he himself thinks this interpretation very hazardous and insecure ; and, in fact, it is improbable that in the division, vers. 13–19, where Job complains of the neglect and indifference which he now experiences from those around him, בני בטני should be the only dead ones among the living, in which case it would moreover be better, after the Arabic version, to translate : " My longing is for, or : I yearn after, the children of my body." Grandchildren (Hirz., Ew., Hlgst., Hahn) might be more readily thought of ; but it is not even probable, that after having introduced the ruin of all of Job's children, the poet would represent their children as still living, some mention of whom might then at least be expected in the epilogue. Others, again (Rosenm., Justi, Gleiss), after the precedent of the LXX. (υἱοὶ παλλακίδων μου), understand the sons of concubines (slaves). Where, however, should a trace be found of the poet having conceived of his hero as a polygamist,—a hero who is even a model of chastity and continence (ch. xxxi. 1) ?

But must בני בטני really signify his sons or grandsons ?

Children certainly are frequently called, in relation to the father, פרי בטנו (*e.g.* Deut. vii. 13), and the father himself can call them פרי בטני (Mic. vi. 7); but בטן in this reference is not the body of the father, but the mother's womb, whence, begotten by him, the children issue forth. Hence " son of my body" occurs only once (Prov. xxxi. 2) in the mother's mouth. In the mouth of Job even (where the first origin of man is spoken of), בטני signifies not Job's body, but the womb that conceived him (*vid.* ch. iii. 10); and thus, therefore, it is not merely possible, but it is natural, with Stuhlm., Ges., Umbr., and Schlottm., to understand בני בטני of the sons of his mother's womb, *i.e.* of her who bare him; consequently, as בני אמי, Ps. lxix. 9, of natural brethren (brothers and sisters, *sorores uterinæ*), in which sense, regarding וחנותי according to the most natural influence of the tone as *infin.*, we transl. : " and my stinking is offensive (supply זרה) to the children of my mother's womb." It is also possible that the expression, as the words seem to be taken by Symmachus (υἰοὺς παιδῶν μου, my slaves' children), and as they are taken by Kosegarten, in comparison with the Arab. بطن in the signification race, subdivision (in the downward gradation, the third) of a greater tribe, may denote those who with him belong in a wider sense to one mother's bosom, *i.e.* to the same clan, although the mention of בני בטני in close connection with אשתי is not favourable to this extension of the idea. The circle of observation is certainly widened in ver. 18, where עֲוִילִים are not Job's grandchildren (Hahn), but the children of neighbouring families and tribes; עֲוִיל (*vid.* ch. xvi. 11) is a boy, and especially (perh. on account of the similarity in sound between מְעַוֵּל and עֲוִיל) a rude, frolicsome, mischievous boy. Even such make him feel their contempt; and if with difficulty, and under the influence of pain which distorts his countenance, he attempts to raise himself (אָקוּמָה, LXX. ὅταν ἀναστῶ, hypothetical cohortative, as ch. xi. 17,

xvi. 6), they make him the butt of their jesting talk (דִּבֶּר בְּ, as Ps. l. 20).

Ver. 19. מְתֵי סוֹדִי is the name he gives those to whom he confides his most secret affairs; סוֹד (*vid.* on Ps. xxv. 14) signifies either with a verbal notion, secret speaking (Arab. *sâwada*, III. form from *sâda*, to press one's self close upon, esp. as *sârra*, to speak in secret with any one), or what is made firm, *i.e.* what is impenetrable, therefore a secret (from *sâda*, to be or make close, firm, compact; cognate root, יָסַד, *wasada*, cognate in signification, *sirr*, a secret, from *sarra*, שָׂרַר, which likewise signifies to make firm). Those to whom he has made known his most secret plans (comp. Ps. lv. 13–15) now abhor him; and those whom he has thus (זֶה, as ch. xv. 17) become attached to, and to whom he has shown his affection,—he says this with an allusion to the three,— have turned against him. They gave tokens of their love and honour to him, when he was in the height of his happiness and prosperity, but they have not even shown any sympathy with him in his present form of distress.[1] His bones cleave (דָּבְקָה, Aq. ἐκολλήθη, LXX. erroneously ἐσάπησαν, *i.e.* רקבה) to his skin, *i.e.* the bones may be felt and seen through the skin, and the little flesh that remains is wasted away almost to a skeleton (*vid.* ch. vii. 15). This is not contradictory to the primary characteristic symptom of

[1] The disease which maims or devours the limbs, *dâ'u el-gudhâm* [*vid. supra*, p. 69], which generically includes Arabian leprosy, cancer, and syphilis, and is called the " first-born of death" in ch. xviii. 13, is still in Arabia the most dreaded disease, in the face of which all human sympathy ceases. In the steppe, even the greatest personage who is seized with this disease is removed at least a mile or two from the encampment, where a *charbûsh*, *i.e.* a small black hair-tent, is put up for him, and an old woman, who has no relations living, is given him as an attendant until he dies. No one visits him, not even his nearest relations. He is cast off as *muqâtal ollah*.—WETZST. The prejudice combated by the book of Job, that the leper is, as such, one who is smitten by the wrath of God, has therefore as firm hold of the Arabian mind in the present day as it had centuries ago.

the *lepra nodosa;* for the wasting away of the rest of the body may attain an extraordinarily high degree in connection with the hypertrophy of single parts. He can indeed say of himself, that he is only escaped (*se soit échappé*) with the skin of his teeth. By the "skin of his teeth" the gums are generally understood. But (1) the gum is not skin, and can therefore not be called "skin of the teeth" in any language; (2) Job complains in ver. 17 of his offensive breath, which in itself does not admit of the idea of healthy gums, and especially if it be the result of a scorbutic ulceration of the mouth, presupposes an ulcerous destruction of the gums. The current translation, "with my gums," is therefore to be rejected on account both of the language and the matter. For this reason Stickel (whom Hahn follows) takes עוֹר as *inf.* from עָרַר, and translates: "I am escaped from it with my teeth naked" [lit. with the being naked of my teeth], *i.e.* with teeth that are no longer covered, standing forward uncovered. This explanation is pathologically satisfactory; but it has against it (1) the translation of עוֹר, which is wide of the most natural interpretation of the word; (2) that in close connection with וָאֶתְמַלְּטָה one expects the mention of a part of the body that has remained whole. Is there not, then, really a skin of the teeth in the proper sense? The gum is not skin, but the teeth are surrounded with a skin in the jaw, the so-called periosteum. If we suppose, what is natural enough, that his offensive breath, ver. 17, arises from ulcers in the mouth (in connection with scorbutus, as is known, the breath has a terribly offensive smell), we obtain the following picture of Job's disease: his flesh is in part hypertrophically swollen, in part fearfully wasted away; the gums especially are destroyed and wasted away from the teeth, only the periosteum round about the teeth is still left to him, and single remnants of the covering of his loose and projecting teeth. Thus we interpret עוֹר שִׁנָּי in the first signification of the words,

and have also no need for supposing that ver. 20*b* is a proverbial phrase for "I have with great care and difficulty
escaped the extreme." The declaration perfectly corresponds
to the description of the disease ; and it is altogether needless with Hupfeld, after ch. xiii. 14, to read עוֹר בִּשְׂנִי, *vitam
solam et nudam vix reportavi,* which is moreover inappro-
priate, since Job regards himself as one who is dying.
Symm. alters the position of the בְּ similarly, since he translates after the Syriac Hexapla : καὶ ἐξέτιλλον (ותלישת) τὸ

δέρμα τοῖς ὀδοῦσιν μου, from מלט = מרט, ܠܶܛ, *nudare pilis,*

which J. D. Michaelis also compares ; the sense, however,
which is thereby gained, is beneath all criticism. On the
aoristic וָאֶתְמַלְּטָה, *vid.* on ch. i. 15. Stickel has on this passage an excursus on this *ah,* to which he also attributes, in
this addition to the historic tense, the idea of striving after a
goal : " I slip away, I escape ; " it certainly gives vividness to
the notion of the action, if it may not always have the force
of direction towards anything. Therefore : with a destroyed
flesh, and indeed so completely destroyed that there is even
nothing left to him of sound skin except the skin of his
teeth, wasted away to a skeleton, and become both to sight
and smell a loathsome object;—such is the sufferer the friends
have before them,—one who is tortured, besides, by a dark
conflict which they only make more severe,—one who now
implores them for pity, and because he has no pity to expect
from man, presses forward to a hope which reaches beyond
the grave.

21 *Have pity upon me, have pity upon me, O ye my friends,*
   For the hand of Eloah hath touched me.
22 *Wherefore do ye persecute me as God,*
   And are never satisfied with my flesh?
23 *Oh that my words were but written,*

That they were recorded in a book,
24 *With an iron pen, filled in with lead,*
Graven in the rock for ever!
25 *And I know : my Redeemer liveth,*
And as the last One will He arise from the dust.

In ver. 21 Job takes up a strain we have not heard previously. His natural strength becomes more and more feeble, and his voice weaker and weaker. It is a feeling of sadness that prevails in the preceding description of suffering, and now even stamps the address to the friends with a tone of importunate entreaty which shall, if possible, affect their heart. They are indeed his friends, as the emphatic אַתֶּם רֵעָי affirms ; impelled towards him by sympathy they are come, and at least stand by him while all other men flee from him. They are therefore to grant him favour (חָנַן, prop. to incline to) in the place of right ; it is enough that the hand of Eloah has touched him (in connection with this, one is reminded that leprosy is called נֶגַע, and is pre-eminently accounted as *plaga divina;* wherefore the suffering Messiah also bears the significant name חִוָּרָא דְבֵי רַבִּי, " the leprous one from the school of Rabbi," in the Talmud, after Isa. liii. 4, 8), they are not to make the divine decree heavier to him by their uncharitableness. Wherefore do ye persecute me—he asks them in ver. 22—like as God (כְּמוֹ־אֵל, according to Saad. and Ralbag = כמו־אֵלֶּה, which would be very tame) ; by which he means not merely that they add their persecution to God's, but that they take upon themselves God's work, that they usurp to themselves a judicial divine authority, they act towards him as if they were superhuman (*vid.* Isa. xxxi. 3), and therefore inhumanly, since they, who are but his equals, look down upon him from an assumed and false elevation. The other half of the question : wherefore are ye not full of my flesh (*de ma chair*, with מִן, as ch. xxxi. 31), but still continue to devour it? is founded upon a common Semitic figurative expression, with which may be compared our [Germ.] expression, "to gnaw with the tooth of slander" [comp. Engl. "backbiting"]. In Chaldee, אֲכַל קַרְצוֹהִי דִי, to eat the pieces of (any one), is equivalent to, to slander him; in Syriac, *ochelqarsso* is the name of Satan, like διάβολος. The Arabic here, as almost everywhere in the book of Job, presents a still closer parallel; for أَكَلَ لَحْمَ signifies to eat any one's flesh, then (different from אכל בשׂר, Ps. xxvii. 2) equivalent to, to slander,[1] since an evil report is conceived of as a wild beast, which delights in tearing a neighbour to pieces, as the friends do not refrain from doing, since, from the love of their assumption that his suffering must be the retributive punishment of heinous sins, they lay sins to his charge of which he is not conscious, and which he never committed. Against these uncharitable and groundless accusations he wishes (vers. 23 sq.) that the testimony of his innocence, to which they will not listen, might be recorded in a book for posterity, or because a book may easily perish, graven in a rock (therefore not on leaden plates) with an iron style, and the addition of lead, with which to fill up the engraved letters, and render them still more imperishable. In connection with the remarkable fidelity with which the poet throws himself back into the pre-Israelitish patriarchal time of his hero, it is of no small importance that he ascribes to him an acquaintance not only with monumental writing, but also with book and documentary writing (comp. ch. xxxi. 35).

The *fut.*, which also elsewhere (ch. vi. 8, xiii. 5, xiv. 13,

---

[1] *Vid.* Schultens' *ad Prov. Meidanii*, p. 7 (where "to eat his own flesh," equivalent to "himself," without allowing others to do it, signifies to censure his kinsmen), and comp. the phrase أَكَلَ الاعراض (*aclu-l-a'râdhi*) in the signification *arrodere existimationem hominum* in Makkari, i. 541, 13.

once the *præt.*, ch. xxiii. 3, *noverim*) follows מִי־יִתֵּן, *quis dabat*
= *utinam*, has *Waw consec.* here (as Deut. v. 26 the *præt.*) ;
the arrangement of the words is extremely elegant, בַּסֵּפֶר
stands *per hyperbaton* emphatically prominent. כְּתָב and חָקַק
(whence *fut. Hoph.* יֻחָקוּ with *Dag. implicitum* in the ח, comp.
ch. iv. 20, and the *Dag.* of the ק omitted, for יֻחְקְקוּ, according
to Ges. § 67, rem. 8) interchange also elsewhere, Isa. xxx. 8.
סֵפֶר, according to its etymon, is a book formed of the skin of
an animal, as Arab. *sufre*, the leathern table-mat spread on
the ground instead of a table. It is as unnecessary to read
לְעֵד (comp. ch. xvi. 8, LXX., εἰς μαρτύριον) instead of לָעַד
here, as in Isa. xxx. 8. He wishes that his own declaration, in
opposition to his accusers, may be inscribed as on a monument,
that it may be immortalized,[1] in order that posterity may behold it, and, it is to be hoped, judge him more justly than
his cotemporaries. He wishes this, and is certain that his
wish is not vain. His testimony to his innocence will not
descend to posterity without being justified to it by God, the
living God.

Thus is וַאֲנִי יָדַעְתִּי connected with what precedes. ידעתי is
followed, as in ch. xxx. 23, Ps. ix. 21, by the *oratio directa*.
The monosyllable tone-word חָי (on account of which גֹּאֲלִי has
the accent drawn back to the *penult.*) is 3 *præt.*: I know :
my redeemer liveth ; in connection with this we recall the
name of God, חי העולם, Dan. xii. 7, after which the Jewish
oath *per Anchialum* in Martial is to be explained. גֹּאֵל might
(with Umbr. and others), in comparison with ch. xvi. 18, as
Num. xxxv. 12, be equivalent to גֹּאֵל הַדָּם : he who will redeem, demand back, avenge the shedding of his blood and
maintain his honour as of blood that has been innocently

---

[1] לָעַד is differently interpreted by Jerome: evermore hewn in the rock;
for so it seems his *vel certe* (instead of which *celte* is also read, which
is an old northern name for a chisel) *sculpantur in silice* must be explained.

shed; in general, however, גאל signifies to procure compensation for the down-trodden and unjustly oppressed, Prov. xxiii. 11, Lam. iii. 58, Ps. cxix. 154. This Rescuer of his honour lives and will rise up as the last One, as one who holds out over everything, and therefore as one who will speak the final decisive word. To אַחֲרוֹן have been given the significations Afterman in the sense of *vindex* (Hirz., Ewald), or Rearman in the sense of a second [*lit.* in a duel,] (Hahn), but contrary to the usage of the language: the word signifies *postremus, novissimus*, and is to be understood according to Isa. xliv. 6, xlviii. 12, comp. xli. 4. But what is the meaning of עַל־עָפָר? Is it: upon the dust of the earth, having descended from heaven? The words may, according to ch. xli. 25 [Hebr., Engl. xli. 33], be understood thus (without the accompanying notion, formerly supposed by Umbreit, of *pulvis* or *arena* = *palæstra*, which is Classic, not Hebraic); but looking to the process of destruction going on in his body, which has been previously the subject of his words, and is so further on, it is far more probable that על־עפר is to be interpreted according to ch. xvii. 16, xx. 11, xxi. 26, Ps. xxx. 10. Moreover, an Arab would think of nothing else but the dust of the grave if he read عَلَى تُرَابٍ in this connection.[1]

Besides, it is unnecessary to connect קוּם עַל, as perhaps 2 Chron. xxi. 4, and the Arab. قَامَ عَلَى (to stand by, help): על־עפר is first of all nothing more than a defining of locality. To affirm that if it refer to Job it ought to be עפרי, is unfounded. Upon the dust in which he is now soon to be laid,

---

[1] In Arabic عَفَر belongs only to the ancient language (whence 'afarahu, he has cast him into the dust, placed him upon the sand, inf. 'afr); غُبَار (whence the Ghobar, a peculiar secret-writing, has its name) signifies the dry, flying dust; تُرَاب, however, is dust in gen., and particularly the dust of the grave, as *e.g.* in the forcible proverb: nothing but the *turâb* fills the eyes of man. So common is this signification, that a tomb is therefore called *turbe*

into which he is now soon to be changed, will He, the Rescuer of his honour, arise (קוּם, as in Deut. xix. 15, Ps. xxvii. 12, xxxv. 11, of the rising up of a witness, and as *e.g.* Ps. xii. 6, comp. xciv. 16, Isa. xxxiii. 10, of the rising up and interposing of a rescuer and help) and set His divine seal to Job's own testimony thus made permanent in the monumental inscription. Oetinger's interpretation is substantially the same : " I know that He will at last come, place himself over the dust in which I have mouldered away, pronounce my cause just, and place upon me the crown of victory."

A somewhat different connection of the thought is obtained, if וַאֲנִי is taken not progressively, but adversatively : " Yet I know," etc. The thought is then, that his testimony of his innocence need not at all be inscribed in the rock ; on the contrary, God, the ever living One, will verify it. It is difficult to decide between them ; still the progressive rendering seems to be preferable, because the human vindication after death, which is the object of the wish expressed in vers. 23 sq., is still not essentially different from the divine vindication hoped for in ver. 25, which must not be regarded as an antithesis, but rather as a perfecting of the other designed for posterity. Ver. 25 is, however, certainly a higher hope, to which the wish in vers. 23 sq. forms the stepping-stone. God himself will avenge Job's blood, *i.e.* against his accusers, who say that it is the blood of one who is guilty ; over the dust of the departed He will arise, and by His majestic testimony put to silence those who regard this dust of decay as the dust of a sinner, who has received the reward of his deeds.

But is it perhaps this his hope of God's vindication, expressed in vers. 25–27, which (as Schlottmann and Hahn,[1]

---

[1] Hahn, after having in his pamphlet, *de spe immortalitatis sub V.T. gradatim exculta*, 1845, understood Job's confession distinctly of a future beholding in this world, goes further in his *Commentary*, and entirely deprives this confession of the character of hope, and takes all as an expression of what is present. We withhold our further assent.

though in other respects giving very different interpretations, think) is, according to Job's wish, to be permanently inscribed on the monument, in order to testify to posterity with what a stedfast and undismayed conviction he had died? The high-toned *introitus*, vers. 23 sq., would be worthy of the important inscription it introduces. But (1) it is improbable that the inscription would begin with ואני, consequently with *Waw*,—a difficulty which is not removed by the translation, " Yea, I know," but only covered up ; the appeal to Ps. ii. 6, Isa. iii. 14, is inadmissible, since there the divine utterance, which begins with *Waw*, *per aposiopesin* continues a suppressed clause; כי אני would be more admissible, but that which is to be written down does not even begin with כי in either Hab. ii. 3 or Jer. xxx. 3. (2.) According to the whole of Job's previous conduct and habitual state of mind, it is to be supposed that the contents of the inscription would be the expression of the stedfast consciousness of his innocence, not the hope of his vindication, which only here and there flashes through the darkness of the conflict and temptation, but is always again swallowed up by this darkness, so that the thought of a perpetual preservation, as on a monument, of this hope can by no means have its origin in Job; it forms everywhere only, so to speak, the golden weft of the tragic warp, which in itself even resists the tension of the two opposites : Job's consciousness of innocence, and the dogmatic postulate of the friends ; and their intensity gradually increases with the intensity of this very tension. So also here, where the strongest expression is given both to the confession of his innocence as a confession which does not shun, but even desires, to be recorded in a permanent form for posterity, and also at the same time in connection with this to the confidence that to him, who is misunderstood by men, the vindication from the side of God, although it may be so long delayed that he even dies, can nevertheless not be wanting. Accordingly, by מִלָּי we understand not what immediately follows, but the words concerning his innocence which have already been often repeated by him, and which remain unalterably the same ; and we are authorized in closing one strophe with ver. 25, and in beginning a new one with ver. 26, which indeed is commended by the prevalence of the decastich in this speech, although we do not allow to this observance of the strophe division any influence in determining the exposition. It is, however, of use in our exposition. The strophe which now follows developes the chief reason of believing hope which is expressed in ver. 25 ; comp. the hexastich ch. xii. 11–13, also there in vers. 14 sqq. is the expansion of ver. 13, which expresses the chief thought as in the form of a thema.

26 *And after my skin, thus torn to pieces,*
   And without my flesh shall I behold Eloah,
27 *Whom I shall behold for my good,*
   And mine eyes shall see Him and no other—
   My veins languish in my bosom.
28 *Ye think: " How shall we persecute him ?"*
   Since the root of the matter is found in me—
29 *Therefore be ye afraid of the sword,*
   For wrath meeteth the transgressions of the sword,
   That ye may know there is a judgment !

If we have correctly understood עַל־עָפָר, ver. 25*b*, we cannot in this speech find that the hope of a bodily recovery is expressed. In connection with this rendering, the oldest representative of which is Chrysostom, מִבְּשָׂרִי is translated either : free from my flesh = having become a skeleton (Umbr., Hirz., and Stickel, in *comm. in Iobi loc. de Goële*, 1832, and in the transl., Gleiss, Hlgst., Renan), but this מבשרי, if the מן is taken as privative, can signify nothing else but fleshless = bodiless ; or : from my flesh, *i.e.* the flesh when made whole again (viz. Eichhorn in the Essay, which has exercised considerable influence, to his *Allg. Bibl. d. bibl. Lit.* i. 3, 1787, von Cölln, BCr., Knapp, von Hofm.,[1] and others), but hereby the relation of ver. 26*b* to 26*a* becomes a contrast, without there being anything to indicate it. Moreover, this rendering, as מבשׂרי may also be explained, is in itself contrary to the spirit and plan of the book ; for the character of Job's present state of mind is, that he looks for certain death, and will hear nothing of the consolation of recovery (ch. xvii. 10–16), which sounds to him as mere mockery ; that he, however, notwithstanding, does not despair of God, but, by the consciousness of his innocence and the uncharitableness of the friends, is more and more impelled from the God of wrath and caprice to the God of love, his future Redeemer ; and that then, when at the end of the course of suffering the actual proof of God's love breaks through the seeming manifestation of wrath, even that which Job had not ventured to hope is realized : a return of temporal prosperity beyond his entreaty and comprehension.

On the other hand, the mode of interpretation of the older translators and expositors, who find an expression of the hope of a resurrection at the end of the preceding strophe or the beginning of this, cannot be accepted. The LXX., by reading יקים instead of יקום, and connecting יקים עורי נקפו זאת, translates : ἀναστήσει δέ (*Cod. Vat.* only ἀναστῆσαι) μου τὸ σῶμα (*Cod. Vat.* τὸ δέρμα μου) τὸ ἀναντλοῦν μοι (*Cod. Vat. om. μοι) ταῦτα, —but how can any one's skin be said to awake (Italic : *super terram resurget cutis mea*),[2] and whence does the verb נקף obtain

---

[1] Von Hofmann (*Schriftbeweis*, ii. 2, 503) translates: "I know, however, my Redeemer is living, and hereafter He will stand forth [which must have been יעמד instead of יקום] upon the earth and after my skin, this surrounding (נקפו, Chaldaism, instead of נקפות after the form עקשׁות), and from my flesh shall I behold God, whom I shall behold for myself, and my eyes see [Him], and He is not strange."

[2] Stickel therefore maintains that this ἀνιστάναι of the LXX. is to be

the signification *exhaurire* or *exantlare*? Jerome's translation
is not less bold : *Scio enim quod redemptor meus vivit et in
novissimo die de terra surrecturus sum*, as though it were אָקוּם,
not יְקוּם, and as though אַחֲרוֹן could signify *in novissimo die* (in
favour of which Isa. viii. 23 can only seemingly be quoted) !
The Targ. translates : "I know that my Redeemer liveth, and
hereafter His redemption will arise (become a reality) over
the dust (into which I shall be dissolved), and after my skin
is again made whole (thus[1] אִתְּפַח seems to require to be translated, not *intumuit*) this will happen ; and from my flesh I
shall again behold God." It is evident that this is intended
of a future restoration of the corporeal nature that has become dust, but the idea assigned to נִקְּפוּ is without foundation.
Luther also cuts the knot by translating : (But I know that
my Redeemer liveth), and He will hereafter raise me up out
of the ground, which is an impossible sense that is word for
word forced upon the text. There is just as little ground
for translating ver. 26a with Jerome : *et rursum circumdabor
pelle mea* (after which Luther : and shall then be surrounded
with this my skin); for נִקְּפוּ can as *Niph.* not signify *circumdabor*, and as *Piel* does not give the meaning *cutis mea
circumdabit* (*scil. me*), since נקפו cannot be predicate to the
sing. עוֹרִי. In general, נקפו cannot be understood as *Niph.*,
but only as *Piel;* the *Piel* נִקַּף, however, signifies not : to
surround, but : to strike down, *e.g.* olives from the tree, Isa.
xvii. 6, or the trees themselves, so that they lie felled on the
ground, Isa. x. 34, comp. نَقَفَ, to strike into the skull and
injure the soft brain, then : to strike forcibly on the head
(gen. on the upper part), or also : to deal a blow with a lance

understood not of being raised from the dead, but of being restored to
health ; *vid.* on the contrary, Umbreit in *Stud. u. Krit.* 1840, i., and
Ewald in *d. Theol. Jahrbb.*, 1843, iv.

[1] In this signification, to recover, prop. to recover one's self, אִתְּפַח is
used in Talmudic ; *vid.* Buxtorf, פוח and תפח. The rabbinical expositors
ignore this Targum, and in general furnish but little that is useful here.

or stick.[1] Therefore ver. 26a, according to the usage of the Semitic languages, can only be intended of the complete destruction of the skin, which is become cracked and broken by the leprosy; and this was, moreover, the subject spoken of above (ver. 20, comp. xxx. 19). For the present we leave it undecided whether Job here confesses the hope of the resurrection, and only repel those forced misconstructions of his words which arbitrarily discern this hope in the text. Free from such violence is the translation: and after this my skin is destroyed, *i.e.* after I shall have put off this my body, from my flesh (*i.e.* restored and transfigured), I shall behold God. Thus is מבשׂרי understood by Rosenm., Kosegarten (*diss. in Iob,* xix., 1815), Umbreit (*Stud. u. Krit.* 1840, i.), Welte, Carey, and others. But this interpretation is also untenable. For, 1. In this explanation ver. 26a is taken as an antecedent; a *præpos.*, however, like אַחַר or עַד, used as a *conj.*, has, according to Hirzel's correct remark, the verb always immediately after it, as ch. xlii. 7, Lev. xiv. 43; whereas 1 Sam. xx. 41, the single exception, is critically doubtful. 2. It is not probable that the poet by עורי should have thought of the body, which disease is rapidly hurrying on to death, and by בשׂרי, on the other hand, of a body raised up and glorified. 3. Still more improbable is it that בשׂר should be so used here as in the church's term, *resurrectio carnis,* which is certainly an allowable expression, but one which exceeds the meaning of the language of Scripture. בשׂר, σάρξ, is in general, and especially in the Old Testament, a notion which has grown up in almost inseparable connection with the marks of frailty

---

[1] Thus, according to the Turkish Kamus: to sever the skull from (عن) the brain, *i.e.* so that the brain is laid bare, or also *e.g.* to split the coloquintida [or bitter cucumber], so that the seeds are laid bare, or: to crack the bones and take out the marrow, cognate with نقف, for the act of piercing an egg is called both *naqaba* and *naqafa-l-beidha.* In Hebrew נקף coincides with נגף, not with נקב.

and sinfulness. And 4. The hope of a resurrection as a settled principle in the creed of Israel is certainly more recent than the Salomonic period. Therefore by far the majority of modern expositors have decided that Job does not indeed here avow the hope of the resurrection, but the hope of a future spiritual beholding of God, and therefore of a future life; and thus the popular idea of Hades, which elsewhere has sway over him, breaks out. Thus, of a future spiritual beholding of God, are Job's words understood by Ewald, Umbreit (who at first explained them differently), Vaihinger, Von Gerlach, Schlottmann, Hölemann (*Sächs. Kirchen- u. Schulbl.* 1853, Nos. 48, 50, 62), König (*Die Unsterblichkeitsidee im B. Iob*, 1855), and others, also by the Jewish expositors Arnheim and Löwenthal. This rendering, which is also adopted in the Art. *Hiob* in Herzog's *Real-Encyklopädie*, does not necessitate any impossible misconstruction of the language, but, as we shall see further on, it does not exhaust the meaning of Job's confession.

First of all, we will continue the explanation of each expression. אַחַר is a *præpos.*, and used in the same way as the Arabic بَعْدَ is sometimes used : after my skin, *i.e.* after the loss of it (comp. ch. xxi. 21, אַחֲרָיו, after he is dead). נִקְּפוּ is to be understood relatively : which they have torn in pieces, *i.e.* which has been torn in pieces (comp. the same use of the 3 *pers.*, ch. iv. 19, xviii. 18) ; and זֹאת, which, according to Targ., Koseg., Stickel *de Goële*, and Ges. *Thes.*, ought to be taken inferentially, equivalent to *hoc erit* (this, however, cannot be accepted, because it must have been וְזֹאת אַחַר וגו', وَذٰلِكَ بَعْدَ أَنْ, *idque postquam*, and moreover would require the words to be arranged אַחַר נִקְּפוּ עוֹרִי), commonly however taken together with עוֹרִי (which is nevertheless *masc.*), is understood as pointing to his decayed body, seems better to be taken adverbially : in this manner (Arnheim, Stickel in his translation, von Gerl., Hahn) ; it is the *acc.* of reference, as ch. xxxiii. 12. The מִן of מִבְּשָׂרִי is the negative מִן: free from my flesh (prop. away, far from, Num. xv. 25, Prov. xx. 3),—a rather frequent way of using this preposition (*vid.* ch. xi. 15, xxi. 9 ; Gen. xxvii. 39 ; 2 Sam. i. 22 ; Jer. xlviii. 45). Accordingly, we translate : " and after my skin, which they tear to pieces thus, and free from my flesh, shall I behold Eloah." That Job, after all, is permitted to behold God in this life, and also in this life receives the testimony of his justification, does not, as already observed, form any objection to this rendering of ver. 26 : it is the reward of his faith, which, even in the face of certain death, has not despaired of God, that he does not fall into the power of death at all, and that God forthwith condescends to him in love. And that Job here holds firm, even beyond death, to the hope of beholding God in the future as a witness to his innocence, does not, after ch. xiv. 13–15, xvi. 18–21, come unexpectedly ; and it is entirely in accordance with the inner progress of the drama, that the thought of a redemption from Hades, expressed in the former passage, and the demand expressed in the latter passage, for the rescue of the honour of his blood, which is even now guaranteed him by his witness in heaven, are here comprehended, in the confident certainty that his blood and his dust will not be declared by God the Redeemer as innocent, without his being in some way conscious of it, though freed from this his decaying body. In ver. 27 he declares how he will behold God : whom I shall behold to me, *i.e.* I, the deceased one, as being *for* me (לְ, like Ps. lvi. 10, cxviii. 6), and my eyes see Him, and not a stranger. Thus (*neque alius*) LXX., Targ., Jerome, and most others translate ; on the other hand, Ges. *Thes.*, Umbr., Vaih., Stick., Hahn, and von Hofm. translate : my eyes see Him, and indeed not as an enemy ; but זָר signifies *alienus* and *alius*, not however *adversarius*, which latter meaning it in

general obtains only in a national connection ; here (used as
in Prov. xxvii. 2) it excludes the three : none other but Job,
by which he means his opponents, will see God rising up for
him, taking up his cause. רָאוּ is *præt.* of the future, therefore *præt. propheticum,* or *præt. confidentiæ* (as frequently in
the Psalms). His reins within him pine after this vision of
God. Hahn, referring to ch. xvi. 13, translates incorrectly :
" If even my reins within me perish," which is impossible,
according to the syntax ; for Ps. lxxiii. 26 has כלה in the
sense of *licet defecerit* as hypothetical antecedent. The Syriac
version is altogether wrong : my reins (*culjot*) vanish completely away by reason of my lot (בְּחֻקִּי). It would be expressed in Arabic exactly as it is here : *culája* (or, dual,
culatája) *tadhûbu,* my reins melt ; for in Arab. also, as in
the Semitic languages generally, the reins are considered as
the seat of the tenderest and deepest affections (*Psychol.* S.
268, *f*), especially of love, desire, longing, as here, where
כָּלָה, as in Ps. cxix. 123 and freq., is intended of wasting
away in earnest longing for salvation.

Having now ended the exposition of the single expressions,
we inquire whether those do justice to the text who understand it of an absolutely bodiless future beholding of God.
We doubt it. Job says not merely that he, but that his eyes,
shall behold God. He therefore imagines the spirit as clothed
with a new spiritual body instead of the old decayed one ;
not so, however, that this spiritual body, these eyes which
shall behold in the future world, are brought into combination with the present decaying body of flesh. But his faith
is here on the direct road to the hope of a resurrection ; we
see it germinating and struggling towards the light. Among
the three pearls which become visible in the book of Job above
the waves of conflict, viz. ch. xiv. 13–15, xvi. 18–21, xix.
25–27, there is none more costly than this third. As in the
second part of Isaiah, the fifty-third chapter is outwardly and

inwardly the middle and highest point of the 3 × 9 prophetic utterances, so the poet of the book of Job has adorned the middle of his work with this confession of his hero, wherein he himself plants the flag of victory above his own grave.

Now in ver. 28 Job turns towards the friends. He who comes forth on his side as his advocate, will make Himself felt by them to be a judge, if they continue to persecute the suffering servant of God (comp. ch. xiii. 10–12). It is not to be translated : for then ye will say, or : forsooth then will ye say. This would be כִּי אָז תֹּאמְרוּ, and certainly imply that the opponents will experience just the same theophany, that therefore it will be on the earth. Oehler (in his *Veteris Test. sententia de rebus post mortem futuris,* 1846) maintains this instance against the interpretation of this confession of Job of a future beholding; it has, however, no place in the text, and Oehler rightly gives no decisive conclusion.[1] For ver. 28, as is rightly observed by C. W. G. Köstlin (in his Essay, *de immortalitatis spe, quæ in l. Iobi apparere dicitur,* 1846) against Oehler, and is even explained by Oetinger, is the antecedent to ver. 29 (comp. ch. xxi. 28 sq.) : if ye say : how, *i.e.* under what pretence of right, shall we prosecute him (נִרְדָּף־לֹו, prop. pursue him, comp. Judg. vii. 25), and (so that) the root of the matter (treated of) is found in me (בִּי, not בֹּו, since the *oratio directa,* as in ch. xxii. 17, passes into the *oratio obliqua,* Ew. § 338, *a*) ; in other words : if ye continue to seek the cause of my suffering in my guilt, fear ye the sword, *i.e.* God's sword of vengeance (as ch. xv. 22, and perhaps as Isa. xxxi. 8 : a sword, without the *art.* in order to combine the idea of what is boundless, endless, and terrific with the indefinite—the indetermination *ad amplificandum* described on Ps. ii. 12). The confirmatory substantival

---

[1] He remains undecided between a future spiritual and a present beholding of God: *harum interpretationum utra rectior sit, vix erit dijudicandum, nam in utramque partem facile potest disputari.*

clause which follows has been very variously interpreted. It is inadmissible to understand חֵמָה of the rage of the friends against Job (Umbr., Schlottm., and others), or עֲוֹנוֹת חֶרֶב of their murderous sinning respecting Job; both expressions are too strong to be referred to the friends. We must explain either: the glow, *i.e.* the glow of the wrath of God, are the expiations which the sword enjoins (Hirz., Ew., and others); but apart from עָוֹן not signifying directly the punishment of sin, this thought is strained; or, which we with Rosenm. and others prefer: glow, *i.e.* the glow of the wrath of God, are the sword's crimes, *i.e.* they carry glowing anger as their reward in themselves, wrath overtakes them. Crimes of the sword are not such as are committed with the sword—for such are not treated of here, and, with Arnh. and Hahn, to understand חרב of the sword " of hostilely mocking words," is arbitrary and artificial—but such as have incurred the sword. Job thinks of slander and blasphemy. These are even before a human tribunal capital offences (comp. ch. xxxi. 11, 28). He warns the friends of a higher sword and a higher power, which they will not escape: "that ye may know it." שַׁדִּין, for which the *Keri* is שַׁדוּן. An ancient various reading (in Pinkster) is יִדְעוּן (instead of תֵּדְעוּן). The LXX. shows how it is to be interpreted: θυμὸς γὰρ ἐπ' ἀνόμους (*Cod. Alex.* —οις) ἐπελεύσεται, καὶ τότε γνώσονται. According to *Cod. Vat.* the translation continues ποῦ ἔστιν αὐτῶν ἡ ὕλη (שַׁדִּין, comp. ch. xxix. 5, where שָׁדִי is translated by ὑλώδης); according to *Cod. Alex.* ὅτι οὐδαμοῦ αὐτῶν ἡ ἰσχύς ἐστιν (שַׁדִּין from שָׁדַד). Ewald in the first edition, which Hahn follows, considers, as Eichhorn already had, שַׁדִּין as a secondary form of שַׁדַּי; Hlgst. wishes to read שַׁדַּי at once. It might sooner, with Raschi, be explained: that ye might only know the powers of justice, *i.e.* the manifold power of destruction which the judge has at his disposal. But all these explanations are unsupported by the usage of the language, and

Ewald's conjecture in his second edition : אֵי שָׁדְּכֶם (where is your violence), has nothing to commend it ; it goes too far from the received text, calls the error of the friends by an unsuitable name, and gives no impressive termination to the speech. On the other hand, the speech could not end more suitably than by Job's bringing home to the friends the fact that there is a judgment ; accordingly it is translated by Aq. ὅτι κρίσις; by Symm., Theod., ὅτι ἔστι κρίσις. שׁ is=אֲשֶׁר once in the book of Job, as probably also once in the Pentateuch, Gen. vi. 3. דִּין or דוּן are infinitive forms; the latter from the *Kal*, which occurs only in Gen. vi. 3, with *Cholem*, which being made a substantive (as *e.g.* בּוּז), signifies the judging, the judgment. Why the *Keri* substitutes דִן, which does not occur elsewhere in the signification *judicium*, for the more common דִין, is certainly lost to view, and it shows only that the reading שֶׁדוּן was regarded in the synagogue as the traditional. דִּין has everywhere else the signification *judicium*, *e.g.* by Elihu, ch. xxxvi. 17, and also often in the book of Proverbs, *e.g.* ch. xx. 8 (comp. in the Arabizing supplement, ch. xxxi. 8). The final judgment is in Aramaic דִּינָא רַבָּא; the last day in Hebrew and Arabic, יוֹם הַדִּין, *jaum ed-dîn*. To give to " שֶׁדִין, that [there is] a judgment," this dogmatically definite meaning, is indeed, from its connection with the historical recognition of the plan of redemption, inadmissible; but there is nothing against understanding the conclusion of Job's speech according to the conclusion of the book of Ecclesiastes, which belongs to the same age of literature.

The speech of Job, now explained, most clearly shows us how Job's affliction, interpreted by the friends as a divine retribution, becomes for Job's nature a wholesome refining crucible. We see also from this speech of Job, that he can only regard his affliction as a kindling of divine wrath, and God's meeting him as an enemy (ch. xix. 11). But the more decidedly the friends affirm this, and describe the root of the

manifestation as lying in himself, in his own transgression ;
and the more uncharitably, as we have seen it at last in Bildad's
speech, they go to an excess in their terrible representations of
the fate of the ungodly with unmistakeable reference to him :
the more clearly is it seen that this indirect affliction of misconstruction must tend to help him in his suffering generally
to the right relation towards God.   For since the consolation
expected from man is changed into still more cutting accusation, no other consolation remains to him in all the world but
the consolation of God ; and if the friends are to be in the
right when they persist unceasingly in demonstrating to him
that he must be a heinous sinner, because he is suffering so
severely, the conclusion is forced upon him in connection with
his consciousness of innocence, that the divine decree is an
unjust one (ch. xix. 5 sq.).   From such a conclusion, however, he shrinks back ; and this produces a twofold result.
The crushing anguish of soul which the friends inflict on
him, by forcing upon him a view of his suffering which is as
strongly opposed to his self-consciousness as to his idea of
God, and must therefore bring him into the extremest difficulty of conscience, drives him to the mournful request,
" Have pity upon, have pity upon me, O ye my friends "
(ch. xix. 21) ; they shall not also pursue him whom God's
hand has touched, as if they were a second divine power in
authority over him, that could dispose of him at its will and
pleasure ; they shall, moreover, cease from satisfying the insatiable greed of their nature upon him.   He treats the
friends in the right manner ; so that if their heart were not
encrusted by their dogma, they would be obliged to change
their opinion.   This in Job's conduct is an unmistakeable
step forward to a more spiritual state of mind.   But the stern
inference of the friends has a beneficial influence not merely
on his relation to them, but also on his relation to God.   To
the wrathful God, whom they compel him to regard also as

unjust, he cannot in itself cling. He is so much the less able to do this, as he is compelled the more earnestly to long for vindication, the more confidently he is accused.

When he now wishes that the testimony which he has laid down concerning his innocence, and which his cotemporaries do not credit, might be graven in the rock with an iron pen, and filled in with lead, the memorial in words of stone is but a dead witness; and he cannot even for the future rely on men, since he is so contemptuously misunderstood and deceived by them in the present. This impels his longing after vindication forward from a lifeless thing to a living person, and turns his longing from man below to God above. He has One who will acknowledge his misjudged cause, and set it right,—a *Goël*, who will not first come into being in a later generation, but *liveth*—who has not to come into being, but *is*. There can be no doubt that by the words נאל חי he means the same person of whom in ch. xvi. 19 he says: " Behold, even now *in heaven* is my Witness, and One who acknowledges me is *in the heights*." The חי here corresponds to the נם עתה in that passage; and from this—that the heights of heaven is the place where this witness dwells—is to be explained the manner in which Job (ch. xix. 25*b*) expresses his confident belief in the realization of that which he (ch. xvi. 20 sq.) at first only importunately implores: as the Last One, whose word shall avail in the ages of eternity, when the strife of human voices shall have long been silent, He shall stand forth as finally decisive witness over the dust, in which Job passed away as one who in the eye of man was regarded as an object of divine punishment. And after his skin, in such a manner destroyed, and free from his flesh, which is even now already so fallen in that the bones may be seen through it (ch. xix. 20), he will behold Eloah; and he who, according to human judgment, has died the death of the unrighteous, shall behold Eloah on his side, *his* eyes shall see and not a stranger; for entirely for his profit, in order that he may bask in the light of His countenance, will He reveal himself.

This is the picture of the future, for the realization of which Job longs so exceedingly, that his reins within him pine away with longing. Whence we see, that Job does not here give utterance to a transient emotional feeling, a merely momentary flight of faith; but his hidden faith, which during the whole controversy rests at the bottom of his soul, and over which the waves of despair roll away, here comes forth to view. He knows, that although his outward man may decay, God cannot, however, fail to acknowledge his inner man. But does this confidence of faith of Job really extend to the future life? It has, on the contrary, been observed, that if the hope expressed with such confidence were a hope respecting the future life, Job's despondency would be trifling, and to be rejected; further, that this hope stands in contradiction to his own assertion, ch. xiv. 14: "If man dies, shall he live again? All the days of my warfare would I wait, till my change should come;" thirdly, that Job's character would be altogether wrongly drawn, and would be a psychological caricature, if the thought slumbering in Job's mind, which finds utterance in ch. xix. 25–27, were the thought of a future vision of God; and finally, that the unravelling of the knot of the puzzle, which continually increases in entanglement by the controversy with the friends, at the close of the drama, is effected by a theophany, which issues in favour of one still living, not, as ought to be expected by that rendering, a celestial scene unveiled over the grave of Job. But such a conclusion was impossible in an Old Testament book. The Old Testament as yet knew nothing of a heaven peopled with happy human spirits, arrayed in white robes (the *stola prima*). And at the time when the book of Job was composed, there was also neither a positive revelation nor a dogmatic confession of the resurrection of the dead, which forms the boundary of the course of this world, in existence. The book of Job, however, shows us how, from the conflict concerning the mystery of this present life, faith struggled forth towards a future solution. The hope which Job expresses is not one prevailing in his age—not one that has come to him from tradition—not one embracing mankind, or even only the righteous in general. All the above objections would be really applicable, if it were evident here that Job was acquainted with the doctrine of a beholding of God after death, which should recompense the pious for the sufferings of this present time. But such is not the case. The hope expressed is not a finished and believingly appropriating hope; on the contrary, it is a hope which is first conceived and begotten under the pressure of divinely decreed sufferings, which make him appear to be a transgressor, and of human accusations which charge him with transgression. It is impossible for him to suppose that God should remain, as now, so hostilely turned from him, without ever again acknowledging him. The truth must at last break through the false appearance, and wrath again give place to love. That it should take place after his death, is only the extreme which his faith assigns to it.

If we place ourselves on the standpoint of the poet, he certainly here gives utterance to a confession, to which, as the book of Proverbs also shows, the Salomonic Chokma began to rise in the course of believing thought; but also on the part of the Chokma, this confession was primarily only a *theologoumenon*, and was first in the course of centuries made sure under the combined agency of the progressive perception of the revelation and facts connected with redemption; and it is first of all in the New Testament, by the descent to Hades and the ascension to heaven of the Prince of Life, that it became a fully decided and well-defined element of the church's creed. If, however, we place ourselves on the standpoint of the hero of the drama, this hope of future vindication which flashes through the fierceness of the conflict, far from making it a caricature,[1] gives to the delineation of his faith, which does not forsake God, the final perfecting stroke. Job is, as he thinks, meeting certain death. Why then should not the poet allow him to give utterance to that demand of faith, that he, even if God should permit him apparently to die the sinner's death, nevertheless cannot remain unvindicated? Why should he not allow him here, in the middle of the drama, to rise from the thought, that the cry of his blood should not ascend in vain, to the thought that this vindication of his blood, as of one who is innocent, should not take place without his being consciously present, and beholding with his own eyes the God by whose judicial wrath he is overwhelmed, as his Redeemer? This hope, regarded in the light of the later perception of the plan of redemption, is none other than the hope of a resurrection; but it appears here only in the germ, and comes forward as purely personal: Job rises from the dust, and, after the storm of wrath is passed, sees Eloah, as one who acknowledges him in love, while his surviving opponents fall before the tribunal of this very God. It is therefore not a share in the resurrection of the righteous (in Isa. xxvi., which is uttered prophetically, but first of all nationally), and not a share in the general resurrection of the dead (first expressed in Dan. xii. 2), with which Job consoled himself; he does not speak of what shall happen at the end of the days, but of a purely personal matter after his death. Considering himself as one who must die, and thinking of himself as deceased, and indeed, according to appearance, overwhelmed by the

---

[1] If Job could say, like Tobia, ch. ii. 17 sq., Vulg.: *filii sanctorum sumus et vitam illam exspectamus, quam Deus daturus est his qui fidem suam nunquam mutant ab eo*, his conduct would certainly be different; but what he expresses in ch. xix. 25–27 is very far removed from this confession of faith of Tobia.

punishment of his misdeeds, he would be compelled to despair of God, if he were not willing to regard even the incredible as unfailing, this, viz., that God will not permit this mark of wrath and of false accusation to attach to his blood and dust. That the conclusion of the drama should be shaped in accordance with this future hope, is, as we have already observed, not possible, because the poet (apart from his transferring himself to the position and consciousness of his patriarchal hero) was not yet in possession, as a dogma, of that hope which Job gives utterance to as an aspiration of his faith, and which even he himself only at first, like the psalmists (*vid.* on Ps. xvii. 15, xlix. 15 sq., lxxiii. 26), had as an aspiration of faith ;[1] it was, however, also entirely unnecessary, since it is indeed not the idea of the drama that there is a life after death, which adjusts the mystery of the present, but that there is a suffering of the righteous which bears the disguise of wrath, but nevertheless, as is finally manifest, is a dispensation of love.

If, however, it is a germinating hope, which in this speech of Job is urged forth by the strength of his faith, we can, without anachronistically confusing the different periods of the development of the knowledge of redemption, regard it as a full, but certainly only developing, preformation of the later belief in the resurrection. When Job says that with his own eyes he shall behold Eloah, it is indeed possible by these eyes to understand the eyes of the spirit ;[2] but it is just as possible to understand him to mean the eyes of his renewed body (which the old theologians describe as *stola secunda*, in distinction from the *stola prima* of the intermediate state); and when Job thinks of him-

---

[1] The view of Böttcher, *de inferis*, p. 149, is false, that the poet by the conclusion of his book disapproves the hope expressed, as *dementis somnium*.

[2] Job's wish, ch. xix. 23 sq., is accomplished, as *e.g.* James v. 11 shows, and his hope is realized, since he has beheld God the Redeemer enter Hades, and is by Him led up on high to behold God in heaven. We

self (ver. 25*b*) as a mouldering corpse, should he not by his eyes, which shall behold Eloah, mean those which have been dimmed in death, and are now again become capable of seeing? While, if we wish to expound grammatical-historically, not practically, not homiletically, we also dare not introduce the definiteness of the later dogma into the affirmation of Job. It is related to eschatology as the protevangelium is to soteriology; it presents only the first lines of the picture, which is worked up in detail later on, but also an outline, sketched in such a way that every later perception may be added to it. Hence Schlottmann is perfectly correct when he considers that it is justifiable to understand these grand and powerful words, in hymns, and compositions, and liturgies, and monumental inscriptions, of the God-man, and to use them in the sense which "the more richly developed conception of the last things might so easily put upon them." It must not surprise us that this sublime hope is not again expressed further on. On the one hand, what Sanctius remarks is not untrue: *ab hoc loco ad finem usque libri aliter se habet Iobus quam prius;* on the other hand, Job here, indeed in the middle of the book, soars triumphantly over his opponents to the height of a believing consciousness of victory, but as yet he is not in that state of mind in which he can attain to the beholding of God on his behalf, be it in this world or in the world to come. He has still further to learn submission in relation to God, gentleness in relation to the friends. Hence, inexhaustibly rich in thought and variations of thought, the poet allows the controversy to become more and more involved, and the fire in which Job is to be proved, but also purified, to burn still longer.

assume the historical reality of Job and the consistence of his history with the rest of Scripture, which we have treated in. *Bibl. Psychol.* ch. vi. § 3, on the future life and redemption. Accordingly, one might, with the majority of modern expositors, limit Job's hope to the beholding of God in the intermediate state; but, as is further said above, such particularizing is unauthorized.

Zophar's Second Speech.—Chap. xx.

Schema : 8. 12. 10. 8. 12. 7. 2.

[Then began Zophar the Naamathite, and said :]
2 *Therefore do my thoughts furnish me with a reply,*
    And indeed by reason of my feeling within me.
3 *The correction of my reproach I must hear,*
    Nevertheless the spirit of my understanding informeth me.
4 *Knowest thou this which is from everlasting,*
    Since man was placed upon the earth :
5 *That the triumphing of the evil-doer is not long,*
    And the joy of the godless is but for a moment ?

All modern expositors take ver. 2 as an apology for the opposition which follows, and the majority of them consider בַּעֲבוּר as elliptical for בעבור זאת, as Tremell., Piscator, and others have done, partly (but wrongly) by referring to the *Rebia mugrasch.* Ewald observes : " בעבור stands without addition, because this is easily understood from the כן in לָכֵן." But although this ellipsis is not inadmissible (comp. לכן = לכן אשר, ch. xxxiv. 25 ; בעל, Isa. lix. 18), in spite of it ver. 2*b* furnishes no meaning that can be accepted. Most expositors translate : " and hence the storm within me " (thus *e.g.* Ewald) ; but the signification *perturbatio animi*, proposed by Schultens for חוּשִׁי, after the Arab. حاش, is too remote from the usage of Hebrew. Moreover, this حاش signifies prop. to scare, hunt, of game ; not, however : to be agitated, to storm, —a signification which even the corresponding Hebr. חוּשׁ, *properare*, does not support. Only a few expositors (as Umbreit, who translates : because of my storm within me) take בעבור (which occurs only this once in the book of Job) as *præpos.*, as it must be taken in consideration of the infin. which follows (comp. Ex. ix. 16, xx. 20 ; 1 Sam. i. 6 ; 2 Sam. x. 3). Further, לָכֵן (only by Umbreit translated by " yet," after the Arab. *lákin, lákinna,* which it never signifies in Hebr., where לְ is not = לֹא, but = לְ with *Kametz* before the tone) with that which follows is referred by several expositors to the preceding speech of Job, *e.g.* Hahn: "under such circumstances, if thòu behavest thus;" by most, however, it is referred to ver. 3, *e.g.* Ew.: "*On this account* he feels called upon by his thoughts to answer, and *hence* his inward impulse leaves him no rest: *because* he hears from Job a contemptuous wounding reproof of himself." In other words: in consequence of the reproach which Job casts upon him, especially with his threat of judgment, Zophar's mind and feelings fall into a state of excitement, and give him an answer to which he now gives utterance. This prospective sense of לכן may at any rate be retained, though בעבור is taken as a preposition (wherefore . . . and indeed on account of my inward commotion); but it is far more natural that the beginning of Zophar's speech should be connected with the last word of Job's. Ver. 2 may really be so understood if we connect חושׁי, not with חושׁ, حاش, to excite, to make haste (after which also Saad. and Aben-Ezra: on account of my inward hastening or urging), but with حسّ, to feel; in this meaning חשׁ is usual in all the Semitic dialects, and is even biblical also; for Eccles. ii. 25 is to be translated: who hath feeling (pleasure) except from Him (read ממנו)? *i.e.* even in pleasure man is not free, but has conditions fixed by God.

With לכן (used as in ch. xlii. 3) Zophar draws an inference from Job's conduct, esp. from the turn which his last speech has taken, which, as שְׂעִיפַּי יְשִׁיבוּנִי[1] affirms, urges him involuntarily and irresistibly forward, and indeed, as he adds with

---

[1] Thus it is to be read according to the Masoretic note, לית ומלא (*i.e. plene,* as nowhere else), which occurs in Codd., as is also attested by Kimchi in his Gramm., *Moznajim,* p. 8; Aben-Ezra in his Gramm., *Zachoth* 1, *b ;* and the punctuator Jekuthiël, in his *Darche ha-Nikkud* (chapter on the letters יהוא).

Waw explic. : on account of the power of feeling dwelling
in him, by which he means both his sense of truth and his
moral feeling, in general the capacity of direct perception,
not perception that is only attained after long reflection. On
שְׂעִפִּי, of thoughts which, as it were, branch out, *vid.* on ch.
iv. 13, and *Psychol.* S. 181. הֵשִׁיב signifies, as everywhere, to
answer, not causative, to compel to answer. חוּשִׁי is *n. actionis*
in the sense of רְגִישָׁתִי (Targ.), or הרגישי (Ralbag), which also
signifies "my feeling (αἴσθησις)," and the combination חוּשִׁי בִי
is like ch. iv. 21, vi. 13. Wherein the inference consists is
self-evident, and proceeds from vers. 4 sq. In ver. 3 expression is given to the ground of the conclusion intended in
לָכֵן : the chastisement of my dishonour, *i.e.* which tends to my
dishonour (comp. Isa. liii. 5, chastisement which conduces to
our peace), I must hear (comp. on this modal signification of
the future, *e.g.* ch. xvii. 2) ; and in ver. 3*b* Zophar repeats
what he has said in ver. 2, only somewhat differently applied :
the spirit, this inner light (*vid.* ch. xxxii. 8; *Psychol.* S. 154, *f*),
answers him from the perception which is peculiar to himself,
i.e. out of the fulness of this perception it furnishes him with
information as to what is to be thought of Job with his
insulting attacks, viz. (this is the substance of the הָשִׁיב of the
thoughts, and of the עֲנוֹת of the spirit), that in this conduct of
Job only his godlessness is manifest. This is what he warn-
ingly brings against him, vers. 4 sq. : knowest thou indeed
(which, according to ch. xli. 1, 1 Kings xxi. 19, sarcastically
is equivalent to : thou surely knowest, or in astonishment :
what dost thou not know ?!) this from the beginning, *i.e.* this
law, which has been in operation from time immemorial (or
as Ew. : *hoccine scis æternum esse,* so that מִנִּי־עַד is not a
virtual adj., but virtual predicate-acc.), since man was placed
(שִׂים *infin.,* therefore prop., since one has placed man) upon
the earth (comp. the model passage, Deut. iv. 32), that the
exulting of the wicked is מִקָּרוֹב, from near, *i.e.* not extending

far, enduring only a short time (Arab. قَرِيبٌ often directly
signifies *brevis*); and the joy of the godless עֲדֵי־רָגַע, only for a
moment, and continuing no longer?

> 6 *If his aspiration riseth to the heavens,*
>   *And he causeth his head to touch the clouds :*
> 7 *Like his dung he perisheth for ever ;*
>   *Those who see him say : Where is he?*
> 8 *As a dream he flieth away, and they cannot find him ;*
>   *And he is scared away as a vision of the night.*
> 9 *The eye hath seen him, and never again,*
>   *And his place beholdeth him no more.*
> 10 *His children must appease the poor,*
>   *And his hands give up his wealth.*
> 11 *His bones were full of youthful vigour ;*
>   *Now it is laid down with him in the dust.*

If the exaltation of the evil-doer rises to heaven, and he
causes his head to reach to the clouds, *i.e.* to touch the clouds,
he notwithstanding perishes like his own dung. We are here
reminded of what Obadiah, ver. 4, says of Edom, and Isaiah,
ch. xiv. 13–15, says of the king of Babylon. שִׂיא is equivalent
to נִשִׂיא, like שׂוֹא, Ps. lxxxix. 10 = נִשׂוֹא ; the first weak radical
is cast away, as in כִּילַי = נְכִילַי, *fraudulentus, machinator,* Isa.
xxxii. 5, and according to Olsh. in שִׁיבָה = יְשִׁיבָה, 2 Sam. xix.
33. הִגִּיעַ is to be understood as causative (at least this is the
most natural) in the same manner as in Isa. xxv. 12, and
freq. It is unnecessary, with Ew., Hirz., and Hlgst., after
Schultens, to transl. בְגֻלְלוֹ, ver. 7*a*, according to the Arab.
جلال (whence the name *Gelál-ed-din*): *secundum majestatem
suam,* or with Reiske to read בְגֻלְלוֹ, *in magnificentia sua,* and it
is very hazardous, since the Hebrew גלל has not the meaning
of جلّ, *illustrem esse.* Even Schultens, in his *Commentary,*
has retracted the explanation commended in his *Animadv.,*

and maintained the correctness of the translation, *sicut stercus suum* (Jer. *sicut sterquilinium*), which is also favoured by the similar figurative words in 1 Kings xiv. 10: as one burneth up (not : brushes away) dung (הַגָּלָל), probably cow-dung as fuel, until it is completely gone. גֶּלְלוֹ (or גֶּלֲלוֹ with an audible *Sh'vá*) may be derived from גָּלָל, but the analogy of צְלָלוֹ favours the primary form גָּל (Ew. § 255, *b*) ; on no account is it גֵּל. The word is not low, as Ezek. iv. 12, comp. Zeph. i. 17, shows, and the figure, though revolting, is still very expressive; and how the fulfilment is to be thought of may be seen from an example from 2 Kings ix. 37, according to which, " as dung upon the face of the field shall it be, so that they cannot say: this is Jezebel."[1] The continuation here, ver. 7*b*,

[1] In Arabic, *gille* (גִּלָּה) and *gelle* (גֶּלָּה) is the usual and preferred fuel (hence used as synon. of *hhattab*) formed of the dung of cows, and not indeed yoke-oxen (*baqar 'ammále*), because they have more solid fodder, which produces no material for the *gelle*, but from cattle that pasture in the open fields (*baqar bat.tále*), which are almost entirely milking cows. This dung is collected by women and children in the spring from the pastures as perfectly dry cakes, which have the green colour of the grass. Every husbandman knows that this kind of dung—the product of a rapid, one might say merely half, digestion, even when fresh, but especially when dry—is perfectly free from smell. What is collected is brought in baskets to the forming or pressing place (*mattba'a*, מַטְבָּעָה), where it is crumbled, then with water made into a thick mass, and, having been mixed with chopped straw, is formed by the women with the hand into round cakes, about a span across, and three fingers thick. They resemble the tanners' tan-cakes, only they are not square. Since this compound has the form of a loaf it is called *qurss* (which also signifies a loaf of bread) ; and since a definite form is given to it by the hand, it is called *ttabbu'* (טַבּוּעַ), collective *ttébábi'*, which צְפִיעֵי (צְפִיעִי), Ezek. iv. 15, resembles in meaning; for *ssaf''*, צפע (cogn. *ssaf hh*, צפח), signifies to beat anything with the palm of the hand. First spread out, then later on piled up, the *gelle* lies the whole summer in the *mattba'a*. The domes (*qubeb*) are not formed until a month before the rainy season, *i.e.* a circular structure is built up of the cakes skilfully placed one upon another like bricks ; it is made from six to eight yards high, gradually narrowed and finished with a vaulted dome, whence this structure has its name, *qubbe* (קֻבָּה). Below it measures about eight or ten paces, it is always hollow,

is just the same : they who saw him (*partic.* of what is past,
Ges. § 134, 1) say : where is he ? As a dream he flieth away,
so that he is not found, and is scared away (יֻדַּד *Hoph.*, not
יֵדַד *Kal*) as a vision of the night (חִזָּיוֹן everywhere in the book
of Job instead of חָזוֹן, from which it perhaps differs, as *visum*
from *visio*), which one banishes on waking as a trick of his
fancy (comp. Ps. lxxiii. 20, Isa. xxix. 7 sq.). Eyes looked
upon him (שְׁזָף only in the book of Job in this signification of
a fixed scorching look, cogn. שָׂרַף, *adurere,* as is manifest from
Cant. i. 6), and do it no more ; and his place (מְקוֹמוֹ construed
as *fem.*, as Gen. xviii. 24, 2 Sam. xvii. 12, *Cheth.*) shall not
henceforth regard him (שׁוּר, especially frequent in the book of
Job, prop. to go about, cogn. תּוּר, then to look about one).
The *futt.* here everywhere describe what shall meet the evil-
doer. Therefore Ewald's transl., " his fists smote down the
weak," cannot be received. Moreover, חָפְנָיו, which must then

and is filled from beneath by means of an opening which serves as a door.
The outside of the *qubbe* is plastered over with a thick solution of dung ;
and this coating, when once dried in the sun, entirely protects the
building, which is both storehouse and store, against the winter rains.
When they begin to use the fuel, they take from the inside first by
means of the doorway, and afterwards (by which time the heavy rains are
over) they use up the building itself, removing the upper part first by
means of a ladder. By the summer the *qubbe* has disappeared. Many
large households have three or four of these stores. Where walled-in
courts are spacious, as is generally the case, they stand within ; where
not, outside. The communities bordering on the desert, and exposed to
attacks from the Arabs, place them close round their villages, which
gives them a peculiar appearance. When attacked, the herds are driven
behind these buildings, and the peasants make their appearance between
them with their javelins. Seetzen reckons the *gelle* among the seven
characteristics of the district of *Haurân* (*Basan*).
    It appears that Ezek. iv. 12 sqq.—where the prophet is allowed the
usual cow-dung, the flame of which has no smell whatever, and its ashes,
which smoulder for a long time, are as clean as wood ashes, instead of the
cakes (גְּלְלֵי) of human dung—is to be explained according to this custom.
My fellow-travellers have frequently roasted mushrooms (*futtr*) and
truffles (*faq', פְּקַע) in the early spring in the glowing ashes of the *gelle*.
On the other hand, it would be an error to infer from this passage that

be read instead of בָּנָיו, does not occur elsewhere in this athletic
signification; and it is quite unnecessary to derive יְרַצּוּ from
a רָצָה = רָצַץ (to crush, to hurl to the ground), or to change it
to יָרֹצוּ (Schnurrer) or יְרַצְצוּ (Olsh.); for although the thought,
filios ejus vexabunt egeni (LXX. according to the reading
θλάσειαν, and Targ. according to the reading יְרַעֲעוּן), is not
unsuitable for ver. 10*b*, a sense more natural in connection
with the position of בניו, and still more pleasing, is gained if
רָצָה is taken in the usual signification: to conciliate, appease,
as the Targ. according to the reading יְרַעוּן (Peschito-word for
ἀποκαταλλάσσειν), and Ges., Vaih., Schlottm., and others,
after Aben-Ezra, Ralbag, Merc.: *filii ejus placabunt tenues,
quos scilicet eorum pater diripuerat, vel eo inopiæ adigentur, ut
pauperibus sese adjungere et ab illis inire gratiam cogantur.*
Its retributive relation to ver. 19*a* is also retained by this rendering. The children of the unfeeling oppressor of the poor

the Semites made use of human dung for fuel; the Semites (including
the Nomads) are the most scrupulously particular people respecting clean-
liness. According to the above, Zeph. i. 17 may be explained: "their
flesh shall become like dung," *i.e.* be burned or destroyed like dung. And
also we understand the above passage in the book of Job, "as his heap
of dung-cakes shall he be consumed away," exactly like 1 Kings xiv. 10:
"I will burn (take away) the remnant of the house of Jeroboam, as a
man burneth the dung-cakes until they are consumed." The suff. in
כְּגֶלְלוֹ refers to the habitation of the evil-doer, above whose grovelling joy
the high dome of the dung-cakes rises, which, before one becomes aware
of it, has disappeared; and throughout the description of the sudden
destruction of the evil-doer, vers. 8, 9, the reader must keep the figure
of this dome and its disappearing before his mind. If it be objected
that by such a rendering כְּגֶלָלָיו would be expected, 1 Kings xiv. 10 shows
that גֵּלֶל (גֵּל) was also used as a collective, and the Arabic *gelle* is never
used in any other way, which is the more remarkable, as one from the
first regards its termination as the " ÿ of unity." My attendants on my
journey from Damascus (where there is no *gelle*, and consequently the word
is not used) always took it so, and formed the plural *gellât* and the col-

lective *gilel*, and were always laughed at and corrected: say أقْرَاص جلّة

or طبابيع جلّة !—WETZST.

will be obliged, when the tyrant is dead, to conciliate the destitute; and his hands, by means of his children, will be obliged to give back his property, *i.e.* to those whom his covetousness had brought to beggary (אוֹן, exertion, strength, ch. xviii. 7, then as הוֹן, and synon. חַיִל, wealth, prob. from the radical meaning to breathe, which is differently applied in the Arabic *aun*, rest, and *haun*, lightness). Carey thinks that the description is retrospective: even he himself in his lifetime, which, however, does not commend itself, since here it is throughout the deceased who is spoken of. As in ver. 9, so now in ver. 11 also, *perf.* and *fut.* interchange, the former of the past, the latter of the future. Jerome, by an amalgamation of two distinct radical significations, translates: *ossa ejus implebuntur* (it should be *impleta erant*) *vitiis adolescentiæ ejus*, which is to be rejected, because עָלוּם, Ps. xc. 8, is indeed intended of secret sin, but signifies generally that which is secret (veiled). On the contrary, עֲלוּמִים, ch. xxxiii. 25, certainly signifies

adolescentia (Arab. غُلَمَة), and is accordingly, after LXX., Targ., and Syr., to be translated: his bones were full of youthful vigour. In ver. 11*b*, תִּשְׁכָּב, as ch. xiv. 19, can refer to the purely plural עַצְמוֹתָיו, but the predicate belonging to it would then be plur. in ver. 11*a*, and sing. in ver. 11*b*; on which account the reference to עֲלוּמוּ, which is in itself far more suitable, is to be preferred (Hirz., Schlottm.) : his youthful vigour, on which he relied, lies with him in the dust (of the grave).

12 *If wickedness tasted sweet in his mouth,*
    He hid it under his tongue ;
13 *He carefully cherished it and did not let it go,*
    And retained it in his palate :
14 *His bread is now changed in his bowels,*
    It is the gall of vipers within him.

15 *He hath swallowed down riches and now he spitteth them*
     out,
   God shall drive them out of his belly.
16 *He sucked in the poison of vipers,*
   The tongue of the adder slayeth him.

The evil-doer is, in vers. 12 sq., likened to an epicure; he
keeps hold of wickedness as long as possible, like a delicate
morsel that is retained in the mouth (Renan : *comme un
bonbon qu'on laisse fondre dans la bouche*), and seeks to
enjoy it to the very last. הִמְתִּיק, to make sweet, has here
the intransitive signification *dulcescere*, Ew. § 122, c. הִכְחִיד,
to remove from sight, signifies elsewhere to destroy, here to
conceal (as the *Piel*, ch. vi. 10, xv. 18). חָמַל, to spare, is
construed with עַל, which is usual with verbs of covering and
protecting. The conclusion of the hypothetical antecedent
clauses begins with ver. 14 ; the *perf.* נֶהְפָּךְ (with *Kametz* by
Athnach) describes the suddenness of the change ; the מְרוֹרַת
which follows is not equivalent to לִמְרוֹרַת (Luther : *His food
shall be turned to adder's gall in his body*), but ver. 14b expresses
the result of the change in a substantival clause. The bitter
and poisonous are synonymous in the ancient languages; hence
we find the meanings poison and gall (ver. 25) in מְרֹרָה, and
רֹאשׁ signifies both a poisonous plant which is known by its
bitterness, and the poison of plants like to the poison of serpents (ver. 16 ; Deut. xxxii. 33). חַיִל (ver. 15) is property,
without the accompanying notion of forcible acquisition
(Hirz.), which, on the contrary, is indicated by the בָּלַע. The
following *fut. consec.* is here not *aor.*, but expressive of the
inevitable result which the performance of an act assuredly
brings : he must vomit back the property which he has swallowed down ; God casts it out of his belly, *i.e.* (which is
implied in הוֹרִישׁ, *expellere*) forcibly, and therefore as by the
pains of colic. The LXX., according to whose taste the

mention of God here was contrary to decorum, transl. ἐξ οἰκίας (read κοιλίας, according to *Cod. Alex.*) αὐτοῦ ἐξελκύσει αὐτὸν ἄγγελος (Theod. δυνάστης). The *perf.*, ver. 15*a*, is in ver. 16*a* changed into the *imperf. fut.* יְרַצֵּ֑ם, which more strongly represents the past action as that which has gone before what is now described ; and the ἀσυνδέτως, *fut.*, which follows, describes the consequence which is necessarily and directly involved in it. Ps. cxl. 4 may be compared with ver. 16*a*, Prov. xxiii. 32 with 16*b*. He who sucked in the poison of low desire with a relish, will meet his punishment in that in which he sinned : he is destroyed by the poisonous deadly bite of the serpent, for the punishment of sin is fundamentally nothing but the nature of sin itself brought fully out.

17 *He shall not delight himself in streams,*
     Like to rivers and brooks of honey and cream.
18 *Giving back that for which he laboured, he shall not swal-*
     *   low it ;*
     He shall not rejoice according to the riches he hath gotten.
19 *Because he cast down, let the destitute lie helpless ;*
     He shall not, in case he hath seized a house, finish building
     *   it.*
20 *Because he knew no rest in his craving,*
     He shall not be able to rescue himself with what he most
     *   loveth.*

As poets sing of the *aurea ætas* of the paradise-like primeval age : *Flumina jam lactis, jam flumina nectaris ibant*,[1] and as the land of promise is called in the words of Jehovah in

---

[1] Ovid, *Metam.* i. 112, comp. Virgil, *Ecl.* iv. 30 :
           Et duræ quercus sudabant roscida mella ;
and Horace, *Epod.* xvi. 47 :
           Mella cava manant ex ilice, montibus altis
           Levis crepante lympha desilit pede.

the Thora, " a land flowing with milk and honey," the puffed-
up prosperity to which the evil-doer has attained by injustice
is likened to streams (פְּלַגּוֹת, prop. dividings, and indeed perhaps of a country = districts, Judg. v. 15 sq., or as here, of a
fountain = streams) of rivers, of brooks (two *gen. appositionis*
which are co-ordinate, of which Hupfeld thinks one must be
crossed out ; they, however, are not unpoetical, since, just as
in Ps. lxxviii. 9, the flow of words is suspended, Ew. § 289, *c*)
of honey and cream (comp. cream and oil, ch. xxix. 6), if
נהרי נחלי is not perhaps (which is more in accordance with
the accentuation) intended as an explanatory permutative of
בפלגות : he shall not feast himself upon streams, streamings
of rivers of honey and cream (Dachselt) ; and by אַל־יֵרֶא (*seq.*
Beth, to fasten one's gaze upon anything = feast one's self
upon it), the prospect of enjoying this prosperity, and indeed,
since the moral judgment and feeling are concerned in the
affirmation of the fact (אַל, as ch. v. 22, Ps. xli. 3, Prov. iii.
3, 25), the privilege of this prospect, is denied.   This thought,
that the enjoyment aimed at and anticipated shall not follow
the attainment of this height of prosperity, is reiterated in a
twofold form in ver. 18.

Ver. 18*a* is not to be translated : He gives back that
which he has gained without swallowing it down, which must
have been יָשִׁיב ; the syntactic relation is a different one : the
Waw of וְלֹא is not expressive of detail ; the detailing is
implied in the *partic.*, which is made prominent as an antecedent, as if it were : because, or since, he gives out again that
which he has acquired (יָנַע only here instead of יְנִיעַ, ch. x. 3
and freq.), he has no pleasure in it, he shall or may not
altogether swallow it down (Targ. incorrectly ולא־יגמר, after
the Arabic بلغ, to penetrate, attain an object).   The formation of the clause corresponds entirely with ver. 18*b*.   All
attempts at interpretation which connect כְּחֵיל תְּמוּרָתוֹ with
מֵשִׁיב, ver. 18*a*, are to be objected to : (he gives it back again) as

property of his restitution, *i.e.* property that is to be restored (Schlottm.), or the property of another (Hahn). Apart from the unsuitableness of the expression to the meaning found in it, it is contrary to the relative independence of the separate lines of the verse, which our poet almost always preserves, and is also opposed by the interposing of ולא יבלע. The explanation chosen by Schult., Oet., Umbr., Hirz., Renan, and others, after the Targ., is utterly impossible: as his possession, so his exchange (which is intended to mean: restitution, giving up); this, instead of כְּחֵיל, must have been not merely כְּחֵיל, but כְּחֵילוֹ. The designed relation of the members of the sentence is, without doubt, that כחיל תמורתו is a nearer defining of ולא יעלס, after the manner of an antecedent clause, and from which, that it may be emphatically introduced, it begins by means of *Waw apod.* (to which Schult. not unsuitably compares Jer. vi. 19, 1 Kings xv. 13). The following explanation is very suitable: according to the power, *i.e.* entire fulness of his exchange, but not in the sense of "to the full amount of its value" (Carey, as Rosenm.), connected with מֵשִׁיב, but connected with what follows: "how great soever his exchange (gain), still he does not rejoice" (Ew.). But it is not probable that חֵיל here signifies power = a great quantity, where property and possessions are spoken of. The most natural rendering appears to me to be this: according to the relation of the property of his exchange (תמורה from מור, Syr. directly *emere*, cogn. מחר, מחר, and perhaps also מכר, here of exchange, barter, or even acquisition, as ch. xv. 31; comp. xxviii. 17, of the means of exchange), *i.e.* of the property exchanged, bartered, gained by barter by him, he is not to enjoy, *i.e.* the rejoicing which might have been expected in connection with the greatness of the wealth he has amassed, departs from him.

Jerome is not the only expositor who (as though the Hebrew tenses were subject to no rule, and might mean everything) translates ver. 19, *domum rapuit et non œdificavit eam* (equivalent to *quam non œdificaverat*). Even Hupfeld translates thus, by taking וְלֹא יִבְנֵהוּ as imperfect = וְהוּא לֹא בְנָהוּ; but he, of course, fails to furnish a grammatical proof for the possibility of inferring a *plusquamperfectum* sense. It might sooner be explained : instead of building it (*Lit. Central-blatt*, 1853, Nr. 24). But according to the syntax, ver. 19*a* must be an antecedent clause: because he crushed, left (there-fore : crushed by himself) the destitute alone ;[1] and 19*b* the conclusion : he has pillaged a house, and will not build it, *i.e.* in case he has plundered a house, he will not build it up. For בַּיִת גָּזָל, according to the accents, which are here correct, is not to be translated : *domus, quam rapuit*, but hypotheti-cally : *si (ἐὰν) domum rapuit*, to which וְלֹא יִבְנֵהוּ is connected by *Waw apod.* (comp. ch. vii. 21*b*) ; and בָּנָה signifies here, as frequently, not : to build, but : to build round, build addi-tions to, continue building (comp. 2 Chron. xi. 5, 6 ; Ps. lxxxix. 3, 5). In ver. 20 similar periodizing occurs : be-cause he knew not שָׁלֵו (neutral = שַׁלְוָה, Prov. xvii. 1 ; Ew. § 293, *c*), contentment, rest, and sufficiency (comp. Isa. lix. 8, לֹא יָדַע שָׁלוֹם) in his belly, *i.e.* his craving, which swallows up everything : he will not be able to deliver himself (מִלֵּט like פִּלֵּט, ch. xxiii. 7, as intensive of *Kal :* to escape, or also = מִלֵּט נַפְשׁוֹ, which Amos ii. 25 seems to favour) with (בְּ as ch. xix. 20) his dearest treasure (thus *e.g.* Ewald), or : he will not be able to rescue his dearest object, prop. not to effect a rescue with his dearest object, the obj., as ch. xvi. 4, 10, xxxi. 12, conceived of as the instrument (*vid. e.g.* Schlottm.). The former explanation is more natural and simple. חָמוּד,

---

[1] The Targ. translates : because he brought to ruin the business of the poor (עזב after עִזָּבוֹן in Ezekiel) ; and Parchon : because he brought to ruin the courts of the poor (after the Mishna-word מְעַזֵּיבָה, a paved floor) ; but עזב, according to the Masora on Isa. lviii. 2 (comp. Kimchi, *Michlol*, p. 35), is to be read עָזַב, as a verb.

that which is exceedingly desired (Ps. xxxix. 12, of health
and pleasantness ; Isa. xliv. 9, of idols, as the cherished
objects of their worshippers), is the dearest and most precious
thing to which the sinner clung with all his soul, not, as
Böttch. thinks, the soul itself.[1]

> 21 *Nothing escaped his covetousness,*
>   *Therefore his prosperity shall not continue.*
> 22 *In the fulness of his need it shall be strait with him,*
>   *Every hand of the needy shall come upon him.*
> 23 *It shall come to pass : in order to fill his belly,*
>   *He sendeth forth the glow of His anger into him,*
>   *And He causeth it to rain upon him into his flesh.*
> 24 *He must flee from an iron weapon,*
>   *Therefore a brazen bow pierceth him through.*
> 25 *It teareth, then it cometh forth out of his body,*
>   *And the steel out of his gall,*
>   *The terrors of death come upon him.*

The words of ver. 21*a* are : there was nothing that escaped

(שָׂרִיד, as ch. xviii. 19, from שָׂרַד, شرد, *aufugere*) his eating
(from אָכַל, not from אֹכֶל), *i.e.* he devoured everything without sparing, even to the last remnant; therefore טוּבוֹ, his
prosperity, his abundant wealth, will not continue or hold out
(יָחִיל, as Ps. x. 5, to be solid, powerful, enduring, whence

---

[1] Hupfeld interprets : *non fruitur securus ventre suo h. e. cibo quo venter
potitus erat et deliciis quas non salvas retinebit* (or also ver. 20*b* as a clause
by itself : *cum deliciis suis non evadet*), but without any proof that יָדַע בְּ
can signify *frui*, and בטן metonymically food, whereas the assertion that
שְׁלֵו cannot be equivalent to שָׁלֵו, and cannot be used of rest with reference to the desire, is unfounded. In Hebrew the neuter adj. can be used
as a substantive, just as in Greek, *e.g.* τὸ ἀσφαλές, security, τὸ εὐτυχές,
success (comp. *e.g.* the combination בתמים ואמת), and שׁלו signifies
release and ease (Arab. followed by عن), without distinction of what
disturbs, be it danger, or pain, or any kind of emotion whatever.

חַיִל, حَوْل, حِيلَة). Hupf. transl. differently: *nihil ei superstes ad vescendum, itaque non durant ejus bona;* but שָׂרִיד signifies first *elapsum,* and עַל־כֵּן *propterea;* and we may retain these first significations, especially since ver. 21a is not future like 21b. The tone of prediction taken up in ver. 21b is continued in what follows. The *inf. constr.* מְלֹאות (prop. מְלֹאות, but with *Cholem* by the *Aleph,* since the *Waw* is regarded as יָתִיר, superfluous), formed after the manner of the verbs *Lamed He* (Ew. 238, *c*), is written like קְרֹאות, Judg. viii. 1 (comp. on the other hand the *scriptio defectiva,* Lev. viii. 33, xii. 4); and שְׂפָקוֹ (with *Sin,* as Norzi decides after Codd., Kimchi, and Farisol, not *Samech*) is to be derived from שָׂפֵק (סֶפֶק), *sufficientia* (comp. the verb, 1 Kings xx. 10): if his sufficiency exists in abundance, not from שָׂפֵק = سَفْقَة, صَفْقَة, *complosio,* according to which Schultens explains: if his joyous clapping of hands has reached its highest point (Elizabeth Smith: "while clapping the hands in the fulness of joy"), to which מְלֹאות is not suitable, and which ought at least to be שֵׂפֶק כַּפָּיו. Therefore: in the fulness of his need shall he be straitened (יֵצַר with the tone drawn back for יֵצַר on account of the following monosyllable, although also apocopated *futt.* follow further on in the strict future signification, according to poetic usage), by which not merely the fearful foreboding is meant, which just in the fullest overflow makes known his impending lot, but the real calamity, into which his towering prosperity suddenly changes, as ver. 22b shows: All the hands of the destitute come upon him (בּוֹא *seq. acc.: invadere*) to avenge on him the injustice done to the needy. It is not necessary to understand merely such as he has made destitute, it is כָּל־יַד; the assertion is therefore general: the rich uncompassionate man becomes a defenceless prey of the proletaries.

Ver. 23. The יְהִי which opens this verse (and which also
occurs elsewhere, e.g. ch. xviii. 12, in a purely future signification), here, like וַיְהִי, 2 Sam. v. 24 (Ew. § 333, b), serves to
introduce the following יְשַׁלַּח (it shall happen : He shall send
forth) ; וַיְהִי (e.g. Gen. xl. 1) frequent in the historical style,
and וְהָיָה in the prophetical, are similarly used.   In order to
fill his belly, which is insatiable, God will send forth against
him His glowing wrath (comp. Lam. i. 13, from on high hath
He sent fire into my bones), and will rain upon him into
his flesh, or his plumpness (Arab. fi lachmihi).   Thus we
believe בִּלְחוּמוֹ must be understood by referring to Zeph. i.
17; where, perhaps not without reference to this speech of
Zophar, the כַּגְּלָלִים, which serves to explain ver. 7, coincides
with וּלְחֻמָּם, which serves to explain this בלחומו; and the right
meaning is not even missed by the LXX., which translates
καὶ τὰς σάρκας αὐτῶν ὡς βόλβιτα.[1]   A suitable thought is
obtained if לְחוּם is taken in the signification, food : He will
rain upon him his food, i.e. what is fit for him (with Beth of
the instrument instead of the accusative of the object), or :
He will rain down (His wrath) upon him as his food (with
Beth essent., according to which Ew. : what can satisfy him ;
Bridel : pour son aliment ; Renan : en guise de pain) ; but we
give the preference to the other interpretation, because it is
at once natural in this book, abounding in Arabisms, to sup-

pose for לחום the signification of the Arab. لَحْم, which is also
supported in Hebrew by Zeph. i. 17 ; further, because the
Targ. favours it, which transl. בְּשִׁלְדֵיהּ, and expositors, as Aben-
Ezra and Ralbag, who interpret by בבשרו ; finally, because it
gives an appropriate idea, to which Lam. i. 13 presents a
commendable parallel, comp. also James v. 3, and Koran,

---

[1] This passage is translated : and their blood is poured forth as dust,
i.e. useless rubbish (Arab. el-ghabra אלעברה), and their flesh as filth.
The form of inflection לְחֻמָּם is referable to לְחֹם after the form לְאֹם.

Sur. 2, 169 : " those who hide what God has sent down by the Scripture, and thereby obtain a small profit, eat only fire into their belly." That עָלֵימוֹ can be used pathetically for עָלָיו is unmistakeably clear from ch. xxii. 2, comp. xxvii. 23, and on Ps. xi. 7 ; the morally indignant speech which threatens punishment, intentionally seeks after rare solemn words and darksome tones. Therefore : Upon his flesh, which has been nourished in unsympathizing greediness, God rains down, *i.e.* rain of fire, which scorches it. This is the hidden background of the lot of punishment, the active principle of which, though it be effected by human agency, is the punitive power of the fire of divine wrath. Vers. 24 sq. describe, by illustration, how it is worked out. The evil-doer flees from a hostile superior power, is hit in the back by the enemy's arrows; and since he, one who is overthrown, seeks to get free from them, he is made to feel the terrors of inevitably approaching death.

Ver. 24. The two *futt.* may be arranged as in a conditional clause, like Ps. xci. 7*a*, comp. Amos ix. 2–4 ; and this is, as it seems, the mutual relation of the two expressions designed by the poet (similar to Isa. xxiv. 18) : if he flee from the weapons of iron, *i.e.* the deadly weapon in the thick of the fight, he succumbs to that which is destructive by and by : the bow of brass (נְחוּשָׁה poet. for נְחֻשֶׁת, as Ps. xviii. 35, although it might also be an adj., since *eth*, as the Arab. قَوْس shows, is really a feminine termination) will pierce him through (*fut. Kal* of חָלַף, خلف, to press further and further, press after, here as in Judg. v. 26). The flight of the disheartened is a punishment which is completed by his being hit while fleeing by the arrow which the brazen bow sends with swift power after him. In ver. 25 the Targ. reads מִגְוָה with *He mappic.*, and translates : he (the enemy, or God) draws (*stringit*), and it (the sword) comes out of its sheath, which is to be rejected because גֵּו cannot signify *vagina*. Kimchi and most Jewish expositors interpret מִגְוָה by מִגּוּף; the LXX. also translates it σῶμα. To understand it according to גֵּו (back), of the hinder part of the body, gives no suitable sense, since the evil-doer is imagined as hit in the back, the arrow consequently passing out at the front;[1] whereas the signification body is suitable, and is also made sufficiently certain by the cognate form גְּוִיָּה. The verb שָׁלַף, however, is used as in Judg. iii. 22 : he who is hit draws the arrow out, then it comes out of his body, into which it is driven deep; and the glance, *i.e.* the metal head of the arrow (like לַהַב, Judg. iii. 22, the point in distinction from the shaft), out of his gall (מְרֹרָה = מְרֵרָה, ch. xvi. 13, so called from its bitterness, as χολή, χόλος, comp. χλόος, χλωρός, from the green-yellow colour), since, as the Syriac version freely translates, his gall-bladder is burst.[2] Is יַהֲלֹךְ, as a parallel word to וַיֵּצֵא, to be connected with ממררתו, or with what follows? The accentuation varies. The ordinary interpunction is ובֵרָק with *Dechî*, ממררתו *Mercha*, or more correctly *Mercha-Zinnorith*, יהלך *Rebia mugrasch* (according to which, Ew., Umbr., Vaih., Welte, Hahn, Schlottm., and Olsh. divide) ; ממררתו is, however, also found with *Athnach*. Although the latter mode of accentuation is only feebly supported, we nevertheless consider it as the more correct, for עָלָיו אֵמִים, in the mind of the poet, can hardly have formed

---

[1] Thus sings the warrior *Cana'an Têjâr* (died about 1815) after the loss of his wife :—

" My grief for her is the grief of him whose horse is dashed in pieces in the desert.

The way is wild, and there is no help from the travellers who have hurried on before.

My groaning is like the groaning of one who, mortally wounded between the shoulders,

Will flee, and trails after him the lance that is fastened in him."

—Wetzst.

[2] Abulwalid (in Kimchi) understands the red gall, *i.e.* the gall-bladder, by מרורה, after the Arabic *marâre*. If this is pierced, its contents are emptied into the lower part of the body, and the man dies.

a line of the verse. If, however, יהלך עליו אמים is now taken together, it is a matter for inquiry whether it is to be explained : he passes away, since terrors come upon him (Schult., Rosenm., Hirz., Von Gerl., Carey), or : terrors come upon him (LXX., Targ., Syr., Jer., Ramban). We consider the latter as the only correct interpretation ; for if יהלך ought to be understood after ch. xiv. 20, xvi. 22, the poet would have expressed himself ambiguously, since it is at least as natural to consider אמים as the subject of יהלך, as to take עליו אמים as an adverbial clause. The former, however, is both natural according to the syntax (*vid.* Ges. § 147, *a*) and suitable in matter : terrors (*i.e.* of certain death to him in a short time) draw on upon him, and accordingly we decide in its favour.

> 26 *All darkness is reserved for his treasured things,*
> *A fire that is not blown upon devoureth him ;*
> *It feedeth upon what is left in his tent.*
>
> 27 *The heavens reveal his iniquity,*
> *And the earth riseth up against him.*
>
> 28 *The produce of his house must vanish,*
> *Flowing away in the day of God's wrath.*
>
> . . . .
>
> 29 *This is the lot of the wicked man from Elohim,*
> *And the heritage decreed for him from God.*

As in Ps. xvii. 14 God's store of earthly goods for the children of men is called צָפוּן (צָפִין), so here the stores laid up by man himself are called צְפוּנָיו. Total darkness, which will finally destroy them, is decreed by God against these stores of the godless, which are brought together not as coming from the hand of God, but covetously, and regardless of Him. Instead of טָמוּן it might also have been צָפוּן (ch. xv. 20, xxi. 19, xxiv. 1), and instead of לִצְפוּנָיו also לִטְמוּנָיו (Deut. xxxiii. 19) ; but טָמוּן is, as ch. xl. 13 shows, better suited to darkness (on account of the ט, this dull-toned *muta*, with which the word begins). כָּל־חֹשֶׁךְ signifies sheer darkness, as in Ps. xxxix. 6, כל־הבל, sheer nothingness; Ps. xlv. 14, כל־כבודה, sheer splendour ; and perhaps Isa. iv. 5, כל־כבוד, sheer glory. And the thought, expressed with somewhat of a play upon words, is, that to the θησαυρίζειν of the godless corresponds a θησαυρίζειν of God, the Judge (Rom. ii. 5 ; James v. 3) : the one gathers up treasures, and the other nothing but darkness, to whom at an appointed season they shall be surrendered. The תְּאָכְלֵהוּ which follows is regarded by Ges. as *Piel* instead of תְּאַכְּלֵהוּ, but such a resolving of the characteristic sharpened syllable of *Piel* is unsupportable ; by Hirz., Olsh. § 250, *b*, as *Pual* instead of תְּאֻכְּלֵהוּ, but אָכַל signifies to be eaten, not (so that it might be connected with an accusative of the obj.) to get to eat ; by Ew., Hupf., as *Kal* for תֹּאכְלֵהוּ, which is possible both from the letters and the matter (*vid.* on Ps. xciv. 20) ; but more correctly it is regarded as *Poel*, for such *Poel* forms from strong roots do occur, as שֹׁפֵט (*vid.* on ch. ix. 15), and that the *Cholem* of these forms can be shortened into *Kametz-chatuph* is seen from וְדֹרְשׁוּ, Ps. cix. 10 (*vid. Psalter in loc.*).[1] The *Poel* is in the passage before us the intensive of *Kal*: a fire which is not blown upon shall eat him up. By this translation נֻפַּח is equivalent to נֻפְּחָה, since attention is given to the gender of אֵשׁ in the verb immediately connected with it, but it is left out of consideration in the verbs נפח and יֵרַע which stand further from it, which Olshausen thinks doubtful ; there are,

---

[1] Such a contraction is also presented in the readings תִּרְצָחוּ, Ps. lxii. 4 ; מְלָשְׁנִי, Ps. ci. 5 ; and וַיְּחָלְקֵם, 1 Chron. xxiii. 6, xxiv. 3. All these forms are not resolved forms of *Piel* (Ges., Berth., Olsh. § 248, *a*), but contracted forms of *Poel* with *Kametz-chatuph* instead of *Cholem*. תְּהָתְּלוּ, ch. xiii. 9, is not a resolved form of *Piel*, but a non-syncopated *Hiphil*. [It should be observed that the *Chateph-Kametz* in "*wedorschu*" above and at p. 153 is used as an unmistakeable sign of the ŏ.—Tr.]

however, not a few examples which may be adduced in
favour of it, as 1 Kings xix. 11, Isa. xxxiii. 9; comp. Ges. §
147, rem. 1. Certainly the relative clause נֻפַּח לֹא may also be
explained by supplying בָּהּ : into which one has not blown, or
that one has not blown on (Symm., Theod., ἄνευ φυσήματος) :
both renderings are possible, according to Ezek. xxii. 20, 22 ;
but since the masc. יֵרַע follows, having undoubtedly אִשׁ as its
subject, we can unhesitatingly take the *Synallage gen.* as beginning even with נֻפַּח. A fire which needs no human help
for its kindling and its maintenance is intended (comp. on
לֹא בְיָד, ch. xxxiv. 20) ; therefore "fire of God," ch. i. 16.
This fire feasts upon what has escaped (שָׂרִיד, as ver. 21, ch.
xviii. 19), *i.e.* whatever has escaped other fates, in his tent.
יֵרַע (*Milel*) is *fut. apoc. Kal;* the form of writing יֵרַע (*fut.*
apoc. Niph.) proposed by Olsh. on account of the change of
gender, *i.e.* it is devoured, is to be rejected for the reason
assigned in connection with נֻפַּח. The correct interpretation
has been brought forward by Schultens.

It is not without reference to ch. xvi. 18, 19, where Job
has called upon earth and heaven as witnesses, that in ver. 27
Zophar continues : " the heavens reveal his guilt, and the
earth rises against him;" heaven and earth bear witness to
his being an abhorrence, not worthy of being borne by the
earth and shone upon by the light of heaven ; they testify
this, since their powers from below and above vie with one
another to get rid of him. מִתְקוֹמְמָה is connected closely with
לוֹ (which has *Lamed raphatum*) by means of *Mercha-Zinnorith*,
and under the influence of the law, according to which before
a monosyllabic accented word the tone is drawn back from
the last syllable of the preceding word to the *penultima* (Ew.
§ 73, 3), is accented as *Milel* on account of the pause.[1] In

---

[1] This mode of accentuation, which is found in Codd. and is attested
by grammarians (*vid.* Norzi), is grammatically more intelligible than
that of our editions, which have the *Mercha* with the final syllable. For

ver. 28, Ges., Olsh., and others translate : the produce of his
house, that which is swept together, must vanish away in the
day of His wrath ; נִגָּרוֹת corrasæ (opes), Niph. from גָּרַר.   But
first, the suff. is wanting to נגרות ; and secondly, בְּיוֹם אַפּוֹ has no
natural connection in what precedes.   The Niph. נגרות in the
signification diffluentia, derived from נָגַר, to flow away (comp.
جرى, to flow), is incomparably better suited to the passage
(comp. 2 Sam. xiv. 14, where Luther transl. : as water which
glides away into the earth).   The close of the description is
similar to Isa. xvii. 11 : "In the day that thou plantedst, thou
causedst it to increase, and with the morning thy seed was
in flower—a harvest-heap in the day of deep wounding and
deadly sorrow."   So here everything that the evil-doer hoards
up is spoken of as "vanishing in the day of God's wrath."

The speech now closes by summing up like Bildad's, ch.
xviii. 21 : "This is the portion or inheritance of, i.e. the lot
that is assigned or falls to, the wicked man (אָדָם רָשָׁע, a rare
application of אדם, comp. Prov. vi. 12, instead of which אִישׁ
is more usual) from Elohim, and this the heritage of his
(i.e. concerning him) decree from God."   אֵמֶר (אֹמֶר) with an
objective suff., which also occurs elsewhere of the almighty
word or command of God (vid. on Hab. iii. 9), signifies here
God's judicial arrangement or order, in this sense just as
Arabic as Hebraic, for also in Arab. amr (plur. awâmir)
signifies command and order.

The speech of Zophar, ch. xx., is his ultimatum, for in the
third course of the controversy he takes no part.   We have
already seen from his first speech, ch. xi., that he is the most
impassioned of the friends.   His vehemence is now the less
excusable, since Job in his previous speech has used the truly

while מִתְקוֹמְמָה, as Milel, is the pausal-form of the fem. part. Hithpalel
for מִתְקוֹמְמָה (מִתְקוֹמֶמֶת) with pausal â instead of ê, it ought to be as
Milra, a passive form ; but the Hithpalal has no meaning here, and is in
general not firmly supported within the range of biblical Hebrew.

spiritual language of importunate entreaty and earnest warning in reply to the friends. The friends would now have
done well if they had been silent, and still better if they had
recognised in the sufferer the tried and buffeted servant of
God, and had withdrawn their charges, which his innermost
nature repudiates. But Zophar is not disposed to allow the
reproach of the correction which they received to rest upon
him; in him we have an illustration of the fact that a man
is never more eloquent than when he has to defend his injured
honour, but that he is also never more in danger of regarding
the extravagant images of natural excitement as a higher in-
spiration, or, however, as striking justifications coming from
the fulness of a superior perception. It has been rightly
remarked, that in Zophar the poet describes to us one of those
hot-heads who pretend to fight for religion that is imperilled,
while they are zealous for their own wounded vanity. Instead of being warned by Job's threat of judgment, he thrusts
back his attempt at producing dismay by a similar attempt.
He has nothing new to bring forward in reply to Job; the
poet has skilfully understood how to turn the heart of his
readers step by step from the friends, and in the same degree
to gain its sympathy for Job. For they are completely spent
in their one dogma; and while in Job an endless multitude of
thoughts and feelings surge up one after another, their heart
is as hermetically closed against every new perception and
emotion. All that is new in the speech of Zophar, and in
those of the friends generally, in this second course of the
controversy, is, that they no longer try to lure Job on to
penitence by promises, but endeavour to bring him to a right
state of mind, or rather to weaken his supposedly-mad assault
upon themselves, by presenting to him only the most terrible
images. It is not possible to illustrate the principle that the
covetous, uncompassionate rich man is torn away from his
prosperity by the punishment God decrees for him, more

fearfully and more graphically than Zophar does it; and this terrible description is not overdrawn, but true and appropriate, —but in opposition to Job it is the extreme of uncharitableness which outdoes itself : applied to him, the fearful truth becomes a fearful lie. For in Zophar's mind Job is the godless man, whose rejoicing does not last long, who indeed raises himself towards heaven, but as his own dung must he perish, and to whom the sin of his unjust gain is become as the poison of the viper in his belly. The arrow of God's wrath sticks fast in him; and though he draw it out, it has already inflicted on him a deservedly mortal wound! The fire of God which has already begun to consume his possessions, does not rest until even the last remnant in his tent is consumed. The heavens, where in his self-delusion he seeks the defender of his innocence, reveal his guilt, and the earth, which he hopes to have as a witness in his favour, rises up as his accuser. Thus mercilessly does Zophar seek to stifle the new trust which Job conceives towards God, to extinguish the faith which bursts upwards from beneath the ashes of the conflict. Zophar's method of treatment is soul-destroying; he seeks to slay that life which germinates from the feeling of death, instead of strengthening it. He does not, however, succeed; for so long as Job does not become doubtful of his innocence, the uncharitableness of the friends must be to him the thread by which he finds his way through the labyrinth of his sufferings to the God who loves him, although He seems to be angry with him.

Job's Third Answer.—Chap. xxi.

Schema: 10. 10. 10. 11. 10. 10. 5. 2.

[Then began Job, and said :]
2 *Hear, oh hear, my speech,*
  And let this be instead of your consolations.

3 *Suffer me, and I will speak,*
  And after I have spoken thou mayest mock.
4 *As for me, then, doth my complaint concern man,*
  Or wherefore should I not become impatient?
5 *Turn ye to me and be astonished,*
  And lay your hand upon your mouth.
6 *Even if I think of it I am bewildered,*
  And my flesh taketh hold on trembling—:

The friends, far from being able to solve the enigma of Job's affliction, do not once recognise the mystery as such. They cut the knot by wounding Job most deeply by ever more and more frivolous accusations. Therefore he entreats them to be at least willing to listen (שִׁמְעוּ with the gerund) to his utterance (מִלָּה) respecting the unsolved enigma; then (*Waw apodosis imper.*) shall this attention supply the place of their consolations, *i.e.* be comforting to him, which their previous supposed consolations could not be. They are to bear with him, *i.e.* without interruption allow him to answer for himself (שָׂאוּנִי with *Kametz* before the tone, as Jonah i. 12, comp. קָחֻהוּ, 1 Kings xx. 33, not as Hirz. thinks under the influence of the distinctive accent, but according to the established rule, Ges. § 60, rem. 1); then he will speak (אנכי contrast to the "ye" in שאוני without further force), and after he has expressed himself they may mock. It is, however, not תַּלְעִיגוּ (as Olshausen corrects), but תַּלְעִיג (in a voluntative signific. = תַּלְעֵג), since Job here addresses himself specially to Zophar, the whole of whose last speech must have left the impression on him of a bitter sarcasm (σαρκασμός from σαρκάζειν in the sense of ch. xix. 22*b*), and has dealt him the freshest deep blow. In ver. 4 שִׂיחִי is not to be understood otherwise than as in ch. vii. 13, ix. 27, x. 1, xxiii. 2, and is to be translated " my complaint." Then the prominently placed אָנֹכִי is to be taken, after Ezek. xxxiii. 17, Ges. § 121, 3, as an emphatic

strengthening of the "my" : he places his complaint in contrast with another. This emphasizing is not easily understood,
if one, with Hupf., explains : *nonne hominis est querela mea*,
so that הֲ is equivalent to הֲלֹא (which here in the double
question is doubly doubtful), and לְ is the sign of the cause.
Schultens and Berg, who translate לְאָדָם *more humano*, explain
similarly, by again bringing their suspicious לְ *comparativum*[1]
here to bear upon it. The לְ by שִׂיחִי (if it may not also be
compared with ch. xii. 8) may certainly be expected to denote
those to whom the complaint is addressed. We translate :
As for me, then, does my complaint concern men? The
אָנֹכִי which is placed at the beginning of the sentence comes
no less under the rule, Ges. § 145, 2, than § 121, 3. In
general, sufferers seek to obtain alleviation of their sufferings
by imploring by words and groans the pity of sympathizing
men ; the complaint, however, which the three hear from
him is of a different kind, for he has long since given up the
hope of human sympathy,—his complaint concerns not men,
but God (comp. ch. xvi. 20).[2] He reminds them of this by
asking further : or (וְאִם, as ch. viii. 3, xxxiv. 17, xl. 9, not :
and if it were so, as it is explained by Nolde contrary to the
usage of the language) why (interrogative upon interrogative :
an quare, as Ps. xciv. 9, אִם הֲלֹא, *an nonne*) should not my
spirit (disposition of mind, θυμός) be short, *i.e.* why should
I not be short-tempered (comp. Judg x. 16, Zech. xi. 8,
with Prov. xiv. 29) = impatient? Dürr, in his *commentatio
super voce* רוּחַ, 1776, 4, explains the expression *habito simul*

---

[1] In the passage from Ibn-Kissaï quoted above, p. 325, Schultens,
as Fleischer assures me, has erroneously read لمنخاليب instead of
كمنخاليب, having been misled by the frequent failing of the upper
stroke of the ک, and in general ل is never = ك, and also לְ never = כ, as
has been imagined since Schultens.

[2] An Arabian proverb says : "The perfect patience is that which
allows no complaint to be uttered *ila el-chalq* against creatures (men)."

halitus, qui iratis brevis esse solet, respectu, but the signification breath is far from the nature of the language here; רוח
signifies emotional excitement (comp. ch. xv. 13), either long
restrained (with אָרֹךְ), or not allowing itself to be restrained
and breaking out after a short time (קצר). That which causes
his vexation to burst forth is such that the three also, if they
would attentively turn to him who thus openly expresses himself, will be astonished and lay their hand on their mouth
(comp. ch. xxix. 9, xl. 4), *i.e.* they must become dumb in
recognition of the puzzle,—a puzzle insoluble to them, but
which is nevertheless not to be denied. הֵשַׁמּוּ is found in
Codd. and among grammarians both as *Hiph.* הָשַׁמּוּ *hashammu*
(Kimchi) and as *Hoph.* הֲשַׁמּוּ, or what is the same, הָשַׁמּוּ *hŏsh-
shammu* (Abulwalid) with the sharpening of the first radical,
which also occurs elsewhere in the *Hoph.* of this verb (Lev.
xxvi. 34 sq.) and of others (Olsh. § 259, *b*, 260). The pointing as *Hiph.* (הָשַׁמּוּ for הֵשַׁמּוּ) in the signification *obstupescite*
is the better attested. Job himself has only to think of this
mystery, and he is perplexed, and his flesh lays hold on
terror. The expression is like ch. xviii. 20. The emotion is
conceived of as a want arising from the subject of it, which
that which produces it must as of necessity satisfy.

In the following strophe the representation of that which
thus excites terror begins. The divine government does not
harmonize with, but contradicts, the law maintained by the
friends.

7 *Wherefore do the wicked live,*
   Become old, yea, become mighty in power?
8 *Their posterity is established before them about them,*
   And their offspring before their eyes.
9 *Their houses have peace without fear,*
   And the rod of Eloah cometh not upon them.
10 *His (the evil-doer's) bull gendereth and faileth not;*

His cow calveth easily, and casteth not her calf.
11 *They let their little ones run about as a flock,*
   And their children jump about.

The question in ver. 7 is the same as that which Jeremiah also puts forth, ch. xii. 1–3. It is the antithesis of Zophar's thesis, ch. xx. 5, and seeks the reason of the fact established by experience which had also well-nigh proved the ruin of Asaph (Ps. lxxiii. comp. Mal. iii. 13–15), viz. that the ungodly, far from being overtaken by the punishment of their godlessness, continue in the enjoyment of life, that they attain to old age, and also a proportionately increasing power and wealth. The verb עָתַק, which in ch. xiv. 18, xviii. 4 (comp. the *Hiph.* ch. ix. 5, xxxii. 15); we read in the signification *promoveri*, has here, like the Arabic 'ataqa, 'atuqa, the signification to become old, *ætate provehi*; and גָּבַר חַיִל, to become strong in property, is a synonym of הִשְׂגָּה חַיִל, to acquire constantly increasing possessions, used in a similar connection in Ps. lxxiii. 12. The first feature in the picture of the prosperity of the wicked, which the pang of being bereft of his own children brings home to Job, is that they are spared the same kind of loss: their posterity is established (נָכוֹן, *constitutus*, elsewhere standing in readiness, ch. xii. 5, xv. 23, xviii. 12, here standing firm, as *e.g.* Ps. xciii. 2) in their sight about them (so that they have to mourn neither their loss by death nor by separation from their home), and their offspring (צֶאֱצָאִים, a word common only to the undisputed as well as to the disputed prophecies of Isaiah and the book of Job) before their eyes; נכון must be carried over to ver. 8*b* as predicate: they are, without any loss, before their eyes. The description passes over from the children, the corner-stones of the house (*vid.* Ges. *Thes.*, *s.v.* בנה), to the houses themselves. It is just as questionable here as in ch. v. 24, Isa. xli. 3, and elsewhere, whether שָׁלוֹם is a subst. (= בשלום) or an adj.; the substantival rendering is at least equally admissible in such an elevated poetic speech, and the plur. subject בָּתֵּיהֶם, which, if the predicate were intended to be taken as an adj., leads one to expect שְׁלוּמִים, decides in its favour. On מִפַּחַד, without (far from) terrifying misfortune, as Isa. xxii. 3, מִקֶּשֶׁת, without a bow, vid. on ch. xix. 26. That which is expressed in ver. 9a, according to external appearance, is in ver. 9b referred to the final cause; Eloah's שֵׁבֶט, rod, with which He smites in punishment (ch. ix. 34, xxxvii. 13, comp. Isa. x. 24–26, where שׁוֹט, scourge, interchanges with it), is not over them, i.e. threatens and smites them not.

Ver. 10 comes specially to the state of the cattle, after the state of the household in general has been treated of. Since שׁוֹרוֹ and פָּרָתוֹ are interchangeable, and are construed according to their genus, the former undoubtedly is intended of the male, not also ἐπικοίνως of the female (LXX. ἡ βοῦς, Jerome, Saadia), as Rosenm., after Bochart, believes it must be taken, because עבר is never said de mare feminam ineunte, but always de femina quæ concipit. In reality, however, it is with עבר otherwise than with עדה, whose Pael and Aphel certainly signify concipere (prop. transmittere sc. semen in a passive sense). On the other hand, עבר, even in Kal, signifies to be impregnated (whence עוֹבָר, the embryo, and the biblical עָבוּר, like the extra-biblical עַבּוּר, the produce of the land), the Pael consequently to impregnate, whence מְעַבְּרָא (from the part. pass. מְעַבַּר) impregnated (pregnant), the Ithpa. to be impregnated, as Rabb. Pual מְעֻבֶּרֶת, impregnated (by which עֻבֶּרֶת also signifies pregnant, which would be hardly possible if עבר in this sexual sense were not radically distinct from עבר, περ-âν). Accordingly the Targ. translates עַבַּר by מבטין (imprægnans), and Gecatilia translates שׁורו by فَحَالَهُم (admissarius eorum), after which nearly all Jewish expositors explain. This explanation also suits לֹא יַגְעִל, which LXX. translates οὐκ ὠμοτόκησε (Jer. non abortivit), Symm. in a like sense οὐκ ἐξέτρωσε, Aq. οὐκ ἐξέβαλε, Saad. *la julziq.* The reference of שׁוֹרוֹ to the female animal everywhere assumed is incorrect; on the contrary, the bullock kept for breeding is the subject; but proceeding from this, that which is affirmed is certainly referred to the female animal. For גָּעַל signifies to cast out, cast away; the *Hiph.* therefore: to cause to cast out; Rabb. in the specified signification: so to heat what has sucked in that which is unclean, that it gives it back or lets it go (לפלוט הבלוע). Accordingly Raschi explains: " he injects not useless seed into her, which might come back and be again separated (נפלט) from her inward part, without impregnation taking place." What therefore עִבַּר says positively, ולא יגעיל says negatively: *neque efficit ut ejiciat.*[1] It is then further, in ver. 9*b*, said of the female animal which has been impregnated that she does not allow it to glide away, *i.e.* the fruit, therefore that she brings forth (פִּלֵּט as מִלֵּט, הִמְלִיט), and that she does not cause or suffer any untimely birth.

At the end of the strophe, ver. 11, the poet with delicate tact makes the sufferer, who is become childless, return to the joy of the wicked in the abundance of children. שִׁלַּח signifies here, as Isa. xxxii. 20, to allow freedom for motion and exercise. On עֲוִיל, *vid.* on ch. xvi. 11, xix. 18. It has a similar root (عال, *alere*) to the Arab. 'ajjil (collect. 'ijâl), servants, but not a similar meaning. The subj. to ver. 12 are not the children, but the "wicked" themselves, the happy fathers of the flocks of children that are let loose.

12 *They raise their voice with the playing of timbrel and harp,*
   And rejoice at the sound of the pipe.

---

[1] The Aruch under נָעַל quotes a passage of the Tosefta: גיעולי ביצים מותרים באכילה מזורות נפש היפה תאכלם, the cast away (*Würflinge*) eggs (*i.e.* such as have fallen away from the hen from a stroke on the tail or some other cause, and which are not completely formed) are allowed as food; he may eat them who does not loathe them.

13 *They enjoy their days in prosperity,*
    And in a moment they go down to Sheôl.
14 *And yet they said to God : " Depart from us !*
    We desire not the knowledge of Thy ways.
15 *What is the Almighty, that we should serve Him ?*
    And what doth it profit us that we should importune
        Him ?"—
16 *Lo ! they have not their prosperity by their own hand,*
    The thought of the wicked be far from me !

קוֹלָם is to be supplied to יִשְׂאוּ, as in Isa. xlii. 11 ; and instead
of בְּתֹף with בְּ of the musical accompaniment (as Ps. iv. 1,
xlix. 5), it is to be read כְּתֹף after the Masora with Kimchi,
Ramban, Ralbag, and Farisol,[1] but not with Rosenm. to be
explained : *personant velut tympano et cythera,* but : they raise
their voice as the timbrel and harp sound forth simultaneously;
כְּ as Isa. xviii. 4 (which is to be transl. : during the clear
warmth of the sunshine, during the dew-clouds in the heat
of harvest). תֹף (Arabic *duff,* Spanish *adufè*) is τύμπανον
(τύπανον), כִּנּוֹר (Arab. *canâre*) κινύρα or κιθάρα (Dan. iii. 5),

עוּגָב or עֻגָב, ch. xxx. 31 (from עֲגַב, *flare ; vid.* on Gen. iv. 21),
the Pan-pipe (Targ. from a similar root אַבּוּבָא, whence the
name of the *ambubajæ*). In ver. 13*a* the *Keri* gives the more
usual יְכַלּוּ (ch. xxxvi. 11) in place of the *Chethib* יְבַלּוּ, though
יְבַלּוּ occurs in Isa. lxv. 22 without this *Keri ;* יבלו signifies *con-
sument,* and יבלו *usu deterent :* they use up their life, enjoy it
to the last drop. In connection with this one thinks of a coat

---

[1] The Masora observes. לית כותיה (not occurring thus elsewhere), and
accordingly this בתף is distinguished in the Masoretic אב מן חד חד נסבין
כף ברישיה (alphabetic list of words which take at one time the prefix כ
and at another the prefix ב), from בתף, which occurs elsewhere. The
Targ. has read בתף ; the reading of Raschi and Aben-Ezra is questionable.

which is not laid aside until it is entirely worn out. It is therefore not, as the friends say, that the ungodly is swept away before his time (ch. xv. 32), also a lingering sickness does not hand him over to death (xviii. 13 sq.), but בְּרֶגַע, in a moment (comp. ch. xxxiv. 20, not: in rest, *i.e.* freedom from pain, which רֶגַע never signifies), they sink down to Hades (*acc. loci*). The matter does not admit of one's deriving the *fut.* יֵחַתּוּ here, as ch. xxxix. 22, xxxi. 34, from the *Niph.* of the verb חָתַת, *terrore percelli;* it is to be referred to נָחַת or נָחֵת (Aram. for יָרַד), which is the only certain example of a Hebrew verb *Pe Nun* ending with ת, whose *fut.* is יֵנְחַת, Ps. xxxviii. 3, also יֵחַת (Prov. xvii. 10; Jer. xxi. 13), instead of יִחַת, and in the inflexion its ת (after the analogy of יִצְּתוּ, Isa. xxxiii. 12) is doubled; as an exception (*vid. Psalter*, ii. 468), the lengthening of the short vowel (יֵחָתּוּ, Olsh. § 83, *b*) by *Silluk* does not take place, as *e.g.* by *Athnach*, ch. xxxiv. 5.

The *fut. consec.* וַיֹּאמְרוּ, in which ver. 14 is continued, does not here denote temporally that which follows upon and from something else, but generally that which is inwardly connected with something else, and even with that which is contradictory, and still occurring at the same time, exactly as Gen. xix. 9, 2 Sam. iii. 8, comp. Ew. § 231, *b*: they sink down after a life that is completely consumed away, without a death-struggle, into Hades, and yet they denied God, would not concern themselves about His ways (comp. the similar passage, Isa. lviii. 2), and accounted the service of God and prayer (פְּגַע בְּ, *precibus adire*) as useless. The words of the ungodly extend to ver. 15*b*; according to Hirz., Hlgst., Welte, and Hahn, ver. 16*a* resumes the description: behold, is not their prosperity in their hand? *i.e.* is it not at their free disposal? or: do they not everywhere carry it away with them? But ver. 16*b* is not favourable to this interrogative rendering of לֹא (= הֲלֹא). Schlottm. explains more correctly: behold, their prosperity is not in their power; but by taking not only ver. 16a (like Schnurrer), but the whole of ver. 16, as an utterance of an opponent, which is indeed impossible, because the declining of all fellowship with the godless would be entirely without aim in the mouth of the opponent. For it is not the friends who draw the picture of the lot of the punishment of the godless with the most terrible lines possible, who suggest the appearance of looking wishfully towards the godless, but Job, who paints the prosperity of the godless in such brilliant colours. On the other hand, both sides are agreed in referring prosperity and misfortune to God as final cause. And for this very reason Job thinks that בָּרֵךְ אֶת־הָאֱלֹהִים, which he makes the godless, in vers. 14, 15, express in their own words, so horrible.

Ver. 16a is therefore to be taken as Job's judgment, and 16b as the moral effect which it produces upon him. הֵן introduces the true relation of things; טוּבָם signifies, as ch. xx. 21, their prosperity; and לֹא בְיָדָם (the emphatic position of בידם is to be observed) that this is not in *their* hand, *i.e.* arbitrary power, or perhaps better: that it is not by their own hand, *i.e.* that it is not their own work, but a gift from above, the gift even of the God whom they so shamelessly deny. That God grants them such great and lasting prosperity, is just the mystery which Job is not able to bring forth to view, without, however, his abhorrence of this denying of God being in the slightest degree lessened thereby. Not by their own hand, says he, do they possess such prosperity—the counsel (עֵצַת, similar to ch. v. 13, x. 3, xviii. 7: design, principle, and general disposition, or way of thinking) of the wicked be far from me; *i.e.* be it far from me that so I should speak according to their way of thinking, with which, on the contrary, I disavow all fellowship. The relation of the clauses is exactly like ch. xxii. 18, where this formula of detestation is repeated. רָחֲקָה is, according to the meaning, optative or precative (Ew. § 223, b, and Ges. § 126, 4*),

which Hahn and Schlottm. think impossible, without assigning any reason.   It is the *perf.* of certainty, which expresses
that which is wished as a fact, but with an emotional exclamative accent.   In ancient Arabic it is a rule to use the
perf. as optative; and also still in modern Arabic (which
often makes use of the fut. instead of the perf.), they say
e.g. la cân, i.e. he must never have been!   The more detestable the conduct of the prosperous towards Him to whom
they owe their prosperity is, the sooner, one would think, the
justice of God would be called forth to recompense them
according to their deeds; but—

17   *How rarely is the light of the wicked put out,*
       And their calamity breaketh in upon them,
       That He distributeth snares in his wrath,
18   *That they become as straw before the wind,*
       And as chaff which the storm sweepeth away! ?
19   *" Eloah layeth up his iniquity for his children !"*
       May He recompense it to him that he may feel it.
20   *May his own eyes see his ruin,*
       And let him drink of the glowing wrath of the Almighty.
21   *For what careth he for his house after him,*
       When the number of his months is cut off ?

The interrogative כַּמָּה has here the same signification as in
Ps. lxxviii. 40: how often (comp. ch. vii. 19, how long? xiii.
23, how many?), but in the sense of " how seldom ?!"   How
seldom does what the friends preach to him come to pass,
that the lamp of the wicked is put out (thus Bildad, ch.
xviii. 5 sq.), and their misfortune breaks in upon them (יָבֹא,
ingruit; thus Bildad, ch. xviii. 12 : misfortune, אֵיד, prop.
pressure of suffering, stands ready for his fall), that He
distributes (comp. Zophar's " this is the portion of the wicked
man," *i.e.* what is allotted to him, ch. xx. 29) snares in His
wrath.   Hirz., Ew., Schlottm., and others, translate חֲבָלִים,

after the precedent of the Targ. (עָדְבִין, *sortes*), " lots," since
they understand it, after Ps. xvi. 6, of visitations of punishment allotted, and as it were measured out with a measuring-
line; but that passage is to be translated, " the measuring-
lines have fallen to me in pleasant places," and indeed חֶבֶל
can signify the land that is allotted to one (Josh. xvii. 14,
comp. 5); but the plural does not occur in that tropical
sense, and if it were so intended here, חֲבָלִים לָהֶם or חַבְלֵיהֶם
might at least be expected. Rosenm., Ges., Vaih., and
Carey transl. with LXX. and Jer. (ὠδῖνες, *dolores*) " pains,"
but חבלים is the peculiar word for the writhings of those in
travail (ch. xxxix. 3), which is not suited here. Schnurr. and
Umbr. are nearer to the correct interpretation when they
understand חבלים like פחים, Ps. xi. 6, of lightning, as it were
fiery strings cast down from above. If we call to mind in
how many ways Bildad, ch. xviii. 8–10, has represented the
end of the godless as a divinely decreed seizure, it is certainly
the most natural, with Stick. and Hahn, to translate (as if it
were Arabic خِبَالًا) " snares," to be understood after the
idea, however, not of lightning, but generally of ensnaring
destinies (*e.g.* חֶבְלֵי עֳנִי, ch. xxxvi. 8).

Both ver. 17 with its three members and ver. 18 with two,
are under the control of במה. The figure of straw, or rather
chopped straw (Arab. *tibn, tabn*), occurs only here. The
figure of chaff is more frequent, *e.g.* Ps. i. 4. Job here puts
in the form of a question what Ps. i. maintains, being urged
on by Zophar's false application and superficial comprehension
of the truth expressed in the opening of the Psalter. What
next follows in ver. 19*a* is an objection of the friends in vindication of their thesis, which he anticipates and answers;
perhaps the clause is to be spoken with an interrogative
accent: Eloah will—so ye object—reserve his evil for his
children? אוֹנוֹ, not from אָוֶן, strength, wealth, as ch. xviii.

7, 12, xx. 10, xl. 16, but from אָוֶן, wickedness (ch. xi. 11) and
evil (ch. xv. 35), here (without making it clear which) of
wickedness punishing itself by calamity, or of calamity which
must come forth from the wickedness as a moral necessity
[comp. on. ch. xv. 31]. That this is really the opinion of
the friends : God punishes the guilt of the godless, if not in
himself, at least in his children, is seen from ch. xx. 10, v. 4.
Job as little as Ezekiel, ch. xviii., disputes the doctrine of
retribution in itself, but that imperfect apprehension, which,
in order that the necessary satisfaction may be rendered to
divine justice, maintains a transfer of the punishment which
is opposed to the very nature of personality and freedom :
may He recompense him himself, וִֽישַׁלֵּם, that he may feel it,
i.e. repent (which would be in Arab. in a similar sense, fa-
ja'lamu ; יֵדָע as Isa. ix. 8, Hos. ix. 7, Ezek. xxv. 14).

Ver. 20 continues in the same jussive forms ; the ἅπ. γεγρ.
כִּיד signifies destruction (prop. a thrust, blow), in which sense
the Arab. caid (commonly : cunning) is also sometimes used.
The primary signification of the root כד, كد, is to strike, push ;

from this, in the stems كاد, med. Wau and med. Je, كد, كدكد,
the most diversified turns and applications are developed ;
from it the signif. of כִּידוֹד, ch. xli. 11, כִּידוֹן, xxxix. 23, and
according to Fleischer (vid. supra, pp. 263 sq.) also of כִּידוֹר,
are explained. Ver. 20b, as Ps. lx. 5, Obad. 16, refers to the
figure of the cup of the wrath of God which is worked out
by Asaph, Ps. lxxv. 9, and then by the prophets, and by the
apocalyptic seer in the New Testament. The emphasis lies
on the signs of the person in עֵינוֹ (עֵינָיו) and יִשְׁתֶּה. The rather
may his own eyes see his ruin, may he himself have to drink
of the divine wrath ; for what is his interest (what interest
has he) in his house after him ? מה puts a question with a
negative meaning (hence لا is directly used as non) ; חֵפֶץ,
prop. inclination, corresponds exactly to the word "interest"

(*quid ejus interest*), as ch. xxii. 3, comp. Isa. lviii. 3, 13 (following his own interest), without being weakened to the signification, affair, πρᾶγμα, a meaning which does not occur in
our poet or in Isaiah.   Ver. 21*b* is added as a circumstantial
clause to the question in 21*a* : while the number of his own
months . . ., and the predicate, as in ch. xv. 20 (which see),
is in the plur. *per attractionem.*   Schnurr., Hirz., Umbr., and
others explain : if the number of his months is drawn by lot,
i.e. is run out; but חֻצָּץ as *v. denom.* from חֵץ, in the signification to shake up arrows as sticks for drawing lots (Arab. سهم,
an arrow and a lot, just so Persian *tîr*) in the helmet or
elsewhere (comp. Ezek. xxi. 26), is foreign to the usage of
the Hebrew language (for מחצצים, Judg. v. 11, signifies not
those drawing lots, but the archers) ; besides, חֻצָּץ (*pass.*
חֻצָּץ) would signify " to draw lots," not " to dispose of by lot,"
and " disposed of by lot " is an awkward metaphor for "run
out."   Cocceius also gives the choice of returning to חֻצָּץ,
ψῆφος, in connection with this derivation : *calculati sive ad
calculum, i.e. pleno numero egressi,* which has still less ground.
Better Ges., Ew., and others : if the number of his months
is distributed, *i.e.* to him, so that he (this is the meaning
according to Ew.) can at least enjoy his prosperity undisturbed within the limit of life appointed to him.   By this
interpretation one misses the לֹו which is wanting, and an interpretation which does not require it to be supplied is therefore to be preferred.   All the divers significations of the verbs
חָצַץ (to divide, whence Prov. xxx. 27, חֹצֵץ, forming divisions,
i.e. in rank and file, *denom.* to shoot with the arrow, Talm.
to distribute, to halve, to form a partition), חָצָה (to divide, ch.
xl. 30 ; to divide in two equal parts), حصّ (to divide, whence
حصّة, *portio*), and خصّ (to separate, particularize)—to which,
however, خطّ (to draw, write), which Ew. compares here, does

not belong—are referable to the primary signification *scindere*,
to cut through, split (whence חֵץ, an arrow, LXX. 1 Sam. xx.
20, σχίζα); accordingly the present passage is to be explained:
when the number of his months is cut off (Hlgst., Hahn), or
cut through, *i.e.* when a bound is set to the course of his life
at which it ends (comp. בִּצֵּע, of the cutting off of the thread of
life, ch. vi. 9, xxvii. 8, Arab. صرم). Ch. xiv. 21 sq., Eccles.
iii. 22, are parallels to ver. 21. Death is the end of all clear
thought and perception. If therefore the godless receives the
reward of his deeds, he should receive it not in his children,
but in his own body during life. But this is the very thing
that is too frequently found to be wanting.

> 22 *Shall one teach God knowledge,*
> *Who judgeth those who are in heaven?*
> 23 *One dieth in his full strength,*
> *Being still cheerful and free from care.*
> 24 *His troughs are full of milk,*
> *And the marrow of his bones is well watered.*
> 25 *And another dieth with a sorrowing spirit,*
> *And hath not enjoyed wealth.*
> 26 *They lie beside one another in the dust,*
> *And worms cover them both.*

The question, ver. 22, concerns the friends. Since they
maintain that necessarily and constantly virtue is rewarded by
prosperity, and sin by misfortune, but without this law of the
divine order of the world which is maintained by them being
supported by experience: if they set themselves up as teachers
of God, they will teach Him the right understanding of the
conduct which is to be followed by Him as a ruler and judge
of men, while nevertheless He is the Absolute One, beneath
whose judicial rule not merely man, but also the heavenly
spirits, are placed, and to which they must conform and bow.
The verb לְמֵּד, instead of being construed with two acc., as

in the dependent passage Isa. xl. 14, is here construed with
the *dat.* of the person (which is not to be judged according
to ch. v. 2, xix. 3, but according to διδάσκειν τινί τι, to teach
one anything, beside the other prevailing construction). With
והוא a circumstantial clause begins regularly : while He, however, etc. Arnh. and Löwenth. translate : while, however,
He exaltedly judges, *i.e.* according to a law that infinitely
transcends man ; but that must have been מָרוֹם (and even thus
it would still be liable to be misunderstood). Hahn (whom
Olsh. is inclined to support) : but He will judge the proud,
to which first the circumstantial clause, and secondly the
parallels, ch. xxv. 2, xv. 15, iv. 18 (comp. Isa. xxiv. 21), from
which it is evident that רָמִים signifies the heavenly beings (as
Ps. lxxviii. 69, the heights of heaven), are opposed : it is a
fundamental thought of this book, which abounds in allusions
to the angels, that the angels, although exalted above men,
are nevertheless in contrast with God imperfect, and therefore are removed neither from the possibility of sin nor the
necessity of a government which holds them together in unity,
and exercises a judicial authority over them. The rule of the
all-exalted Judge is different from that which the three pre-
sumptuously prescribe to Him.

The one (viz. the evil-doer) dies בְּעֶצֶם תֻּמּוֹ, *in ipsa sua inte-
gritate*, like בעצם היום, *ipso illo die ;* the Arabic would be
في عين, since there the eye, here the bone (comp. Uhlemann,
Syr. Gramm. § 58), denote corporeality, duration, existence,
and therefore identity.   תֹּם is intended of perfect external
health, as elsewhere מָתֹם ; comp. תְּמִימִים, Prov. i. 12.   In ver.
23*b* the pointing שַׁלְאָנַן (*adj.*) and שָׁלְאָנַן (3 *præt.*) are interchanged in the Codd. ; the following verbal adjective favours
the form of writing with *Kametz*. As to the form, however
(which Röd. and Olsh. consider to be an error in writing), it
is either a mixed form from שׁאן and שׁלו with the blended
meaning of both (Ew. § 106, *c*), to which the comparison with

שְׁלֵיו (= שָׁלֵו) is not altogether suitable, or it is formed from שָׁאַן by means of an epenthesis (as זִלְעַף from זָעַף, æstuare, and בִּלְסֹם, βάλσαμον, from בֹּשֶׂם), and of similar but intensified signification; we prefer the latter, without however denying the real existence of such mixed forms (vid. on ch. xxvi. 9, xxxiii. 25). This fulness of health and prosperity is depicted in ver. 24. The ancient translators think, because the bones are mentioned in the parallel line, עֲטִינָיו must also be understood of a part of the body: LXX. ἔγκατα, Jer. viscera; Targ. בִּיזוֹי, his breasts, βυζία[1] (for Hebr. שָׁדַיִם, שֹׁד); Syr. version gabauh (= ganbauh), his sides in regard to עַטְמָא, Syr. ʽattmo = אַטְמָא, side, hip; Saad. audâguhu, his jugular veins, in connection with which (not, however, by this last reudering) חֵלֶב is read instead of חָלָב: his bowels, etc., are full of fat.[2] But the assumption that עטיניו must be a part of the body is without satisfactory ground (comp. against it e.g. ch. xx. 17, and for it xx. 11); and Schlottm. very correctly observes, that in the contrast in connection with the representation of the well-watered marrow one expects a reference to a rich nutritious drink. To this expectation corresponds

---

[1] Vid. Handschriftliche Funde, 2. S. V.

[2] Gesenius in his Thes. corrects the אוּדָאגֶה which was found in Saadia's manuscript translation to אוּדָאעֶה, اودَاعه, which is intended to mean repositoria ejus, but is really not Arabic; whereas אוּדָאגֶה is the correct plur. of ودج: his jugular veins, which occurs not merely of horses, but also of animals and men. Saadia, with reference to the following מָלְאוּ חָלָב, has thought of the metaphorical phrase حلب اوداجه: "he has milked his jugular vein," i.e. he has, as it were, drawn the blood from his jugular veins = eum jugulavit, vid. Bibliotheca Arabo-Sicula, p. ٣١٥: "and with the freshly milked juice of the jugular veins, viz. of the enemy (ومن حلب الاوداج), our infant ready to be weaned is nourished in the midst of the tumult of battle, as soon as he is weaned." The meaning of Saadia's translation is then: his jugular veins are filled with fresh blood, swollen with fulness of blood.—FL.

the translation: "his resting-places (*i.e.* of his flocks) are full of milk," after the Arab. عَطَن or مَعْطَن, which was not first compared by Schultens and Reiske (*epaulia*), but even by Abul-walid, Aben-Ezra, and others. But since the reference of what was intended to be said of the cattle at the watering-places to the places where the water is, possesses no poetic beauty, and the Hebrew language furnished the poet with an abundance of other words for pastures and meadows, it is from the first more probable that עֲטִינָיו are large troughs,—like Talm. מַעֲטָן, a trough, in which the unripe olives were laid in order that they might become tender and give forth oil, that they may then be ready for the oil-press (בַּד), and עֲטָן denotes this laying in itself,—and indeed either milk-tubs or milk-pails (שְׁחוּלְבִין לְתוֹכֵן), or with Kimchi (who rightly characterizes this as more in accordance with the prosperous condition which is intended to be described), the troughs for the store of milk, which also accords better with the meaning of the verb עֲטַן, عَطَن, to lay in, *confire*.[1] From the abundance of nutriment in ver. 24*a*, the description passes over in 24*b* to the well-nourished condition of the rich man himself in consequence

---

[1] The verb عَطَن, compared by the Orientals themselves with وَطَن, cognate in sound and meaning, has the primary signification to lie secure and to lay secure, as عَطَن, a resting-place of camels, sheep, and goats about the watering-places, is only specifically distinct from وَطَن, a cow-shed, cow-stall. The common generic notion is always a resting-place, wherefore the Kamus interprets *ʿattan* by *wattan wa-mebrek*, viz. round about the drinking-places. مَعْطَن as *n. loci*, written *mʿatén* by Barth in his *Wanderungen durch die Küstenländer des Mittelmeeres*, Bd. i. (*vid. Deutsch. Morgenländ. Zeitschrift*, iv. S. 275) S. 500, 517, is similar in meaning. The verb عَطَن impf. *jʿattunu*, also *jʿattina*, n. act. *ʿuttûn*, a v. *intrans.*, signifies, viz. of camels, etc., to lay themselves down around the

of this abundance. מֹחַ (Arab. مخّ, or even نخّ, as נֹף = מֹף, naurag = מוֹרַג) is the marrow in the bones, *e.g.* the spinal marrow, but also the brain as the marrow of the head (*Psychol.* S. 233). The bones (Prov. iii. 8), or as it is here more exactly expressed, their marrow, is watered, when the body is inwardly filled with vigour, strength, and health; Isaiah, ch. lviii. 11, fills up the picture more (as a well-watered garden), and carries it still further in ch. lxvi. 14 (thy bones shall blossom like a tender herb). The counterpart now follows with וְזֶה (and the other, like ch. i. 16). The other (viz. the righteous) dies with a sorrowful soul (comp. Job's lament, ch. vii. 11, x. i.), *i.e.* one which is called to experience the bitterness of a suffering life; he dies and has not enjoyed בַּטּוֹבָה, any of the wealth (with partitive *Beth*, as Ps. cxli. 4, comp. *supra*, ch. vii. 13), has had no portion in the enjoyment of it (comp. Job's lament, ch. ix. 25). In death they are then both, unrighteous and righteous, alike, as the Preacher saith: מקרה אחד comes upon the wise as upon the fool, Eccles. ii. 15, comp. ix. 2 sq. They lie together in the dust, *i.e.* the dust of the grave (*vid.* on ch. xix. 25), and worms cover them. What then is become of the law of retribution in the present world,

drinking-troughs, after or even before drinking from them. On the other hand, عطَن *impf. j̇ attinu*, also *j̇ attunu*, *n. act.* 'attn, a *v. trans.* used by the dresser of skins: to lay the skins in the tan or ooze (French, *confire*; low Latin, *tanare, tannare*, whence French, *tanner*, to tan, *tan*, the bark) until they are ready for dressing, and the hairs will easily scrape off. Hence عطَن

impf. j̇ attanu, n. act. 'attan, a *v. intrans.* used of skins: to become tender by lying in the ooze, and to smell musty, to stink, which is then transferred to men and animals: to stink like a skin in the ooze, comp. *situs*, mould, mildew, rust.—FL. Starting from the latter signification, *macerare pellem*, Lee explains: his bottles (viz. made of leather); and Carey: his half-dressed skins (because the store of milk is so great that he cannot wait for the preparation of the leather for the bottles); but the former is impossible, the latter out of taste, and both are far-fetched.

which the friends maintained with such rigid pertinacity, and so regardless of the deep wound they were inflicting on Job?

27 *Behold I know your thoughts*
     And the stratagems, with which ye overpower me!
28 *When ye say: Where is the house of the tyrant,*
     And where the pavilions of the wicked—:
29 *Have ye not asked those who travel,*
     Their memorable things ye could surely not disown:
30 *That the wicked was spared in the day of calamity,*
     In the day of the outburst of wrath they were led away.
31 *Who liketh to declare to him his way to his face?*
     And hath he done aught, who will recompense it to him?

Their thoughts which he sees through, are their secret thoughts that he is such an evil-doer reaping the reward of his deeds. מְזִמּוֹת (which occurs both of right measures, good wise designs, Prov. v. 2, viii. 12, and of artful devices, malicious intrigues, Prov. xii. 2, xiv. 17, comp. the definition of בַּעַל מְזִמּוֹת, Prov. xxiv. 8) is the name he gives to the delicately developed reasoning with which they attack him; חָמַס (comp. Arab. تحمّس, to act harshly, violently, and overbearingly) is construed with עַל in the sense of forcing, apart from the idea of overcoming. In ver. 28, which is the antecedent to ver. 29, beginning with כִּי תֹאמְרוּ (as ch. xix. 28), he refers to words of the friends like ch. viii. 22, xv. 34, xviii. 15, 21. נָדִיב is prop. the noble man, whose heart impels (ندب, נָדַב) him to what is good, or who is ready and willing, and does spontaneously that which is good (ندب), *vid.*

Psychol. S. 165; then, however, since the notion takes the reverse way of *generosus*, the noble man (princely) by birth and station, with which the secondary notion of pride and

abuse of power, therefore of a despot or tyrant, is easily as
here (parall. רְשָׁעִים, comp. עָשִׁיר, Isa. liii. 9, with the same word
in the parallel) combined (just so in Isa. xiii. 2, and similarly
at least above, ch. xii. 21,—an anomaly of name and conduct,
which will be for the future put aside, according to Isa. xxxii.
5). It is not admissible to understand the double question
as antithetical, with Wolfson, after Prov. xiv. 11; for the
interrogative אַיֵּה is not appropriate to the house of the נדיב,
in the proper sense of the word. Ver. 28, מִשְׁכְּנוֹת is not
an externally but internally multiplying plur.; perhaps the
poet by בַּיִת intends a palace in the city, and by אֹהֶל מִשְׁכְּנוֹת a
tent among the wandering tribes, rendered prominent by its
spaciousness and the splendour of the establishment.[1] Job
thinks the friends reason *a priori* since they inquire thus; the
permanent fact of experience is quite different, as they can
learn from עֹבְרֵי דֶרֶךְ, travellers, *i.e.* here: people who have tra-
velled much, and therefore are well acquainted with the stories
of human destinies. The *Piel* נִכַּר, proceeding from the radical meaning to gaze fixedly, is an ἐναντιόσημον, since it signifies both to have regard to, ch. xxxiv. 19, and to disown,
Deut. xxxii. 27; here it is to be translated: their אֹתֹת ye
cannot nevertheless deny, ignore (as Arab. نكر and انكر).
אֹתֹת are tokens, here: remarkable things, and indeed the
remarkable histories related by them; آية (collective plur.
آي), signs, is also similarly used in the signification of عبرة,
example, historical teaching.

---

[1] Although the tents regularly consist of two divisions, one for the men
and another for the women, the translation " magnificent pavilion"
(*Prachtgezelt*), disputed by Hirz., is perfectly correct; for even in the
present day a Beduin, as he approaches an encampment, knows the tent
of the sheikh immediately: it is denoted by its size, often also by the
lances planted at the door, and also, as is easily imagined, by the rich
arrangement of cushions and carpets. *Vid.* Layard's *New Discoveries*,
pp. 261 and 171.

That the פִּי, ver. 30, as in ver. 28, introduces the view of
the friends, and is the antecedent clause to ver. 31 : *quod (si)*
vos dicitis, in tempora cladis per iram divinam immissæ servari
et nescium futuri velut pecudem eo deduci improbum (Böttcher,
de inf. § 76), has in the double לֹ an apparent support, which
is not to be denied, especially in regard to ch. xxxviii. 23 ; it
is, however, on account of the omission of the indispensable
תאמרו in this instance, an explanation which does violence
to the words.   The פִּי, on the contrary, introduces that which
the accounts of the travellers affirm.   Further, the לֹ in לְיוֹם
indicates here not the *terminus ad quem*, but as in לְעֶרב, in the
evening, the *terminus quo.*   And the verb חָשַׂךְ, *cohibere*,
signifies here to hold back from danger, as ch. xxxiii. 18,
therefore to preserve uninjured.   Ew. translates ver. 30*b*
erroneously : "in the day when the floods of wrath come on."
How tame would this הוּבָל, "to be led near," be!   This
Hoph. signifies elsewhere to be brought and conducted, and
occurs in ver. 32, as in Isa. lv. 12 and elsewhere, of an honourable escort; here, in accordance with the connection : to be
led away out of the danger (somewhat as Lot and his family
by the escort of angels).   At the time, when streams of wrath
(עֶבְרָה, the overflowing of vexation = outburst of wrath, like
the Arab. عبرة, the overflowing of the eye = tears) go forth,
they remain untouched : they escape them, as being under a
special, higher protection.[1]   Ver. 31 is commonly taken as a

---

[1] This interpretation, however, is unsatisfactory, because it does not do
justice to the twofold לֹ, which seems, according to ch. xxxviii. 23, to be
intended to indicate the *terminus ad quem ;* perhaps vers. 29 and 30 are
to be transposed.   If ver. 30 followed ver. 28, it would retain its natural
sense as belonging to the view of the friends : "For the wicked is reserved
for the day of calamity, and to a day of wrath they are led" (יוּבְלוּ as
Isa. liii. 7, Jer. xi. 19).   Then והוּא לִקְבָרוֹת יוּבָל also adds a suitable echo
of the contradiction in Job's mouth.   Böttch. rightly calls attention to
the consonance of יוּבָל with יוּבְלוּ, and of עֲבָרוֹת with קְבָרוֹת.

reflection on the exemption of the evil-doer : God's mode of action is exalted above all human scrutiny, although it is not reconcilable with the idea of justice, ch. ix. 12, xxiii. 13. But the מִי יְשַׁלֶּם־לוֹ, who will recompense it to him, which, used of man in relation to God, has no suitable meaning, and must therefore mean : who, after God has left the evil-doer unpunished—for which, however, הוּא עָשָׂה would be an unsuitable expression—shall recompense him, the evil-doer? is opposed to it. Therefore, against Ew., Hirz., and Hlgst., it must with most expositors be supposed that ver. 31 is a reflection referable not to God, but to the evil-doer : so powerful is the wicked generally, that no one can oppose his pernicious doings and call him to account for them, much less that any one would venture to repay him according to his desert when he has brought anything to a completion (הוּא עָשָׂה, intentionally thus seriously expressed, as elsewhere of God, e.g. Isa. xxxviii. 15). In the next strophe, that which is gathered from the accounts of travellers is continued, and is then followed by a declamatory summing up.

> 32 *And he is brought to the grave,*
>   *And over the tomb he still keepeth watch.*
> 33 *The clods of the valley are sweet to him,*
>   *And all men draw after him,*
>   *As they preceded him without number.*
>
> .   .   .   .
>
> 34 *And how will ye comfort me so vainly !*
>   *Your replies are and remain perfidy.*

During life removed at the time of dire calamity, this unapproachable evil-doer is after his death carried to the grave with all honour (יוּבָל, comp. x. 19), and indeed to a splendid tomb ; for, like מִשְׁכָּנוֹת above, קְברות is also an amplificative plural. It is certainly the most natural to refer יִשְׁקֹד, like יוּבָל, to the deceased. The explanation : and over the tomb one keeps watch (Böttch., Hahn, Röd., Olsh.), is indeed in itself admissible, since that which serves as the efficient subject is often left unexpressed (Gen. xlviii. 2 ; 2 Kings ix. 21 ; Isa. liii. 9 ; comp. *supra*, on ch. xviii. 18) ; but that, according to the prevalent usage of the language, יִשְׁקֹד would denote only a guard of honour at night, not also in the day, and that for clearness it would have required וּגְדִישׁוֹ instead of גְּדִישׁ, are considerations which do not favour this explanation, for שָׁקַד signifies to watch, to be active, instead of sleeping or resting ; and moreover, the placing of guards of honour by graves is an assumed, but not proved, custom of antiquity. Nevertheless, יִשְׁקֹד might also in general denote the watchful, careful tending of the grave, and the *maqâm* (the tomb) of one who is highly honoured has, according to Moslem custom, servants (*châdimîn*) who are appointed for this duty. But though the translation "one watches" should not be objected to on this ground, the preference is to be given to a commendable rendering which makes the deceased the subject of יִשְׁקֹד. Raschi's explanation does not, however, commend itself : "buried in his own land, he also in death still keeps watch over the heaps of sheaves." The LXX. translates similarly, ἐπὶ σωρῶν, which Jerome improperly, but according to a right sentiment, translates, *in congerie mortuorum*. For after the preceding mention of the pomp of burial, גְּדִישׁ, which certainly signifies a heap of sheaves in ch. v. 26, is favoured by the assumption of its signifying a sepulchral heap, with reference to which also in that passage (where interment is likewise the subject of discourse) the expression is chosen. Haji Gaon observes that the dome (קֻבָּה, قبّة, the dome and the sepulchral monument vaulted over by it)[1] erected over graves according to Arab custom is intended ; and Aben-Ezra says,

---

[1] *Vid.* Lane's *Manners and Customs of the Modern Egyptians* (translated by Zenker).

that not exactly this, but in general the grave-mound formed of earth, etc., is to be understood. In reality, נדיש (from the verb נדש, *cumulare*, commonly used in the Talmud and Aramaic) signifies *cumulus*, in the most diversified connections, which in Arabic are distributed among the verbs جدس, كدس, and جدث, especially *tumulus*, Arab. جدث (broader pronunciation جذف). If by grave-mound a mound with the grave upon it can be understood, a beautiful explanation is presented which accords with the preference of the Beduin for being buried on an eminence, in order that even in death he may be surrounded by his relations, and as it were be able still to overlook their encampment : the one who should have had a better lot is buried in the best place of the plain, in an insignificant grave ; the rich man, however, is brought up to an eminence and keeps watch on his elevated tomb, since from this eminence as from a watch-tower he even in death, as it were, enjoys the wide prospect which delighted him so while living.[1] But the signification *collis* cannot be supported ; נדיש signifies the hill which is formed by the grave itself, and ver. 33 indeed directs us to the wady as the place of burial, not to the hill. But if נדיש is the grave-mound, it is also not possible with Schlottm. to think of the pictures on the wall and images of the deceased, as they are found in the Egyptian vaults (although in ch. iii. 14 we recognised an allusion to the pyramids), for it cannot then be a נדיש in the strict sense that is spoken of; the word ought, like the Arabic جدث (which the Arab. translation of the New Testament in the London Polyglott uses of the μνημεῖον of Jesus), with a

---

[1] " Take my bones," says an Arabian poem, " and carry them with you, wherever you go ; and if ye bury them, bury them opposite your encampment ! And bury me not under a vine, which would shade me, but upon a hill, so that my eye can see you ! " *Vid. Ausland*, 1863, Nr. 15 (*Ein Ritt nach Transjordanien*).

mingling of its original signification, to have been used in
the general signification *sepulcrum*. This would be possible,
but it need not be supposed. Job's words are the pictorial
antithesis to Bildad's assertion, ch. xviii. 17, that the godless
man dies away without trace or memorial ; it is not so, but as
may be heard from the mouth of people who have experience
in the world : he keeps watch over his tomb, he continues
to watch although asleep, since he is continually brought
to remembrance by the monument built over his tomb. A
keeping watch that no one approaches the tomb disrespect-
fully (Ew.), is not to be thought of. שָׁקַד is a relative negation of the sleep of death : he is dead, but in a certain manner
he continues to live, viz. in the monument planting forward his
memory, which it remains for the imagination to conceive of
as a mausoleum, or weapons, or other votive offerings hung
upon the walls, etc. In connection with such honour, which
follows him even to and beyond death, the clods of the valley
(*est ei terra levis*) are sweet (מָתְקוּ is accentuated with *Mercha*,
and לוֹ without *Makkeph* with little-*Rebia*) to him ; and if
death in itself ought to be accounted an evil, he has shared
the common fate which all men after him will meet, and
which all before him have met ; it is the common end of
all made sweet to him by the pageantry of his burial and his
after-fame. Most modern expositors (Ew., Hirz., Umbr.,
Hlgst., Welte) understand the יִמְשֹׁךְ, which is used, certainly,
not in the transitive signification : to draw after one's self,
but in the intransitive : to draw towards (LXX. ἀπελεύσεται),
as Judg. iv. 6 (*vid.* Ges. *Thes.*), of an imitative treading of
the same way ; but כָּל־אָדָם would then be an untrue hyperbole,
by which Job would expose himself to the attack of his
adversaries.

In ver. 34 Job concludes his speech ; the *Waw* of וְאֵיךְ,
according to the idea (as *e.g.* the *Waw* in וַאֲנִי, Isa. xliii. 12), is
an inferential *ergo*. Their consolation, which is only avail-

able on condition of penitence, is useless; and their replies, which are intended to make him an evil-doer against the testimony of his conscience, remain מְעַל. It is not necessary to construe: and as to your answers, only מעל remains. The predicate stands *per attractionem* in the sing.: their answers, reduced to their true value, leave nothing behind but מעל, end in מעל, viz. באלהים, Josh. xxii. 22, perfidious sinning against God, *i.e.* on account of the sanctimonious injustice and un charitableness with which they look suspiciously on him.

Job has hitherto answered the accusations of the friends, which they express in ever-increasingly terrible representations of the end of the godless, presenting only the terrible side of their dogma of the justice of God, with a stedfast attestation of his innocence, and with the ever-increasing hope of divine vindication against human accusation. In him was manifest that faith which, being thrust back by men, clings to God, and, thrust back by God, even soars aloft from the present wrath of God to His faithfulness and mercy. The friends, however, instead of learning in Job's spiritual condition to distinguish between the appearance and the reality in this confidence, which comes back to itself, see in it only a constant wilful hardening of himself against their exhortations to penitence. It does not confound them, that he over whom according to their firm opinion, the sword of God's vengeance hangs, warns them of that same sword, but only confirms them still more in their conviction, that they have to do with one who is grievously self-deluded.

Zophar has painted anew the end of the evil-doer in the most hideous colours, in order that Job might behold himself in this mirror, and be astonished at himself. We see also, from the answer of Job to Zophar's speech, that the passionate excitement which Job displayed at first in opposition to the friends has given place to a calmer tone; he has already got over the first impression of disappointed expectation, and the more confidently certain of the infallibility of divine justice he becomes, the more does he feel raised above his accusers. He now expects no further comfort; careful attention to what he has to say shall henceforth be his consolation. He will also complain against and of men no more, for he has long since ceased to hope for anything for himself from men; his vexation concerns the objective indefensibility of that which his opponents maintain as a primeval law of the divine government in the world. The maxim that godlessness always works its own punishment by a calamitous issue, is by no means supported by experience. One sees godless persons who are determined to know nothing of God, and are at the same time prosperous. It is not to be said that God treasures up the punishment they have deserved for their children. The godless ought rather to bear the punishment themselves, since the destiny of their children no longer concerns them after they have enjoyed their fill of life. That law is therefore a precept which human shortsightedness has laid down for God, but one by which, however, He is not guided. The godless who have lived prosperously all their days, and the righteous who have experienced only sorrow, share the common lot of death. One has only to ask persons who have had experience of the world: they can relate instances of notorious sinners who maintained their high position until death, and who, without being overtaken by divine judgments, and without human opposition and contradiction, were carried in honour to the grave, and their memory is immortalized by the monuments erected over their tomb. From this Job infers that the connection into which the friends bring his suffering with supposed guilt, is a false one, and that all their answers are, after all, reducible to an unjust and uncharitable judgment, by which they attack (מָעַל) God.

Job has more than once given expression to the thought,

that a just distribution of prosperity and misfortune is not to be found in the world, ch. ix. 22–24, xii. 6. But now for the first time he designedly brings it forward in reply to the friends, after he has found every form of assertion of his innocence unavailing, and their behaviour towards him with their dogma is become still more and more inconsiderate and rash. Job sins in this speech; but in order to form a correct judgment of this sinning, two things must be attended to. Job does not revel in the contradiction in which this lasting fact of experience stands to the justice of divine retribution, he had rather be ignorant of it; for he has no need of it in order, in spite of his affliction, to be able to hold fast the consciousness of his innocence. No indeed! if he thinks of this mystery he is perplexed, and shuddering comes over him, ch. xxi. 6. And when he depicts the prosperity of sinners, he expresses his horror of the sins of such prosperous men in the words : The counsel of the ungodly be far from me ! (ch. xxi. 16), in order that it may not be erroneously imagined that he lusts after such prosperity.

If we compare Zophar's and Job's speeches one with another, we are obliged to say, that relatively the greater right is on the side of Job. True, the Scriptures confirm what Zophar says of the destruction of the evil-doer in innumerable passages; and this calamitous end of one who has long been prosperous and defiant, is the solution by which the Old Testament Scriptures (Ps. xxxvii. lxxiii.; Jer. xii. 1–3; Hab. i. 13–ii.) remove the stumbling-block of the mysterious phenomenon of the prosperity of the evil-doer. But if we bear in mind that this solution is insufficient, so long as that calamitous end is regarded only outwardly, and with reference to the present world,—that the solution only becomes satisfactory when, as in the book of Ecclesiastes, in reply to a similar doubt to that which Job expresses (Eccles. vii. 15, viii. 14), the end is regarded as the end of all, and as the decision of a final judgment which sets all contradictions right,—that, however, neither Zophar nor Job know anything of a decision beyond death, but regard death as the end whither human destiny and divine retribution tend, without being capable of any further distinction : we cannot deny that Job is most in the right in placing the prosperous life and death of the godless as based upon the incontrovertible facts of experience, in opposition to Zophar's primeval exceptionless law of the terrible end of the godless. The speeches of Zophar and of Job are both true and false,—both one-sided, and therefore mutually supplementary. The real final end of the evil-doer is indeed none other than Zophar describes; and the temporal prosperity of the evil-doer, lasting often until death, is really a frequent phenomenon. If, however, we consider further, that Job is not able to deny the occurrence of such examples of punishment, such revelations of the retributive justice of God, as those which Zophar represents as occurring regularly and without exception ; that, however, on the other hand, exceptional instances undeniably do exist, and the friends *are obliged* to be blind to them, because otherwise the whole structure of their opposition would fall in,—it is manifest that Job is nearer to the truth than Zophar. For it is truer that the retributive justice of God is often, but by far not always, revealed in the present world and outwardly, than that it never becomes manifest.

Wherein, then, does Job's sin in this speech consist ? Herein, that he altogether ignores the palpably just distribution of human destinies, which does occur frequently enough. In this he becomes unjust towards his opponent, and incapable of convincing him. From it, it appears as though in the divine government there is not merely a preponderance of what is mysterious, of what is irreconcilable with divine justice, but as though justice were altogether contradicted.

The reproach with which he reproaches his opponents: Shall one teach God understanding? is one which also applies to himself; for when he says that God, if He punishes, must visit punishment upon the evil-doer himself, and not on his children, it is an unbecoming dictation with regard to God's doing. We should be mistaken in supposing that the poet, in ch. xxi. 19–21, brings forward a concealed contradiction to the Mosaic doctrine of retribution; nowhere in the Old Testament, not even in the Mosaic law, is it taught, that God visits the sins of the fathers on the children, while He allows them themselves to go free, Ex. xx. 5, comp. Deut. xxiv. 16, Ezek. xviii., Jer. xxxi. 29 sq. What Job asserts, that the sinner himself must endure the punishment of his sins, not his children instead of him, is true; but the thought lying in the background, that God does not punish where He ought to punish, is sinful. Thus here Job again falls into error, which he must by and by penitently acknowledge and confess, by speaking unbecomingly of God: the God of the future is again vanished from him behind the clouds of temptation, and he is unable to understand and love the God of the present; He is a mystery to him, the incomprehensibility of which causes him pain. "The joyous thought of the future, which a little before struggled forth, again vanishes, because the present, into the abyss of which he is again drawn down, has remained perfectly dark the whole time, and as yet no bridge has been revealed crossing from this side to that."

THE THIRD COURSE OF THE CONTROVERSY.—
CHAP. XXII.–XXVI.

Eliphaz' Third Speech.—Chap. xxii.

Schema: 8. 8. 4. 6. 8. 4. 10. 10.

[Then began Eliphaz the Temanite, and said :]
2 *Is a man profitable unto God?*
  No, indeed! the intelligent man is profitable to himself.
3 *Hath the Almighty any profit if thou art righteous,*
  Or gain if thou strivest to walk uprightly?
4 *Will He reprove thee for thy fear of God,*
  Will He go with thee into judgment?
5 *Is not thy wickedness great,*
  Thine iniquities infinite?

The verb סָכַן, in the signification to be profitable, is peculiar to the book of Job (although also סֹכֵן and סֹכֶנֶת elsewhere, according to its primary signification, does not differ from מוֹעִיל, מוֹעִילָה, by which it is explained by Kimchi); the correct development of the notion of this verb is to be perceived from the *Hiph.*, which occurs in ver. 21 in this speech of Eliphaz (*vid.* Ges. *Thes.*) : it signifies originally, like שָׁכַן, سكن, to rest, dwell, especially to dwell beside one another, then to become accustomed to one another (comp. שָׁכֵן, a neighbour, and سَكَن, a friend, confidant), and to assist one another, to be serviceable, to be profitable ; we can say both סָכַנְתִּי, I have profit, ch. xxxiv. 9, and סָכַן, it is profitable, ch. xv. 3, xxxv. 3, here twice with a personal subj., and first followed by לְ, then with the עַל, usual also elsewhere in later prose (*e.g.* טוֹב עַל, 1 Chron. xiii. 2, comp. *supra*, ch. x. 3, to be pleasant) and poetry, which gladly adopts Aramaisms (as here and Ps. xvi. 6, שָׁפַר עַל, well-pleased), instead of לְ, whence here עָלֵימוֹ, as ch. xx. 23, pathetic for עָלָיו. The question, which is intended as a negative, is followed by the negative answer (which establishes its negative meaning) with כִּי ; מַשְׂכִּיל is, like Ps. xiv. 2, the intelligent, who wills and does what is good, with an insight into the nature of the extremes in morality, as in Prov. i. 3 independent morality which rests not merely on blind custom is called מוּסַר הַשֵּׂכֶל. הֲיֵה חֵפֶץ לְ, it is to the interest of any one (different from 1 Sam. xv. 22, vid. on ch. xxi. 21), and הֲיֵה בֶצַע לְ, it is to the gain of any one (prop. the act of cutting, cutting off, i.e. what one tears in pieces), follow as synonyms of סכן. On the Aramaizing doubling of the first radical in the *Hiph.* תַּחֵם (instead of תָּחֵם), vid. Ges. § 67, rem. 8, comp. 3. It is translated *an lucrum (ei) si integras facias vias tuas.* The meaning of the whole strophe is mainly determined according to the rendering of הֲמִיּרְאָתְךָ (like המבינתך, ch. xxxix. 26, with *Dechî,* and as an exception with *Munach,* not removed to the place of the *Metheg; vid. Psalter,* ii. 491, Anm. 1). If the suff. is taken objectively (from fear of thee), *e.g.* Hirz., we have the following line of thought: God is neither benefited by human virtue nor injured by human sin, so that when He corrects the sinner He is turning danger from himself; He neither rewards the godly because He is benefited by his piety, nor punishes the sinner because by his sinning he threatens Him with injury. Since, therefore, if God chastises a man, the reason of it is not to be found in any selfish purpose of God, it must be in the sin of the man, which is on its own account worthy of punishment. But the logical relation in which ver. 5 stands to ver. 4 does not suit this: perhaps from fear of thee . . .? no, rather because of thy many and great sins! Hahn is more just to this relation when he explains: " God has no personal profit to expect from man, so that, somewhat from fear, to prevent him from being injurious, He should have any occasion to torment him with sufferings unjustly." But if the personal profit, which is denied, is one that grows out of the piety of the man, the personal harm, which is denied as one which God by punishment will keep far from Himself, is to be thought of as growing out of the sin of the man ; and the logical relation of ver. 5 to 4 is not suited to this, for ver. 5 assigns the reason of the chastisement to the sin, and denies, as it runs, not merely any motive whatever in connection with the sin, but that the reason can lie in the opposite of sin, as it appears according to Job's assertion that, although guiltless, he is still suffering from the wrath of God.

Thus, then, the suff. of המיראתך is to be taken subjectively : on account of thy fear of God, as Eliphaz has used יראתך twice already, ch. iv. 6, xv. 4. By this subjective rendering vers. 4 and 5 form a true antithesis : Does God perhaps punish thee on account of thy fear of God ? Does He go (on that account) with thee into judgment ? No (it would be absurd to suppose that) ; therefore thy wickedness must be great (in proportion to the greatness of thy suffering), and thy misdeeds infinitely many. If we now look at what precedes, we shall have to put aside the thought drawn into vers. 2 and 3 by Ewald (and also by Hahn) : whether God, perhaps with the purpose of gaining greater advantage from piety, seeks to raise it by unjustly decreed sufferings ; for this thought has nothing to indicate it, and is indeed certainly false, but on account of the force of truth which lies in it (there is a decreeing of suffering for the godly to raise their piety) is only perplexing.

First of all, we must inquire how it is that Eliphaz begins his speech thus. All the exhortations to penitence in which the three exhaust themselves, rebound from Job without affecting him. Even Eliphaz, the oldest among them, full of a lofty, almost prophetic consciousness, has with the utmost solicitude allured and terrified him, but in vain. And it is the cause of God which he brings against him, or rather his

own well-being that he seeks, without making an impression
upon him. Then he reminds him that God is in Himself the
all-sufficient One ; that no advantage accrues to Him from
human uprightness, since His nature, existing before and
transcending all created things, can suffer neither diminution
nor increase from the creature ; that Job therefore, since he
remains inaccessible to that well-meant call to penitent humi-
liation, has refused not to benefit Him, but himself ; or, what
is the reverse side of this thought (which is not, however,
expressed), that he does no injury to Him, only to himself.
And yet in what except in Job's sin should this decree of
suffering have its ground ? If it is a self-contradiction that
God should chastise a man because he fears Him, there must
be sin on the side of Job ; and indeed, since the nature of
the sin is to be measured according to the nature of the
suffering, great and measureless sin. This logical necessity
Eliphaz now regards as real, without further investigation,
by opening out this bundle of sins in the next strophe, and
reproaching Job directly with that which Zophar, ch. xx.
19–21, aiming at Job, has said of the רשע. In the next
strophe he continues, with כי explic. :

6 *For thou distrainedst thy brother without cause,*
   And the clothes of the naked thou strippedst off.
7 *Thou gavest no water to the languishing,*
   And thou refusedst bread to the hungry.
8 *And the man of the arm—the land was his,*
   And the honourable man dwelt therein.
9 *Thou sentest widows away empty,*
   And the arms of the orphan are broken.

The reason of exceeding great suffering must be exceeding
great sins. Job must have committed such sins as are here
cited ; therefore Eliphaz directly attributes guilt to him,
since he thinks thus to tear down the disguise of the hypo-

crite. The strophe contains no reference to the Mosaic law : the compassionate Mosaic laws respecting duties towards widows and orphans, and the poor who pledge their few and indispensable goods, may have passed before the poet's mind ; but it is not safe to infer it from the expression. As specific Mohammedan commandments among the wandering tribes even in the present day have no sound, so the poet dare not assume, in connection with the characters of his drama, any knowledge, of the Sinaitic law ; and of this he remains conscious throughout : their standpoint is and remains that of the Abrahamic faith, the primary commands (later called the ten commands of piety, *el-felâhh*) of which were amply sufficient for stigmatizing that to which this strophe gives prominence as sin. It is only the force of the connection of the matter here which gives the *futt.* which follow כי a retrospective meaning. חָבַל is connected either with the accusative of the thing for which the pledge is taken, as in the law, which meets a response in the heart, Ex. xxii. 25 sq. ; or with the accus. of the person who is seized, as here אַחֶיךָ ; or, if this is really (as Bär asserts) a mistake that has gained a footing, which has Codd. and old printed editions against it, rather אָחִיךָ. LXX., Targ., Syr., and Jer. read the word as plural. עֲרוּמִּים (from עָרוֹם), like γυμνοί, James ii. 15, *nudi* (comp. Seneca, *de beneficiis*, v. 13 : *si quis male vestitum et pannosum videt, nudum se vidisse dicit*), are, according to our mode of expression, the half-naked, only scantily (*vid.* Isa. xx. 2) clothed.

Ver. 8. The man of the arm, זְרוֹעַ, is in Eliphaz' mind Job himself. He has by degrees acquired the territory far and wide for himself, by having brought down the rightful possessors by open violence (ch. xx. 19), or even by cunning and unfeeling practices, and is not deterred by any threat of a curse (ch. xv. 28) : לֹו הָאָרֶץ, he looked upon it as his, and his it must become ; and since with his possessions his authority increased, he planted himself firmly in it, filled it out alone, like a stout fellow who takes the room of all others away. Umbr., Hahn, and others think Job's partiality for power and rank is described in ver. 8 ; but both assertions read straight-forward, without any intimation of co-operation. The address is here only suspended, in order to describe the man as he was and is. The all-absorbing love of self regulated his dealings. In possession of the highest power and highest rank, he was not easy of access. Widows and orphans, that they might not perish, were obliged to turn suppliantly to him. But the widows he chased away with empty hands, and the arms of the orphans were crushed. From the address a turn is also here taken to an objective utterance turned from the person addressed, intended however for him ; the construction is like מַצּוֹת יֵאָכֵל, unleavened bread is eaten, Ex. xiii. 7, according to Ew. § 295, b. The arms are not conceived of as stretched out for help (which would rather be יְרֵי), nor as demanding back their perverted right, but the crushing of the arms, as Ps. xxxvii. 17, Ezek. xxx. 22, and frequently implies a total destruction of every power, support, and help, after the analogy of the Arabic phrase compared by Ges. in his *Thes.* pp. 268*b*, 433*b*. The arm, זְרוֹעַ (ذِرَاع, oftener عَضُد or سَاعِد), signifies power, ch. xl. 9, Ps. lxxvii. 16 ; force and violence, ver. 8, ch. xxxv. 9 ; self-help, and help from without, Ps. lxxxiii. 9 (comp. Ps. xliv. 4). Whatever the orphans pos-sessed of goods, honour, and help still available, is not merely broken, it is beaten into fragments.

> 10 *Therefore snares are round about thee,*
> *And fear terrifieth thee suddenly;*
> 11. *Or perceivest thou not the darkness,*
> *And the overflow of waters, which covereth thee?*

On account of this inhuman mode of action by which he

has challenged the punishment of justice, snares are round about him (comp. Bildad's picture of this fate of the evil-doer, ch. xviii. 8–10), destruction encompasses him on every side, so that he sees no way out, and must without any escape succumb to it. And the approaching ruin makes itself known to him time after time by terrors which come suddenly upon him and disconcert him; so that his outward circumstances being deranged and his mind discomposed, he has already in anticipation to taste that which is before him. In ver. 11, לֹא תִרְאֶה is by no means to be taken as an even-tual circumstantial clause, whether it is translated affirma-tively: or darkness (covers thee), that thou canst not see; or interrogatively: or does darkness (surround thee), that thou seest not? In both cases the verb in the principal clause is wanting; apart from the new turn, which אוֹ introduces, being none, it would then have to be explained with Löwenthal: or has the habit of sinning already so dulled thy feeling and darkened thine eye, that thou canst not perceive the enor-mity of thy transgression? But this is a meaning forced from the words which they are not capable of; it must have been at least אוֹ חֹשֶׁךְ בַּעַדְךָ, or something similar. Since אוֹ חֹשֶׁךְ (to be accented without Makkeph with Múnach, Dechî) cannot form a principal clause of itself, תראה is without doubt the verb belonging to it: or (אוֹ as ch. xvi. 3) seest thou not darkness? Because, according to his preceding speeches, Job does not question the magnitude of his sufferings, but acknowledges them in all their fearfulness; therefore Hahn believes it must be explained: or shouldst thou really not be willing to see thy sins, which encompass thee as thick dark clouds, which cover thee as floods of water? The two figures, however, can only be understood of the destruction which entirely shrouds Job in darkness, and threatens to drown him. But destruction, in the sense in which Eliphaz asks if Job does not see it, is certainly intended differently to what it was in Job's complaints. Job complains of it as being unmerited, and therefore mysterious; Eliphaz, on the other hand, is desirous that he should open his eyes that he may perceive in this darkness of sorrow, this flood of suffering, the well-deserved punishment of his heinous sins, and anticipate the worst by penitence. לֹא תְכַסֶּךָ is a relative clause, and belongs logically also to חֹשֶׁךְ, comp. Isa. lx. 2, where שִׁפְעַת is also found in ver. 6 (from שָׁפַע, *abundare;* comp. شفع, ספק, ch. xx. 22). Eliphaz now insinuates that Job denies the special providence of God, because he doubts the exceptionless, just government of God. In the second strophe he has explained his affliction as the result of his uncharitableness ; now he explains it as the result of his unbelief, which is now become manifest.

> 12 *Is not Eloah high as the heavens?*
>   *See but the head of the stars, how exalted!*
> 13 *So then thou thinkest:* " *What doth God know?*
>   *Can He judge through the thick cloud?*
> 14 *Clouds veil Him that He seeth not,*
>   *And in the vault of heaven He walketh at His pleasure.*"

Because Job has denied the distribution of worldly fortune, of outward prosperity and adversity, according to the law of the justice that recompenses like for like, Eliphaz charges him with that unbelief often mentioned in the Psalms (lxxiii. 11, xciv. 7 ; comp. Isa. xxix. 15, Ezek. viii. 12), which denies to the God in heaven, as Epicurus did to the gods who lead a blessed life in the spaces between the worlds, a knowledge of earthly things, and therefore the preliminary condition for a right comprehension of them. The mode of expression here is altogether peculiar. גֹּבַהּ שָׁמָיִם is not *acc. loci,* as the like accusatives in combination with the verb שָׁכַן, Isa. lvii. 15, may be taken : the substantival clause would lead one to expect בְּגֹבַהּ, or better בִּגְבְהֵי (ch. xi. 8) ; it is rather (similar to ch. xi. 8) *nomin. prædicati* : Eloah is the height of the heavens = heaven-high, as high as the heavens, therefore certainly highly, and indeed very highly, exalted above this earth. In this sense it is continued with *Waw explic.* : and behold (= behold then) the head of the stars, that, or how (כִּי as in Gen. xlix. 15, 1 Sam. xiv. 29, *quod = quam*) exalted they are. וּרְאֵה has *Asla* (*Kadma*) in correct texts, and רמו is written רָמּוּ (*râmmu*) with a so-called *Dag. affectuosum* (Olsh. § 83, *b*). It may be received as certain that רֹאשׁ, the head (*vertex*), beside רְאֵה (not סְפֹר), does not signify the sum (Aben-Ezra). But it is questionable whether the genitive that follows רֹאשׁ is *gen. partitivus* : the highest among the stars (Ew., Hirz., Schlottm.), or *gen. epexegeticus* : the head, *i.e.* (in relation to the rest of the universe) the height, which is formed by the stars, or even which they occupy (Ges. *cœlum stellatum*) ; the partitive rendering is to be preferred, for the Semitic perception recognises, as the plural שָׁמַיִם implies, nearer and more distant celestial spheres. The expression "head of the stars" is therefore somewhat like *fastigium cœli* (the extreme height, *i.e.* the middle of the vault of heaven), or *culmen aereum* (of the æther separating the strata of air above) ; the summit of the stars rising up into the extremest spheres is intended (we should say : the fixed stars, or to use a still more modern expression, the milky way), as also the רמו naturally refers to רֹאשׁ כוכבים as one notion (*summitas astrorum = summa astra*).

The connection of what follows with *Waw* is not adversative (Hirz., Ew., and others : and yet thou speakest), it is rather consecutive (Hahn : and since thou speakest ; better : and in consequence of this thou speakest ; or : thus speakest thou, thinkest thou then). The undeniable truth that God is exalted, and indeed absolute in His exaltation, is misapplied by Job to the false conclusion : what does God know, or (since the *perf.* in interrogative sentences frequently corresponds to the Latin conjunctive, *vid.* on Ps. xi. 3) how should God know, or take knowledge, *i.e.* of anything that happens on earth? In ver. 13*b* the potential takes the place of this modal perfect : can He rule judicially behind the dark clouds, *i.e.* over the world below from which He is shut out? בְּעַד (of like verbal origin with the Arab. بعد, *post*, prop. distance, separation, succession, but of wider use) signifies here, as in ch. i. 10, ix. 7, behind, *pone*, with the secondary notion of being encompassed or covered by that which shuts off. Far from having an unlimited view of everything earthly from His absolute height, it is veiled from Him by the clouds, so that He sees not what occurs here below, and unconcerned about it He walks the circle of the heavens (that which vaults the earth, the inhabitants of which seem to Him, according to Isa. xl. 22, as grasshoppers) ; הִתְהַלֵּךְ is here, after the analogy of *Kal*, joined with the accus. of the way over which He walks at His pleasure : *orbem cælum obambulat.* By such unworthy views of the Deity, Job puts himself on a par with the godless race that was swept away by the flood in ancient days, without allowing himself to be warned by this example of punishment.

15 *Wilt thou observe the way of the ancient world,*
   Which evil men have trodden,
16 *Who were withered up before their time,*
   Their foundation was poured out as a stream,
17 *Who said unto God: Depart from us !*
   And what can the Almighty do to them?
18 *And notwithstanding He had filled their houses with good—*
   The counsel of the wicked be far from me !

While in Ps. cxxxix. 24 דרך עולם prospectively signifies a way of eternal duration (comp. Ezek. xxvi. 20, עם עולם, of the people who sleep the interminably long sleep of the grave),

אֹרַח עוֹלָם signifies here retrospectively the way of the ancient
world, but not, as in Jer. vi. 16, xviii. 15, the way of thinking and acting of the pious forefathers which put their posterity to shame, but of a godless race of the ancient world
which stands out as a terrible example to posterity. Eliphaz
asks if Job will observe, *i.e.* keep (שמר as in Ps. xviii. 22),
this way trodden by people (מְתֵי, comp. אַנְשֵׁי, ch. xxxiv. 36)
of wickedness. Those worthless ones were withered up, *i.e.*
forcibly seized and crushed, וְלֹא־עֵת, when it was not yet time
(ולא after the manner of a circumstantial clause : *quum non-
dum*, as Ps. cxxxix. 16), *i.e.* when according to God's creative
order their time was not yet come. On קֻמְּטוּ[1] *vid.* on ch.
xvi. 8 ; LXX. correctly, συνελήφθησαν ἄωροι, nevertheless
συλλαμβάνειν is too feeble as a translation of קמט; for as
قبص signifies to take with the tip of the finger, whereas قبض
signifies to take with the whole bent hand, so קמט, in conformity to the dull, emphatic final consonant, signifies "to bind
firmly together." In ver. 16*b* יוּצַק is not *perf. Pual* for יֻצַּק
(Ew. § 83, *b*), for this exchange, contrary to the law of vowels,
of the sharp form with the lengthened form is without
example ; it must at least have been written יֻצַּק (comp.
Judg. xviii. 29). It is *fut. Hoph.*, which, according to ch. xi.
15, might be יֻצַק ; here, however, it is with a resolving, not
assimilation, of the *Jod*, as in Lev. xxi. 10. The *fut.* has the
signification of the imperfect which it acquires in an historic
connection. It is not to be translated : their place became a
stream which has flowed away (Hirz.), for the היה which
would be required by such an interpretation could not be
omitted ; also not : *flumen effusum est in fundamentum eorum*
(Rosenm., Hahn, and others), which would be לִיסוֹדָם, and
would still be very liable to be misunderstood; also not: whose
foundation was a poured-out stream (Umbr., Olsh.), for then

[1] This קמטו, according to the Masora, is the middle word of the book
of Job (חצי הספר).

there would be one attributive clause inserted in the other;
but: their solid ground became fluid like a stream (Ew.,
Hlgst., Schlottm.), so that נֶהֱרָר, after the analogy of the verbs
with two accusatives, Ges. § 139, 2, is a so-called second acc.
of the obj. which by the passive becomes a nominative (comp.
ch. xxviii. 2), although it might also be an apposition of the
following subj. placed first: a stream (as such, like such a
one) their solid ground was brought into a river; the ground
on which they and their habitations stood was placed under
water and floated away: without doubt the flood is intended;
reference to this perfectly accords with the patriarchal pre-
and extra-Israelitish standpoint of the book of Job; and the
generation of the time of the flood (דור המבול) is accounted
in the holy scriptures of the Old and New Testament as a
paragon of godlessness, the cotemporaries of Noah are the
ἀπειθοῦντες, סוררים, κατ᾽ ἐξοχήν (comp. 1 Pet. iii. 20 with
Ps. lxviii. 19).

Accordingly they are now here also further described (ver.
17) as those who said to God, "Depart from us," and what
could the Almighty do to them (לָמוֹ instead of לָנוּ, which was
to be expected, since, as in ch. xix. 28, there is a change
from the *oratio directa* to *obliqua*)! Olshausen explains with
Hahn: "with respect to what thou sayest: and what then
does the Almighty do to them (for it)? He fills their houses
with prosperity, while the counsel of the wicked is far from
me (notwithstanding I am unfortunate)." But this explanation is as forced (since ומה without a אמרת or תאמר standing
with it is taken as the word of Job) as it is contrary to the
syntax (since the circumstantial clause with והוא is not recognised, and on the other hand וְעֵצַת וגו׳, instead of which it ought
at least to have been וּמִמֶּנִּי וגו׳, is regarded as such an one).
No indeed, just this is an exceedingly powerful effect, that
Eliphaz describes those godless ones who dismiss God with
סור ממנו, to whom, according to Job's assertion, ch. xxi. 13

sq., undimmed prosperity is portioned out, by referring to a memorable fact as that which has fallen under the strict judgment of God ; and that with the very same words with which Job, ch. xxi. 16, declines communion with such prosperous evil-doers : " the counsel of the wicked be far from me," he will have nothing more to do, not with the wicked alone, but, with a side glance at Job, even with those who place themselves on a level with them by a denial of the just government of God in the world.   פְּעָל לֹ, as the following circumstantial clause shows, is intended like Ps. lxviii. 29, comp. xxxi. 20, Isa. xxvi. 12 : how can the Almighty then help or profit them ?   Thus they asked, while He had filled their houses with wealth—Eliphaz will have nothing to do with this contemptible misconstruction of the God who proves himself so kind to those who dwell below on the earth, but who, though He is rewarded with ingratitude, is so just. The truly godly are not terrified like Job, ch. xvii. 8, that retributive justice is not to be found in God's government of the world ; on the contrary, they rejoice over its actual manifestation in their own case, which makes them free, and therefore so joyous.

> 19 *The righteous see it and rejoice,*
>   *And the innocent mock at them :*
> 20 " *Verily our opponent is destroyed,*
>   *And the fire hath devoured their abundance.*"

This thought corresponds to that expressed as a wish, hope, or anticipation at the close of many of the Psalms, that the retributive justice of God, though we may have to wait a long time for it, becomes at length the more gloriously manifest to the joy of those hitherto innocently persecuted, Ps. lviii. 11 sq.   The obj. of יִרְאוּ, as in Ps. cvii. 42, is this its manifestation.   לָמוֹ is not an ethical dative, as in Ps. lxxx. 7, but as in Ps. ii. 4 refers to the ungodly whose mocking pride comes to such an ignominious end. What follow in ver. 20 are the words of the godly; the introductory לֵאמֹר is wanting, as *e.g.* Ps. ii. 3. אִם־לֹא can signify neither *si non*, as ch. ix. 24, xxiv. 25, xxxi. 31, nor *annon*, as in a disjunctive question, ch. xvii. 2, xxx. 25; it is affirmative, as ch. i. 11, ii. 5, xxxi. 36—an Amen to God's peremptory judgment. On נִכְחַד (he is drawn away, put aside, become annulled), *vid. supra,* p. 282. קִימָנוּ (for which Aben-Ezra is also acquainted with the reading קִימֵנוּ with קמץ קטן, *i.e.* צירי) has a pausal *â* springing from *ê*, as ch. xx. 27, מתקוממה for מתקוֹמֲמָה; Ruth iii. 2, מוֹדַעְתָּנוּ; Isa. xlvii. 10, רֹאָנִי (together with the reading רֹאַנִי, comp. 1 Chron. xii. 17, לרמוּתֵנִי). The form קִים is remarkable; it may be more readily taken as *part. pass.* (like שִׂים, *positus*) than as *nom. infin.* (the act of raising for those who raise themselves); perhaps the original text had קמֵינוּ (קָמֵינוּ). יִתְרָם is no more to be translated their remnant (Hirz.) here than in Ps. xvii. 14, at least not in the sense of Ex. xxiii. 11; that which exceeds the necessity is intended, their surplus, their riches. It is said of Job in *b. Megilla,* 28*a :* אִיוֹב וַתְרָן בְּמָמוֹנֵיהּ הֲוָה, he was extravagant (*prodigus*) with his property. The fire devouring the wealth of the godless is an allusion to the misfortune which has befallen him.

After this terrible picture, Eliphaz turns to the exhortation of him who may be now perhaps become ripe for repentance.

21 *Make friends now with Him, so hast thou peace;*
   Thereby good will come unto thee.
22 *Receive now teaching from His mouth,*
   And place His utterances in thy heart.
23 *If thou returnest to the Almighty, thou shalt be built up*
   again;
   If thou puttest away iniquity far from thy tents.
24 *And lay by in the dust the gold ore,*

And under the pebbles of the brooks the gold of Ophir.
25 *So shall the Almighty be to thee gold ore in abundance,*
　　And silver to thee of the brightest lustre.

The relationship of the verbs סָכַן, שָׁכַן, and سكن, has been already discussed on ver. 2 : the *Hiph.* signifies to be on friendly terms with any one ; to enter into, or to stand in, an intimate relationship to any one (Ps. cxxxix. 3) ; then also (as the Greek φιλεῖν) to get accustomed to, to be used to (Num. xxii. 30). The second *imper.* is consecutive, as *e.g.* Prov. iii. 4 : and have as the result of it peace (Arab. فاسلم) = so shalt thou have peace, Ges. § 130, 2. In ver. 21 the first thing to be done is to clear up the form תְּבוּאָתֶךְ or (according to another reading which is likewise well attested) תְּבוּאָתְךָ. Olshausen (in Hirz. and in his *Gramm.*) and Rödiger (in *Thes.* p. 11, *suppl.*) explain this form the same as the other forms which come under consideration in connection with it, viz. תְּבוֹאָתָה (*veniat*), Deut. xxxiii. 16, and וַתְּבֹאתִי, *Keri* וַתָּבֹאת (*et venisses*, addressed to Abigail), 1 Sam. xxv. 34, as errors in writing ; whereas Ew., § 191, *c*, sees in תְּבוּאָתְךָ the erroneous form תְּבוֹא = תְּבוֹאָה with a superfluous feminine termination, in תְּבוֹאָתָה an extension of the double feminine by the unaccented *ah* of intention, and in תְּבֹאתִי a transfer of the inflexion of the perf. to the fut. Confining ourselves to the form which occurs here, we refer to what was said above, p. 187, note 2 : תבואתך is not a *forma mixta* from תְּבוֹאֲךָ and בָּאַתְךָ, but the mistaken double feminine תְּבוֹאָה with suff., the *ah* of which, although the tone is on the *penult.*, is not *He voluntativum*, as Isa. v. 19, but *He femin.* The exception of such double feminines is made as certain in Hebrew by the regular form נִגְלָתָה (= נִגְלָת with a second feminine termination), and by examples like Prov. i. 20, Ezek. xxiii. 20, and also Josh. vi. 17, 2 Sam. i. 26, Amos iv. 3 (comp. even

Olsh. in his *Gramm.* S. 449), as the double plural and its
further formation by a feminine termination in Arabic. It is
therefore unnecessary, with Olsh. and Röd., after the precedent of the ancient versions, to read תְּבוּאָתְךָ (which is found
in 19 Codd. in de Rossi) : *proventus tuus bonus erit.* The
suff. in בָּהֶם, as Isa. lxiv. 4, Ezek. xxxiii. 18, comp. עֲלֵיהֶם,
Isa. xxxviii. 16, is intended as neuter, as the fem. is used elsewhere (*e.g.* Isa. xxxviii. 16, בָּהֵן) : by it, *i.e.* by such conduct,
good (prosperity) shall come to thee, and indeed, as the בוא
construed with the acc. implies, in a sudden change of thy
previous lot, coming about without any further effort on thy
part. In the certainty that it is God's word which he presents
to his friend (the very certainty which Eliphaz also expresses
elsewhere, *e.g.* ch. xv. 11), he further admonishes him (ver.
22) to receive instruction from God's mouth (מִפִּיו as Prov.
ii. 6), and to allow His (God's) utterances a place in his
heart, not to let them die away without effect, but to imprint
them deeply on his mind.

Ver. 23. If he return to the Almighty (שׁוּב עַד as freq., *e.g.*
Isa. xix. 22, comp. xlv. 24, instead of the otherwise usual
שׁוּב אֶל, of thorough and complete conversion), he will be
built up again, by his former prosperity being again raised
from its ruins. בָּנָה, to build, always according to the connection, has at one time the idea of building round about,
continuing to build, or finishing building (*vid.* on ch. xx. 19) ;
at another of building up again (ch. xii. 14 ; Isa. lviii. 12),
referred to persons, the idea of increasing prosperity (Mal.
iii. 15), or of the restoration of ruined prosperity (Jer. xxiv.
6, xxxiii. 7), here in the latter sense. The promissory תִּבָּנֶה
is surrounded by conditional clauses, for ver. 23*b* (comp. ch.
xi. 14) is a second conditional clause still under the government of אִם, which is added for embellishment ; it opens the
statement of that in which penitence must be manifested, if
it is to be thorough. The LXX. translates ἐὰν δὲ ἐπι-

στραφῆς καὶ ταπεινώσῃς, i.e. תֵּעָנֶה, which Ewald considers as the original; the omission of the אִם (which the poet otherwise in such connections has formerly heaped up, e.g. ch. viii. 5 sq., xi. 13 sq.) is certainly inconvenient. And yet we should not on that account like to give up the figure indicated in תבנה, which is so beautiful and so suited to our poet. The statement advanced in the latter conditional clause is then continued in ver. 24 in an independent imperative clause, which the old versions regard as a promise instead of exhortation, and therefore grossly misinterpret. The Targ. translates: and place on the dust a strong city (i.e. thou shalt then, where there is now nothing but dust, raise up such), as if בֶּצֶר could be equivalent to בִּצָרוֹן or מִבְצָר,—a rendering to which Saadia at least gives a turn which accords with the connection: "regard the stronghold (الحصن) as dust, and account as the stones of the valleys the gold of Ophir;" better than Eichhorn: "pull down thy stronghold of violence, and demolish (הפיר) the castles of thy valleys." On the other hand, Gecatilia, who understands בצר proportionately more correctly of treasures, translates it as a promise: so shalt thou inherit treasures (ذخاير) more numerous than dust, and gold ore (تبر) (more than) the stones of the valleys; and again also Rosenm. (repones præ pulvere argentum) and Welte interpret ver. 24 as a promise; whereas other expositors, who are true to the imperative שׁית, explain שׁית æstimare, and עַל־עָפָר pulveris instar (Grot., Cocc., Schult., Dathe, Umbr.), by falsely assigning to עַל here, as to לְ elsewhere, a meaning which it never has anywhere; how blind, on the other hand, since the words in their first meaning, pone super pulverem, furnish an excellent thought which is closely connected with the admonition to rid one's self of unjust possessions. בֶּצֶר, like تبر (by which Abulwalid explains it), is gold and silver ore, i.e. gold and silver as they are broken out of the mine, therefore (since silver is partially pure, gold almost pure, and always containing more or less silver) the most precious metal in its pure natural state before being worked, and consequently also unalloyed (comp. نَضِير and نَصَار, which likewise signifies *aurum argentumve nativum,* but not *ab excidendo,* but *a nitore*) ; and " to lay in the dust" is equivalent to, to part with a thing as entirely worthless and devoid of attraction. The meaning is therefore : put away from thee the idol of precious metal with contempt (comp. Isa. ii. 20), which is only somewhat differently expressed in the parallel : lay the Ophir under the quartz (וּבְצוּר agreeing with בְצר) of the brooks (such as is found in the beds of empty wâdys), *i.e.* place it under the rubble, after it has lost for thee its previous bewitching spell. As cloth woven from the filaments of the nettle is called muslin, from Mossul, and cloth with figures on it " damask, דְּמֶשֶׁק" (Amos iii. 12), from Damascus,[1] and aloes-wood صَنْدَل, from Coromandel; so the gold from Ophir, *i.e.* from the coast of the *Abhîra,* on the north coast of the Runn (Old Indian *Irina, i.e.* Salt Sea), east of the mouth of the Indus,[2] is directly called אוֹפִיר. When Job thus casts from him temporal things, by the excessive cherishing of which he has hitherto sinned, then God himself will be his imperishable treasure, his everlasting higher delight. He frees himself from temporal בֶּצֶר ; and the Almighty, therefore the absolute personality of God himself, will be to him instead of it בְּצָרִים, gold as from the mine, in

---

[1] We leave it undecided whether in a similar manner silk has its name μέταξα (μάταξα), Armenian *metaks,* Aramaic מטכסא, מטקסין, from Damascus (Ewald and Friedr. Müller).

[2] Thus אוֹפִיר has been explained by Lassen in his pamphlet *de Pentapotamia,* and his *Indische Alterthumskunde* (i. 539). The LXX. (*Cod. Vat.*) and Theodot. have Σωφείρ, whence Ges. connects Ophir with Arrian's Οὔππαρα and Edrisi's *Sufâra* in Guzerat, especially since *Sofir* is attested as the Coptic name for India. The matter is still not settled.

rich abundance. This is what the contrast of the *plur*. (בְּצָרֶךָ
without *Jod plur.* is a false reading) with the *sing.* implies;
the LXX., Syriac version, Jerome, and Arabic version err
here, since they take the בְּ of בִּצְרֶיךָ as a preposition.

The ancient versions and lexicographers furnish no explanation of תּוֹעֲפוֹת. The Targ. translates it תְּקוֹף רוּמָא, and
accordingly it is explained by both חסן (strength) and נבה
(height), without any reason being assigned for these significations. In the passage before us the LXX. transl. ἀργύριον
πεπυρωμένον from עף, in the Targum signification to blow,
forge; the Syriac version, *argentum computationum* (חוּשְׁבָּנִין),
from עף in the Targum-Talmudic signification to double
(= Hebr. כפל). According to the usage of the language in
question, יָעֵף, from the *Hiph.* of which תועפות is formed, signifies to become feeble, to be wearied; but even if, starting
from the primary notion, an available signification is attained
for the passage before us (fatigues = toilsome excitement,
synon. יְגִיעַ) and Ps. xcv. 4 (climbings = heights), the use of
the word in the most ancient passages citable, Num. xxiii. 22,
xxiv. 8, כְּתוֹעֲפֹת רְאֵם לוֹ, still remains unexplained; for here the
notion of being incapable of fatigue, invincibility, or another
of the like kind, is required, without any means at hand for
rightly deriving it from יָעֵף, to become feeble, especially as
the radical signification *anhelare* supposed by Gesenius (comp.
אוֹן from the root אן) is unattested. Accordingly, we must go
back to the root יף, וף, discussed on Ps. xcv. 4, which signifies
to rise aloft, to be high, and from which יפע, or with a transposition of the consonants יעף (comp. עָיֵף and יָעֵף), acquires
the signification of standing out, rising radiantly, shining afar
off, since יָעֵף, to become weary, is allied to the Arab. وغف
fut. i; this יעף (יפע), on the other hand, to يفع, *ascendere,
adolescere*, وفع *elatum, adultum esse*, and وفى *eminere*, and
tropically *completum, perfectum esse.* Thus we obtain the
signification *eminentiæ* for תועפות. In Ps. xcv. 4, as a

numerical plur., it signifies the towerings (tops) of the mountains, and here, as in the passages cited from Numbers, either
prominent, eminent attributes, or as an intensive plur. excellence ; whence, agreeing with Ewald, we have translated
" silver of the brightest lustre " (comp. יִפְעָה, *eminentia*,
splendor, Ezek. xxviii. 7).

26 *For then thou shalt delight thyself in the Almighty,*
      And lift up thy countenance to Eloah ;
27 *If thou prayest to Him, He will hear thee,*
      And thou shalt pay thy vows.
28 *And thou devisest a plan, and it shall be established to thee,*
      And light shineth upon thy ways.
29 *If they are cast down, thou sayest, " Arise !"*
      And him that hath low eyes He saveth.
30 *He shall rescue him who is not guiltless,*
      And he is rescued by the purity of thy hands.

כִּי־אָז might also be translated "then indeed" (*vid.* on ch.
xi. 15), as an emphatic resumption of the promissory וְהָיָה
(*tum erit*), ver. 25 ; but what follows is really the confirmation of the promise that God will be to him a rich recompense for the earthly treasures that he resigns ; therefore :
for then thou shalt delight thyself in the Almighty (*vid.* the
primary passage, Ps. xxxvii. 4, and the dependent one, Isa.
lviii. 14 ; comp. *infra*, ch. xxvii. 10), *i.e.* He will become a
source of highest, heartfelt joy to thee (עַל as interchanging
with בְּ by שָׂמַח). Then shall he be able to raise his countenance, which was previously depressed (נִפְלוּ, Gen. iv. 6 sq.),
in the consciousness of his estrangement from God by dearly
cherished sin and unexpiated guilt, free and open, confident
and joyous, to God. If he prays to Him (תַּעְתִּיר may be
thus regarded as the antecedent of a conditional clause,
like יִבְרַח, ch. xx. 24), He will hear him ; and what he has
vowed in prayer he will now, after that which he sup-

plicated is granted, thankfully perform ; the *Hiph.* הֶעְתִּיר (according to its etymon : to offer the incense of prayer) occurs only in Ex. viii.–x. beside this passage, whereas גָּזַר (to cut in pieces, cut off) occurs here for the first time in the signification, to decide, resolve, which is the usual meaning of the word in the later period of the language. On וַתִּגְזַר (with *Pathach*, according to another reading with *Kametz-chatuph*), vid. Ges. § 47, rem. 2. Moreover, the paratactic clauses of ver. 28 are to be arranged as we have translated them ; קוּם signifies to come to pass, as freq. (*e.g.* Isa. vii. 7, in connection with הָיָה, to come into being). That which he designs (אֹמֶר) is successful, and is realized, and light shines upon his ways, so that he cannot stumble and does not miss his aim,—light like moonlight or morning light; for, as the author of the introductory Proverbs, to which we have already so often referred as being borrowed from the book of Job (comp. ch. xxi. 24 with Prov. iii. 8), ingeniously says, ch. iv. 18 : " The path of the righteous is as the morning light (כְּאוֹר נֹגַהּ, comp. Dan. vi. 20), which shineth brighter and brighter unto the height of day (*i.e.* noonday brightness)."

Ver. 29. הִשְׁפִּילוּ refers to דְּרָכֶיךָ ; for if it is translated : in case they lower (Schlottm., Renan, and others), the suff. is wanting, and the thought is halting. As הִשְׁפִּיל signifies to make low, it can also signify to go down (Jer. xiii. 18), and said of ways, " to lead downwards" (Rosenm., Ew., Hahn). The old expositors go altogether astray in ver. 29*a*, because they did not discern the exclamative idea of גֵּוָה. The noun גֵּוָה—which is formed from the verb גָּוָה = גָּאָה, as גֵּאָה, arrogance, Prov. viii. 13 ; גֵּהָה, healing, Prov. xvii. 22 ; כֵּהָה, mitigation, Nah. iii. 19 (distinct from גֵּוָה, the body, the fem. of גֵּו), without the necessity of regarding it as syncopated from גְּאֵוָה (Olsh. § 154, *b*), as שֵׁלָה, 1 Sam. i. 17, from שְׁאֵלָה—does not here signify pride or haughtiness, as in ch. xxxiii. 17, Jer. xiii. 17, but signifies adverbially *sursum* (therefore synon. of

סֶלָה, which, being formed from סַל, *elevatio*, with *He* of direction and *Dag. forte implic.*, as הֶרָה, פֶּדֶנָה = *paddannah, harrah*,—
perhaps, however, it is to be read directly סַלָּה, with *He fem.*,—
is accordingly a substantive made directly into an adverb, like
נֶוֶה): suppose that (כִּי = ἐάν, as אִם = εἰ) thy ways lead downwards, thou sayest: on high! *i.e.* thy will being mighty in
God, thy confidence derived from the Almighty, will all at
once give them another and more favourable direction : God
will again place in a condition of prosperity and happiness,
—which יוֹשִׁעַ (defectively written ; LXX. : σώσει; Jer. and
Syr., however, reading יִוָשֵׁעַ : *salvabitur*), according to its
etymon, Arab. اوسع, signifies,—him who has downcast eyes
(LXX. κύφοντα ὀφθαλμοῖς).

Ver. 30. It may seem at first sight, that by אִי־נָקִי, the
not-guiltless (אִי[1] = אִין = אֵין, *e.g.* Isa. xl. 29, 2 Chron. xiv. 10,
Ges. § 152, 1), Eliphaz means Job himself in his present
condition ; it would then be a mild periphrastic expression
for " the guilty, who has merited his suffering." If thou
returnest in this manner to God, He will—this would be the
idea of ver. 30a—free thee, although thy suffering is not
undeserved. Instead now of proceeding : and thou shalt be
rescued on account of the purity of thy hands, *i.e.* because
thou hast cleansed them from wrong, Eliphaz would say :
and this not-guiltless one will be rescued, *i.e.* thou, the not-
guiltless, wilt be rescued, by the purity of thy hands. But
one feels at once how harsh this synallage would be. Even
Hirzel, who refers ver. 30a to Job, refers 30b to some one
else. In reality, however, another is intended in both cases
(Ew., Schlottm., Hahn, Olsh.) ; and ver. 30a is just so
arranged as to be supplemented by בְּבֹר כַּפֶּיךָ, ver. 30b. Even

---

[1] In Rabbinic also this abbreviated negative is not אִ (as Dukes and
Geiger point it), but according to the traditional pronunciation, אִי, *e.g.*
אִי אֶפְשַׁר (*impossibile*).

old expositors, as Seb. Schmid and J. H. Michaelis, have correctly perceived the relation : *liberabit Deus et propter puritatem manuum tuarum alios, quos propria innocentia ipsos deficiens non esset liberatura.* The purity of the hands (Ps. xviii. 21) is that which Job will have attained when he has put from him that which defiles him (comp. ch. ix. 30 with xvii. 9). Hirzel has referred to Matt. vi. 33 in connection with vers. 24 sq. ; one is here reminded of the words of our Lord to Peter, Luke xxii. 32 : σύ ποτὲ ἐπιστρέψας στήριξον τοὺς ἀδελφούς σου. Eliphaz, although unconsciously, in these last words expresses prophetically what will be fulfilled in the issue of the history in Job himself.

The speech of Eliphaz opens the third course of the controversy. In the first course of the controversy the speeches of the friends, though bearing upon the question of punishment, were embellished with alluring promises ; but these promises were incapable of comforting Job, because they proceeded upon the assumption that he is suffering as a sinner deserving of punishment, and can only become free from his punishment by turning to God. In the second course of the controversy, since Job gave no heed to their exhortations to penitence, the friends drew back their promises, and began the more unreservedly to punish and to threaten, by presenting to Job, in the most terrifying pictures of the ruin of the evil-doer, his own threatening destruction. The misconstruction which Job experiences from the friends has the salutary effect on him of rooting him still more deeply in the hope that God will not let him die without having borne witness to his innocence. But the mystery of the present is nevertheless not cleared up for Job by this glimpse of faith into the future. On the contrary, the second course of the controversy ends so, that to the friends who unjustly and uncharitably deny instead of solving the mystery of his individual lot, Job now presents that which is mysterious in the divine distribution of human fortune in general, the total irreconcilableness of experience with the idea of the just divine retribution maintained by them. In that speech of his, ch. xxi., which forms the transition to the third course of the controversy, Job uses the language of the doubter not without sinning against God. But since it is true that the outward lot of man by no means always corresponds to his true moral condition, and never warrants an infallible conclusion respecting it, he certainly in that speech gives the death-blow to the dogma of the friends. The poet cannot possibly allow them to be silent over it. Eliphaz, the most discreet and intelligent, speaks. His speech, considered in itself, is the purest truth, uttered in the most appropriate and beautiful form. But as an answer to the speech of Job the dogma of the friends itself is destroyed in it, by the false conclusion by which it is obliged to justify itself to itself. The greatness of the poet is manifest from this, that he makes the speeches of the friends, considered in themselves, and apart from the connection of the drama, express the most glorious truths, while they are proved to be inadequate, indeed perverted and false, in so far as they are designed to solve the existing mystery. According to their general substance, these speeches are genuine diamonds; according to their special application, they are false ones.

How true is what Eliphaz says, that God neither blesses the pious because he is profitable to Him, nor punishes the wicked because he is hurtful to Him; that the pious is profitable not to God, but to himself; the wicked is hurtful not to God, but himself; that therefore the conduct of God towards both is neither arbitrary nor selfish! But if we consider the conclusion to which, in these thoughts, Eliphaz only takes a spring, they prove themselves to be only the premises of a false conclusion. For Eliphaz infers from them that God rewards virtue as such, and punishes vice as such; that therefore where a man suffers, the reason of it is not to be sought in any secondary purpose on the part of God, but solely and absolutely in the purpose of God to punish the sins of the man. The fallacy of the conclusion is this, that the possibility of any other purpose, which is just as far removed from self-interest, in connection with God's purpose of punishing the sins of the man, is excluded. It is now manifest how near theoretical error and practical falsehood border on one another, so that dogmatical error is really in the rule at the same time ἀδικία. For after Eliphaz, in order to defend the justice of divine retribution against Job, has again indissolubly connected suffering and the punishment of sin, without acknowledging any other form of divine rule but His justice, any other purpose in decreeing suffering than the infliction of punishment (from the recognition of which the right and true comfort for Job would have sprung up), he is obliged in the present instance, against his better knowledge and conscience, to distort an established fact, to play the hypocrite to himself, and persuade himself of the existence of sins in Job, of which the confirmation fails him, and to become false and unjust towards Job even in favour of the false dogma. For the dogma demands wickedness in an equal degree to correspond to a great evil, unlimited sins to unlimited sufferings. Therefore the former wealth of Job must furnish him with the ground of heavy accusations, which he now expresses directly and unconditionally to Job. He whose conscience, however, does not accuse him of mammon-worship, ch. xxxi. 24 sq., is suffering the punishment of a covetous and compassionless rich man. Thus is the dogma of the justice of God rescued by the unjust abandonment of Job.

Further, how true is Eliphaz' condemnatory judgment against the free-thinking, which, if it does not deny the existence of God, still regards God as shut up in the heavens without concerning himself about anything that takes place on earth! The divine judgment of total destruction came upon a former generation that had thought thus insolently of God, and to the joy of the righteous the same judgment is still executed upon evil-doers of the same mind. This is true, but it does not apply to Job, for whom it is intended. Job has denied the universality of a just divine retribution, but not the special providence of God. Eliphaz sets retributive justice and special providence again here in a false correlation. He thinks that, so far as a man fails to perceive the one, he must at once doubt the other,—another instance of the absurd reasoning of their dogmatic one-sidedness. Such is Job's relation to God, that even if he failed to discover a single trace of retributive justice anywhere, he would not deny His rule in nature and among men. For his God is not a mere notion, but a person to whom he stands in a living relation. A notion falls to pieces as soon as it is found to be self-contradictory; but God remains what He is, however much the phenomenon of His rule contradicts the nature of His person. The rule of God on earth Job firmly holds, although in manifold instances he can only explain it by God's absolute and arbitrary power. Thus he really knows no higher motive in God to which to refer his affliction; but nevertheless he knows that God interests himself about him, and that He who is even now his Witness in heaven will soon arise on the dust of the grave in his behalf. For such utterances of Job's faith Eliphaz has no ear. He knows no faith beyond the circle of his dogma.

The exhortations and promises by which Eliphaz then (ch. xxii. 21-30) seeks to lead Job back to God are in and of themselves true and most glorious. There is also somewhat in them which reflects shame on Job; they direct him to that inward peace, to that joy in God, which he had entirely lost sight of when he spoke of the misfortune of the righteous in contrast with the prosperity of the wicked.[1] But even these beauteous words of promise are blemished by the false assumption from which they proceed. The promise, the Almighty shall become Job's precious ore, rests on the assumption that Job is now suffering the punishment of his avarice, and has as its antecedent: "Lay thine ore in the dust, and thine Ophir beneath the pebbles of the brook." Thus do even the holiest and truest words lose their value when they are not uttered at the right time, and the most brilliant sermon that exhorts to penitence remains without effect when it is prompted by pharisaic uncharitableness. The poet, who in general has regarded the character of Eliphaz as similar to that of a prophet (vid. ch. iv. 12 sqq.), makes him here at the close of his speech against his will prophesy the issue of this controversy. He who now, considering himself as נקי, preaches penitence to Job, shall at last stand forth as אי נקי, and will be one of the first who need Job's intercession as the servant of God, and whom he is able mediatorially to rescue by the purity of his hands.

[1] Brentius: *Prudentia carnis existimat benedictionem extrinsecus in hoc seculo piis contingere, impiis vero maledictionem, sed veritas docet, benedictionem piis in hoc seculo sub maledictione, vitam sub morte, salutem sub damnatione, e contra impiis sub benedictione maledictionem, sub vita mortem, sub salute damnationem contingere.*

END OF VOL. I.